Forty Studies That Changed Psychology

Explorations into the History of Psychological Research

Eighth Edition

Roger R. Hock, Ph.D.
Mendocino College

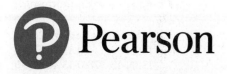

Portfolio Manager: *Tanimaa Mehra*
Content Producer: *Sugandh Juneja*
Portfolio Manager Assistant: *Anna Austin*
Product Marketer: *Marianela Silvestri*
Art/Designer: *SPi Global*
Full-Service Vendor: *SPi Global*
Full-Service Project Manager: *Bhanuprakash Sherla, SPi Global*
Compositor: *SPi Global*
Printer/Binder: *LSC Communications, Inc.*
Cover Printer: *LSC Communications, Inc.*
Cover Design: *Lumina Datamatics, Inc.*
Cover Art: *wenmei Zhou/DigitalVision Vectors/Getty Images*

Library of Congress Cataloging-in-Publication Data
Names: Hock, Roger R., 1948- author.
Title: Forty studies that changed psychology: explorations into the history of psychological research / Roger R. Hock, Ph.D.
Description: Eighth edition. | Hoboken, NJ: Pearson Education, Inc., [2019]
Identifiers: LCCN 2019018574 | ISBN 9780135705063 (print)
Subjects: LCSH: Psychology—Experiments—History—20th century. | Psychology—Experiments—History—21st century.
Classification: LCC BF198.7 .H63 2019 | DDC 150.1—dc23 LC record available at https://lccn.loc.gov/2019018574

1 2019

Rental Edition
ISBN-10:   0-13-570506-1
ISBN-13: 978-0-13-570506-3

Instructor's Review Copy
ISBN-10:   0-13-489763-3
ISBN-13: 978-0-13-489763-9

Brief Contents

Contents

Preface

Welcome to the eighth edition of *Forty Studies That Changed Psychology*. For over 25 years, this book has been a mainstay for many college and high school courses around the world and has been translated into six languages. The majority of the studies included in this edition are the same ones that made up a large part of the first edition. This demonstrates how these landmark studies continue today to exert their influence over psychological thought and research. These original studies and the ones that have been added or changed over the years provide a fascinating glimpse into the birth and growth of the *science of psychology* and into the insights we have acquired trying to unravel the complexities of human nature.

Many studies of human behavior have made remarkable and lasting impacts on the various disciplines that comprise the vast field of psychology. The findings generated from this research have changed our knowledge of human behavior, and they have set the stage for countless subsequent projects and research programs. Even when the results of some of these pivotal studies have later been drawn into controversy and question, their effect and influence in a historical context never diminish. They continue to be cited in new articles, they continue to be the topic of academic discussion, they continue to form the foundation for hundreds of textbook chapters, and they continue to hold a special place in the minds of psychologists.

The concept for this book is originated from my three decades of teaching psychology. Most psychology textbooks are based on key studies that have shaped the science of psychology over its relatively brief history. Textbooks, however, seldom give the original core studies the attention they richly deserve. The original research processes and findings often are summarized and diluted to the point that little of the life and excitement of the discoveries remain. Sometimes, research results are reported in ways that may even mislead the reader about the study's real impact and influence about what we know and how we know it. This is in no way a criticism of the textbook writers who work under length constraints and must make many difficult choices about what gets included and in how much detail. The situation is, however, unfortunate because the foundation of all of modern psychology is scientific research, and through over a century of ingenious and elegant studies, our knowledge and understanding of human behavior have been expanded and refined to the advanced level of sophistication that exists today.

This book is an attempt to fill the gap between all those psychology textbooks and the research that made them possible. It is a journey through the *headline history* of psychology. My hope is that the way the 40 chosen studies are presented will bring every one of them back to life so that you can experience them for yourself. This book is intended for anyone, in any course, who wishes a greater understanding of the true roots of psychology.

Choosing the Studies

The studies included in this book have been carefully chosen from those found in psychology texts and journals and from those suggested by leading authorities in the many branches of psychology. As the studies were selected, 40 seemed to be a realistic number both from a historical point of view and in terms of length. The studies chosen are arguably among the most famous, the most important, or the most influential in the history of psychology. I use the word *arguably* because many who read this book may wish to dispute some of the choices. One conclusion is sure: No *single* list of 40 studies would satisfy *everyone*. However, the studies included here stirred up a great deal of controversy when they were published, sparked the most subsequent related research, opened new fields of psychological exploration, changed dramatically our knowledge of human behavior, and continue to be cited frequently. These studies are organized by chapter according to the major psychology branches into which they best fit: *Biology and Human Behavior; Perception and Consciousness; Learning and Conditioning; Intelligence, Cognition, and Memory; Human Development; Emotion and Motivation; Personality; Psychopathology; Psychotherapy;* and *Social Psychology*.

Presenting the Studies

The original studies themselves are not included in their entirety in this book. Instead, I have discussed and summarized them in a consistent format throughout the book to promote a clear understanding of the studies presented. Each reading contains the following:

1. An exact, readily available reference for where the original study can be found

2. A brief introduction summarizing the background in the field leading up to the study and the reasons the researcher carried out the project

3. The theoretical propositions or hypotheses on which the research rests

4. A detailed account of the experimental design and methods used to carry out the research, including, where appropriate, who the participants were and how they were recruited; descriptions of any apparatus and materials used; and the actual procedures followed in carrying out the research

5. A summary of the results of the study in clear, understandable, nontechnical, nonstatistical, no-jargon language

6. An interpretation of the meaning of the findings based on the author's own discussion in the original article

7. The significance of the study to the field of psychology

8. A brief discussion of supportive or contradictory follow-up research findings and subsequent questioning or criticism from others in the field

9. A sampling of recent applications and citations of the study in others' articles to demonstrate its continuing influence

10. References for additional and updated readings relating to the study

Often, scientists speak in languages that are not easily understood. (Even by other scientists!) The primary goal of this book is to make these discoveries meaningful and accessible to the reader and to allow you to experience the excitement and drama of these remarkable and important discoveries. Where possible and appropriate, I have edited and simplified some of the studies presented here for ease of reading and understanding. However, this has been done carefully so that the meaning and elegance of the work are preserved and the impact of the research is distilled and clarified.

New to the Eighth Edition

This eighth edition of *Forty Studies* offers numerous noteworthy and substantive changes and additions. The *Recent Applications* sections near the end of the readings have been substantively updated. These sections sample recent citations of the 40 studies into the 21st century. The 40 studies discussed in this book are referred to in over 1,000 research articles every year! A small sampling of those articles is briefly summarized throughout this edition to allow you to experience the *ongoing* influence of each or more of these 40 studies that changed psychology. These new studies (that have cited the study under discussion) include the following (only authors and titles are included here—full reference information is available at the end of each main-study discussion):

- Alferink, L., et al., (2010). Brain-(not) based education: Dangers of misunderstanding and misapplication of neuroscience research.

- Cacioppo, S., et al., (2014). Toward a neurology of loneliness.
- Hur, Y. M., et al., (2014). Shared genetic and environmental influences on self-reported creative achievement in art and science.
- Adolph, K. E., et al., (2014). Fear of heights in infants.
- Hobson, J. (2009). REM sleep and dreaming: Towards a theory of protoconsciousness.
- Clercq, T. D. (2017). Embracing Ambiguity in the Analysis of Form in Pop/Rock Music, 1982–1991.
- Moens, E., et al., (2014). How can classical conditioning learning procedures support the taste development in toddlers.
- DeAngelis, T. (2010). Little Albert regains his identity.
- Churchill, A., et al., (2015). The creation of a superstitious belief regarding putters in a laboratory-based golfing task.
- Rubie-Davies, C. M., & Rosenthal, R. (2016). Intervening in teachers' expectations: A random effects meta-analytic approach to examining the effectiveness of an intervention.
- Tsai, Min-Ying, (2016). Research on multiple intelligences of junior high school students with different background variables.
- Moser, E., & Moser, M. B. (2014, March). Mapping your every move.
- Carlson, C. A., et al., (2017). An investigation of the weapon focus effect and the confidence–accuracy relationship for eyewitness identification.
- Berscheid, E. (2010). Love in the fourth dimension.
- Zentall, T. R., & Pattison, K. F. (2016). Now you see it, now you don't: object permanence in dogs.
- Walker, L. J. (2014). Sex differences in moral reasoning.
- Garcia, J. R., et al., (2014). Variation in orgasm occurrence by sexual orientation in a sample of US singles.
- Lawrence, K., et al., (2015). Age, gender, and puberty influence the development of facial emotion recognition.
- Philipa, R., et al., (2012). A systematic review and meta-analysis of the fMRI investigation of autism spectrum disorders.
- Frantzen, K. et al., (2016). Parental self-perception in the autism spectrum disorder literature: a systematic mixed studies review.
- Moses, I., et al., (2016). Gender and gender role differences in student–teachers' commitment to teaching.
- Denollet, J. Et al., (2010). General propensity to psychological distress affects: Cardiovascular outcomes: Evidence from research on the type D (distressed) personality profile.
- Bhandari, S. (2018). Mental health and psychotherapy: Types of psychotherapy.
- Appukutan, D. (2016). Strategies to manage patients with dental anxiety and dental phobia.

- Mondal, A., & Kumar, M. (2015). A study on Rorschach depression index in patients suffering from depression.
- Nagle, Y. K., & Rani, E. K. (2015). Sound apperception test: Development and validation.
- Carson, A. (2018). Bureau of Justice Statistics.
- Parsons, D., (2016). Social conformity to moral dilemmas.
- van Bommel, M., et al., (2016). Booze, bars, and bystander behavior: People who consumed alcohol help faster in the presence of others.
- Griggs, R. A., & Whitehead III, G. I. (2015). Coverage of Milgram's obedience experiments in social psychology textbooks: Where have all the criticisms gone?

As you read through the brief summaries of these studies, you will be able to appreciate the breadth and richness of the contributions still being made today by the 40 studies that comprise this book.

Over the several years since completing the seventh edition, I have continued to enjoy numerous conversations with, and helpful suggestions from, colleagues in many branches of psychological research about potential changes in the selection of studies over the decades of revisions of this book. This has resulted in a selection of 40 studies that represents the history of psychological research *arguably* as well as can be expected.

All the studies, regardless of vintage, discussed in the upcoming pages have one issue in common: research ethics. Perhaps the most important building block of psychological science is a strict understanding and adherence to a clear set of professional ethical guidelines in any research involving humans or animals. Let's consider briefly the ethical principles social scientists work diligently to follow as they make their discoveries.

The Ethics of Research Involving Human or Animal Participants

Without subjects, scientific research is virtually impossible. In physics, the subjects are matter and energy; in botany, they are plant life; in chemistry, they are molecules, atoms, and subatomic particles; and in psychology, the participants are people. Sometimes, certain types of research do not ethically permit the use of human participants, so animal subjects are substituted. However, the ultimate goal of animal research in psychology is to understand human behavior better, not to study the animals themselves. In this book, you will be reading about research involving both human and animal subjects. Some of the studies may cause you to question the ethics of the researchers in regard to the procedures used with the subjects.

When painful or stressful procedures are part of a study, the question of ethics is noted in the chapter. However, because this is such a volatile and topical issue, a brief discussion of the ethical guidelines followed by present-day psychologists in all research is included here in advance of the specific studies described in this book.

Research with Human Participants

The American Psychological Association (APA) has issued strict and clear guidelines that researchers must follow when carrying out experiments involving human participants. A portion of the introduction to those guidelines reads as follows:

> Psychologists strive to benefit those with whom they work and take care to do no harm. In their professional actions, psychologists seek to safeguard the welfare and rights of those with whom they interact. . . . When conflicts occur among psychologists' obligations or concerns, they attempt to resolve these conflicts in a responsible fashion that avoids or minimizes harm. . . . Psychologists uphold professional standards of conduct, clarify their professional roles and obligations, accept appropriate responsibility for their behavior, and seek to manage conflicts of interest that could lead to exploitation or harm. . . . Psychologists respect the dignity and worth of all people, and the rights of individuals to privacy, confidentiality, and self-determination (excerpted from *Ethical Principles of Psychologists and Code of Conduct*, 2003; see http:// apa.org/ethics).

Researchers today take great care to adhere to those principles by following basic ethical principles in carrying out all studies involving human participants. These principles may be compiled and summarized as follows:

1. *Protection from harm.* This may seem overly obvious to you: Of course, researchers have the duty to protect their research participants from harm; don't they? The answer is yes! But this was not always a hard and fast rule. As you will see in a few of the studies in this book, debates have long ensued over whether the rights of the volunteers were violated and whether researchers truly followed the other following guidelines. Moreover, the protection must extend beyond the experiments so that if a participant has any disturbing thoughts later on, he or she may contact the researchers and discuss them.

2. *Informed consent.* A researcher must explain to potential participants what the experiment is about and what procedures will be used so that the individual is able to make an informed decision about whether or not to

participate. If the person then agrees to participate, this is called *informed consent*. As you will see in this book, sometimes the true purposes of an experiment cannot be revealed because this would alter the behavior of the participants and contaminate the results. In such cases, when deception is used, a subject still must be given adequate information for informed consent, and the portions of the experiment that are hidden must be both justifiable based on the importance of the potential findings and revealed to the participants at the end of their involvement in the study. In research involving children or minors, parent or guardian consent is required and the same ethical guidelines apply.

3. *Freedom to withdraw at any time.* Part of informed consent is the principle that all human participants in all research projects must be aware that they may withdraw freely from the study at any time. This may appear to be an unnecessary rule because it would seem obvious that any subject who is too uncomfortable with the procedures can simply leave. However, this is not always so straightforward. For example, undergraduate students are often given course credit for participating as participants in psychological experiments. If they feel that withdrawing will influence the credit they need, they may not feel free to do so. When participants are paid to participate, if they are made to feel that their completion of the experiment is a requirement for payment, this could produce an unethical inducement to avoid withdrawing if they wish to do so. To avoid this problem, participants should be given credit or paid at the beginning of the procedure *just for showing up*.

4. *Confidentiality.* All results based on participants in experiments should be kept in complete confidence unless specific agreements have been made with the participants. This does not mean that results cannot be reported and published, but this is done in such a way that individual data cannot be identified. Often, no identifying information is even acquired from participants, and all data are combined to arrive at *average* differences among groups.

5. *Debriefing.* Most psychological research involves methods that are completely harmless, both during and after the study. However, even seemingly harmless procedures can sometimes produce negative effects, such as frustration, embarrassment, or concern. One common safeguard against those effects is the ethical requirement of debriefing. After participants have completed an experiment, especially one involving any form of deception, they should be debriefed. During debriefing, the true purpose and goals of the experiment are explained to them, and they are given the opportunity to ask any questions about their experiences. If there is any possibility of lingering aftereffects from the experiment, the researchers should provide participants with contact information if participants might have any concerns in the future.

As you read through the studies included in this book, you may find a few studies that appear to have violated some of these ethical principles. Those studies were carried out long before formal ethical guidelines existed and the research could not be replicated under today's ethical principles. The lack of guidelines, however, does not excuse past researchers for abuses. Judgment of those investigators and their actions must now be made by each of us individually, and we must learn, as psychologists have, from past mistakes.

Research with Animal Subjects

One of the hottest topics of discussion inside and outside the scientific community is the question of the ethics of animal research. Animal-rights groups are growing in number and are becoming increasingly vocal and militant. More controversy exists today over animal subjects than human participants, probably because animals cannot be protected, as humans can, with informed consent, freedom to withdraw, or debriefing. In addition, the most radical animal rights activists take the view that all living things are ordered in value by their ability to sense pain. In this conceptualization, animals are equal in value to humans and, therefore, any use of animals by humans is seen as unethical. This use includes eating a chicken, wearing leather, and owning pets (which, according to some animal-rights activists, is a form of slavery).

At one end of the spectrum, many people believe that research with animals is inhumane and unethical and should be prohibited. However, nearly all scientists and most Americans believe that the limited and humane use of animals in scientific research is necessary and beneficial. Many lifesaving drugs and medical techniques have been developed through the use of animal experimental subjects. Animals have also often been subjects in psychological research to study issues such as depression, brain development, overcrowding, and learning processes. The primary reason animals are used in research is that to carry out similar research on humans clearly would be unethical. For example, suppose you wanted to study the effect on brain development and intelligence of raising infants in an enriched environment with many activities and toys, versus an impoverished environment with little to do. To assign human infants to these different conditions would simply not be possible. However, most people would agree that rats could be studied without major ethical concerns to reveal findings potentially important to humans (see Reading 2 on research by Rosenzweig and Bennett).

The APA, in addition to its guidelines on human participants, has strict rules governing research with animal subjects that are designed to ensure humane treatment. These rules require that research animals receive proper housing, feeding, cleanliness, and health care. All unnecessary pain to the animal is prohibited. A portion of the APA's *Guidelines for the Ethical Conduct in the Care and Use of Animals* (2004) reads as follows:

> Animals are to be provided with humane care and healthful conditions during their stay in the facility. . . . Psychologists are encouraged to consider enriching the environments of their laboratory animals and should keep abreast of literature on well-being and enrichment for the species with which they work. . . . When alternative behavioral procedures are available, those that minimize discomfort to the animal should be used. When using aversive conditions, psychologists should adjust the parameters of stimulation to levels that appear minimal, though compatible with the aims of the research. Psychologists are encouraged to test painful stimuli on themselves, whenever reasonable (see http://apa.org/science/anguide.html).

In this book, several studies involve animal subjects. In addition to the ethical considerations of such research, difficulties also arise in applying findings from animals to humans. These issues are discussed in this book within each reading that includes animal research. Each individual, whether a researcher or a student of psychology, must make his or her own decisions about animal research in general and the justifiability of using animal subjects in any specific instance. If you allow for the idea that animal research is acceptable under *some* circumstances, then, for each study involving animals in this book, you must decide if the value of the study's findings supports the methods used.

One final note related to this issue of animal subjects involves a development that is a response to public concerns about potential mistreatment. The city of Cambridge, Massachusetts, one of the major research centers of the world and home to institutions such as Harvard University and the Massachusetts Institute of Technology (MIT), has led the way by creating the position of *Commissioner of Laboratory Animals* within the *Cambridge Health Department* (see http://www.-cambridgepublichealth.org/services/regulatory-activities/lab-animals). This was the first such governmental position in the United States. Cambridge, and the many research universities there, is home to 44 laboratories that house over 200,000 animals. The commissioner's charge is to ensure humane and proper treatment of all animal subjects in all aspects of the research process, from the animals' living quarters to the methods used in administering the research protocols. If a lab is found to be in violation of Cambridge's strict laws concerning the humane care of lab animals, the commissioner is authorized to impose fines of up to $300 per day. As of this writing, only one such fine has been imposed; it amounted to $40,000 (for 133 days in violation) on a facility that appeared to have deliberately disregarded animal treatment laws (Dr. Julie Medley, Commissioner of Laboratory Animals, e-mail, April 15, 2012). In all other cases, any facility that has been found in violation has willingly and quickly corrected the problem. The studies you are about to experience in this book have benefited all of humankind in many ways and to varying degrees. The history of psychological research is a relatively short one, but it is brimming with the richness and excitement of discovering human nature.

Acknowledgments

I would like to express my gratitude to Ashley Dodge, editor in chief at Pearson, for her support and continuing, talented assistance on this project. For this edition, my sincere thanks go out to Tanimaa Mehra, sponsoring editor at Pearson, Sugandh Juneja, the content producer at Pearson, and Bhanuprakash Sherla, the project manager at SPi Global.

Thank you to my psychology colleagues in the field who have taken the time, interest, and effort to communicate to me their comments, suggestions, and wisdom relating to this and previous editions of *Forty Studies*. I have attempted at every opportunity to incorporate their valued insights into each edition.

To my family, my friends, and my students who have participated in the history of this book in so many tangible and intangible ways over the past 20+ years (you know who you are), I extend my continuing best wishes and heartfelt thanks.

Roger R. Hock

Chapter 1
Biology and Human Behavior

 ## Learning Objectives

1.1 Summarize research on the relationship between the right and left sides of the human brain

1.2 Evaluate how Rosenzweig's research on the social environment of rats has influenced analysis and understanding of brain enrichment in humans

1.3 Explain how twin studies are used to study the impact of genetics on human behavior

1.4 Describe applications and results of experimental measurements of depth perception development

Typically, the first or second chapter in general psychology focuses on various aspects of the biology of human behavior. This is simply not due to convention but because basic biological processes, primarily dealing with the brain, underlie *all* behavior. The other branches of psychology rest, to varying degrees, on this biological foundation. The area of psychology that studies these basic physiological functions is usually called *psychobiology, biological psychology, or behavioral neuroscience*. These fields focus on the actions of your brain and nervous system, the processes of receiving stimulation and information from the environment through your senses, the ways your brain organizes sensory information to create your perceptions of the world, and how all of this affects your behavior.

The studies chosen to represent this basic component of psychological research include a wide range of research, are often cited and are among the most influential. The first study discusses a famous research program on right-brain/left-brain specialization that shaped much of our present knowledge about how the brain functions. The second study surprised the scientific community by demonstrating how a stimulating "childhood" might result in a more highly developed brain. The third study represents a fundamental change in the thinking of many psychologists about the basic causes of human behavior, personality, and social interaction—namely, an appreciation for the significance of your *genes' effect* on your behavior. The fourth study is the invention of the famous *visual cliff* method of studying infants' brains to perceive depth. All these studies, along with several others in this book, also address an issue that underlies and connects nearly all areas of psychology and provides the fuel for an ongoing and fascinating debate: the nature–nurture controversy.

1

Reading 1.1: One Brain or Two?

Gazzaniga, M. S. (1967). The split brain in man. *Scientific American, 217*(2), 24–29.

1.1 Summarize research on the relationship between the right and left sides of the human brain

You are probably aware that the two halves (or *hemispheres*) of your brain are not the same and that they perform different functions. For example, in general, the left side of your brain is responsible for movement on the right side of your body, and vice versa. Beyond this, though, the two brain hemispheres have much more elaborate specialized abilities.

It has come to be rather common knowledge that for most of us, the left brain controls our ability to use language while the right is involved in spatial relationships, such as those needed for artistic activities. Stroke or head-injury patients who suffer damage to the left side of the brain will often lose, to varying degrees, their ability to speak (often this skill returns with therapy and training). Some researchers believe that each hemisphere of your brain may actually be a separate mental system with its own individual abilities for learning, remembering, perceiving the world, and feeling emotions. The concepts underlying this view of the brain rest on early scientific research on the effects of splitting the brain into two separate hemispheres.

This research was pioneered by Roger W. Sperry (1913–1994), beginning about 15 years prior to the article examined in this chapter. In his early work with animal subjects, Sperry made many remarkable discoveries. For example, in one series of studies, cats' brains were surgically altered to sever the connection between the two halves of the brain and to alter the optic nerves so that the left eye transmitted information only to the left hemisphere and the right eye only to the right hemisphere. Following surgery, the cats appeared to behave normally and exhibited virtually with no ill effects. Then, with the right eye covered, the cats learned a new behavior, such as walking through a short maze to find food. After the cats became skilled at maneuvering through the maze, the eye cover was shifted to the cats' left eyes. Now, when the cats were placed back in the maze, their right brains had no idea where to turn, and the animals had to relearn the entire maze from the beginning.

Sperry conducted many related studies over the next 30 years, and in 1981 he received the Nobel Prize for his work on the specialized abilities of the two hemispheres of the brain. When his research endeavors turned to human participants in the early 1960s, he was joined in his work at the California Institute of Technology (Caltech) by Michael Gazzaniga. Although Sperry is considered to be the founder of split-brain research, Gazzaniga's article has been chosen here because it is a clear, concise summary of their early collaborative work with human participants and it, along with other related research by Gazzaniga, is cited often in psychology texts. Its selection is in no way intended to overlook or overshadow either Sperry's leadership in this field or his great contributions. Gazzaniga owes his early research, and his discoveries in the area of hemispheric specialization, to Roger W. Sperry (see Sperry, 1968; Puente, 1995).

To understand split-brain research, some knowledge of human physiology is required. The two hemispheres of your brain are in constant communication with one another via the *corpus callosum*, a structure made up of about 200 million nerve fibers (Figure 1.1.1). If your corpus callosum is cut, this major line of communication is disrupted, and the two halves of your brain must function then independently. If we want to study each half of your brain separately, "all" we need to do is surgically sever your corpus callosum.

But can scientists surgically divide the brains of humans for research? That sounds more like something out of a Frankenstein movie than real science! Obviously, research ethics would never allow such drastic methods simply for the purpose of studying the specialized abilities of the brain's two hemispheres. However, in the late 1950s, the field of medicine provided psychologists with a golden opportunity. In some people with very rare and very extreme cases of uncontrollable epilepsy, it was found that seizures

Figure 1.1.1 The corpus callosum.

SOURCE: 3D4Medical/Science Source

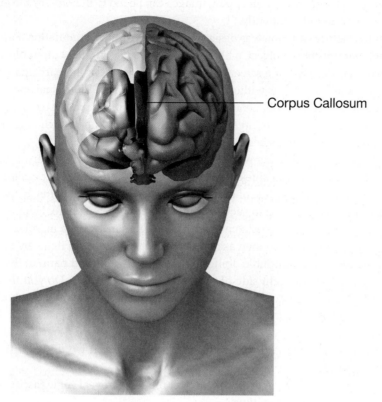

Corpus Callosum

could be greatly reduced or virtually eliminated by surgically severing the patient's corpus callosum. This operation was (and is) successful, as a last resort, for those patients who cannot be helped by any other means. When this article was written in 1966, 10 such operations had been undertaken, and four of the patients consented to participate in examination and testing by Sperry and Gazzaniga to determine how their perceptual and intellectual skills were affected by this surgical treatment.

Theoretical Propositions

The researchers wanted to explore the extent to which the two halves of the human brain are able to function independently as well as whether they have separate and unique abilities. If the information traveling between the two halves of your brain is interrupted, would the right side of your body suddenly be unable to coordinate with the left? If language is controlled by the left side of the brain, how would your ability to speak and understand words be affected by this surgery? Would thinking and reasoning processes exist in both halves separately? If the brain is really two separate brains, would a person be capable of functioning normally when these two brains are no longer able to communicate? Considering that we receive sensory input from both the right and the left brains, how would the senses of vision, hearing, and touch be affected? Sperry and Gazzaniga attempted to answer these and many other questions in their studies of split-brain individuals.

Method

The researchers developed three types of tests to explore a wide range of mental and perceptual capabilities of the patients. One was designed to examine visual abilities. They devised a technique that allowed a picture of an object, a word, or parts of words to be transmitted only to the visual area (called a *field*) in *either* the right or left brain hemisphere, but not to both. Normally, both of your eyes send information to both sides of your brain. However, with exact placement of items or words in front of you, and with your eyes fixed on a specific point, images can be fed to the right or the left visual field of your brain independently.

Another testing situation was designed for tactile (touch) stimulation. Participants could feel, but not see, an object, a block letter, or even a word in cutout block letters. The apparatus consisted of a screen with a space under it for the participant to reach through and touch the items without being able to see them. The visual and the tactile devices could be used simultaneously so that, for example, a picture of a pen could be projected to one side of the brain and the same object could be searched for by either hand among various objects behind the screen (see Figure 1.1.2).

Testing auditory abilities was trickier. When sound enters either of your ears, sensations are sent to both sides of your brain. Therefore, it is not possible to limit auditory input to only one side of the brain even in split-brain patients. However, it is possible to limit the *response* to such input to one brain hemisphere. Here is how this was done: Imagine that several common objects (a spoon, a pen, a marble) are placed into a cloth bag and you are then asked, verbally, to find certain items by touch. You would probably have no trouble doing so. If you place your left hand in the bag, it is being controlled by the right side of your brain, and vice versa. Do you think either side of your brain could do this task alone? As you will see in a moment, both halves of the brain are not equally capable of responding to this auditory task. What if you are not asked for specific objects but are asked to reach into the bag and identify objects by touch? Again, this would not be difficult for you, but it would be difficult for a split-brain patient.

Gazzaniga combined all these testing techniques to reveal some fascinating findings about how the brain functions.

Results

First, know by following this radical brain surgery, the patients' intelligence level, personality, typical emotional reactions, and so on were relatively unchanged. They were happy and relieved that they were now free of seizures. Gazzaniga reported that one patient, while still groggy from surgery, joked that he had "a splitting headache." When testing began, however, these participants demonstrated many unusual mental abilities.

VISUAL ABILITIES   One of the first tests involved a board with a horizontal row of lights. When a patient sat in front of this board and stared at a point in the middle of the lights, the bulbs would flash across both the right and left visual fields. However, when the patients were asked to explain what they saw, they said only the lights on the right side of the board had flashed. Next, when the researchers flashed only the lights on the

---

Figure 1.1.2 A typical visual testing device for split-brain participants.

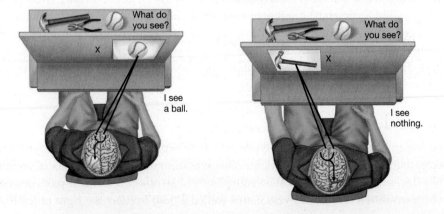

left side of the visual field, the patients claimed to have seen nothing. A logical conclusion from these findings was that the right side of the brain was blind. Then an amazing thing happened. The lights were flashed again, only this time the patients were asked to point to the lights that had flashed. Although they had said they only saw the lights on the right, they pointed to all the lights in both visual fields. Using this method of pointing, it was found that both halves of the brain had seen the lights and were equally skilled in visual perception. The important point here is that when the patients failed to *say* that they had seen all the lights, it was not because they didn't see them but because the center for speech is located in the brain's left hemisphere. In other words, for you to say you saw something, the object has to have been seen by the left side of your brain.

TACTILE ABILITIES   You can try this test yourself. Put your hands behind your back. Then have someone place familiar objects (a spoon, a pen, a book, a watch) in either your right or your left hand and see if you can identify the object. You would not find this task to be very difficult, would you? This is basically what Sperry and Gazzaniga did with the split-brain patients. When an object was placed in the right hand in such a way that the patient could not see or hear it, messages about the object would travel to the left hemisphere and the patient was able to name the object and describe it and its uses. However, when the same objects were placed in the left hand (connected to the right hemisphere), the patients could not name them or describe them in any way. But did the patients *know* in their right brain what the object was? To find out, the researchers asked the participants to match the object in their left hand (without seeing it, remember) to a group of various objects presented to them. This they could do as easily as you or I could. Again, this places verbal ability in the left hemisphere of the brain. Keep in mind that the reason you are able to name unseen objects in your left hand is that the information from the right side of your brain is transmitted via the corpus callosum to the left side, where your center for language says, "That's a spoon!"

VISUAL PLUS TACTILE TESTS   Combining these two types of tests provided support for the preceding findings and also offered additional interesting results. If participants were shown a picture of an object to the right hemisphere only, they were unable to name it or describe it. In fact, they might display no verbal response at all or even deny that anything had been presented. However, if the patients were allowed to reach under the screen with their left hand (still using only the right hemisphere) and touch a selection of objects, they were always able to find the one that had been presented visually.

The right hemisphere can think about and analyze objects as well. Gazzaniga reported that when the right hemisphere was shown a picture of an item such as a cigarette, the participants could touch 10 objects behind the screen, all of which did not include a cigarette, and select an object that was most closely related to the item pictured—in this case, an ashtray. He further explained:

> Oddly enough, however, even after their correct response, and while they were holding the ashtray in their left hand, they were unable to name or describe the object or the picture of the cigarette. Evidently, the left hemisphere was completely divorced, in perception and knowledge, from the right. (p. 26)

Other tests were conducted to shed additional light on the language-processing abilities of the right hemisphere. One very famous, ingenious, and revealing use of the visual apparatus came when the word HEART was projected to the patients so that HE was sent to the right visual field and ART was sent to the left. Now, keeping in mind (your connected mind) the functions of the two hemispheres, what do you think the patients verbally reported seeing? If you said ART, you were correct. However, and here is the revealing part, when the participants were presented with two cards with the words HE and ART printed on them and asked to point with the left hand to the word they had seen, they all pointed to HE! This demonstrated that the right hemisphere is able to comprehend language although it does so in a different way from the left: in a nonverbal way.

The auditory tests conducted with the patients produced similar results. When patients were asked to reach with their left hand into a grab bag hidden from view and pull out certain specific objects (a watch, a marble, a comb, a coin), they had no trouble. This demonstrated that the right hemisphere was comprehending language. It was even possible to describe a related aspect of an item with the same accurate results. An example given by Gazzaniga was when the patients were asked to find in a grab bag full of plastic fruit "the fruit monkeys like best," they retrieved a banana. Or when told "Sunkist sells a lot of them," they pulled out an orange. However, if these same pieces of fruit were placed out of view in the patients' left hand, they were unable to say what they were. In other words, when a verbal response was required, the right hemisphere was unable to speak.

One last example of this amazing difference between the two hemispheres involved plastic block letters on the table behind the screen. When patients were asked to spell various words by feel with the left hand, they had an easy time doing so. Even if three or four letters that spelled specific words were placed behind the screen, they were able, left-handed, to arrange them correctly into words. However, immediately after completing this task, the participants could not name the word they had just spelled. The left hemisphere of the brain is superior to the right for speech (in some left-handed people, this is reversed). But in what skills, if any, does the right hemisphere excel? Sperry and Gazzaniga found in this early work that visual tasks involving spatial relationships and shapes were performed with greater proficiency by the left hand (even though these patients were all right-handed). As seen in Figure 1.1.3, participants who copy three-dimensional drawings (using the pencil behind the screen) were much more successful when using their left hand.

The researchers wanted to explore emotional reactions of split-brain patients. While performing visual experiments, Sperry and Gazzaniga suddenly flashed a picture of a

---

Figure 1.1.3 Drawings made by split-brain patients.

SOURCE: Adapted from p. 27, "The Split Brain in Man," by Michael S. Gazzaniga.

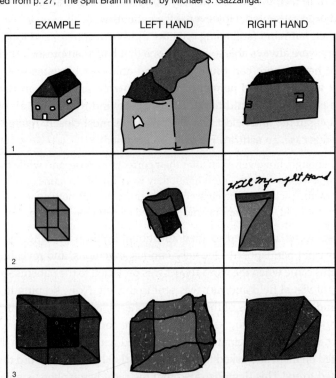

nude woman to either the left or right hemisphere. In one instance when this picture was shown to the left hemisphere of a female patient:

> She laughed and verbally identified the picture of a nude. When it was later presented to the right hemisphere, she said . . . she saw nothing, but almost immediately a sly smile spread over her face and she began to chuckle. Asked what she was laughing at, she said: "I don't know . . . nothing . . . oh—that funny machine." Although the right hemisphere could not describe what it had seen, the sight nevertheless elicited an emotional response like the one evoked in the left hemisphere. (p. 29).

Discussion

The overall conclusion drawn from the research reported in this article was that two different brains exist within each person's cranium—each with complex abilities. Gazzaniga notes the possibility that if our brain is really two brains, then perhaps we have the potential to process twice as much information if the two halves are divided. Some research evidence suggests that split-brain patients have the ability to perform two cognitive tasks as fast as a normal person can carry out one.

Significance of Findings

These findings and subsequent research carried out by Sperry, Gazzaniga, and others were significant and far-reaching. They demonstrated that the two halves of your brain have many specialized skills and functions. Your left brain is "better" at speaking, writing, mathematical calculation, and reading, and it is the primary center for language. Your right hemisphere, however, possesses superior capabilities for recognizing faces, solving problems involving spatial relationships, symbolic reasoning, and artistic activities. In the years since Sperry and Gazzaniga's "split-brain" discoveries, psychobiological researchers have continued to uncover the amazing complexities of the human brain. Our brains are far more divided and compartmentalized than merely two hemispheres. We now know that a multitude of specific structures within the brain serve very specialized cognitive and behavioral functions.

Our increased knowledge of the specialized functioning of the brain allows us to treat victims of stroke or head injury more effectively. By knowing the location of the damage, we can predict what deficits are likely to exist as a patient recovers. Through this knowledge, therapists can employ appropriate relearning and rehabilitation strategies to help patients recover fully and quickly.

Gazzaniga and Sperry, after years of continuous work in this area, suggested that each hemisphere of your brain really is a mind of its own. In a later study, split-brain patients were tested on much more complex problems than have been discussed here. One question asked was "What profession would you choose?" A male patient verbally (left hemisphere) responded that he would choose to be a draftsman, but his left hand (right hemisphere) spelled, by touch in block letters, *automobile racer* (Gazzaniga & LeDoux, 1978). Gazzaniga has taken this theory a step further. He has proposed that even in people whose brains are normal and intact, the two hemispheres may not be in complete communication (Gazzaniga, 1985). For example, if certain bits of information, such as those forming an emotion, are not stored in a linguistic format, the left hemisphere may not have access to it. The result of this is that you may feel sad and not be able to say why. As this is an uncomfortable cognitive dilemma, the left hemisphere may try to *find* a verbal reason to explain the sadness (after all, language is its main job). However, because your left hemisphere does not have all the necessary data, its explanation may actually be wrong!

Criticisms

The findings from the split-brain studies carried out over the years by Sperry, Gazzaniga, and others have rarely been disputed. The main body of criticism about this research has focused instead on the way the idea of right- and left-brain specialization has filtered down to popular culture and the media.

A widely believed myth states that some people are more *right-brained* or more *left-brained*, or that one side of your brain needs to be developed in order for you to improve certain skills (more on this next). Jerre Levy, a psychobiologist at the University of Chicago, has been in the forefront of scientists trying to dispel the notion that we have two separately functioning brains. She claims that it is precisely because each hemisphere has separate functions that they must integrate their abilities instead of separating them as is commonly believed. Through such integration, your brain is able to perform in ways that are greater than and different from the abilities of either side alone.

When you read a story, for example, your right hemisphere is specializing in emotional content (humor, pathos), picturing visual descriptions, keeping track of the story structure as a whole, and appreciating artistic writing style (such as the use of metaphors). While all this is happening, your left hemisphere understands the written words, deriving meaning from the complex relationships among words and sentences, and translating words into their phonetic sounds so that they can be understood as language. The reason you are able to read, understand, and appreciate a story is that your brain functions as a single, integrated structure (Levy, 1985).

In fact, Levy explains that no human activity uses only one side of the brain: "The popular myths are interpretations and wishes, not the observations of scientists. Normal people have not half a brain, nor two brains, but one gloriously differentiated brain, with each hemisphere contributing its specialized abilities" (Levy, 1985, p. 44).

Recent Applications

The continuing influence of the split-brain research by Sperry and Gazzaniga echoes the quote from Levy. A review of recent medical and psychological literature reveals numerous articles in various fields referring to the early work and methodology of Roger Sperry, as well as to more recent findings by Gazzaniga and his associates. For example, a study from 1998 conducted in France (Hommet & Billard, 1998) has questioned the foundations of the Sperry and Gazzaniga studies—namely, that severing the corpus callosum actually divides the hemispheres of the brain. The French study found that children born without a corpus callosum (a rare brain malformation) demonstrated that information was being transmitted between their brain hemispheres. The researchers concluded that significant connections other than the corpus callosum must exist in these children. Whether such subcortical connections are present in split-brain individuals remains unclear.

Recent research has sounded an additional note of caution in how educators might be tempted to apply Gazzaniga's findings (Alferink & Farmer-Dougan, 2010). The widespread belief that different brain hemispheres control distinct cognitive functions has been clearly demonstrated only in a *selected* number of patients who, for specific medical reasons have undergone the surgical procedure of severing the corpus callosum, we should not assume that the findings from these individuals should apply to everyone whose brains are intact. To leap from the assumption that different brain hemispheres are responsible for unique tasks to formulating education models based on these findings is risky. The point some researchers make is that the patients on whom this research was based displayed non typical brain function even before the surgery. Therefore, to assume that educational methodology should focus on one hemisphere or the other for those with normal nonsevered brain functioning should be avoided.

Researchers continue to explore the idea that our two brain hemispheres have separate, yet distinct, functions and influences. One such study (Morton, 2003) demonstrated how your dominant hemisphere may lead you toward specific interests and professions. Morton's research made two discoveries in this regard. Using a special written test called "The Best Hand Test," which measures *hemisphericity* (whether a person is right- or left-brain oriented), Morton found that among 400 students enrolled in first-year, general college courses, 56% were left-brain oriented. However, when the same methods applied to 180 students in various, *specialized* upper-level courses, the range of left-brain students ranged from 38% to 65%. This difference indicated that something about a person's brain hemispheres was associated with spreading students out over a variety of college degrees and interests. Second, and more revealing, Morton employed the same method in determining the hemispheric orientation of members of various professions in university settings. The findings indicated that hemispheric specialization appears to be predictive of professional choices. For example, among biochemists, Morton found that 83% were left-brain oriented, while among astronomers only 29% showed a left-brain preference (p. 319). You can see how this would make sense in relation to Sperry and Gazzaniga's work. Biology and chemistry rely more heavily on linguistic abilities whereas astronomers must have greater abilities in spatial relationships (no pun intended).

Conclusion

Gazzaniga (now at the University of California at Santa Barbara) and his associates continued to study hemispheric specialization and continued to make new discoveries. Using new, sophisticated imaging and analysis techniques, a study in his lab found that healthy individuals (those with intact brains) appear to have more trouble processing language that is projected only to their right brain, *even though the two hemispheres are connected*. The researchers showed participants either a real word or a non word that looked like a word (not just gibberish) to left or right hemispheres and found that when shown to the right side the participants had more trouble distinguishing between the real and fake words. These findings shed light on the types of connections that function in transferring information between the two sides of your brain (Gallessich, 2012).

Other behavioral scientists have carried this separate-brain idea a step further and applied it to some psychological disorders, such as dissociative, multiple personality disorder (e.g., Schiffer, 1996). The idea behind this notion is that in some people with intact, "nonsplit" brains, the right hemisphere may be able to function at a greater-than-normal level of independence from the left, and it may even take control of a person's consciousness for periods of time. Is it possible that multiple personality disorder might be the expression of hidden personalities contained in our right hemispheres? It's something to think about . . . with *both* of your hemispheres.

Alferink, L., & Farmer-Dougan, V. (2010). Brain-(not) based education: Dangers of misunderstanding and misapplication of neuroscience research. *Exceptionality, 18*, 42–52.

Gallessich, G. (2012). UCSB scientists report 'new beginning' in split-brain research, using new analytical tools. *The UC Santa Barbara Current, November 1*. Retrieved from www.news.ucsb.edu/2012/013395/ucsb-scientists-report-%E2%80%98new-beginning-split-brain-research-using-new-analytical-tools.

Gazzaniga, M. S. (1985). *The social brain*. New York: Basic Books.

Gazzaniga, M. S., & LeDoux, J. E. (1978). *The integrated mind*. New York: Plenum Press.

Hommet, C., & Billard, C. (1998). Corpus callosum syndrome in children. *Neurochirurgie, 44*(1), 110–112.

Levy, J. (1985, May). Right brain, left brain: Fact and fiction. *Psychology Today*, 42–44.

Morton, B. E. (2003). Line bisection-based hemisphericity estimates of university students and professionals: Evidence of sorting during higher education and career selection. *Brain and Cognition, 52*(3), 319–325.

Puente, A. E. (1995). Roger Wolcott Sperry (1913–1994). *American Psychologist, 50*(11), 940–941.

Schiffer, F. (1996). Cognitive ability of the right-hemisphere: Possible contributions to psychological function. *Harvard Review of Psychiatry, 4*(3), 126–138.

Sperry, R. W. (1968). Hemisphere deconnection and unity in conscious awareness. *American Psychologist, 23,* 723–733.

Reading 1.2: More Experience = Bigger Brain

Rosenzweig, M. R., Bennett, E. L., & Diamond, M. C. (1972). Brain changes in response to experience. *Scientific American, 226*(2), 22–29.

1.2 Evaluate how Rosenzweig's research on the social environment of rats has influenced analysis and understanding of brain enrichment in humans

If you were to enter the baby's room in a typical American home today, you would probably see a crib and baby's room full of stuffed animals and various colorful toys dangling directly over or within reach of the infant. Some of these toys may light up, move, play music, or do all three. What do you suppose is the parents' reasoning behind providing infants with so much to see and do? Aside from the fact that babies seem to enjoy and respond positively to these toys, most parents believe, whether they verbalize it or not, that children need a stimulating environment for optimal intellectual development and brain growth.

The question of whether certain experiences produce physical changes in the brain has been a topic of conjecture and research among philosophers and scientists for centuries. In 1785, Vincenzo Malacarne, an Italian anatomist, studied pairs of dogs from the same litter and pairs of birds from the same batches of eggs. For each pair, he would train one participant extensively over a long period of time while the other would be equally well cared for but untrained. He discovered later, in autopsies of the animals, that the brains of the trained animals appeared more complex, with a greater number of folds and fissures. However, this line of research was discontinued for unknown reasons. In the late 19th century, attempts were made to relate the circumference of the human head with the amount of learning a person had experienced. Although some early findings claimed such a relationship, later research determined that this was not a valid measure of brain development.

By the 1960s, new technologies had been developed that gave scientists the ability to measure brain changes with precision using high-magnification techniques and assessment of levels of various brain enzymes and neurotransmitter chemicals. Mark Rosenzweig and his colleagues Edward Bennett and Marian Diamond, at the University of California at Berkeley, incorporated those technologies in an ambitious series of 16 experiments over a period of 10 years to try to address the issue of the effect of experience on the brain. Their findings were reported in the article discussed in this chapter. For reasons that will become obvious, they did not use humans in their studies, but rather, as in many classic psychological experiments, their subjects were rats.

Theoretical Propositions

Because psychologists are ultimately interested in humans, not rats, the validity of using nonhuman subjects must be demonstrated. In these studies, the authors explained that for several reasons, using rodents rather than higher mammals such as primates was scientifically sound as well as more convenient. The part of the brain that is the main focus of this research is smooth in the rat, not folded and complex as it is in higher animals. Therefore, it can be examined and measured more easily. In addition, rats are small and inexpensive, which is an important consideration in the world of research laboratories (usually underfunded and lacking in space). Rats bear large litters, and this allows for members from the same litters to be assigned to different experimental conditions. The authors point out that various strains of inbred rats have been produced, and this allows researchers to include the effects of genetics in their studies if desired.

The main hypothesis implicit in Rosenzweig's research was the idea that animals raised in highly stimulating environments will demonstrate differences in brain growth and chemistry when compared with animals reared in plain or dull circumstances. In each of the experiments reported in this article, 12 sets of 3 male rats, each set from the same litter, were studied.

Method

Three male rats were chosen from each litter. They were then randomly assigned to one of three conditions. One rat remained in the laboratory cage with the rest of the colony, another was assigned to what Rosenzweig termed the "enriched" environment cage, and the third was assigned to the "impoverished" cage. Remember, 12 rats were placed in each of these conditions for each of the 16 experiments (that's 576 rats).

The three different environments (Figure 1.2.1) were described as follows:

1. The standard laboratory colony cage contained several rats in an adequate space with food and water always available.

2. The impoverished environment was a slightly smaller cage isolated in a separate room in which the rat was placed alone with adequate food and water.

3. The enriched environment was virtually a rat's Disneyland (no offense intended to Mickey!). Six to eight rats lived in a large cage furnished with a variety of objects with which they could play. A new set of rat toys, from a selection 25 objects, was placed in the cage each day, so the enriched rats experienced a lot of variety or play activities.

The rats were allowed to live in these different environments for various periods of time, ranging from 4 to 10 weeks. Following this differential treatment period, the experimental rodents were examined to determine if any differences had developed in

Figure 1.2.1 Rosenzweig's three cage environments.

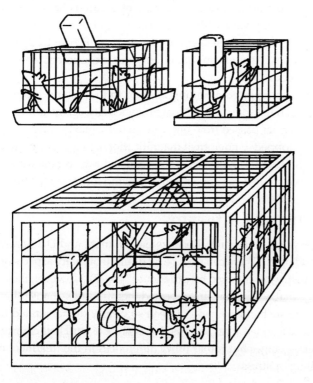

brain development. To be sure that no experimenter bias would occur, the examinations were done in random order by code number so that the person doing the autopsy would not know in which condition the rat was raised in order to avoid any unintentional bias.

The rats' brains were then measured, weighed, and analyzed to determine the amount of cell growth and levels of neurotransmitter activity. In this latter measurement, one brain enzyme was of particular interest: *acetylcholinesterase* (abbreviated AChE). This brain chemical is important because it allows for faster and more efficient transmission of impulses among brain cells.

Did Rosenzweig and his associates find differences in the brains of rats raised in enriched versus impoverished environments? The following are their results.

Results

Results indicated that the brains of the enriched rats were indeed different from those of the impoverished rats in many ways. The *cerebral cortex* (the part of the brain that responds to experience and is responsible for movement, memory, learning, and sensory input: vision, hearing, touch, taste, and smell) of the enriched rats was significantly heavier and thicker. Also, greater activity of the nervous system enzyme acetylcholinesterase, mentioned previously, was found in the brain tissue of the rats with the enriched experience.

Although no significant differences were found between the two groups of rats in the number of brain cells (*neurons*), the enriched environment produced larger neurons. Related to this was the finding that the ratio of RNA to DNA, the two most important brain chemicals for cell growth, was greater for the enriched rats. This implied that a higher level of chemical activity had taken place in the enriched rats' brains.

Rosenzweig and his colleagues stated that "although the brain differences induced by environment are not large, we are confident that they are genuine. When the experiments are replicated, the same pattern of differences is found repeatedly. . . . The most consistent effect of experience on the brain that we found was the ratio of the weight of the cortex to the weight of the rest of the brain: the sub-cortex. It appears that the cortex increases in weight quite readily in response to experience, whereas the rest of the brain changes little" (p. 25). This measurement of the ratio of the cortex to the rest of the brain was the most accurate measurement of brain changes because the overall weight of the brain may vary with the overall weight of each animal. By considering this ratio, such individual differences are canceled out. Figure 1.2.2 illustrates this finding for all 16 studies. As you can see, in only one experiment was the difference *not* statistically significant.

The researchers reported a finding relating to the two rat groups' brain *synapses* (the points at which neurons meet). Most brain activity occurs at the synapse, where a nerve impulse is either passed from one neuron to the next so that it continues on, or it is inhibited and stopped. Under great magnification using the electron microscope, the researchers found that the synapses of the enriched rats' brains were 50% larger than those of the impoverished rats, potentially allowing for increased brain activity.

Discussion and Criticisms

After nearly 10 years of research, Rosenzweig, Bennett, and Diamond were willing to state with confidence, "There can now be no doubt that many aspects of brain anatomy and brain chemistry are changed by experience" (p. 27). However, they were also quick to acknowledge that, when they first reported their findings, many other scientists were skeptical because such effects had not been so clearly demonstrated in past research. Some criticism contended that perhaps it was not the enriched environment that produced the brain changes but rather other differences in the treatment of the rats, such as mere handling or stress.

Figure 1.2.2 Ratio of cortex to the rest of the brain: enriched compared with impoverished environment. (Results in experiments 2 through 16 were statistically significant.)

SOURCE: Adapted from Rosenzweig, Bennett, & Diamond, p. 26.

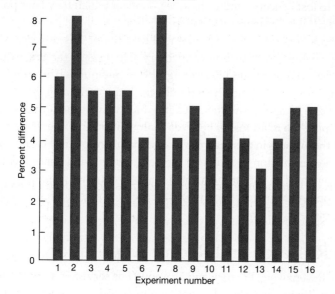

The criticism of differential handling was a valid one in that the enriched rats were handled twice each day when they were removed from the cage as the toys were being changed, but the impoverished rats were not handled. It was possible, therefore, that the handling alone might have caused the results and not the enriched environment. To respond to this potentially confounding factor, the researchers handled one group of rats every day and did not handle another group of their littermates (all were raised in the same environment). Rosenzweig and his associates found no differences in the brains of these two groups. In addition, in their later studies, both the enriched and impoverished rats were handled equally and, still, the same pattern of results was found.

As for the criticisms relating to stress, the argument was that the isolation experienced by the impoverished rats was stressful, and this was the reason for their less-developed brains. Rosenzweig et al. cited other research that had exposed rats to a daily routine of stress (cage rotation or mild electric shock) and had found no evidence of changes in brain development due to stress alone.

One of the problems of any research carried out in a laboratory is that it is nearly always an artificial environment. Rosenzweig and his colleagues were curious about how various levels of stimulation might affect the brain development of animals in their *natural* environments. They pointed out that laboratory rats and mice often have been raised in artificial environments for as many as a hundred generations and bear little genetic resemblance to rats in the wild. To explore this intriguing possibility, they began studying wild deer mice. After the mice were trapped, they were randomly placed in either natural outdoor conditions or the enriched laboratory cages. After 4 weeks, the outdoor mice showed greater brain development than did those in the enriched laboratory environment: "This indicates that even the enriched laboratory environment is indeed impoverished in comparison with a natural environment" (p. 27).

The most important criticism of any research involving animal subjects is the question of its application, if any, to humans. Without a doubt, this line of research could never be performed on humans, but it is nevertheless the responsibility of the researchers to address this issue, and these scientists did so.

The authors explained that it is difficult to generalize from the findings of one set of rats to another set of rats, and consequently it is much more difficult to try to apply rat findings to monkeys or humans. And, although they report similar findings with several species of rodents, they admit that more research would be necessary before any assumptions could be made responsibly about the effects of experience on the human brain. They proposed, however, that the value of this kind of research on animals is that "it allows us to test concepts and techniques, some of which may later prove useful in [ethical] research with human subjects" (p. 27).

The authors suggested several potential benefits of this research. One possible application pertained to the study of memory. Changes in the brain due to experience might lead to a better understanding of how memories are stored in the brain. This could, in turn, lead to new techniques for improving memory and preventing memory loss due to aging. Another area in which this research might prove helpful was in explaining the relationship between malnutrition and intelligence. The concept proposed by the authors in this regard was that malnutrition may be a person's responsiveness to the stimulation available in the environment and consequently may limit brain development. The authors also noted that other studies suggested that the effects of malnutrition on brain growth may be either reduced by environmental enrichment or increased by deprivation.

Related Research and Recent Applications

This work by Rosenzweig, Bennett, and Diamond has served as a catalyst for continued research in this developmental area that continues today. Over the decades since the publication of their article, these scientists and many others have continued to confirm, refine, and expand their findings. For example, research has demonstrated that learning itself is enhanced by enriched environmental experiences and that even the brains of adult animals raised in impoverished conditions can be improved when placed in an enriched environment (see Bennett, 1976, for a complete review).

Some evidence exists to indicate that experience does indeed alter brain development in humans. Through careful autopsies of humans who have died naturally, it appears that as a person develops a greater number of skills and abilities, the brain actually becomes more complex and heavier. Other findings have come from examinations during autopsies of the brains of people who were unable to have certain experiences. For example, in a blind person's brain, the portion of the cortex used for vision is significantly less developed, less convoluted, and thinner than in the brain of a person with normal sight.

Marian Diamond, one of the authors of this original article, has applied the results of work in this area to the process of human intellectual development throughout life. She says, "For people's lives, I think we can take a more optimistic view of the aging brain. . . . The main factor is stimulation. The nerve cells are designed for stimulation. And I think curiosity is a key factor. If one maintains curiosity for a lifetime, that will surely stimulate neural tissue and the cortex may in turn respond. . . . I looked for people who were extremely active after 88 years of age. I found that the people who use their brains don't lose them. It was that simple" (in Hopson, 1984, p. 70).

Two recent studies have elaborated on Rosenzweig, Diamond, and Bennett's notions of environmental influences on brain development in very diverse applications. Weiss and Bellinger (2006) expanded on the research by suggesting that studies of the effects of environmental toxins on early brain development in humans must encompass not only the toxicity of the chemical but also should consider all the factors present within the individual's overall life context, including genetic tendencies and enriched or impoverished environments. The authors proposed that, in humans, the effects of exposure to toxic substances tend to be directly related to growing up in an enriched versus an impoverished environment. In other words, when children are raised in poverty, not only is their developmental environment likely to be impoverished, but they may also be at a greater risk of exposure to neurotoxic chemicals. Moreover, the environmental factors that are present can affect the outcome of the toxic exposure on brain development. Weiss and Bellinger asserted that when researchers have studied environmental toxins, the tendency has been to focus on the toxic substance itself and to minimize the accompanying situational variables. As the authors stated,

> We argue that the outcomes of exposure to neurotoxic chemicals early in life are shaped by the nature of a child's social environment, including that prevailing before birth. . . . We contend that a true evaluation of toxic potential and its neurobehavioral consequences is inseparable from the ecologic setting [such as environmental richness] in which they act and which creates unique, enduring individual vulnerabilities. (p. 1497)

Another article cites Rosenzweig's 1972 study in critiquing some recent attempts to oversimplify enrichment strategies in attempts to enhance children's brain development (Jones & Zigler, 2002). As you can imagine, when the public learns about research such as Rosenzweig's, a popular movement may be born that sounds attractive but has little basis in scientific fact. One of these from the 1990s, which you may have heard about, has become known as the "Mozart Effect." This fad began with some preliminary research showing that when children listen to Mozart (but not other classical composers) they become better learners. This idea has grown to the point that entire Web sites are devoted to the benefits of the "Mozart Effect" for children and adults alike, involving claims that certain music can enhance overall health, improve memory, treat attention deficit disorder, reduce depression, and speed healing from physical injuries; none of which rests on a scientific foundation (no matter what you have heard!)

Conclusion

However, Rosenzweig's research continues to be cited in a wide variety of interesting and potentially useful research. For example, think about the negative effect we feel from social isolation and especially loneliness. A study by Cacioppo, Capitanio and Cacioppo (2014) explored the connection between situations such as Rosenzweig's impoverished rats and the human emotion of loneliness. It's not difficult to see the parallels: loneliness is an impoverished social environment that has been shown to alter brain structures and processing, not unlike the effects found in the impoverished rats.

Bennett, E. L. (1976). Cerebral effects of differential experience and training. In M. R. Rosenzweig & E. L. Bennett (Eds.), *Neural mechanisms of learning and memory.* Cambridge, MA: MIT Press.

Cacioppo, S., Capitanio, J., & Cacioppo, J. (2014). Toward a neurology of loneliness. *Psychological Bulletin, 140*(6), 1464–1504.

Hopson, J. (1984). A love affair with the brain: A PT conversation with Marian Diamond. *Psychology Today, 11,* 62–75.

Weiss, B., & Bellinger, D. C. (2006). Social ecology of children's vulnerability to environmental pollutants. (Commentary). *Environmental Health Perspectives, 114,* 1479–1485.

Reading 1.3: Are You A "Natural?"

Bouchard, T., Lykken, D., McGue, M., Segal, N., & Tellegen, A. (1990). Sources of human psychological differences: The Minnesota study of twins reared apart. *Science, 250,* 223–229.

1.3   Explain how twin studies are used to study the impact of genetics on human behavior

This study represents a relatively recent and ongoing fundamental change in the way many psychologists view human nature in its broadest sense. You can relate to this change in a personal way by first taking a moment to answer in your mind the following question: "Who are you?" Think for a moment about some of your individual characteristics: your "personality traits." Are you high strung or laid-back? Are you shy or outgoing? Are you adventurous, or do you seek out comfort and safety? Are you easy to get along with, or do you tend toward the disagreeable? Are you usually optimistic or more pessimistic about the outcome of future events? Think about yourself in terms of these or any other questions you feel are relevant. Take your time. . . . Finished? Now, answer this next, and, for this reading, more important question: "*Why* are you who you are?" In other words, what factors contributed to "creating" the person you are today?

If you are like most people, you will point to the child-rearing practices of your parents and the values, goals, and priorities they instilled in you. You might also credit the influences of brothers, sisters, grandparents, aunts, uncles, peers, teachers, and other mentors who played key roles in molding you. Still others of you will focus on key life-changing events, such as an illness, the loss of a loved one, or the decision to attend a specific college, choose a major or take a particular life course that seemed to lead you toward becoming your current self. All these influences share one characteristic: They are all *environmental* phenomena. Hardly anyone ever replies to the question "Why are you who you are?" with "I was born to be who I am; it's all in my genes."

Everyone acknowledges that physical attributes, such as height, hair color, eye color, and body type, are primarily inherited—they are a product of your genes. In addition, the medical world is discovering more and more that your tendencies toward many illnesses, such as cancer, heart disease, and high blood pressure, have significant genetic components. However, almost no one thinks of genes as the main force behind who they are *psychologically*. This may strike you as odd when you stop to think about it, but in reality, very understandable reasons explain our "environmental bias."

First of all, psychology during the second half of the 20th century was dominated by the *behaviorism* theory of human nature. Basically, that theory states that all human behavior is controlled by environmental factors, including the stimuli that provoke behaviors and the consequences that follow response choices. Strict behaviorists believed that the internal psychological workings of the human mind were not only impossible to study scientifically but also that such study was unnecessary and irrelevant to a complete explanation for human behavior. Whether the wider culture accepted or even understood formal theories of behaviorism is not as important as the reality of their influence on today's firmly entrenched popular belief that *experience* is the primary or exclusive architect of human nature.

Another reason for the pervasive acceptance of environmental explanations of behavior is that genetic and biological factors usually do not provide visible evidence of their influence. It's easy for someone to say "I became a writer because I was deeply inspired and encouraged by my seventh-grade composition teacher." You remember those sorts of influences; you see them, you experience them. They are part of your past and present conscious experiences. You would find it much more difficult to recognize biological influences and say "I became a writer because my DNA contains a gene that has been expressed in me that predisposes me to write well." You can't see, touch, or remember the influence of your genes, and you don't even know where in your body they might be located!

In addition, many people are uncomfortable with the idea that they might be the product of their genes rather than the choices they have made in their lives. Such ideas smack of determinism and a lack of free will. Most people have a strong dislike for any theory that might in some way limit their conscious ability to determine the outcomes in their lives. Consequently, genetic causes of behavior and personality tend to be avoided or rejected by many. In reality, genetic influences *interact* with experience to mold a complete human, and the only question is this: Which is more dominant? Or, to phrase, the question as it frequently appears in the media, "*Is it nature or nurture?*"

This article by Thomas Bouchard, David Lykken, and their associates at the University of Minnesota in Minneapolis is a review of research that began in 1979 to examine the question of how much influence your genes have in determining your personal psychological qualities. This research grew out of a need for a scientific method to separate genetic influences (nature) from environmental forces (nurture) on people's behavior and personality. This is no simple task when you consider that nearly every one of you, assuming you were not adopted, grew up and developed under the direct environmental influence of your genetic donors (your parents). You might, for example, have the same sense of humor as your father (no offense!) because you learned it from him (nurture) or because you inherited his "sense-of-humor" gene (nature). No systematic approach can tease those two influences apart, right?

Well, Bouchard and Lykken would say "wrong." They have found a way to determine with a reasonable degree of confidence which psychological characteristics appear to be determined primarily by genetic factors and which are molded more by your environment.

Theoretical Propositions

It's simple, really (if not easy!). All you have to do is take two humans who have exactly the same genes, separate them at birth, and raise them in significantly different environments. Then you can assume that those behavioral and personality characteristics they have in common as adults must be genetic. But how on earth can researchers possibly find pairs of *identical people?* (Don't say "cloning"; we're not there yet!) And even if they could, it would be unethical to force them into diverse environments, wouldn't it? As you've already guessed, the researchers didn't have to do that. Society and biology had already done it for them.

Identical twins have virtually the same genetic structure. They are called *monozygotic twins* (one zygote) because they start as one fertilized egg, called a *zygote*, and then split into two identical embryos. Fraternal twins are the result of two separate eggs fertilized by two separate sperm cells and are referred to as *dizygotic twins* (two zygotes). Fraternal twins are only as genetically similar as any two nontwin siblings. As unfortunate as it sounds, twin infants are sometimes given up for adoption and placed in separate homes. Adoption agencies will try to keep siblings, especially twins, together, but the more important goal is to find good homes for them even if it means separation. Over time, thousands of identical and fraternal twins have been adopted into separate homes and raised, sometimes without the knowledge that they were a twin, in different and often contrasting environmental settings.

In 1983, Bouchard and Lykken began to identify, locate, and bring together pairs of these twins. This 1990 article reports on results from 56 pairs of monozygotic twins raised in different home environments—monozygotic twins reared-apart (MZA)—from the United States and seven other countries who agreed to participate in weeklong sessions of intensive psychological and physiological tests and measurements (that this research is located in Minneapolis, one half of "the Twin Cities" is an irony that has not, by any means, gone unnoticed). These twins were compared with monozygotic twins reared together, in the same home environment (MZT). The surprising findings continue to reverberate throughout the biological and behavioral sciences.

Method

PARTICIPANTS   The first challenge for this project was to find sets of monozygotic twins who were separated early in life, reared apart for all or most of their lives, and reunited as adults. Most of the participants were found through word of mouth as news of the study began to spread. The twins themselves or their friends or family members would contact the research institute—the *Minnesota Center for Twin and Adoption Research*—various social services professionals in the adoption arena would serve as contacts, or in some cases, one member of a twin-pair would contact the center for assistance in locating and reuniting with his or her sibling. All twins were tested to ensure that they were indeed monozygotic before beginning their participation in the study.

PROCEDURE The researchers wanted to be sure they obtained as much data as possible during the twins' one-week visit. Each twin completed approximately 50 hours of testing on nearly every human dimension you might imagine. They completed four personality trait scales, three aptitude and occupational interest inventories, and two intelligence tests. In addition, the participants filled in checklists of household belongings (such as power tools, telescope, original artwork, and unabridged dictionary) to assess the similarity of their family resources and a family environment scale that measured how they felt about the parenting they received from their adoptive parents. They were also administered a life history interview, a psychiatric interview, and a sexual history interview. All these assessments were carried out individually so that it was not possible for one twin to inadvertently influence the answers and responses of the other.

As you might imagine, the hours of testing created a huge database of information. The most important and surprising results are discussed here.

Results

Table 1.3.1 summarizes the similarities for some of the characteristics measured in the monozygotic twins reared apart (MZA) and includes the same data for monozygotic twins reared together (MZT). The degree of similarity is expressed in the table as correlations or *r* values. The larger the correlation, the greater the similarity. The logic here is that if environment is responsible for individual differences, the MZT twins who shared the same environment as they grew up *should be* significantly more similar than the MZA twins. As you can see, this is *not* what the researchers found.

The last column in Table 1.3.1 expresses the difference in similarity by dividing the MZA correlation on each characteristic by the MZT correlation. If both correlations were the same, the result would be 1.00; if they were entirely dissimilar, the result could be as low as 0.00. Examining column 4 in the table carefully, you'll find that the correlations for characteristics were remarkably similar—that is, close to 1.00 and no lower than .700 for MZA and MZT twin pairs.

Discussion and Implications of Findings

These findings indicate that genetic factors (or the *genome*) appear to account for most of the variations in a remarkable variety of human characteristics. This finding was demonstrated by the data in two important ways. One is that genetically identical humans (monozygotic twins), who were raised in separate and often very different settings, grew into adults who were extraordinarily similar, not only in appearance, but also in basic psychology and personality. The second demonstration in this study of the dominance of genes is the fact that there appeared to be *little* effect of the environment on identical twins who *were* raised in the same setting. Bouchard and Lykken found that for almost every behavioral (or personality) trait they studied (comparing MZT and MZA), including twins' reaction times to how religious they were, a large percentage of the variation between the twins turns out to be associated with genetic variation (Table 1.3.1). This fact need no longer be subject to debate; rather, it is time to consider its implications.

Some will argue with Bouchard and Lykken's notion that the time to debate these issues is over. Some varying views are discussed in the next section. However, a discussion of the implications of this and other similar studies by these same researchers is clearly warranted. In what ways do the genetic findings reported in this study change psychologists' and, for that matter, all of our views of human nature? As mentioned

Table 1.3.1 Comparison of Correlations (r) of Selected Characteristics for Identical Twins Reared Apart (MZA) and Identical Twins Reared Together (MZT)

Characteristic	r (MZA)	r (MZT)	Similarity r (MZA) ÷ r (MZT)*
Physiological	—	—	—
Brain wave activity	.80	.81	.987
Blood pressure	.64	.70	.914
Heart rate	.49	.54	.907
Intelligence	—	—	—
WAIS IQ	.69	.88	.784
Raven Intelligence Test	.78	.76	1.03
Personality	—	—	—
Multidimensional Personality Questionnaire (MPQ)	.50	.49	1.02
California Personality Inventory	.48	.49	.979
Psychological interests	—	—	—
Strong Campbell Interest Inventory	.39	.48	.813
Minnesota Occupational Interest Scale	.40	.49	.816
Social attitudes	—	—	—
Religiosity	.49	.51	.961
Nonreligious social attitudes	.34	.28	1.21

SOURCE: Adapted from Table 4, p. 226.

*1.00 would imply that MZA twin pairs were found to be exactly as similar as MZT twin pairs.

previously, psychology and Western culture have been dominated for over 50 years by environmental thinking. Many of our basic beliefs about parenting, education, crime and punishment, psychotherapy, skills and abilities, interests, occupational goals, and social behavior, just to name a few, have been interpreted from the perspective that people's experience molds their personalities, not their genes. Very few of us look at someone's behavior and think, "That person was *born* to behave like that!" We *want* to believe that people *learned* their behavior patterns because that allows us to feel some measure of confidence that parenting makes a difference; that positive life experiences can win out over negative ones; and that unhealthy, ineffective behaviors can be *unlearned*. The notion that personality is a done deal the moment we are born leaves us with the temptation to say "Why bother?" Why bother working hard to be good parents? Why bother trying to help those who are down and out? Why bother trying to offer quality education? And so on. Bouchard and Lykken would want to be the first to disagree with such an interpretation of their findings. In this article, they offer three of their own implications of their provocative conclusions:

1. Clearly, intelligence is primarily determined by genetic factors (70% of the variation in intelligence appears to be due to genetic influence). However, as the authors state very clearly,

    > [T]hese findings do not imply that traits like IQ cannot be enhanced. . . . A survey covering 14 countries has shown that the average IQ test score has increased in recent years. The present findings, therefore, do not define or limit what might be conceivably achieved in an optimal environment. (p. 227)

    Basically, what the authors are saying is that although 70% of the variation in IQ is due to naturally occurring genetic variation, 30% of the variation remains subject to increases or decreases due to environmental influences. These influences include many that are well-known, such as education, family setting, toxic substances, and socioeconomic status.

2. The basic underlying assumption in Bouchard and Lykken's research is that human characteristics are determined by some combination of genetic and environmental influences. When the environment exerts less influence, differences must be

attributed more to genes. The converse is also true: As environmental forces create a stronger influence on differences in a particular characteristic, genetic influences will be weaker. For example, most children in the United States have the opportunity to learn to ride a bicycle. This implies that the environment's effect on bicycle riding is somewhat similar for all children, so differences in riding ability will be more affected by genetic forces. On the other hand, variation in, say, food preferences in the United States are more likely to be explained by environmental factors because food and taste experiences in childhood and throughout life are very diverse and will, therefore, leave less room for genetic forces to function. Here's the interesting part of the researchers' point: They maintain that personality is more like bicycle riding than food preferences.

The authors are saying, in essence, that family environments exert *less* influence over who the kids grow up to be than do the genes they inherit from birth. Understandably, most parents do not want to hear or believe this. They are working hard to be good parents and to raise their children to be happy individuals and good citizens. The only parents who might take some comfort from these findings are those who are nearing their wits' end with out-of-control or incorrigible sons or daughters and would appreciate being able to take less of the blame! However, Bouchard and Lykken are quick to point out that genes are not necessarily destiny and that devoted parents can still influence their children in positive ways, even if they are only working on a small percentage of the total variation.

3. The most intriguing implication that Bouchard and Lykken suggest is that it's *not* the environment primarily influencing people's characteristics, but vice versa. That is, people's genetic tendencies actually mold their environments! The following is an example of the idea behind this theory.

The fact that some people are more affectionate than others is usually seen as evidence that some parents were more affectionate with their children than were other parents. In other words, affectionate kids come from affectionate environments. When this kind of assumption has been studied, it is usually found to be true. Affectionate people have, indeed, received more affection from their parents. Bouchard and Lykken are proposing, however, that variation in "affectionateness" may be, in reality, genetically determined so that some children are just born more affectionate than others. Their inborn tendency toward affectionate behavior causes them to *respond* to affection from their parents in ways that reinforce the parents' behavior much more than genetically nonaffectionate children. This, in turn, *produces* the affectionate behavior in the parents, not the other way around. The researchers contend that genes function in this way for many, if not most, human characteristics. They state it this way:

> The proximal [most immediate] cause of most psychological variance probably involves learning through experience, just as radical environmentalists have always believed. The effective experiences, however, to an important extent are self-selected, and that selection is guided by the steady pressure of the genome. (p. 228)

Criticisms and Related Research

As you might imagine, a great many related studies have been carried out using the database of twins developed by Bouchard and Lykken. In general, the findings continue to indicate that many human personality characteristics and behaviors are strongly influenced by genes. Many attributes that have been seen as stemming largely or completely from environmental sources are being reevaluated as twin studies reveal that heredity contributes either the majority of the variation or a significantly larger proportion than was previously contemplated.

For example, studies from the University of Minnesota team found not only that the vocation you choose is largely determined by your genes but also that about 30% of the variation in your overall job satisfaction and work ethic appear to be due to genetic factors (Arvey et al., 1989, 1994) even when the physical requirements of various professions were held constant. Other studies comparing identical (monozygotic) twins with fraternal (dizygotic) twins, both reared together and reared apart, have focused more directly on specific personality traits that are thought to be influential and stable in humans (Bouchard, 1994; Loehlin, 1992). These and other studies' findings determined that the people's variation on the characteristics of extraversion–introversion (outgoing versus shy), neuroticism (tendency to suffer from high anxiety and extreme emotional reactions), and conscientiousness (degree to which a person is competent, responsible, and thorough) is explained more (65%) by genetic differences than by environmental factors.

Of course, not everyone in the scientific community is willing to accept these findings at face value. The criticisms of Bouchard and Lykken's work take several directions (see Billings et al., 1992). Some studies claim that the researchers are not publishing their data as fully and completely as they should, and therefore, their findings cannot be independently evaluated. These same critics also claim that many articles are reporting on case studies demonstrating strong environmental influences on twins that Bouchard and Lykken fail to consider.

In addition, some researchers have voiced a major criticism of one aspect of twin research in general, referred to as the "equal environment assumption" (e.g., Joseph, 2002). This argument maintains that many of the conclusions drawn by Bouchard and Lykken about genetic influence assume that monozygotic and dizygotic twins raised together develop in identical environments. These critics maintain that such an assumption is not valid and that fraternal twins are treated far more differently than are identical twins. This, they contend, draws the entire method of twin research as a determinant of genetic influences into question. However, several other articles have refuted this criticism and supported the "equal environment assumption" (e.g., Kendler et al., 1993).

Recent Applications

In 1999, Bouchard reviewed the nature–nurture evidence from the Minnesota twin registries (Bouchard, 1999). He concluded that, overall, 40% of the variability in personality and 50% of the variability in intelligence appears to be genetically based. He also reiterated his position, discussed previously, that your genes drive your selection of environments and your selection or avoidance of specific personality-molding environments and behaviors.

Research at the Minnesota Center for Twin and Adoption Research continues to be very active. Some fascinating research has examined very complex human characteristics and behaviors that few would have even guessed to be genetically driven, such as love, divorce, and even death (see Minnesota Twin Family Study, 2007). These researchers have studied people's selection of a mate to see if "falling in love" with Mr. or Ms. Right is genetically predisposed. It turns out that it is not. However, the researchers have found a genetic link to the likelihood of divorce, eating disorders, and age at the time of death.

A recent study of achievement in art and science further demonstrated the heritable qualities of personality characteristics (Hur, Y. M., Jeong, H. U., & Piffer). The research examined 79 pairs of identical twins and 90 pairs of same-sex fraternal twins. The researchers found that there was an overall correlation between creative and scientific achievement of .54, which is significant in itself. However, 70% of that correlation was due to the monozygotic (identical) pairs of twins. And the difference was remarkable: The identical twins' correlated at .71, while the fraternal twins' correlation was only .36! This clearly suggests that genes are responsible for a large portion of our artistic and scientific abilities.

Bouchard and Lykken's research has been applied to the larger philosophical discussion of human cloning (see Agar, 2003). If a human being is ever successfully cloned, the question is, as you are probably thinking, to what extent will a person's essence—an individual's *personality*—be transferred to his or her clone? The fear that human identity might be changed, degraded, or lost has been a common argument of those opposed to cloning. On the other hand, results of twin studies, such as those of Bouchard and Lykken suggest that "the cloned person may, under certain circumstances, be seen as surviving, to some degree, in the clone. . . . However . . . rather than warranting concern, the potential for survival by cloning ought to help protect against the misuse of the technology" (Agar, 2003, p. 9). In a separate study examining the issue of identical twins and cloning (Prainsack & Spector, 2006), researchers found that identical twins rarely consider the genetic aspects of their real-life experience of being identical twins. In addition, from a personal perspective, they did not view the idea of human cloning as unnatural or immoral but were more concerned about the ethics underlying the *reasons* for human cloning. Of course, this is a philosophical discussion so far, but as the prospect of human cloning looms ever closer, it becomes increasingly important and interesting food for thought.

Agar, N. (2003). Cloning and identity. *Journal of Medicine and Philosophy, 28,* 9–26.

Arvey, R., Bouchard, T., Segal, N., & Abraham, L. (1989). Job satisfaction: Environmental and genetic components. *Journal of Applied Psychology, 74*(2), 187–195.

Arvey, R., McCall, B., Bouchard, T., & Taubman, P. (1994). Genetic influences on job satisfaction and work value. *Personality and Individual Differences, 17*(1), 21–33.

Billings, P., Beckwith, J., & Alper, J. (1992). The genetic analysis of human behavior: A new era? *Social Science and Medicine, 35*(3), 227–238.

Bouchard, T. (1994). Genes, environment, and personality. *Science, 264*(5166), 1700–1702.

Bouchard, T. (1999). Genes, environment, and personality. In S. Ceci, et al. (Eds.), *The nature–nurture debate: The essential readings,* pp. 97–103. Malden, MA: Blackwell.

Hur, Y. M., Jeong, H. U., & Piffer, D. (2014). Shared genetic and environmental influences on self-reported creative achievement in art and science. *Personality and Individual Differences, 68,* 18–22.

Joseph, J. (2002). Twin studies in psychiatry and psychology: Science or pseudoscience? *Psychiatric Quarterly, 73,* 71–82.

Kendler K., Neale M., Kessler R., Heath A., & Eaves L. (1993). A test of the equal environment assumption in twin studies of psychiatric illness. *Behavioral Genetics, 23,* 21–27.

Loehlin, J. (1992). *Genes and environment in personality development.* Newbury Park, CA: Sage Publications.

Minnesota Twin Family Study. (2007). What's special about twins to science? Retrieved March 10, 2007, from http://www.psych.umn.edu/psylabs/mtfs/special.htm.

Prainsack, B., & Spector, T. D. (2006). Twins: a cloning experience. *Social Science & Medicine, 63*(10), 2739–2752.

Reading 1.4: Watch Out for the Visual Cliff!

Gibson, E. J., & Walk, R. D. (1960). The "visual cliff." *Scientific American, 202*(4), 67–71.

1.4 Describe applications and results of experimental measurements of depth perception development

One of the most often told anecdotes in psychology concerns a man called S. B. (initials used to protect his privacy). S. B. had been blind his entire life until the age of 52 when he underwent a newly developed operation (the now-common corneal transplant) and his sight was restored. However, S. B.'s new ability to see did not mean that he automatically perceived what he saw the way the rest of us do. One important example of this became evident soon after the operation before his vision had cleared completely. S. B. looked out his hospital window and was curious about the small objects he could see moving on the ground below. He began to crawl out on his window ledge, thinking he would lower himself down by his hands and have a look. Fortunately, the hospital staff prevented him from trying this. He was on the fourth floor, and those small moving things were cars! Even though S. B. could now see, he was not able to perceive depth.

Our visual ability to sense and interpret the world around us is an area of interest to experimental psychologists because, obviously, it affects our behavior in important ways. In addition, within this ability lies the central question of whether our sensory processes are inborn or learned: the nature–nurture issue once again. Many psychologists believe that our most important visual skill is depth perception.

You can imagine how difficult, and probably impossible, survival of the human species would have been if we did not evolve to perceive depth. We might have run headlong into things, been unable to judge how far away a predator was or stepped right off cliffs. Therefore, it might be logical to assume that depth perception is an inborn survival mechanism that does not require experience to develop. However, as Eleanor Gibson and Richard Walk point out in their article,

> Human infants at the creeping and toddling stage are notoriously prone to falls from more or less high places. They must be kept from going over the brink by side panels on their cribs, gates on stairways, and the vigilance of adults. As their muscular coordination matures, they begin to avoid such accidents on their own. Common sense might suggest that the child learns to recognize falling-off places by experience—that is, by falling and hurting himself. (p. 64)

These researchers wanted to study this visual ability of depth perception scientifically in the laboratory. To do this, they conceived of and developed a remarkable research tool they called the *visual cliff*.

Theoretical Propositions

If you wanted to find out at what point in the early developmental process animals or people are able to perceive depth, one way to do this would be to put them on the edge of a cliff and see if they are able to avoid falling off. This is a ridiculous suggestion because of the ethical considerations of the potential injury to participants who may be were unable to perceive depth (or, more specifically, height). The *visual cliff* avoids this problem because it presents the participant with what appears to be a drop-off when no drop-off actually exists. Exactly how this is done will be explained shortly, but it is important first to recognize that the importance of this apparatus lies in the fact that human or animal infants can be placed on the visual cliff to see if they are able to perceive the drop-off and avoid it. If they are unable to do this and step off the "cliff," there is no danger of falling.

Gibson and Walk took a "nativist" position on this topic: They believed that depth perception and the avoidance of a drop-off appear *automatically* as part of our original biological equipment and are not, therefore, products of experience. The opposing view, held by *empiricists*, contends that such abilities are learned through experience in the environment. Gibson and Walk's visual cliff allowed them to ask these questions: At what stage in development can a person or animal respond effectively to the stimuli of depth and height? Do these responses appear at different times with animals of different species and habitats? Are these responses preprogrammed at birth or do they develop as a result of experience and learning?

Method

The visual cliff is comprised of a table about 4 feet high with a top made from a piece of thick, clear glass (Figures 1.4.1 and 1.4.2). Directly under half of the glass on the table (the shallow side) is a solid surface with a red-and-white checkered pattern. Under the other half is the same pattern, but it is down at the level of the floor underneath the table (the deep side). At the edge of the shallow side, then, is the appearance of a sudden drop-off to the floor, although, in reality, the glass extends all the way across. Between the shallow and the deep sides is a center board about a foot wide. The process of testing infants using this device was extremely simple.

The participants for this study were 36 infants between the ages of 6 and 14 months. The mothers of the infants also participated. Each infant was placed on the center board of the visual cliff and was then called and enticed to approach the "cliff" by the mother or father, first from the deep side and then from the shallow side.

The researchers also wanted to compare the development of depth perception in humans with that in other baby animals; the visual cliff allowed for similar tests with other species (without a mother's beckoning, however). The baby animals were placed on the center board and observed to see if they could discriminate between the shallow and deep sides and avoid stepping off the "cliff." You can imagine the rather unique situation in the psychology labs at Cornell University when the various baby animals were brought in for testing. They included chicks, turtles, rats, lambs, kids (baby goats, that is), pigs, kittens, and puppies. One has to wonder if they were all tested on the same day in a sort of menagerie setting!

Remember that the goal of this research was to examine whether depth perception is learned or innate. What makes this method so ingenious is that it allowed that question to at least begin to be answered. Infants, whether human or animal, cannot be *asked* if they perceive depth, and, as mentioned, human infants cannot be tested on real drops. In psychology, answers to perplexing questions are often found through the development of new methods for studying the questions. The results of Gibson and Walk's early study provide an excellent example of this.

Figure 1.4.1 Gibson and Walk's visual cliff.

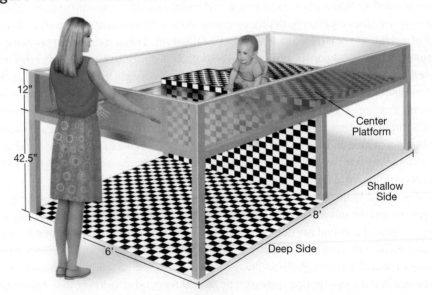

Figure 1.4.2 The visual cliff in a testing situation.

SOURCE: Mark Richards/PhotoEdit, Inc.

Results and Discussion

Nine children in the study refused to move at all off the center board at all. This was not explained by the researchers, but perhaps it was just infant stubbornness. When the mothers of the other 27 called to them from the *shallow* side, all the infants crawled off the board and crossed the glass. Only three of them, however, crept, with great hesitation, off the brink of the visual cliff when called by their mothers from the *deep* side. When called from the "cliff" side, most of the children either crawled away from the mother onto the shallow side or cried in frustration at being unable to reach the mother without moving over the "cliff." There was little question that the children were perceiving the depth of the "cliff": "Often they would peer down through the glass of the deep side and then back away. Others would pat the glass with their hands, yet despite this tactile assurance of solidity would refuse to cross" (p. 64).

Do these results prove that humans' ability to perceive depth is innate rather than learned? It does not because all the children in this study had at least 6 months of life experience in which to learn about depth through trial and error. However, human infants cannot be tested in this way prior to 6 months of age because they do not have adequate locomotor abilities. It was for this reason that Gibson and Walk decided to test various other animals as a comparison. As you know, most nonhuman animals gain the ability to move about much sooner than humans. The results of the animal tests were extremely interesting in that the ability of the various animals to perceive depth developed in relation to when the species needed such a skill for survival.

For example, baby chickens must begin to scratch for their own food soon after hatching. When they were tested on the visual cliff at less than 24 hours of age, they never made the mistake of stepping off onto the deep side.

Kids and lambs are able to stand and walk very soon after birth. From the moment they first stood up, their response on the visual cliff was as accurate and predictable as that of the chicks. Not one error was made. When one of the researchers placed a one-day-old baby goat on the deep side of the glass, the goat became frightened and froze in a defensive posture. If it was then moved over the shallow side, it would relax and jump forward onto the solid surface. This indicated that the visual sense was in complete control and that the animals' ability to *feel* the solidity of the glass on the deep side had no effect on the response.

For the rats, it was a different story. They did not appear to show any significant preference for the shallow side of the table. Why do you suppose they found this difference? Before you conclude that rats are just stupid and willing to walk off a cliff, consider Gibson and Walk's much more likely explanation: A rat does not depend very much on vision to survive. Because it is nocturnal, a rat locates food by smell and moves around in the dark using cues from the stiff whiskers on its nose. So, when a rat was placed on the center board, it was not fooled by the visual cliff because it was not using vision to decide which way to go. To the rat's whiskers, the glass on the deep side felt the same as the glass on the shallow side, and thus, the rat was just as likely to move off the center board to the deep side as to the shallow side (if it had been an actual drop, they would never had done this).

You might expect the same results from kittens. They are basically nocturnal and have sensitive whiskers. However, cats are predators, not scavengers like rats. Therefore, they depend more on vision. And, accordingly, kittens were found to have excellent depth perception as soon as they were able to move on their own: at about 4 weeks.

Although at times this research article, and this discussion, risk sounding like a children's animal story, it has to be reported that the species with the worst performance on the visual cliff was the turtle. The baby turtles chosen to be tested were of the aquatic variety because the researchers expected that they might prefer the deep side of the "cliff" because their natural environment is water. However, it appeared that the turtles were "smart" enough to know that they were not in water: 76% of them crawled off onto the shallow side, while 24% went "over the edge": "The relatively large minority that chose the deep side suggests either that this turtle has poorer depth perception than other animals, or its natural habitat gives it less occasion to 'fear' a fall" (p. 67). Clearly, if you live your life in water, the survival value of depth perception, in terms of avoiding falls, would be diminished—if you fell, you'd just float away.

Gibson and Walk pointed out that all of their observations were consistent with evolutionary theory. That is, all species of animals, if they are to survive, need to develop the ability to perceive depth by the time they achieve independent movement. For humans, this does not occur until around 6 months of age; for chickens and goats, it is nearly immediate (by 1 day old); and for rats, cats, and dogs, it is about 4 weeks of age. Therefore, Gibson and Walk conclude that the development this capacity is inborn because to learn it through trial and error would cause too many potentially fatal accidents and the species would probably not survive.

If we are so well prepared biologically, why do children take so many falls? Gibson and Walk explained that human infants' perception of depth matures sooner than their skill in movement. During testing, many of the infants supported themselves on the deep side of the glass as they turned on the center board, and some even backed up onto the deep side as they began to crawl toward the mother across the shallow side. If the glass had not been there, some of the children would have fallen off the "cliff"!

Criticisms and Subsequent Research

The most common criticism of the researchers' conclusions revolves around the question of whether they really proved that depth perception is innate in humans. As mentioned, by the time infants were tested on the visual cliff, they had already learned to avoid such situations. A later study placed younger infants, ages from 2 to 5 months, on the glass over the deep side of the visual cliff. When this happened, all the babies showed a decrease in heart rate. Such a decrease is thought to be a sign of interest, not fear, which is accompanied by heart rate increases (Campos et al., 1978). This indicates that these younger infants had not yet learned to fear the drop-off and would learn the avoidance behavior somewhat later.

It is important to notice, however, that although there was and still is controversy over just when we are able to perceive depth (the nativists vs. the empiricists), much of the research that is done to find the answer incorporates the visual cliff apparatus developed by Gibson and Walk. In addition, other related research using the visual cliff has turned up some fascinating findings.

One example is the work of Sorce et al. (1985), who put 1-year-old infants on a visual cliff for which the drop-off was neither shallow nor deep but in between (about 30 in.). As a baby crawled toward the "cliff," it would stop and look down. On the other side, as in the Gibson and Walk study, the mother was waiting. Sometimes the mother had been instructed to maintain an expression of fear on her face, while other times the mother looked happy and interested. When infants saw the expression of fear, they refused to crawl any farther. However, most of the infants who saw their mother looking happy checked the "cliff" again and crawled across. When the drop-off was made flat, the infants did not check with the mother before crawling across. This method of nonverbal communication used by infants in determining their behavior is called *social referencing*.

Recent Applications

Gibson and Walk's groundbreaking invention of the visual cliff still exerts a major influence on current studies of human development, perception, emotion, and even mental health. The following is a brief sample.

A study by Berger and Adolph (2003) cited Gibson and Walk's early study in their research on how toddlers analyze the characteristics of tasks involving heights, specifically crossing over a bridge. The researchers coaxed very young toddlers (16 months) to cross bridges of various widths, some with handrails; some without. They found that the children were significantly more likely to cross wider bridges than narrower ones (pretty smart for 16 months!). More interesting, however, was the finding that the toddlers were more likely to attempt the narrow bridge if it had handrails: "Infants who explored the bridge and handrail before stepping onto the bridge and devised alternative bridge-crossing strategies were more likely to cross successfully. These results challenge traditional conceptualizations of tools: babies used the handrail [a tool] as a means for augmenting balance and for carrying out an otherwise impossible goal-directed task" (p. 594).

How about using the concept of a *virtual* visual cliff to help people with severe *acrophobia* (an irrational fear of heights)? This is a very common phobia affecting about 1 in 20 people. If you are a therapist and would like to have your acrophobic clients "face their fear of heights," from high up, you will not have very many customers. Why? Because they are too scared! When someone has a true phobia, he or she will do *anything* to avoid the feared object or situation. One study incorporating Gibson and Walk's study found that the therapeutic effectiveness of a virtually reality drop, while still eliciting fear in the acrophobe so it could be treated, found it was less threatening for the client, which allowed for more effective therapy to reduce the irrational fear without ever leaving the therapist's office (Coelho et al., 2009).

Finally, a study from 2014 suggested that perhaps it is not it's not actually fear that the infants felt on the visual cliff, by "thoughtful avoidance." (Adopph, Kretch, and LoBue, 2014). This research proposed that the infants in this study were cognitively skilled enough to perceive the cliff for what it was, but were not afraid of it. Instead, they did a sort of "baby analysis" and determined that they did not have the motor skills to navigate the drop off.

Conclusion

Through the inventiveness of Gibson and Walk, behavioral scientists have been able to study depth perception in a clear and systematic way. Behavioral scientists continue to debate the question of whether this and other perceptual abilities are innate or learned. The truth may lie in a compromise that proposes an interaction between nature and nurture. Perhaps, as various studies have indicated, depth perception is present at birth, but fear of falling and avoidance of danger are learned through experience after the infant is old enough to crawl around enough to "get into trouble." But whatever the questions are, elegant methodological advances such as the visual cliff allow us to continue to search for answers.

Adolph, K. E., Kretch, K. S., & LoBue, V. (2014). Fear of heights in infants? *Current Directions in Psychological Science, 23*(1), 60–66.

Berger, S., & Adolph, K. (2003). Infants use handrails as tools in a locomotor task. *Developmental Psychology, 39,* 594–605.

Campos, J., Hiatt, S., Ramsay, D., Henderson, C., & Svejda, M. (1978). The emergence of fear on the visual cliff. In M. Lewis & L. A. Rosenblum (Eds.), *The development of affect.* New York: Plenum Press.

Coelho, C., Waters. A., Hine, T., & Wallis, G. (2009). The use of virtual reality in acrophobia research and treatment. *Journal of Anxiety Disorders, 23,* 563–574.

Sorce, J., Emde, R., Campos, J., & Klinnert, M. (1985). Maternal emotion signaling: Its effect on the visual cliff behavior of 1-year-olds. *Developmental Psychology, 21,* 195–200.

Chapter 2
Perception and Consciousness

 Learning Objectives

2.1 Explain how measuring infant interest changed the scientific understanding of perception by newborns

2.2 Outline the early history of REM research

2.3 Relate human biological abilities to the origin of concepts

2.4 Analyze the role of hypnosis as a goal-directed behavior rather than an altered state of consciousness

The study of perception and consciousness is of great interest to psychologists because these activities define and reveal much of your psychological interaction with your environment. Think for a moment about how your senses are bombarded constantly by millions of pieces of information from the combined stimuli that surround you at any given moment. It is impossible for your brain to process all of it, so your brain organizes this barrage of sensory data into sets of information that yield form and meaning. That's what psychologists refer to as *perception*.

Clearly, your level of *consciousness*, also commonly referred to as your *state of awareness*, governs to a large extent what you perceive and how your brain organizes it. As you go through your day, night, week, year, and life, you experience many and varied states of awareness: you concentrate (or not), daydream, fantasize, sleep, dream; maybe you've been hypnotized at some point or used psychoactive drugs (even caffeine and nicotine are psychoactive drugs!). These varying mental conditions are all altered states of consciousness that produce changes in your perceptions of the world that influence your behavior.

Within the research areas of perception and consciousness, some of the most influential and interesting studies have focused on perceptual abilities in early childhood, sleep, dreams, and hypnosis. This section begins with a famous and influential study that contributed a brilliant and remarkable method that allows researchers to study the thinking processes, the *perceptions*, of preverbal infants as young as a few days old. This method, called *preference looking*, provides insights into the functioning of infants' brains and how they conceptualize the world. The second reading contains two articles that changed psychology because they (1) discovered rapid eye movement (REM) sleep and (2) revealed the relationship between REM and dreaming. Third is an influential and controversial study proposing that dreams are not mysterious messages from your unconscious, as Freud and others suggested (and as you probably believe), but rather that dreams are the result of purely random, electrochemical impulses firing off in your brain while you sleep. Fourth is one of many studies that have influenced traditional psychological thinking by making a case *against* the widespread belief that hypnosis is a unique and powerful altered state of consciousness. This last study offers evidence suggesting that hypnotized people are no different from normally awake people—they are just a bit more motivated to behave in certain ways.

Reading 2.1: Take a Long Look

Fantz, R. L. (1961). The origin of form perception. *Scientific American*, *204*(May), 61–72.

2.1 Explain how measuring infant interest changed the scientific understanding of perception by newborns

If you want to know about other people's perceptions of the world around them, an easy way to find out is to simply ask them. Depending, of course, on exactly what you ask, they will often tell and maybe explain to you what they are perceiving at any particular moment. But have you ever tried to ask this of an infant? As much as infants may seem, at times, to be *trying* to tell you what they are thinking and perceiving, they cannot. They can't talk; they probably could not tell you very much if they could; and, most likely, they couldn't even understand your question!

If you have had the opportunity to spend time around infants (and you likely have to varying degrees), you may have often thought to yourself, "I wonder what this baby is thinking!" or "If only this baby could talk. . . . " Unfortunately, that's not going to happen. But psychologists' interest in studying and understanding infants' thoughts and perceptions has been a top priority throughout psychology's history (this book contains seven studies that focused on infants).

However, in Robert Fantz's discoveries, which we will discuss in this chapter, the questions that plagued the researchers were "How can we study an infant's cognitive processes?" and "How can we catch a real glimpse inside very young babies' brains to see what might be going on, what they are perceiving, and how much they really understand?"

In the 1950s, Robert L. Fantz, a psychologist at Western Reserve University in Cleveland (now, Case Western Reserve University), noticed something very interesting about infants; however, these were not human infants but newly hatched chicks—that's right, chickens. Fantz reported that almost immediately upon breaking out of their shell, chicks perceive their environment well enough to begin searching and pecking for food. (See "Watch Out for the Visual Cliff!" in the previous group of readings for more about the perceptual talents of chicks.) This suggested to Fantz that chicks, in some ways, actually have superior perceptual abilities than human infants, making the chicks ideal subjects for research in this area. That said, it is important to note that when psychologists study nonhuman animals, their *ultimate* goal is to apply what they learn from the animals to our understanding of *human* behavior, but we will further discuss that issue later.

Theoretical Propositions

Prior to Fantz's studies, research had clearly demonstrated that human infants are able to perceive the world around them in some rudimentary ways, such as the ability to see light, discriminate basic colors, detect movement, turn their heads at sounds. However, as Fantz pointed out, "It has often been argued that they cannot respond to such stimuli as shape, pattern, size, or solidity; in short, they cannot perceive *form*" (p. 66). But Fantz was skeptical of this argument, so in the late 1950s and early 1960s, he set about developing a new research technique that would allow researchers to study in greater detail what infants can perceive, to pinpoint when perceptual skills develop, and to determine the degree of complexity of their perceptual and mental skills. He proposed that human infants, from the moment of birth, not entirely unlike newly hatched chicks, are actually able to perceive various forms, and this can be demonstrated by observing how babies "analyze" their world—that is, *what* they look at and for *how long* they look at it. This method of studying infants' mental abilities, called *preferential looking*, swept through the psychology world and began a revolution, which continues today, into understanding the minds of infants.

Method

It wasn't difficult for Fantz to demonstrate some of what newly hatched chicks could and could not perceive. Fantz simply presented the chicks, before they had any experience pecking for real food, with objects of different shapes and sizes and recorded how often they pecked at each one. They pecked significantly more often at round shapes versus pyramid shapes; circles more than triangles; spheres more than flat disks; and when shapes of various sizes of circles were presented, they preferred those that were about $\frac{1}{8}$ inch in diameter over larger or smaller sizes. Without any previous learning, chicks were able to perceive form, and they clearly preferred shapes most like potential food: seeds or grain.

Fantz expressed in his article what you are probably thinking right now: "Of course, what holds true for birds [especially chickens!] does not necessarily apply to human beings" (p. 67). He considered the possibility that this innate ability in birds to perceive form (and this is true of many bird species) may not have developed during the evolution of primates (including humans), or that perhaps primates acquire such abilities only after a period of development or learning following birth. So, when Fantz turned his attention to primate infants, he needed a new research method because, obviously, primate infants do not peck at anything, and they don't have the motor development to do so even if they are so inclined (which they aren't because infants don't like grain and seeds very much).

Infants do engage in one behavior, however, that might allow them to be tested in a similar way to the chicks: They *stare* at things. If Fantz could figure out a way to see if they stare at some forms predictably more often or longer than others, the only explanation would be that they could tell the difference—that they could perceive some sort of form. Working at first with infant chimpanzees, the primate genetically most closely related to humans, Fantz and his associates developed what he called a "looking chamber," which was basically a padded, comfortable bassinette inside of a large, plain box. In the top panel of the box were two openings for presenting objects to the infants and peepholes allowing the researchers to observe the looking behavior of infants. When the researchers ascertained that infant chimps appeared to show a systematic preference for certain objects over others (determined by duration of staring), they applied the same basic techniques to studying human babies.

The researchers did nothing to interfere with the babies' usual schedule or activities but simply placed the infants into the comfortable, padded viewing box and presented various pairs of object for them to look at. The infants ranged in age from 1 to 15 weeks of age. The stimuli presented to the babies included solid and textured disks, spheres, an oval with a human face, an oval with the features of a human face jumbled up, and shapes and patterns of varying complexity (see Figure 2.1.1). The researchers revealed the objects in various paired combinations and observed the total amount of time during each 1-minute trial the infants spent staring at the different pairs of objects, as well as which object from each pair they "preferred" (stared at longer). Their findings provided powerful evidence that babies of *all* ages possess the ability to perceive and discriminate among diverse forms.

Results

For their first round of testing, the babies saw pairs of various black-and-white test patterns, including a square with horizontal stripes and a square with a bull's-eye; a checkerboard and a plain, patternless square; a wide plus sign and a circle; and a pair of identical triangles as control stimuli. The results are graphically illustrated in Figure 2.1.1. Clearly, the infants "preferred" the forms with the greatest complexity (the bull's-eye, stripes, and checkerboard). This degree of preference was the same,

Figure 2.1.1 Infants' interest in form pairs as a function of average looking time for 220 tests.

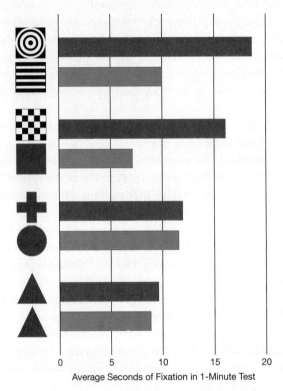

Average Seconds of Fixation in 1-Minute Test

regardless of the infant's age, which indicates that the ability to discriminate among these forms is innate—present at birth. Beginning at approximately 8 weeks of age, the infants preferred the bull's-eye to the stripes and the checkerboard to the plain square. This time delay implies that either some learning has occurred in those 2 months or that maturation of the brain and/or visual system accounted for the change.

As interesting as these findings were, an important link between the infants' abilities and the earlier studies of the chicks was still missing. If human infants are born with an unlearned, natural ability to discriminate form, we must ask why. For chicks, the answer appears rather straightforward: They perceive the forms that allow them to find nourishment and to survive. How could such an innate ability to perceive specific forms have survival value for human infants? Maybe it is for a similar reason. Fantz wrote the following:

> In the world of the infant, people have an importance that is perhaps comparable to the importance of grain in the chick's world. Facial pattern is the most distinctive aspect of a person . . . for distinguishing a human being from other objects and identifying him. So, a facelike pattern might be expected to bring out selective perception in an infant if anything could. (p. 70)

In other words, human infants do not depend upon form perception for nourishment and survival; they depend on other *people* to care for them. Just as chicks can perceive specific shapes best, it would make sense that infants' perceptual tendencies should favor the human face. And they do.

Fantz's team presented 49 infants between 4 days and 6 months old with three identically sized oval disks. One was painted with the features of a human face; another with those same features scrambled; and the third, the control disk, an oval with just a patch of black at one end equal to the total area of the facial features on the other two disks (see Figure 2.1.2). The infants clearly showed greater interest in the ovals with

Figure 2.1.2 Fantz's Facial Figure Test. Infants preferred A over B, and strongly preferred A and B over C.

a   *b*   *c*

the facial features and stared at them intently while virtually ignoring the control oval. Moreover, this preference was approximately the same strength for all infants *regardless of age*, demonstrating again that basic form perception is present at birth and ruling out a learning or developmental factor.

In the final study reported in this article, the researchers tested the human infants again for their ability to recognize facial forms. The infants were presented with six flat disks, each 6 inches in diameter with the following designs: (1) a human face; (2) a bull's-eye; (3) a random fragment of a printed page (such as a newspaper or textbook); (4) an entirely red disk; (5) an entirely fluorescent yellow disk; and (6) a plain white disk. The time of the infants' first look at each disk was recorded. Which one do you think they looked at the most? If you said "the face," you are correct; they gazed at the human face disk far more than any other form or color (see Figure 2.1.3). Fantz had found a way for us to enter a baby's brain and see what thought processes are going on.

Subsequent Research and Recent Applications

This study, like so many in this book, significantly changed psychology for two reasons: the groundbreaking discoveries that were made, and the method the researcher developed to make those discoveries possible. Until the middle of the 20th century, many behavioral and biomedical researchers assumed that babies were born with few,

Figure 2.1.3 Infants' looking time for patterns and colors (black bars = 8–12 months; grey bars = over 12 months of age).

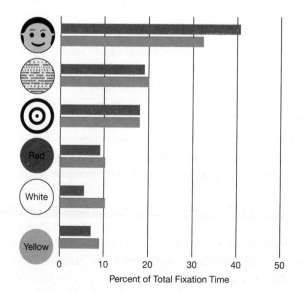

if any perceptual or sensory abilities and that they developed or learned most, if not all, of these skills as they interacted with their environment over time. This idea of the psychologically "empty" newborn was relatively easy to accept because we did not, at the time, possess the necessary research methodologies to reveal very young infants' true capabilities. Fantz gave us preferential-looking methods that, quite literally, opened the doors to the mind of the infant. These methods are used so commonly today that they are to psychology what a microscope is to biology: one of the first tools researchers turn to when they want to study how babies think. Of course, the discovery that infants come into the world with various perceptual skills does not reduce the importance of learning and development. But the *inborn* skills researchers have discovered using Fantz's methods appear to set the stage for an infant's future survival and growth. As Fantz points out,

> Innate knowledge of the environment is demonstrated by the preference of newly hatched chicks for forms likely to be edible and by the interest of young infants in kinds of forms that will later aid in object recognition, social responsiveness, and spatial orientation. This primitive knowledge provides a foundation for the vast accumulation of knowledge through experience. (p. 72)

Fantz's discoveries ignited a research revolution into the perceptual abilities of infants. You can see the influence of Fantz's methodological ingenuity throughout the fields of developmental and cognitive psychology. For example, some of the leading researchers in the world in the area of infant cognition, such as Renee Baillargeon at the University of Illinois's Infant Cognition Lab and Elizabeth Spelke at Harvard's Laboratory for Developmental Studies, have made extensive use of Fantz's preferential-looking research strategies in many studies (see Talbot, 2006, for a review of this work). In addition, Fantz's work helped clarify when and how well babies can perceive depth and drop-offs as studied in greater detail by Gibson and Walk in their classic research incorporating the visual cliff (see Chapter I).

Probably, the most important extension of Fantz's work is credited to Frances Horowitz at the University of Kansas, who discovered that in addition to preferential looking, babies also become bored seeing the same stimulus over and over (Horowitz, & Paden et al., 1972). When you show infants a novel visual pattern (such as those used in Fantz's studies), they gaze at it for a given amount of time, but as you repeatedly present the same stimulus, the amount of time they look predictably decreases. This is called *habituation*. If you then change or alter the pattern, their interest appears to revive and they look at it longer, a response known as *dishabituation*. By combining preferential looking, habituation, and dishabituation methodologies, researchers can now learn a great deal about what very young infants, even newborns, "know" about their world.

For example, in a recent study, researchers wanted to see when humans acquire the ability to distinguish between "possible" objects and "impossible" objects (Shuwairi, Albert, & Johnson, 2007; see also Baillargeon, 1994). You undoubtedly have seen so-called impossible objects that we often refer to as optical illusions. Figure 2.1.4 exemplifies the difference between a possible and impossible object. You looked longer at the impossible one, didn't you? So do babies. Using preferential-looking and duration-of-gaze methods, the researchers found that infants as young a 4 months old indicate an awareness of the difference in that they stared at the impossible object longer, as if to say, "I can see something's wrong with this object, and I need to try to figure it out!"

This is just a sample of hundreds of studies conducted every year by developmental psychologists and other behavioral scientists whose fundamental methodologies rest on Robert Fantz's discoveries. These methods are allowing us to peek inside the minds of infants as never before to see what they perceive and how they think. Virtually, every time we take another look, we discover that they are "smarter" and perceive more of their world than we ever expected.

Figure 2.1.4 Babies can distinguish between a possible (a) and impossible (b) object at 4 months old.

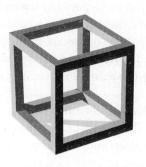 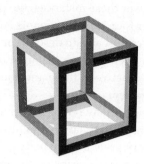

Baillargeon, R. (1994). Physical reasoning in young infants: Seeking explanations for impossible events. *British Journal of Developmental Psychology, 12(1)*, 9–33.

Horowitz, F. D., Paden, L., Bhana, K., & Self, P. (1972). An infant-controlled procedure for studying infant visual fixations. *Developmental Psychology, 7*, 90.

Shuwairi, S., Albert, M., & Johnson, S. (2007). Discrimination of possible and impossible objects in infancy. *Psychological Science, 18(4)*, 303–307.

Talbot, M. (2006, September 4). The baby lab. *The New Yorker, 82(27)*, 91–101.

Reading 2.2: To Sleep, No Doubt to Dream . . .

Aserinsky, E., & Kleitman, N. (1953). Regularly occurring periods of eye mobility and concomi tant phenomena during sleep. *Science, 118*, 273–274.

Dement, W. (1960). The effect of dream deprivation. *Science, 131*, 1705–1707.

2.2 Outline the early history of REM research

As you can see, this section is somewhat different from the others in that *two* articles are discussed; this is because the first study discovered a basic phenomenon about sleeping and dreaming that made the second study possible. The primary focus is William Dement's work on dream deprivation, but to prepare you for that, Aserinsky's findings must be addressed first.

In 1952, Eugene Aserinsky, although a graduate student, was studying sleep. Part of his research involved observing sleeping infants. He noticed that as these infants slept, active eye movements occurred periodically. During the remainder of the night, only occasional slow, rolling eye movements occurred. He theorized that these periods of active eye movements might be associated with dreaming. However, infants could not tell him whether they had been dreaming or not. To test this idea, he expanded his research to include adults.

Aserinsky and his coauthor, Nathaniel Kleitman, employed 20 normal adults to serve as participants. Sensitive electronic measuring devices were connected by electrodes to the muscles around the eyes of these participants. The leads from these electrodes stretched into the next room, where the participants' sleep could be monitored. The participants were then allowed to fall asleep normally (participants participated on more than one night each). During the night, participants were awakened and interrogated, either during periods of eye activity or during periods when little or no eye movement was observed. The idea was to wake the participants and ask them if they had been dreaming and if they could remember the content of the dream. The results were quite revealing.

For all the participants combined, a total of 27 awakenings were done during periods of sleep accompanied by REMs. Of these, 20 reported detailed visual dreams. The other 7 reported "the feeling of having dreamed" but could not recall the content in detail. During periods of no eye movement, 23 awakenings were instigated; in 19 of these instances, the participants did not report any dreaming, while in the other four, the participants felt vaguely as if they might have been dreaming, but they were not able to describe any dreams. On some occasions, participants were allowed to sleep through the night uninterrupted. It was found that the latter group experienced between three and four periods of eye activity during the average of 7 hours of sleep.

Although it may not have seemed so remarkable at the time, Aserinsky had discovered what is very familiar to most of us now: REM sleep or dreaming sleep. From his discovery grew a huge body of research on sleep and dreaming that continues to expand. Over the years, as research methods and physiological recording devices have become more sophisticated, we have been able to refine Aserinsky's findings and unlock many of the mysteries of sleep.

For example, we now know that after you fall asleep, you sleep in four stages, beginning with the lightest sleep (Stage 1) and progressing into deeper and deeper stages. After you reach the deepest stage (Stage 4), you begin to move back up through the stages: Your sleep becomes lighter and lighter. As you approach Stage 1 again, you enter REM, which is a very different kind of sleep. You do most of your dreaming during REM sleep. However, contrary to popular belief, research has revealed that you do not move around very much during REM. Your body is immobilized by electrochemical messages from your brain that paralyze your muscles. This is most likely an evolutionary survival mechanism that prevents you from acting out your dreams and possibly injuring yourself or worse.

Following a short period in REM, you proceed back into the four stages of sleep called non-rapid eye movement sleep (NON-REM, or NREM). During the night, you cycle between NREM and REM about five or six times (your first REM period comes about 90 minutes after falling asleep), with NREM becoming shorter and REM becoming longer (thereby causing you to dream more toward morning). (By the way, everyone dreams. Although a small percentage of individuals never remember dreams, sleep research has determined that we all have them.)

All this knowledge springs from the discovery of REM by Aserinsky in the early 1950s. One of the leading researchers who followed Aserinsky in giving us this wealth of information on sleeping and dreaming is William Dement of Stanford University. Around the same time of Aserinsky's findings, Dement was beginning his decades of groundbreaking research into sleeping and dreaming.

Theoretical Propositions

What struck Dement as most significant was the discovery that dreaming occurs every night in everyone. As Dement states in his article, "Since there appear to be no exceptions to the nightly occurrence of a substantial amount of dreaming in every sleeping person, it might be asked whether or not this amount of dreaming is in some way a necessary and vital part of our existence" (p. 1705). This led him to ask some obvious questions: "Would it be possible for human beings to continue to function normally if their dream life were completely or partially suppressed? Should dreaming be considered necessary in a psychological sense or a physiological sense or both?" (p. 1705).

Dement tried to answer these questions by studying participants who had somehow been deprived of the chance to dream. At first, he tried using depressant drugs to prevent dreaming, but the drugs themselves produced too great an effect on the participants' sleep patterns to allow for valid results. Finally, he decided on a novel method of preventing dreaming by waking participants up every time they entered REM sleep during the night.

Method Drastic

Dement's article reported on the first eight participants in an ongoing sleep and dreaming a research project. The participants were all males ranging in age from 23 to 32. A participant would arrive at the sleep laboratory around his usual bedtime. Small electrodes were attached to the scalp and near the eyes to record brain wave patterns and eye movements. As in the Aserinsky study, the wires to these electrodes ran into the next room so that the participant could sleep in a quiet, darkened room.

The procedure for the study was as follows: For the first several nights, the participant was allowed to sleep normally for the entire night. This was done to establish a baseline for each participant's usual amount of dreaming and overall sleep pattern. Once this information was obtained, the next step was to deprive the participant of REM or dream sleep. Over the next several nights (the number of consecutive deprivation nights ranged from three to seven for the various participants), the experimenter would awaken the participant every time the information from the electrodes indicated that he had begun to dream. The participant was required to sit up in bed and demonstrate that he was fully awake for several minutes before being allowed to go back to sleep.

An important point mentioned by Dement was that the participants were asked not to sleep at any other times during the dream study. This was because if participants slept or napped, they might dream, and this could contaminate the findings of the study.

Following the nights of dream deprivation, participants entered the *recovery phase* of the experiment. During these nights, the participants were allowed to sleep undisturbed throughout the night. Their periods of dreaming continued to be monitored electronically, and the amount of dreaming was recorded as usual.

Next, each participant was given several nights off (something they were very glad about, no doubt!). Then, six of them returned to the lab for another series of interrupted nights. These awakenings "exactly duplicated the dream-deprivation nights in number of nights and number of awakenings per night. The only difference was that the participant was awakened in the intervals between eye-movement (dream) periods. Whenever a dream period began, the participant was allowed to sleep on without interruption and was awakened only after the dream had ended spontaneously" (p. 1706). Participants again had the same number of recovery nights as they did following the dream-deprivation phase. These were called *control recovery* and were included to eliminate the possibility that any effects of dream deprivation were not due simply to being awakened many times during the night, whether dreaming or not.

Results

Table 2.2.1 summarizes the main findings reported. During the baseline nights, when participants were allowed to sleep undisturbed, the average amount of sleep per night was 6 hours and 50 minutes. The average amount of time the participants spent dreaming was 80 minutes or 19.5% (see Table 2.2.1, column 1). Dement discovered in these results from the first several nights that the amount of time spent dreaming was remarkably similar from participant to participant. In fact, the amount of variation among the dreamers was only plus or minus 7 minutes!

The main point of this study was to examine the effects of being deprived of dreaming, or REM, sleep. The first finding to address this was the number of awakenings required to prevent REM sleep during the dream-deprivation nights. As you can see in Table 2.2.1 (column 3a), on the first night, the experimenter had to awaken the participants between 7 and 22 times in order to block REM. However, as the study progressed, participants had to be awakened more and more often in order to prevent them from dreaming. On the last deprivation night, the number of forced awakenings ranged from 13 to 30 (column 3b). On average, there were twice as many attempts to dream at the end of the deprivation nights.

Table 2.2.1 Summary of Dream-Deprivation Results

Participant	1. Percent Dream Time: Baseline	2. Number of Dream Deprivation Nights	3a. & 3b. Number of Awakenings		4. Percent Dream Time: Recovery	5. Percent Dream Time: Control
			First Night	Last Night		
1.	19.5	5	8	14	34.0	15.6
2.	18.8	7	7	24	34.2	22.7
3.	19.5	5	11	30	17.8	20.2
4.	18.6	5	7	23	26.3	18.8
5.	19.3	5	10	20	29.5	26.3
6.	20.8	4	13	20	29.0	—
7.	17.9	4	22	30	19.8 (28.1)*	16.8
8.	20.8	3	9	13	—**	—
Average	19.5	4.38	11	22	26.6	20.1

*Second recovery night.

**Participant dropped out of study before recovery nights. (Adapted from data on p. 1707.)

The next and perhaps most revealing result was the increase in dreaming time after the participants were prevented from dreaming for several nights. The numbers in Table 2.2.1 (column 4) reflect the first recovery night. The average total dream time on this night was 112 minutes, or 26.6% (compared with 80 minutes and 19.5% during baseline nights in column 1). Dement pointed out that two participants did not show a significant increase in REM (participants 3 and 7). If they are excluded from the calculations, the average total dream time is 127 minutes, or 29%. This is a 50% increase over the average for the baseline nights.

Although only the first recovery night is reported in Table 2.2.1, it was noted that most of the participants continued to show elevated dream time (compared with baseline amounts) for five consecutive nights.

Now you're thinking, "Wait a minute!" Maybe this increase in dreaming has nothing to do with REM deprivation at all. Maybe it's just because these participants were awakened so often. You'll remember that Dement planned for your astute observation. Six of the participants returned after several days of rest and repeated the procedure exactly, except they were awakened between REM periods (the same number of times). This produced no significant increases in dreaming. The average time spent dreaming after the control awakenings was 88 minutes, or 20.1% of the total sleep time (column 5). When compared to 80 minutes, or 19.5%, in column 1, no significant difference was found.

Discussion

Dement tentatively concluded from these findings that we need to dream. When we are not allowed to dream, there seems to be some kind of pressure to dream that increases over successive dream-deprivation nights. This was evident in his findings from the increasing number of attempts to dream following deprivation (column 3a versus column 3b) and in the significant increase in dream time (column 4 versus column 1). He also notes that this increase continues over several nights so that it appears to make up in quantity the approximate amount of lost dreaming. Although Dement did not use the phrase at the time, this important finding has come to be known as the *REM-rebound* effect.

Several interesting additional discoveries were made in this brief, yet remarkable article. If you return to Table 2.2.1 for a moment, you'll see that two participants, as mentioned before, did not show a significant REM-rebound effect (participants 3 and 7). It is always important in research incorporating a relatively small number of participants to attempt to explain these exceptions. Dement found that the small increase in participant 7 was not difficult to explain: "His failure to show a rise on the first recovery night was in all likelihood due to the fact that he had imbibed several cocktails at a party before coming to the laboratory, so the expected increase in dream time was offset by the depressing effect of the alcohol" (p. 1706).

Participant 3, however, was more difficult to reconcile. Although he showed the largest increase in the number of awakenings during deprivation (from 7 to 30), he did not have any REM rebound on any of his five recovery nights. Dement acknowledged that this participant was the one exception in his findings and theorized that perhaps he had an unusually stable sleep pattern that was resistant to change.

The eight participants were monitored for any behavioral changes that they might experience due to the loss of REM sleep. All the participants developed minor symptoms of anxiety, irritability, or difficulty concentrating during the REM interruption period. Five of the participants reported a clear increase in appetite during the deprivation, three of whom gained 3 to 5 pounds. None of these behavioral symptoms appeared during the period of control awakenings.

Significance of the Findings and Subsequent Research

More than 40 years after this preliminary research by Dement, we know a great deal about sleeping and dreaming. Some of this knowledge was discussed briefly and previously in this chapter. We know that most of what Dement reported in his 1960 article has stood the test of time. We all dream, and if we are somehow prevented from dreaming one night, we dream more the next night. There does indeed appear to be something basic in our need to dream. In fact, the REM-rebound effect can be seen in many animals.

One of Dement's *accidental* findings, which he reported only as a minor anecdote, now has greater significance. One way that people may be deprived of REM sleep is through the use of alcohol or other drugs, such as amphetamines and barbiturates. Although these drugs increase your tendency to fall asleep, they suppress REM sleep and cause you to remain in the deeper stages of NREM for greater portions of the night. For this reason, many people are unable to break the habit of taking sleeping pills or alcohol in order to sleep. As soon as they stop, the REM-rebound effect is so strong and disturbing that they become afraid to sleep and return to the drug to avoid dreaming. An even more extreme example of this problem occurs with alcoholics who may have been depriving themselves of REM sleep for years. When they stop drinking, the onset of REM rebound may be so powerful that it can occur while they are *awake!* This may be an explanation for the phenomenon known as *delirium tremens* (DTs), which usually involve terrible and frightening hallucinations during withdrawal (Greenberg & Perlman, 1967).

Dement spent decades following up on his early preliminary findings regarding the behavioral effects of dream deprivation. In his later work, he deprived participants of REM for much longer periods of time and found no evidence of harmful changes. He concluded that "[a] decade of research has failed to prove that substantial ill effects result even from prolonged selective REM deprivation" (Dement, 1974).

Research with its origins in Dement's early work reported here suggests that a greater synthesis of proteins takes place in the brain during REM sleep than during NREM sleep. Some believe these chemical changes may represent the process of integrating new information into the memory structures of the brain and may even be the organic basis for new developments in personality (Rossi, 1973).

Recent Applications

Most experts in the field of sleep and dreaming credit Aserinsky with the discovery of REM sleep. Studies relating to sleeping, dreaming, or sleep disorders attribute that basic fact to him. Consequently, his early work with Kleitman is frequently cited in many recent scientific articles.

Dement's extension of Aserinsky's work continues to be referred to frequently in a wide range of research articles relating to sleep patterns. One such recent study made the remarkable discovery that humans may dream during NREM sleep more than we thought (Suzuki et al., 2004). Using daytime napping, during which we tend to enter NREM sleep sooner than during normal nighttime sleep, the researchers found that when participants were asked to report on dreams during naps consisting only of NREM sleep, they were frequently able to do so. However, the researchers also found that "dream reports from NREM naps were less notable in quantity, vividness, and emotions than those from REM naps" (p. 1486).

Another study relating to Dement and Aserinsky's foundational research contends that humans develop during REM sleep a kind of *protoconscious,* a basic biological form of brain organization necessary for normal consciousness (Hobson, 2009). This basic human brain development is thought to begin before birth and continues throughout childhood. Hobson's research proposes that early REM sleep provides us with a virtual model of our waking world that assists us in carrying out the tasks of our normal life while awake. The theory might help explain two phenomena: why infants spend more time in REM sleep than do adults, and why the human brain *insists* on obtaining a minimum amount of REM sleep every night.

Conclusion

William Dement retired from Stanford at the end of 2015, but his sleep center, The Stanford Center for Sleep Sciences and Medicine continues actively pursuing research on sleep and dreaming. In 2000, the latest edition of Dement's book was published, *The Promise of Sleep: A Pioneer in Sleep Medicine Explores the Vital Connection between Health, Happiness and a Good Night's Sleep.* In this book, written for the nonscientist, Dement draws upon his four decades of research on sleep and applies his vast accumulation of knowledge to helping all of us understand the vital importance of quality sleep and how to achieve it. In his book, Dement (2000) describes us as a "sleep-sick society" and sets forth his goals as a sleep researcher:

> For most of my career . . . I have worked unceasingly to change the way society deals with sleep. Why?
>
> Because the current way, or nonway, is so very bad . . . It greatly saddens me to think about the millions, possibly billions, of people, whose lives could be improved if they understood a few simple principles.
>
> Changing the way society and its institutions deal with sleep will do more good than almost anything else I can conceive, or certainly that was ever remotely in my grasp to accomplish. (pp. 4–5)
>
> To learn more about Dement's ongoing work at Stanford, see https://web.stanford.edu/~dement/sleepless.html.

Dement, W. C. (1974). *Some must watch while some must sleep.* San Francisco, CA: Freeman.

Dement, W. C. (2000). *The promise of sleep: A pioneer in sleep medicine explores the vital connection between health, happiness and a good night's sleep.* New York: Dell.

Greenberg, R., & Perlman, C. (1967). Delirium tremens and dreaming. *American Journal of Psychiatry, 124,* 133–142.

Hobson, J. (2009). REM sleep and dreaming: Towards a theory of protoconsciousness. *Neuroscience, 10,* 803–813.

Rossi, E. I. (1973). The dream protein hypothesis. *American Journal of Psychiatry, 130,* 1094–1097.

Suzuki, H., Uchiyama, M., & Tagaya, H., et al. (2004). Dreaming during non-rapid eye movement sleep in the absence of prior rapid eye movement sleep. *Sleep, 27*(8), 1486–90.

Reading 2.3: As a Category, It's a Natural

Rosch, Eleanor H. (1973). Natural categories. *Cognitive Psychology, 4*, 328–350.

2.3 Relate human biological abilities to the origin of concepts

In the 1934 Shirley Temple movie, *Stand Up and Cheer,* the great film actor and dancer who went by the name of "Stepin Fetchit," sat on the porch steps of an old house examining one of his old, beat-up pieces of footwear, and lamented philosophically, "Why's a shoe called a shoe?" His character often wondered why things were called what they were called, and in various ways psychologists have wondered the same thing. The behavioral scientists who focus on these sorts of questions study human *cognition* (thinking) and *perception* (humans' interpretation of the world around them).

One of the basic building blocks of these areas of research is the idea of *concepts.* Concepts are mental representations of your experience of the world that allow you to classify objects (furniture, vegetables, animals, professions, shoes, etc.) according to the characteristics they have in common. Concepts are extremely useful because they allow you to group objects into categories for efficient processing of information. For example, you know that a certain piece of furniture is a chair because it fits your "concept" of a chair. Therefore, it is not necessary for you to learn that a specific chair is called a chair each time you see an unfamiliar style so long as it fits into your category for chairs.

Because it has come up in our conversation here, you are now thinking of a chair (right?). What features comprise your "chair concept"? You probably think of a chair as having legs, a seat, and a back to lean against. Even though some chairs violate your rules (recliners and rocking chairs don't really have legs), they still fit into your chair category well enough. However, if you were to encounter a bean bag "chair" without knowing what it was, you probably would not call it a chair. In fact, you might not be sure what to call it.

The question that has most interested cognitive psychologists is as follows: Where do you get your categories for objects? The traditional or "classical" view that was widely accepted prior to 1970 held that categories are a function of the language we speak. In other words, categories exist because we have words for them. For example, we have a category for animals that lay eggs, fly, have feathers, and chirp; the category is "bird." This traditional view maintained that if we did not have a word for bird, the category or concept for bird would not exist.

Therefore, concepts and categories should vary from culture to culture due to variations in language. And there is evidence of this. A frequently cited example is that the Inuit who live in far northern latitudes have 12 words in their native language for "snow," whereas in English there are only one or two. Obviously, the Inuit need greater flexibility in communicating about snow due to the climate in which they live, and this is reflected in their language. South Pacific Islanders have no word at all in their language for snow; therefore, scientists have assumed that such a concept would not exist for them.

For many years, this theory of the origin of concepts was taken for granted by scientists throughout the social sciences in psychology, anthropology, linguistics, and sociology. During the early 1970s, Eleanor Rosch, at the University of California at Berkeley, published a series of studies that challenged the classical view and turned the field of cognitive psychology upside down. She is considered to have revolutionized the study of categorization. She proposed that categories do not necessarily arise from the language, but exist naturally on their own, in relation to humans' biological abilities of perception.

Her landmark study presented here involved two separate experiments and some rather technical procedures. For the sake of clarity and space limitations, a summary of the first experiment reported in the article previously cited will be detailed here.

Theoretical Propositions

Rosch theorized that if the prevailing theory were correct, all objects belonging to a certain category would have approximately equal status in that category—that is, they would fit into it equally well. She observed, however, that this is not the case. Instead, some "members" of a category are perceived by people to be better examples of the category than others (she called these *prototypes*). As an example of this, consider again the category of "bird." Now, quickly, picture a bird in your mind. You probably pictured something like a robin, blue jay, wren, or sparrow (maybe a crow or an eagle). It is quite unlikely that you thought immediately of a goose, a chicken, an ostrich, or a penguin. According to Rosch, this is because a robin fits your *prototype* (or "ideal example") of a bird better than a chicken. In other words, a robin exhibits all or most of the features that describe your category of bird and you, therefore, judged it higher in "birdiness." Conversely, an ostrich has few of these features—it doesn't fly, doesn't chirp, is too big, etc.—and, consequently, an ostrich does not fit most people's prototype for a bird very well at all.

What Rosch argued was that most categories do not have clear boundaries as to what fits and what does not, but rather, our mental category borders are "fuzzy." We decide if an object fits into a category by comparing it to our category *prototypes*. She also believed that categories can exist and are psychologically real even when there are *no words* in a person's language with which to name them.

To test this theory, in the late 1960s, Rosch traveled to New Guinea where a society of people live called the "Dani" (see the discussion of the study by Ekman in Reading 6.2 for other research within this country's cultures). The Dani, until recently, existed, in essence, as a Stone Age culture and communicated in a language that did not include certain concepts that now exist in all modern cultures. Rosch's early studies, including the one discussed here, focused on categories relating to color. English speakers use 11 major color categories: red, yellow, green, blue, black, gray, white, purple, orange, pink, and brown. Research has determined that speakers of English are able to agree on certain "focal colors": those that are the best examples (or *color prototypes*) of each color category. For example, English speakers know "fire engine red" is the "focal color" for the category of red (you could say it is the "most" redlike), and it is identified as red much more quickly and easily than other "reddish" or off-red colors. More on this in a moment. . .

The Dani, however, only possess two color categories: "mili," which describes dark, cool colors and "mola," used for light, warm colors. Rosch theorized that if the original, "classical" view of categorization was correct—that language determines concepts— the Dani should possess only two color concepts. However, Rosch contended that *all* humans possess from birth—that is, have "preprogrammed" into our brains through evolution—many more than two color categories.

To test this, she decided to teach the Dani new words for either eight focal (proto-type) colors or eight nonfocal colors. She hypothesized that many more than two focal color categories were "psychologically" real for the Dani culture, even though names for them had never existed in their language. If this were true, focal colors (i.e., color pro-totypes) should be able to be learned by the Dani faster and easier than nonfocal colors.

Method

PARTICIPANTS The participants for her study were young Dani males who were all pretested to be sure no one was color-blind. They were also tested to confirm that their knowledge of color terms was restricted to "mili" (dark) and "mola" (light). Interestingly, the Dani do not measure age, so based on size and general physical maturity, the researchers judged all the participants to be at approximately 12 to 15 years of age. The participants volunteered to join in the study and were paid for their participation.

After they had completed the color-learning part of the procedure, they were divided into several groups of 12 participants each. The two most important experimental groups will be discussed here.

COLOR STIMULI   Glossy color chips, similar to those you might obtain from the paint store when you are repainting your house, were used as the stimuli for the colors to be learned.

These chips, however, were developed scientifically to represent specific colors of exacting wave lengths. The color categories used were pink, red, yellow, orange, brown, green, blue, and purple. For one group of participants, the colors were the focal, prototype hue for each color (such as fire-engine red). These were the colors that Rosch theorized to be *universally* represented by natural categories and, therefore, easily identifiable, regardless of culture or language.

For the other group, the hues of the eight color chips fell in between focal colors so that an English-speaker might call them "red-brown" or "yellow-green." These were called ambiguous or "nonfocal colors."

Procedure

The first challenge Rosch and her associates faced was to assign names in the Dani language for the various colors. This was not as easy as it might sound because the names needed to be words that were all equally frequent, familiar, and meaningful to the participants, so as to avoid built-in bias. Rosch discovered that the Dani use many names for what they call "sibs." A *sib* was described by Rosch as a family group similar to a clan. (The English language uses the same word, which is a shortened version of *siblings*.) These names met her requirements for stand-ins for colors and so were used to represent the different color categories to be learned by the participants. To avoid a preference or bias, a participant's own sib name was not used as a color category.

Each participant was told that the task involved learning a new language that the experimenter would teach to him. At the beginning of the first day, the colors were presented to the participant and the name assigned to each color was spoken by the researcher and repeated by the participant. Then, the colors were shuffled and presented again. Each time the participant named the color correctly, he was praised or if he was incorrect, he was told the correct name. Over a period of five to twelve days, the participants were tested on their learning of the color categories and their progress was recorded until all the participants were able to name all the colors without error.

Upon completion of the learning period, an additional task was performed by all participants to determine if this new ability was truly understood as a general concept and would transfer to new situations or was limited only to the specific colors learned.

To test for this, each participant was shown a group of many colors and asked to identify eight of them that had *not* been part of the training categories. The success rate of this "transfer" task (determining if the learning would transfer to a different setting) was calculated for the participants in both groups.

Results

If humans possess inborn, preprogrammed abilities to perceive certain categories of colors (as Rosch hypothesized), then the results of the Dani's learning task should demonstrate faster learning for the focal color categories than for the nonfocal colors because focal colors are better prototypes of the color concept. Figure 2.3.1 summarizes the learning progress of the two groups over the testing period.

The average number of *errors* over the entire learning period was 8.54 for the prototype color group compared to 18.96 for the ambiguous color group. This difference was highly statistically significant. If you consult Figure 2.3.1, you can see that the group presented with the colors that most members of Western cultures consider central to a particular color category were able to learn the names of the colors in only five days compared to eleven days for the group trying to learn the nonfocal color categories.

Rosch believed that it was important to demonstrate the skill of recognizing color categories had been acquired in such a way that it would transfer to new situations—that it was not only a result of the study but also had become a "usable" concept. On the task in which participants were asked to identify colors that were not part of the learning, correct responses would be expected only about 12% of the time (the percentage correct due to chance alone) if the concept did not transfer. The participants in Rosch's study correctly identified the colors *not* used with 90% accuracy.

An additional informal finding reported by Rosch was that four of the participants in the nonfocal color group became very frustrated during the learning period and wanted to quit before learning all the color names. It took a great deal of persuasion to convince them to continue until they completed the task. This problem was not encountered with the focal color group who generally seemed to enjoy the experimental process.

All this may seem like a long way to go for rather simple findings, but, as mentioned at the beginning of this chapter, the results from this and additional studies by Rosch and others had a profound effect on our knowledge of how the brain works. First, Rosch's discussion of her findings will be summarized followed by a brief glimpse of the huge amount of subsequent, related research.

Discussion

Rosch had found a way to test a theory that, on the surface, would seem nearly impossible to test. Can you think of a concept or category of objects that does not exist for speakers of English (or any other language) in the way color categories are missing from the Dani language? There may be some, but they are difficult to find and even more difficult to test. The notion to locate and study a culture that does not acknowledge

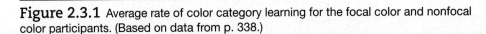

Figure 2.3.1 Average rate of color category learning for the focal color and nonfocal color participants. (Based on data from p. 338.)

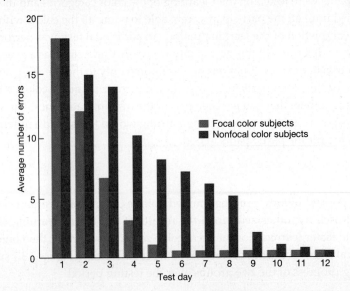

color categories was ingenious in itself. But the weight of her contributions lies more in what she discovered.

The main finding was that people from a culture that did not possess concepts for colors could learn colors that comprised hypothesized prototypes faster than nonprototype colors. This finding indicated that certain concepts exist in the brains of *all* humans regardless of the language they speak or whether they have ever used the concepts. This was a major discovery. Because these concepts appear to be part of the biological structure of humans, Rosch called them "natural categories" (the title of her article). The reason this study had such an impact on psychological research was that suddenly the nearly universally accepted idea that language produces concepts had been changed to the radically opposing view that linguistic concepts stem from and form around these naturally occurring categories.

Rosch concludes her article by suggesting further implications of her findings:

> In short, the evidence which has been presented regarding the structure and learning of color categories may have implications beyond the domain of color: (a) there may be other domains which are organized into natural categories and (b) even in nonperceptual categories, artificial prototypes (the best examples of nonperceptual categories) once developed, may affect learning and processing of categories in that domain in a manner similar to the effects of natural prototypes. (p. 349)

What this means, is that most of what you perceive is analyzed and categorized by your brain according to how well or poorly it matches an appropriate prototype (natural or not), rather than how well it meets the criteria of a formal linguistic definition.

Subsequent Research

Various studies that followed Rosch's early research supported the existence of natural categories and the use of prototypes in concept formation. Rosch and her colleagues as well as others expanded on the early findings reported in this chapter to demonstrate its broader implications.

For example, she further demonstrated that concepts do not have the clear, distinct boundaries that might exist if we used a strict linguistic definition to categorize objects, but rather, as mentioned earlier in this chapter, concepts are indeed fuzzy and somewhat overlapping (see Rosch, 1975). If we return once again to our example of your concept of "bird," would you say a kiwi is a bird? How about a bat? You may have formal knowledge that a kiwi is a bird (even though it doesn't fly, or chirp, or sit in trees), but when you think of a BIRD, a kiwi rarely comes to mind (well, maybe *now* it will!).

On the other hand, you know that a bat is not a bird and yet it flies, makes a sort of a chirping sound, and some of them live in trees. So, some people may, on some level, conceive of bats as birds. As another example, consider your category for "fruit." What fruits are you thinking of? Apples, oranges, or bananas are usually the ones named first. What about a tomato? A tomato may be a fruit, but it is a poor example (compared to your prototype) of one because it is quite distant in resemblance to your prototypical fruit. Remember, psychologists are interested more in *how* you think than whether you are technically correct. (By the way, a kiwi is not only a bad example of a bird; it is also a bad example of a prototype of a fruit!)

Recent Applications

Various research techniques to reveal how people conceptualize the world around them have been developed since Rosch first demonstrated the existence of natural categories with the Dani in New Guinea (for a complete discussion see Rosch, 1978). One method simply asks participants (from any culture) to use a number scale (such as from one

We all know that a French bulldog is a dog, but you would be unlikely to think of this particular breed when asked about dogs because it does not fit your prototype of a dog very well (unless you own one!). (Tatiana Katsai/Shutterstock)

to ten) to rate how well an object fits into a certain category (meaning how well it matches your prototype for that category). For the category "dog," a German Sheppard might rate 10, but a French Bulldog might get a 3 (this has nothing to do with the quality of the breed, just how "doggy" people think they are). Another research technique uses reaction time to measure how well something fits into a mental category (e.g., Dovidio, 1986; Rosch & Mervis, 1975; Unyk, 1990).

One of the ways this is done is that you, as a participant, see or hear a statement, such as, "A turkey is a bird" and then press a button for true or false as fast as you can. Findings from this line of research demonstrate that the closer the category example matches your prototype of the category, the faster you will respond. "A turkey is a bird" will produce a significantly slower reaction time than, "A robin is a bird."

A third method involves asking participants to produce examples of category members either by listing them or making line drawings. In a given amount of time, the participants will produce a far greater number of the more representative members of a category. For example, if you are asked to draw pieces of furniture, you will probably draw a chair, a couch, or a table, before you will draw a hutch or a bookcase. Or, if asked to list human emotions, *happiness* and *anger* might come to mind faster than, say, *confusion* or *rage* (e.g., Fehr & Russell, 1984).

Just as is true of many of the studies summarized in this book, Rosch's discoveries relating to natural categories and prototypes changed psychology's view of your use of concepts, but over the 40 years since her findings, other research has appeared that either expands or questions her results. For example, some research has suggested that, although Rosch's prototype theory appears to be valid, this does not mean researchers have abandoned our use of strict linguistic definitions. For example, one 2010 study, although acknowledging Rosch's study discussed here, reported that other studies, including one with participants from another Papua subculture, do not appear to base their color perception primarily on prototypes within categories, but rather on linguistic cues (Tylen et al., 2010).

The "truth" appears to be (if we can ever actually know the truth) that people will invoke linguistic definitions when that level of precision is necessary. Returning to the category of fruit provides an excellent example. If someone says to you, "Would you like a piece of fruit?" you do not think, "Fruit: The ripened seed-bearing structure of a plant." Instead, you immediately access your prototype for "fruit," which is most likely something such as an apple, an orange, or a banana. You would be quite surprised if you answered, "Yes!" and someone tossed you a pine cone (which is, technically, a fruit from a pine tree)! However, sometimes a formal, linguistic definition of fruit might be useful, such as, say, when you are on a nature walk and come upon an unusual plant with strange objects growing on it. Even though the objects on this plant bear little resemblance to your fruit prototype, your formal, linguistic definition might allow you to say, "Look! This plant is bearing fruit."

In conclusion, let's demonstrate just how broadly Rosch's work has influenced diverse fields of research by ending this discussion on a recent study that cited her work in an analysis of pop/rock music – yes – music (de Clercq, 2017). The study focused on how such songs are divided into sections and the *categorizing* of the sections into a relatively standard set of labels. However, the study found that the categories have fuzzy and overlapping boundaries, just as Rosch's categories for other types of objects. What are these fuzzy boundaries (or ambiguities) in pop/rock music according to this researcher? If you know a little about music, you will recognize them as the *verse*, the *chorus*, and the *bridge*.

Dovidio, J. (1984). Concept of emotion viewed from a prototype perspective. *Journal of Experimental Psychology: General, 113*, 464–486. doi: 10.1037/0096-3445.113.3.464

Fehr, B., & Russell, J. (1986). Racial stereotypes: The contents of their cognitive representations. *Journal of Experimental Social Psychology, 22*, 22–37.

deClercq, T. D. (2017). Embracing Ambiguity in the Analysis of Form in Pop/Rock Music, 1982–1991. *Music Theory Online, 23*(3).

Rosch, E., & Mervis, C. (1975). Family resemblances: Studies in the internal structure of categories. *Cognitive Psychology, 7*, 573–605.

Rosch, E. H. (1975). Cognitive representations of semantic categories. *Journal of Experimental Psychology: General, 104*, 192–233.

Rosch, E. H. (1978). Principles of categorization. In E. Rosch & B. Lloyd (Eds.), *Cognition and categorization*. NJ: Lawrence Erlbaum.

Tylen, E., Weed, E., Wallentin, M., Roepstorff, A., & Frith, C. (2010). Language as a tool for interacting minds. *Mind & Language, 25*, 3–29.

Unyk, A. (1990). An information-processing analysis of expectancy in music cognition. *Psychomusicology, 9*, 229–240.

Reading 2.4: Acting As If You Are Hypnotized

Spanos, N. P. (1982). Hypnotic behavior: A cognitive, social, psychological perspective. *Research Communications in Psychology, Psychiatry, and Behavior, 7*, 199–213.

2.4 Analyze the role of hypnosis as a goal-directed behavior rather than an altered state of consciousness

The alterations in consciousness with which we are all most familiar are related to sleep and dreaming. Another phenomenon relating to altered states of consciousness is hypnosis. Some of you have probably had the experience of being hypnotized. Most people see hypnosis as a mysterious and powerful process of controlling the mind. The phrases and words that surround hypnosis, such as *going under* and *trance,* indicate that it is commonly considered to be a separate and unique state of awareness, different from both waking and sleep. Many psychologists support this view to varying degrees. However, Nicholas Spanos (1942–1994) led an opposing view that hypnosis is, in reality, nothing more than an increased degree of motivation to perform certain behaviors and can be explained fully *without* invoking notions of trances or altered states.

The beginnings of hypnosis are usually traced back to the middle of the 18th century, a time when mental illness was first recognized by some as stemming from supernatural rather than psychological causes. One of the many influential individuals who helped bring psychology out of the realm of witchcraft and devil possession was Franz Anton Mesmer (1733–1815). He believed that "hysterical disorders," as they were referred to then, were a result of imbalances in a "universal magnetic fluid" present in the human body (we do not fully understand his conceptualization of this fluid). During strange gatherings in his laboratory, soft music would play; the lights would dim; and Mesmer, costumed rather like Dumbledore, would take iron rods from bottles of various chemicals and touch parts of afflicted patients' bodies. He believed that these elements and chemicals would transmit what he called the "animal magnetism" into the patients and provide relief from their symptoms. Interestingly, history has recorded that in many cases this treatment appears to have been successful (due, of course, to placebo effects). It is from Mesmer that we acquired the word *mesmerize,* and many believe that his treatment included some of the techniques we now associate with hypnosis.

Throughout the history of psychology, hypnosis (named after *Hypnos,* the Greek god of sleep) has played a prominent role, especially in the treatment of psychological disorders, and it was a major component in Freud's psychoanalytic techniques. Ernest

Hilgard (1904–2001) was at the forefront of modern researchers who support the position that hypnosis is an altered psychological state (see Hilgard, 1978; Kihlstrom, 1998). His and others' descriptions of hypnosis have included characteristics such as increased susceptibility to suggestion, involuntary performance of behaviors, improvements in recall, increased intensity of visual imagination, dissociation (the psychological separation from a person's current environmental reality), and analgesia (lowered sensitivity to pain). Until the 1970s, the idea that hypnosis is capable of producing thoughts, ideas, and behaviors that would otherwise be impossible, and that it is an altered state of consciousness, was virtually undisputed.

However, it is the job of scientists to look upon the status quo with a critical eye and, whenever they see fit, to attempt to debunk popular, questionable beliefs. Social psychologist Nicholas Spanos suggested that the major assumptions underlying hypnosis, as set forth by Hilgard and others, should be questioned. In this article, Spanos wrote, "The positing of special processes to account for hypnotic behavior is not only unnecessary, but also misleading. . . . Hypnotic behavior is basically similar to other social behavior and, like other social behavior, can be usefully described as strategic and goal-directed" (p. 200). In other words, Spanos contended that hypnotized participants are actually engaging in *voluntary* behavior designed to produce a desired consequence. He further maintained that although such behavior may result from increased motivation, it does *not* involve an altered state of consciousness.

Theoretical Propositions

Spanos theorized that the behaviors commonly attributed to a hypnotic trance state are within the normal, voluntary abilities of humans. He maintained that the only reason people define themselves as having been hypnotized is that they have interpreted their own behavior under hypnosis in ways that are consistent with their *expectations* about being hypnotized. Spanos viewed the process of hypnosis as a ritual that in Western cultures carries a great deal of meaning. Participants expect to relinquish control over their own behavior, and as the process of hypnotic induction develops, they begin to believe that their voluntary acts are becoming automatic, involuntary events. An example of this that Spanos offered is that voluntary instructions are given early in the hypnotic procedure to the participant, such as "Relax the muscles in your legs," but later these become involuntary suggestions, such as "Your legs feel limp and heavy."

In collaboration with various colleagues and associates, Spanos devoted nearly a decade of research prior to this 1982 article, demonstrating how many of the effects commonly attributed to hypnotic trances could be explained just as readily (or even more simply) in less mysterious or mind-altering ways.

Method

This article does not report on one specific experiment but rather summarizes a group of studies conducted by Spanos and his associates prior to 1982, which were designed to support his position countering Hilgard's contention (and the popular belief) that hypnosis is a unique state of consciousness. Most of the findings reported were taken from 16 studies in which Spanos was directly involved and that offered interpretations of hypnotically produced behavior other than the common assumption of a unique altered state of being.

Results and Discussion

Spanos claimed that two key aspects of hypnosis lead people to perceive it as an altered state of consciousness. One is that participants interpret their behavior during hypnosis as caused by something other than the self, thus making their actions *seem* involuntary. The second aspect is the belief discussed previously that the "hypnosis ritual" creates expectations in participants, which in turn motivate them to behave in ways that are consistent with their expectations. The findings of the research Spanos reports in this article focus on how these frequently cited claims about hypnosis may be drawn into question.

THE BELIEF THAT BEHAVIOR IS INVOLUNTARY As participants are being hypnotized, they are usually asked to take various tests to determine if a hypnotic state has been induced. Spanos claimed that these tests are often carried out in such a way as to invite the participants to convince themselves that something out of the ordinary is happening. Hypnotic tests involve suggestions, such as "Your arm is heavy and you cannot hold it up"; "Your hands are being drawn together by some force and you cannot keep them apart"; "Your arm is as rigid as a steel bar and you cannot bend it"; or "Your body is so heavy that you cannot stand up." Spanos interpreted these test suggestions as containing two interrelated requests. One request asks participants to do something, and the other asks them to interpret the action as having occurred involuntarily. Some participants fail completely to respond to the suggestion. Spanos claimed that these participants do not understand that they must voluntarily do something to initiate the suggested behavior and instead simply wait for their arms or body to start moving. Other participants respond to the suggestion but are aware that they are behaving voluntarily. Still other participants agree to both requests; they respond to the suggestion and interpret their response as beyond their control.

Spanos suggested that whether participants interpret their behavior to be voluntary or involuntary depends on the way the suggestion is worded. In one of his studies, Spanos put two groups of participants through a hypnosis induction procedure. Then to one group he made various behavior suggestions, such as "Your arm is very light and is rising." To the other group, he gave direct instructions for the same behaviors, such as "Raise your arm." Afterward, he asked the participants if they thought their behaviors were voluntary or involuntary. The participants in the suggestion group were more likely to interpret their behaviors as involuntary than were those in the direct instruction group.

Right now, while you are reading this page, hold your left arm straight out and keep it there for a couple of minutes. You will notice that it begins to feel heavy. This heaviness is neither due to hypnosis nor due to gravity! If you are *hypnotized* and given the suggestion that your outstretched arm is becoming heavy, it would be very easy for you to attribute your action of lowering your arm to involuntary forces (you want to lower it anyway!). But what if you are given the suggestion that your arm is light and rising? If you raise your arm, it should be more difficult to interpret that action as involuntary because you would have to ignore the contradictory feedback provided by gravity. Spanos tested this idea and found that such an interpretation was more difficult. Participants who believed they were hypnotized were significantly more likely to define as involuntary their behavior of arm lowering than that of arm raising. In the traditional view of hypnosis, the direction of the arm in the hypnotic suggestion should not make any difference; it should always be considered involuntary.

Suggestions made to hypnotic participants often ask them to imagine certain situations to produce a desired behavior. If you were a participant, you might be given the suggestion that your arm is rigid and you cannot bend it. To reinforce this suggestion, it might be added that your arm is in a plaster cast. Spanos believed that some people may become absorbed in these imaginal strategies more than others, which could have the effect of leading them to believe that their response (the inability to move their arm) was involuntary. His reasoning was that if you are highly absorbed, you will not be able to focus on information that alerts you to the fact that the fantasy is not real. The more vividly you imagine the cast, its texture and hardness, how it got there, and so on, the less likely you are to remember that this is only your imagination at work. If this deep absorption happens, you might be more inclined to believe that your rigid-arm behavior was involuntary when actually it was not. In support of this, Spanos found that when participants were asked to rate how absorbed they were in a suggested imagined scenario, the higher the absorption rating, the more likely they were to interpret their related behavior as occurring involuntarily (some people appear to become absorbed in these suggestions more easily than others, which renders them more "hypnotizable") Spanos also noted that a person's susceptibility to hypnosis correlates with his or her general tendency to become absorbed in other activities, such as books, music, or daydreaming. Consequently, these individuals are more likely to willingly cooperate with the kind of suggestions involved in hypnosis.

CREATION OF EXPECTATIONS IN HYPNOTIC PARTICIPANTS   Spanos claimed that the beliefs most people have about hypnosis are adequate in themselves to produce what is typically seen as hypnotic behavior. He further contended that these beliefs are strengthened by the methods used to induce and study hypnosis. He cited three examples of research showing how people might engage in certain behaviors under hypnosis because they think they should rather than because of an altered state of awareness.

First, Spanos referred to a study in which a lecture about hypnosis was given to two groups of students. The lectures were identical except that one group was told that arm rigidity was a spontaneous event during hypnosis. Later, both groups were hypnotized. In the group that had heard the lecture including the information about arm rigidity, some of the participants exhibited this behavior *spontaneously,* without any instructions to do so. However, among the participants in the other group, not one arm became rigid. According to Spanos, this demonstrated how people will enact their experience of hypnosis according to how they believe they are supposed to behave.

The second hypnotic event that Spanos used to illustrate his position involved research findings that hypnotized participants claim the visual imagery they experienced under hypnosis was more intense, vivid, and real than similar imaginings when not hypnotized. Here is how these studies typically have been done: Participants are asked to imagine scenes or situations in which they are performing certain behaviors. Then, these same participants are hypnotized and again asked to visualize the same or similar situations (the hypnotized and nonhypnotized trials can be in any order). These participants generally report that the imagery in the hypnotized condition was significantly more intense. Spanos and his associates found, however, that when two different groups of participants are used, one hypnotized and one not, their average intensity ratings of the visual imagery are approximately equal. The difference between the two methods is explained by the fact that when two different groups are tested, the participants do not have anything to use for comparison. However, when the same participants are used in both conditions, they can compare the two experiences and rate one against the other. Because participants nearly always rate the hypnotic imagery as more intense, this supports the idea that hypnosis is really an altered state, right? If you could ask Spanos, he would say, "Wrong!" In his view, the participants who participate in both conditions expect the ritual of hypnosis to produce more intense imagery, and therefore, they rate it accordingly.

The third and perhaps most interesting demonstration of hypnosis addressed by Spanos was the claim that hypnosis can cause people to become insensitive to pain (the *analgesia effect*). One way that pain can be tested in the laboratory without causing damage to the participant is by using the "cold pressor test." If you are a participant in such a study, you would be asked to immerse your arm in freezing water (0°C) and leave it there as long as you could. After first 10 seconds or so, this becomes increasingly painful, and most people will remove their arm within a minute or two. Hilgard (1978) reported that participants who received both waking and hypnotic training in analgesia (pain reduction) reported significantly less cold-pressor pain during the hypnotized trials. His explanation for this was that during hypnosis, a person is able to dissociate the

pain from awareness. In this way, Hilgard contended a part of the person's consciousness experiences the pain, but this part is hidden from awareness by what he called an
"amnesic barrier."

Again, Spanos rejected a hypnotic explanation for these analgesic findings and
offered evidence to demonstrate that reduction in perceived pain during hypnosis is a
result of the participants' motivation and expectations. All the research on hypnosis uses
participants who have scored high on measures of hypnotic susceptibility. According
to Spanos, these individuals "have a strong investment in presenting themselves in the
experimental setting as good hypnotic subjects" (p. 208). The participants know that a
waking state is being compared to a hypnotic state and want to demonstrate the effectiveness of hypnosis. Spanos, working with his associate H. J. Stam, performed a similar
study involving cold-pressor pain but with one major difference: Some participants were
told that they would first use waking analgesia techniques (such as self-distraction) and
would then be tested using hypnotic pain-reduction methods, but other participants
were not told of the later hypnotic test (see also Stam and Spanos, 1980).

Figure 2.4.1 summarizes what Stam and Spanos found. When participants
expected the hypnosis condition to follow the waking trials, they rated the analgesic
effect lower in order to, as the authors state, "leave room" for improvement under
hypnosis. Stam and Spanos claimed that this demonstrated how even the hypnotic
behavior of pain insensitivity could be attributed to the participants' need to respond
to the demands of the situation rather than automatically assuming a dissociated state
of consciousness.

The most important question concerning all these findings reported by Spanos
is whether we should reevaluate the phenomenon called hypnosis. And what does it
mean if we were to decide that hypnosis is not the powerful mind-altering force that
popular culture, and many psychologists, have portrayed it to be?

Figure 2.4.1 Waking versus hypnotic analgesia: expectation versus no expectation.

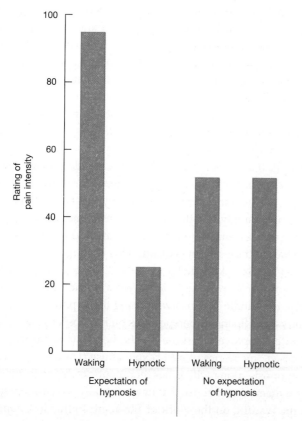

Implications of the Findings

In evaluating Spanos's research, you should remember that his goal was not to prove that hypnosis does not exist but, rather, to demonstrate that what we call *hypnotic behaviors* are the result of highly motivated, goal-directed social behavior, not an altered and unique state of consciousness. It is well accepted among most behavioral scientists that people cannot be hypnotized against their will. Furthermore, under hypnosis, participants will not engage in acts they believe are antisocial, and they are not able to perform feats of superhuman strength or endurance. In this article, Spanos has demonstrated how many of the more subtle aspects of hypnosis may be explained in less mysterious and more straightforward ways than that of the hypnotic trance.

What would be the implications of accepting Spanos's contention that hypnosis does not exist? The answer to this question is "Perhaps none." Whether the effects of hypnosis are produced by an altered state of awareness or by increased motivation does not change the fact that hypnosis is often a useful method of helping people improve something in their lives. One reason that there continues to be such widespread and unquestioning acceptance of the power of the hypnotic trance may be that humans need to feel that there is a way out, a last resort to solve their problems if all else fails—something so omnipotent that they can even change against their own resistance to such change.

Whether or not hypnosis is an altered state of consciousness remains a highly controversial issue. But whatever hypnosis is, it is not the panacea most people would like to find. Several studies have shown that hypnosis is no more effective than other methods of treatment to help people stop abusing alcohol and tobacco, improve their memory, or lose weight (see Lazar & Dempster, 1981, for a review of this research).

Recent Applications

If, given the chance, would you readily agree to be hypnotized or would you rather avoid it? A study based on Spanos's research examined *reluctant* candidates for hypnosis (Capafons et al., 2005). The findings, as you will see, could be used either to dispute or confirm Spanos's research. These hesitant participants, once convinced to agree to the hypnotic experience, were assigned to three groups: One group was given almost no information about what to expect from a hypnotic experience (the control group). Another group was given "cognitive-behavioral" information about the hypnotic experience—that is, what to expect about how they would think and behave while under hypnosis. The third group was told what a hypnotic trance was like: an altered state of consciousness (a trance) accompanied by *cognitive dissociation* (a separation of the consciousness from normal self-awareness).

One might think that among those who were avoidant about being hypnotized to begin with, the *cognitive-behavioral* and the *trance* groups would be more resistant to the hypnotic procedure and the results of the hypnosis would be less obvious (or nonexistent). But, surprisingly, just the opposite was found. Both the cognitive-behavioral group and the trance group demonstrated greater hypnotic suggestibility than the control group. What do these findings mean? This is not particularly clear. They may indicate the old saying that "knowledge is power." That is, people who receive more information about an "unknown" experience, *feel* a greater level of perceived control, and feel more able to "handle" themselves during the hypnotic procedure.

Another study cited Spanos's perspectives on hypnosis to question certain therapeutic practices often employed by some psychotherapists to induce clients to recover ostensibly "repressed" memories of past sexual abuse (Lynn et al., 2003). The authors contended that hypnosis, along with other therapeutic techniques, may distort memories or even create memories of abuse that never actually took place, especially in early childhood (see the reading on the work of Elizabeth Loftus in Chapter IV for more about recovered memories). The researchers point out, based on Spanos's research, that "adults' memory reports from 24 months of age or earlier are likely to represent confabulations, condensations, and constructions of early events, as well as current concerns and stories heard about early events" (p. 42). In other words, the belief that hypnosis somehow allows clients to retrieve accurate memories of early traumatic experiences is misguided and may be subject to all the memory errors that exist in a nonhypnotized state. This, the authors contend, may in some cases, lead to false memories and accusations of abuse that never happened. Spanos elaborated his perspective on this potential misuse of hypnotic techniques in his 1994 book, *Multiple Identities & False Memories: A Sociocognitive Perspective.*

Conclusion

Clearly, the debate goes on. Spanos continued his research until his untimely death in a plane crash in June 1994 (see McConkey & Sheehan, 1995). A summary of his early work on hypnosis can be found in his 1989 book, *Hypnosis: The Cognitive-Behavioral Perspective.* Nicholas Spanos was a prolific and well-respected behavioral scientist who has been missed greatly by his colleagues and by all those who learned and benefited from his work (see Baker, 1994, for a eulogy to Nick Spanos). And, clearly, his research legacy will be carried on by others. His work on hypnosis changed psychology in that he offered an experimentally based, alternative explanation for an aspect of human consciousness and behavior that was virtually unchallenged for nearly 200 years.

Baker, R. (1994). In memoriam: Nick Spanos. *Skeptical Inquirer, 18*(5), 459.

Capafons, A., Cabañas, F., Alarcón, A., Espejo, B., Mendoza, E., Chaves, J., & Monje, A. (2005). Effects of different types of preparatory information on attitudes toward hypnosis. *Contemporary Hypnosis, 22,* 67–76.

Hilgard, E. (1978). Hypnosis and consciousness. *Human Nature, 1,* 42–51.

Kihlstrom, J. F. (1998). Attributions, awareness, and dissociation: In memoriam Kenneth S. Bowers, 1937–1996. *American Journal of Clinical Hypnosis, 40*(3), 194–205.

Lazar, B., and Dempster, C. (1981). Failures in hypnosis and hypnotherapy: A review. *American Journal of Clinical Hypnosis, 24*(1), 48–54.

Lynn, S., Loftus, E., Lilienfeld, S., & Lock, T. (2003). Memory recovery techniques in psychotherapy: Problems and pitfalls. *Skeptical Inquirer, 27,* 40–46.

McConkey, K., & Sheehan, P. (1995). Nicholas Spanos: Reflections with gratitude. *Contemporary Hypnosis, 12,* 36–38.

Spanos, N. P. (1989). *Hypnotic behavior: The cognitive, social, psychological perspective.* Amherst, NY: Prometheus Books.

Spanos, N. P. (1994). *Multiple identities & false memories: A sociocognitive perspective.* Washington, DC: American Psychological Association.

Spanos, N. P., & Chaves, J. F. (1989). *Hypnosis: The cognitive–behavioral perspective.* New York: Prometheus.

Stam, H. J., & Spanos, N. P. (1980). Experimental designs, expectancy effects, and hypnotic analgesia. *Journal of Abnormal Psychology, 89,* 751–762.

Chapter 3
Learning and Conditioning

 Learning Objectives

3.1 Explain how the theory of classical conditioning was developed and applied

3.2 Evaluate the ethics and outcomes of Watson's Little Albert experiment

3.3 Characterize superstition according to Skinner

3.4 Explain how children learn to be aggressive according to social learning theory

The area of psychology, concerned with learning, has produced a well-defined body of literature explaining the process underlying how animals and humans learn. Some of the most famous names in the history of psychology have made their most influential discoveries in this field-names that are easily recognized by those both inside and outside the behavioral sciences, such as Pavlov, Watson, Skinner, and Bandura. Picking a few of the most significant studies from this branch of psychology and from these researchers is no easy task, but the articles selected here can be found in nearly every introductory psychology textbook and are representative of the enormous contributions of these scientists.

For, Ivan Pavlov, we take a journey back to the early 1900s to review his work with dogs, metronomes, bells, salivation, and the discovery of the *conditioned reflex*. Second, John Watson, known for many contributions, is probably most famous (notorious?) for his 1920 ethically challenged experiment with Little Albert, which demonstrated for the first time how emotions could be shown to be a product of the environment rather than purely internal processes. For the third study in this section, we discuss B. F. Skinner's famous demonstration of superstitious behavior in a pigeon and his explanation for how humans become superstitious in exactly the same way. Fourth, we examine the well-known "Bobo Doll Study," in which Albert Bandura established that children could learn aggressive behaviors through their modeling of adult violence.

Reading 3.1: It's Not Just About Salivating Dogs!

Pavlov, I. P. (1927). *Conditioned reflexes.* London: Oxford University Press.

3.1   Explain how the theory of classical conditioning was developed and applied

Have you ever walked into a dentist's office where the odor of the disinfectant made your teeth hurt? If you have, it was probably because the odor triggered an association that had been conditioned in your brain between that smell and your past experiences at the dentist. When you hear "The Star Spangled-Banner" played at the Olympic Games, does your heart beat a little faster? That happens to most Americans. Does the same thing happen when you hear the Italian national anthem? Unless you were raised in Italy, most likely it does not, because you have been conditioned to respond physically to one anthem but not to the other. And why do some people squint and become nervous if you inflate a balloon near them? It is because they have learned to associate the expanding balloon with something fear producing (such as a loud *pop!*). These are just a few of countless human behaviors that exist because of a process known as *classical conditioning.*

The classical conditioning theory of learning was developed and articulated nearly 100 years ago in Russia by one of the most familiar names in the history of psychology, Ivan Petrovich Pavlov (1849–1946). Unlike most of the research presented in this book, Pavlov's name and his basic ideas of learning by association are widely recognized in popular culture. (even a Rolling Stones song from the 1970s contained the line "I salivate like a Pavlov dog"). However, how Pavlov came to make his landmark discoveries and the true significance of his work are not so widely understood.

Although Pavlov's contributions to psychology were among some of the most important ever made, and are included in every psychology text, he was not a psychologist at all but rather a prominent Russian physiologist studying digestive processes. In 1904, his research on digestion earned him the Nobel Prize for science. Yet the discoveries that dramatically changed his career, and the history of psychology, began virtually by accident. In the late 1800s, psychology was a very young field of scientific study and was considered by many to be something less than a true science. Therefore, Pavlov's decision to make such a radical turn from the more solid and respected science of physiology to the fledgling study of psychology was a risky career move. He wrote about this dilemma facing any scientist thinking about studying psychology in the early 1900s:

> It is logical that in its analysis of the various activities of living matter, physiology should base itself on the more advanced and more exact sciences, physics and chemistry. But if we attempt an approach from this science of psychology . . . we shall be building our superstructure on a science that has no claim to exactness. . . . In fact, it is still open to discussion whether psychology is a natural science, or whether it can be regarded as a science at all. (p. 3)

Looking back on Pavlov's discoveries, it was fortunate for the advancement of psychological science and for our understanding of human behavior that he took the risk and made the change.

Pavlov's physiological research involved the use of dogs as subjects for studying the role of salivation on digestion. He or his assistants would introduce various types of food or nonfood substances into a dog's mouth and observe the rate and amount of salivation. To measure salivation scientifically, minor surgery was performed on the dogs so that a salivary duct was redirected through an incision in the dog's cheek and connected to a tube that would collect the saliva. Throughout this research, Pavlov made many new and fascinating discoveries. For example, he found that when a dog received moist food, only a small amount of saliva would be produced, compared with a heavy flow when dry food was presented. The production of saliva under these varying conditions was regarded by Pavlov as a reflex, that is, a response that occurs *automatically* to a specific stimulus without the need for any learning. If you think about it, salivation is purely reflexive for humans, too. Suppose I ask you, as you read this sentence, to salivate as heavily as you can. You cannot do it. But if you are hungry and find yourself sitting in front of your favorite food, you will salivate whether you want to or not.

As Pavlov continued his research, he began to notice strange events that were totally unexpected. The dogs began to salivate *before* any food reached their mouths and even before the smell of food was present. After a while, the dogs were salivating at times when no salivary stimulus was present at all. Somehow, the reflexive action of the salivary glands had been altered through the animals' experience in the lab: "Even the vessel from which the food has been given is sufficient to evoke an alimentary reflex (of salivation) complete in all its details; and, further, the secretion may be provoked even by the sight of the person who has brought the food vessel, or by the sound of his footsteps" (p. 13).

This was the crossroads for Pavlov. He had observed digestive responses occurring to stimuli seemingly unrelated to digestion, and pure physiology could not explain this. To his chagrin, he realized that the answer had to be found in *psychology*.

Theoretical Propositions

Pavlov theorized that the dogs had learned from experience in the lab to expect food following the appearance of certain signals. Although these *signal stimuli* do not naturally produce salivation, the dogs came to associate them with food and, thus, responded to them with salivation. Consequently, Pavlov determined two kinds of reflexes must exist.

Unconditioned reflexes are inborn and automatic, they require no learning (conditioning), and are generally the same for all members of a particular species. Salivating when food enters the mouth, jumping at the sound of a loud noise, and the dilation of your pupils in low light are examples of unconditioned reflexes. *Conditioned reflexes,* on the other hand, are acquired through experience or learning and may vary a great deal among individual members of a species. A dog salivating at the sound of footsteps, or you feeling pain in your teeth when you smell dental disinfectant, are conditioned reflexes.

Unconditioned reflexes are caused by an *unconditioned stimulus* (UCS) producing an *unconditioned response* (UCR). In Pavlov's studies, the UCS was food and the UCR was salivation. Remember, "unconditioned" means no learning is required for the response. *Conditioned reflexes* consist of a *conditioned stimulus* (CS), such as the footsteps, producing a *conditioned response* (CR), salivation. You will notice that the response in both these examples is salivation, but when the salivation results from hearing footsteps, it is the *learning*, and not the dog's natural reflex, that produced it.

Pavlov wanted to answer this question: Conditioned reflexes are not inborn, so exactly how are they acquired? He proposed that if a particular stimulus in the dog's environment was often present when the dog was fed, this stimulus would become associated in the dog's brain with food; it would *signal* the approaching food. Prior to being paired with the food, the environmental stimulus did not produce any important response. In other words, to the dogs, it was a *neutral stimulus* (NS). When the dogs first arrived at the lab, the assistant's footsteps might have produced a response of curiosity (Pavlov called it the "What is it?" response), but hearing the footsteps certainly would not have caused the dogs to salivate. The footsteps, then, were an NS. However, over time, as the dogs heard the same footsteps just prior to being fed every day, they would begin to associate the sound with food. Eventually, according to the theory, the footsteps alone would cause the dogs to salivate. Pavlov proposed that the process by which an NS becomes a CS could be diagrammed as follows:

Step 1			UCS (food)	⟶	UCR (salivation)
Step 2	NS (footsteps)	+ +	UCS (food)	⟶	UCR (salivation)
Step 3	(Repeat step 2 several times)				
Step 4			CS (footsteps)	⟶	CR (salivation)

Now that he had a theory to explain his observations, Pavlov began a series of experiments to prove that it was correct. It is commonly believed that Pavlov conditioned dogs to salivate at the sound of a bell, which was true of his later studies. But as you will see, his early experiments involved a metronome (nearly anything could be used as a stimulus).

Method and Results

Pavlov was able to build a special laboratory at the Institute of Experimental Medicine in Petrograd (which became Leningrad following Lenin's death and has now returned to its original name of St. Petersburg) with funds donated by a philanthropic businessman from Moscow. This soundproof lab allowed for complete isolation of the subjects from the experimenters and from all extraneous stimuli during the experimental procedures. Therefore, a specific stimulus could be administered and responses could be recorded without any direct contact between the experimenters and the animals.

After Pavlov had established this controlled research environment, the procedure was simple. Pavlov chose *food* as the UCS. As explained previously, food will elicit the UCR of salivation. Then, Pavlov needed to find an NS that was, for the dogs, completely unrelated to food. For this, he used the sound of the metronome. Over several conditioning trials, the dog was exposed to the ticking of the metronome and then was immediately presented with food: "A stimulus which was neutral of itself had been superimposed upon the action of the inborn alimentary reflex (salavation). We observed that after several repetitions of the combined stimulation, (the food and the metronome) the sounds of the metronome had acquired the property of stimulating salivary secretion" (p. 26). In other words, the metronome had become a CS for the conditioned response of salivation.

Pavlov and his associates elaborated on this preliminary finding by using different unconditioned and neutral stimuli. For example, they presented the odor of vanilla (NS) to the subjects prior to placing a lemon juice-like solution in the dog's mouth (the UCS). The juice caused heavy salivation (UCR). After 20 repetitions of the pairing, the vanilla alone produced salivation. For a visual test, the dogs were exposed to an object that began to rotate just prior to the presentation of food. After only five pairings, the rotating object by itself (CS) caused the dogs to salivate (CR).

The importance and application of Pavlov's work extends far beyond salivating dogs. His theories of classical conditioning explained a major portion of human behavior and helped to launch psychology as a true science.

Significance of the Findings

The theory of classical conditioning (also called *Pavlovian conditioning*) is universally accepted and has remained virtually unchanged since its conception through Pavlov's work. It is used to explain and interpret a wide range of human behavior, including where phobias come from, why you dislike certain foods, the source of your emotions, how advertising works, why you feel anxiety before a job interview or an exam, and what arouses you sexually. Several later studies dealing with some of these applications are discussed here.

Classical conditioning focuses on reflexive behavior: those behaviors that are not under your voluntary control. Any reflex can be conditioned to occur to a previously NS. You can become classically conditioned so that your left eye blinks when you hear a doorbell, your heart rate increases at the sight of a flashing blue light, or you experience sexual arousal when you eat strawberries. The doorbell, blue light, and strawberries were all neutral in relation to their conditioned responses until they somehow became associated with unconditioned stimuli for eye blinking (e.g., a puff of air into the eye), heart rate increase (e.g., a sudden loud noise), and sexual arousal (e.g., romantic caresses).

To experience firsthand the process of classical conditioning, here is an experiment you can perform on yourself. All you will need is a bell, a mirror, and, to serve as your temporary laboratory, a room that becomes completely dark when the light is switched off. The pupils of your eyes dilate and constrict reflexively according to changes in light intensity. You have no voluntary control over this, and you did not have to learn how to do it. If I say to you "Please dilate your pupils now," you would be unable to do so. However, when you walk into a dark theater, they dilate immediately. Therefore, a decrease in light would be considered an UCS for pupil dilation, the UCR. In your temporary lab, ring the bell and, immediately after, turn off the light. Wait in the total darkness about 15 seconds and turn the light back on. Wait another 15 seconds and repeat the procedure: bell . . . light off . . . wait 15 seconds . . . light on. . . . Repeat this pairing of the NS (the bell) with the UCS (the darkness) 10–20 times, making sure that the bell *only* rings just prior to the sudden darkness. Now, with the lights on, watch your eyes closely in the mirror and ring the bell. You will see your pupils dilate slightly even though there is no change in light! The bell has become the CS and pupil dilation the conditioned response.

Related Research and Recent Applications

Two other studies presented in this book rest directly on Pavlov's theory of classical conditioning. In the next article, John B. Watson conditioned 11-month-old Little Albert to fear a white rat (and other furry things) by employing the same principles Pavlov used to condition salivation in dogs. By doing so, Watson demonstrated how emotions, such as fear, are formed. Later, Joseph Wolpe (see Chapter IX: *Psychotherapy: Reading 9.2*) developed a therapeutic technique for treating intense fears (phobias) by applying the concepts of classical conditioning. His work was based on the idea that the association between the CS and the UCS must be broken to reduce the fearful response.

This line of research on classical conditioning and phobias continues to the present. For example, studies have found that children whose parents have phobias may develop the same phobias to objects such as snakes and spiders through "vicarious" conditioning from mom and dad without any direct exposure to the feared object (Fredrikson, Annas, & Wik, 1997). The countless applications of Pavlov's theory in the psychological and medical literature are far too numerous to summarize in any detail here. Instead, a few additional examples of the more notable findings are discussed.

A common problem that plagues ranchers around the world is that of predatory animals, usually wolves and coyotes, killing and eating their livestock. In the early 1970s, studies were conducted that attempted to apply Pavlovian conditioning techniques to solve the problem of the killing of sheep by coyotes and wolves without the need for killing the predators (see Gustafson et al., 1974). Wolves and coyotes were given pieces of mutton (meat from sheep) containing small amounts of lithium chloride (UCS), a chemical that if ingested, makes an animal sick. When the animals ate the meat, they became dizzy, with severe nausea and vomiting (UCR). After recovering, these same hungry predators were placed in a pen with a live sheep. The wolves and coyotes began to attack the sheep (CS), but as soon as they smelled their prey, they stopped and stayed as far away from the sheep as possible. When the gate to the pen was opened, the wolves and coyotes ran away from the sheep! Based on this and other related research, ranchers commonly use this method of classical conditioning to keep wolves and coyotes away from their herds.

Another potentially vital area of research involving classical conditioning is in the field of behavioral medicine. Studies have suggested that the activity of the immune system can be altered using Pavlovian principles. Ader and Cohen (1985) gave mice water flavored with saccharine (mice love this water). They then paired the saccharine water with an injection of a drug that weakened the immune system of the mice. Later, when these conditioned mice were given the saccharine water but no injection, they showed signs of immunosuppression, a weakening of the immune response. Research is underway (primarily within a psychology subfield called *psychoneuroimmunology*) to study if the reverse is also possible—if immune *enhancing* responses may be classically conditioned. Overall, research is demonstrating that classical conditioning may indeed hold promise for increasing the effectiveness of immune system responses in humans (Miller & Cohen, 2001). Just imagine: In the future, you may be able to strengthen your resistance to illness by exposing yourself to a *nonmedical* CS. For example, imagine you feel the beginnings of a cold or the flu, so you tune into your special classically conditioned "immune response enhancement music" on your phone. As the music fills your ears, your resistance rises as a conditioned response to this stimulus and stops the disease in its tracks.

Pavlov's theories have even been applied to helping parents condition a liking of fruits and vegetables in their toddlers (Moens et. al., 2014).

As a demonstration of the continuing impact of Pavlov's discoveries on today's psychological research, consider the following. Since 2000, more than a thousand scientific articles have cited Pavlov's work that forms the basis for this discussion. One especially fascinating recent study demonstrated how your psychological state at the time of conditioning and extinction may play a part in the treatment of classically conditioned irrational fears, called *phobias* (Mystkowski et al., 2003). Researchers used desensitization techniques to treat participants who were terrified of spiders. Some received the treatment after ingesting caffeine, while others ingested a placebo. A week later, all participants were retested—some receiving caffeine and others a placebo. Those who were given the placebo during treatment, but received real caffeine at the follow-up, *and* those who had received real caffeine during treatment, but received a placebo at the follow-up, experienced a relapse of the fear response. In other words, changing the characteristics of a stimulus situation lessens the effect of extinction. However, those who were in the same drug condition, either caffeine or placebo, at treatment *and* follow-up, continued to experience a lowered fear response to spiders. This finding implies that if a classically conditioned behavior is successfully placed on extinction, the response may return if the CS is encountered in a new and different situation.

Conclusion

These examples demonstrate how extensive Pavlov's influence has been on many scientific and research disciplines. For psychology, in particular, few scientists have had as much impact in any single discipline. Classical conditioning is one of the fundamental theories on which modern psychology rests. Without Pavlov's contributions, behavioral scientists still might have uncovered most of these principles over the decades. It is unlikely, however, that such a cohesive, elegant, and well-articulated theory of the conditioned reflex would ever have existed if Pavlov had not made the decision to risk his career and venture into the untested, uncharted, and highly questionable science of 19th-century psychology.

Ader, R., & Cohen, N. (1985). CNS immune system interactions: Conditioning phenomena. *Behavioral and Brain Sciences, 8,* 379–394.

Fredrikson, M., Annas, P., & Wik, G. (1997). Parental history, aversive exposure, and the development of snake and spider phobias in women. *Behavior Research and Therapy, 35*(1), 23–28.

Gustafson, C. R., Garcia, J., Hawkins, W., & Rusiniak, K. (1974). Coyote predation control by aversive conditioning. *Science, 184,* 581–583.

Miller, G., & Cohen, S. (2001). Psychological interventions and the immune system: a meta-analytic review and critique. *Health Psychology, 20,* 47–63.

Moens, E., Verbeken, S., Vandeweghe, L., Vervoort, L., Goossens, L., & Braet, C. (2014). How can classical conditioning learning procedures support the taste development in toddlers: Rationale, design and methods. Improving Infant and Child Eating Habits, Encouraging Fruit and Vegetable Intake: Translating Evidence into Practical Recommendations. From The HABEAT Conference, Dijon, France. https://biblio.ugent.be/publication/4420245.

Mystkowski, J., Mineka, S., Vernon, L., & Zinbarg, R. (2003). Changes in caffeine states enhance return of fear in spider phobia. *Journal of Consulting and Clinical Psychology, 71*, 243–250.

Reading 3.2: Little Emotional Albert

Watson, J. B., & Rayner, R. (1920). Conditioned emotional responses. *Journal of Experimental Psychology, 3*, 1–14.

3.2   Evaluate the ethics and outcomes of Watson's Little Albert experiment

Have you ever wondered where your emotions come from? If you have, you're not alone. The source of our emotions has fascinated behavioral scientists throughout psychology's history (and philosophers for thousands of years). Part of the evidence for this fascination can be found in this book; four studies are included that relate directly to emotional responses (Chapter V, Harlow, 1958; Chapter VI, Ekman & Friesen, 1971; Chapter VIII, Seligman & Meier, 1967; and Chapter IX, Wolpe, 1961). This study by Watson and Rayner on conditioned emotional responses was a strikingly powerful piece of research when it was published nearly a century ago, and it continues to exert influence today. You would be hard pressed to pick up a textbook on general psychology or on learning and behavior without finding a summary of this study's findings.

The historical importance of this study is not solely due to the research findings but also to the new psychological territory it pioneered. If we could be transported back to the turn of the century and get a feel for the state of psychology at the time, we would find it nearly completely dominated by the work of Sigmund Freud (see the reading on Anna Freud in Chapter VIII). Freud's psychoanalytic view of human behavior was based on the idea that we are motivated by unconscious instincts and repressed conflicts from early childhood. In simplified Freudian terms, behavior, thoughts, and emotions are generated internally through biological and instinctual processes.

In the 1920s, a new movement in psychology known as behaviorism, spearheaded by Pavlov (as discussed in the previous study) and Watson took hold. The behaviorists' viewpoint was radically opposed to the psychoanalytic school and proposed that behavior is generated *outside* the person through various environmental or situational stimuli. Therefore, Watson theorized, emotional responses exist in us because we have been conditioned to respond emotionally to certain stimuli that we encounter. In other words, we *learn* our emotional reactions. Watson (1913) believed that all human behavior was a product of learning and conditioning, as he proclaimed in his famous statement,

> Give me a dozen healthy infants, well-formed, and my own special world to bring them up in, and I'll guarantee to take anyone at random and train him to become any type of specialist I might select—doctor, lawyer, artist, merchant-chief, and, yes, beggar man and thief.

This was, for its time, an extremely revolutionary view. Most psychologists, as well as public opinion in general, were not ready to accept these new ideas. This was especially true for emotional reactions, which seemed to be generated from within the person. Watson set out to demonstrate that specific emotions could be conditioned without regard for any internal forces.

Theoretical Propositions

Watson theorized that if a stimulus automatically produces a certain emotion in you (such as fear) and that stimulus is repeatedly experienced at the same moment as something else, such as a rat, the rat will become associated in your brain with the fear. In other words, you will eventually become conditioned to be afraid of the rat (this view reflects Pavlov's theory of classical conditioning). He maintained that we are not born to fear rats but that such fears are learned through conditioning. This formed the theoretical basis for his most famous experiment, which involved a participant named "Little Albert."

Method and Results

The participant, "Albert B.," was recruited for this study at the age of 9 months from a hospital where he had been raised as an orphan from birth. The researchers and the hospital staff judged him to be very healthy, both emotionally and physically. To see if Albert was naturally afraid of certain stimuli, the researchers presented him with a white rat, a rabbit, a monkey, a dog, masks with and without hair, and white cotton wool. Albert's reactions to these stimuli were closely observed. Albert was interested in the various animals and objects and would reach for them and sometimes touch them, but he never showed the slightest fear of them. Because they produced no fear, these are referred to as *neutral stimuli.*

The next phase of the experiment involved determining if a fear reaction could be produced by exposing Albert to a loud noise. This was not difficult because all humans, and especially infants, will exhibit fear reactions to loud, sudden noises. Because no learning is necessary for this response to occur, the loud noise is called an *unconditioned stimulus.* In this study, a steel bar 4 feet in length was struck with a hammer just behind Albert. This noise startled and frightened him and made him cry.

Now, the stage was set for testing the idea that the emotion of fear could be conditioned in Albert. The actual conditioning tests were not done until the child was 11 months old. The researchers were hesitant to create fear reactions in a child experimentally, but they made the decision to proceed based on what was, in retrospect, questionable ethical reasoning. (This is discussed in conjunction with the overall ethical problems of this study, later in this review.)

As the experiment began, Watson and his graduate research assistant, Rosalie Rayner, presented Albert with the white rat. At first, Albert was interested in the rat and reached out to touch it. As he did this, the metal bar was struck, which startled and frightened Albert. This process was repeated three times. One week later, the same procedure was followed. After a total of seven pairings of the noise and the rat, the rat was presented to Albert alone, without the noise. As you've probably guessed by now, Albert reacted with extreme fear to the rat. He began to cry, turned away, rolled over on one side away from the rat, and began to crawl away so fast that the researchers had to rush to catch him before he crawled off the edge of the table! A fear response had been conditioned to an object that had not been feared only 1 week earlier.

The researchers then wanted to determine if this learned fear would transfer to other objects. In psychological terms, this transfer is referred to as *generalization.* If Albert showed fear of other similar objects, then the learned behavior is said to have generalized. The next week, Albert was tested again and was still found to be afraid of the rat. Then, to test for generalization, an object similar to the rat (a white rabbit) was presented to Albert. In the author's words,

> Negative responses began at once. He (Albert) leaned as far away from the animal as possible, whimpered, then burst into tears. When the rabbit was placed in contact with him, he buried his face in the mattress, then got up on all fours and crawled away, crying as he went. (p. 6)

Table 3.2.1 Sequence of Stimulus Presentations to Albert on Fourth Day of Testing

Stimulus Presented	Reaction Observed
1. Blocks	Played with blocks as usual
2. Rat	Fearful withdrawal (no crying)
3. Rat + Noise	Fear and crying
4. Rat	Fear and crying
5. Rat	Fear, crying, and crawling away
6. Rabbit	Fear, but less strong reaction than on former presentations
7. Blocks	Played as usual
8. Rabbit	Same as 6
9. Rabbit	Same as 6
10. Rabbit	Some fear, but also wanted to touch rabbit
11. Dog	Fearful avoidance
12. Dog + Noise	Fear and crawling away
13. Blocks	Normal play

Remember, Albert was *not* afraid of the rabbit prior to conditioning and had not been conditioned to fear the rabbit specifically.

Little Albert was presented over the course of this day of testing with a dog, a white fur coat, a package of cotton, and Watson's own head of gray hair. He reacted to all of these items with fear. One of the most well-known tests of generalization that made this research as infamous as it is famous occurred when Watson presented Albert with a Santa Claus mask. The reaction? Yes . . . fear! After another 5 days, Albert was tested again. The sequence of presentations on this day is summarized in Table 3.2.1.

Another aspect of conditioned emotional responses Watson wanted to explore was whether the learned emotion would transfer from one situation to another. If Albert's fear responses to these various animals and objects occurred only in the experimental setting and nowhere else, the significance of the findings would be greatly reduced. To test this, later on, the day outlined in Table 3.2.1, Albert was taken to an entirely different room with brighter lighting and more people present. In this new setting, Albert's reactions to the rat and rabbit were still clearly fearful.

The final test that Watson and Rayner wanted to make was to see if Albert's newly learned emotional responses would persist over time. Albert had been adopted and was scheduled to leave the hospital in the near future. Therefore, all testing was discontinued for a period of 31 days. At the end of this time, he was once again presented with the Santa Claus mask, the white fur coat, the rat, the rabbit, and the dog. After a month, Albert remained very afraid of all these objects.

Watson and his colleagues had planned to attempt to *recondition* Little Albert and eliminate these fearful reactions. However, Albert left the hospital on the day these last tests were made, and, as far as anyone knows, no reconditioning ever took place.

Discussion and Significance of Findings

Watson had two fundamental goals in this study and in virtually all his work: (a) to demonstrate that human behavior stems from learning and conditioning and (b) to demonstrate that the Freudian conception of human nature, that our behavior stems from unconscious processes, was wrong. This study, with all its methodological flaws and serious breaches of ethical conduct, succeeded to a large extent in convincing many in the psychological community that emotional behavior could be conditioned through simple stimulus-response techniques. This finding helped, in turn, to launch one of the major schools of thought in psychology: behaviorism. Here, something as complex and personal as an emotion was shown to be subject to conditioning, just as Pavlov demonstrated that dogs learn to salivate at the sound of a metronome.

A logical extension of this is that other emotions, such as anger, joy, sadness, surprise, or disgust, may be learned in the same manner. In other words, the reason you are sad when you hear that old song, nervous when you have a job interview or a public speaking engagement, happy when spring arrives, or afraid when you hear a dental drill is that you have developed an association in your brain between these stimuli and specific emotions through conditioning. Other more extreme emotional responses, such as phobias and sexual fetishes, may also develop through similar sequences of conditioning.

Watson was quick to point out that his findings could explain human behavior in rather straightforward and simple terms, compared with the complexities of the psychoanalytic notions of Freud and his followers. As Watson and Rayner explained in their article, a Freudian would explain thumb sucking as an expression of the original pleasure-seeking instinct. Albert, however, would suck his thumb whenever he felt afraid. As soon as his thumb entered his mouth, his fear lessened. Therefore, Watson interpreted thumb sucking as a conditioned device for blocking fear-producing stimuli.

An additional questioning of Freudian thinking in this article concerned how Freudians in Albert's future, given the opportunity, might analyze Albert's fear of a white fur coat. Watson and Rayner claimed that Freudian analysts "will probably tease from him the recital of a dream which, upon their analysis, will show that Albert at three years of age attempted to play with the pubic hair of the mother and was scolded violently for it" (p. 14). Their main point was that they had demonstrated with Little Albert that emotional disturbances in adults cannot always be attributed to sexual traumas in childhood, as the Freudian view maintained.

Questions and Criticisms

As you have been reading this, you have probably been concerned or even angered over the experimenter's treatment of this innocent child. This study clearly violated current standards of ethical conduct in research involving humans. It would be highly unlikely that any institutional review board at any research institution would approve this study today. A century ago, however, such ethical standards did not formally exist, and it is not unusual to find reports in the early psychological literature of what now appear to be questionable research methods. It must be pointed out that Watson and his colleagues were not sadistic or cruel people and that they were engaged in a new, unexplored area of research. They acknowledged their considerable hesitation in proceeding with the conditioning process but decided that it was justifiable because, in their opinion, some such fears would arise anyway when Albert left the sheltered hospital environment. Even so, is it ever appropriate to frighten a child to this extent, regardless of the importance of the potential discovery? Today nearly all behavioral scientists would agree that it is not.

Another important point regarding the ethics of this study was the fact that Albert was allowed to leave the research setting and was never reconditioned to remove his fears. Watson and Rayner contended in their article that such emotional conditioning may persist over a person's lifetime. If they were correct on this point, it is extremely difficult, from an ethical perspective, to justify allowing someone to grow into adulthood fearful of all these objects (and who knows how many others!).

Several researchers have criticized Watson's assumption that these conditioned fears would persist indefinitely (e.g., Harris, 1979). Others claim that Albert was not conditioned as effectively as the authors maintained (e.g., Samelson, 1980). Researchers have frequently demonstrated that behaviors acquired through conditioning can be lost because of other experiences or simply because of the passage of time. Imagine, for example, that when Albert turned age five, he was given a pet white rabbit for a birthday present. At first, he might have been afraid of it (no doubt baffling his adoptive parents). As he continued to be exposed to the rabbit without anything frightening occurring (such as that loud noise), he would probably slowly become less and less afraid until the rabbit no longer caused a fear response. This is a well-established process in learning psychology called *extinction*, and it happens routinely as part of the constant learning and unlearning, conditioning and unconditioning processes we experience throughout our lives. However, it appears this was not true for Albert.

Recent research by a team of graduate students that took over 7 years has finally shed light on who the child called "Albert" truly was: a mystery that has persisted for decades. "Albert has been identified as Douglas Merritte, the son of Arvilla Merritte, a nurse at the Johns Hopkins University Hospital department called the Harriet Lane Home during the years when Watson's studies were carried out. She was paid $1.00 for her permission for her son to be studied (see DeAngelis, 2010). The saddest part of these newly discovered aspects of the study was that Douglas died at the age of 6 from *hydrocephalus*, a condition involving a buildup of fluid in and around the brain. Today, many treatments exist for this serious condition, but in the 1920s, it was often fatal. Consequently, the question of whether "Albert" was ever able to overcome the fears that Watson had conditioned in him, remains unknown. Furthermore, as long as we are in the "criticisms" section of this reading, Watson was dismissed from the Johns Hopkins University around the time of this study for engaging in an affair with his graduate assistant, Rosalie Rayner.

Recent Applications

Watson's 1920 article, its ethical flaws notwithstanding, continues to be cited in research in a wide range of applications, including theories of effective parenting and psychotherapy. One study examined the facial expressions of emotion in infants (Sullivan & Lewis, 2003). We know that facial expressions corresponding to specific emotions are consistent among all adults and across cultures (see the reading on Ekman's research in Chapter VI). This study, however, extended this research to how such expressions develop in infants and what the various expressions mean at very young ages. A greater understanding of infants' facial expressions might be of great help in adults' efforts to communicate with and care for babies. The authors noted that their goal in their research was "to provide practitioners with basic information to help them and the parents they serve become better able to recognize the expressive signals of the infants and young children in their care" (p. 120). These authors' use of Watson's findings offers us a degree of comfort in that his-questionable research tactics with Little Albert, may, in the final analysis, allow us to develop greater sensitivity and perception into the feelings and needs of infants.

As mentioned previously in this discussion, one emotion—fear—in its extreme form, can produce serious negative consequences known as *phobias*. Many psychologists believe that phobias are conditioned much like Little Albert's fear of furry animals (see the discussion of Wolpe's research on the treatment of phobias in Chapter IX: *Psychotherapy*). Watson's research has been incorporated into many studies about the origins and treatments of phobias. One such article discussed phobias from the nature–nurture perspective and found some remarkable results. Watson's approach is rooted completely in the environmental or nurture side of the argument, and most people would view phobias as learned.

However, a study by Kendler, Karkowski, and Prescott (1999) provided compelling evidence that the development of phobias may include a substantial genetic component. The researchers studied phobias and unreasonable fears in more than 1,700 female twins (see the discussion of Bouchard's twin research in Chapter I). They claim to have found that a large percentage of the variation in phobias was due to *inherited* factors. The authors concluded that, although phobias may be molded by an individual's personal experiences, the role of a person's family in the development of phobias is primarily genetic, not environmental. Imagine: *Born to be phobic!* This view flies directly in the face of Watson's theory and should provide plenty of fuel for the ongoing nature–nurture debate in psychology and throughout the behavioral sciences.

DeAngelis, T. (2010). Little Albert regains his identity. *Monitor on Psychology, 41,* 10.

Harris, B. (1979). What ever happened to Little Albert? *American Psychologist, 34,* 151–160.

Kendler, K., Karkowski, L., & Prescott, C. (1999). Fears and phobias: reliability and heritability. *Psychological Medicine, 29*(3), 539–553.

Samelson, F. (1980). Watson's Little Albert, Cyril Burt's twins, and the need for a critical science. *American Psychologist, 35,* 619–625.

Sullivan, M., & Lewis, M. (2003). Emotional expressions of young infants and children: A practitioner's primer. *Infants and Young Children, 16,* 120–142.

Watson, J. B. (1913). Psychology as the behaviorist views it. *Psychological Review, 20,* 158–177.

Reading 3.3: Knock Wood!

Skinner, B. F. (1948). Superstition in the pigeon. *Journal of Experimental Psychology, 38,* 168–172.

3.3 Characterize superstition according to Skinner

In this reading, we examine one study from a *huge* body of research carried out by one of the most influential and most widely known figures in the history of psychology: B. F. Skinner (1904–1990). Deciding how to present Skinner and which of his multitude of studies to explore is a difficult task. It is impossible to represent adequately in one short article Skinner's contributions to the history of psychology. After all, Skinner is considered by most to be the father of radical behaviorism, he was the inventor of the famous (or infamous) Skinner Box, and he was the author of over 20 books and many hundreds of scientific articles. This article, with the funny-sounding title, "Superstition in the Pigeon," has been selected from all his work because it allows for a clear discussion of Skinner's basic theories, provides an interesting example of his approach to studying behavior, and offers a "Skinnerian" explanation of a behavior with which we are all familiar (in humans): superstition.

Skinner is referred to as a *radical behaviorist* because he believed that all behaviors—including public (or external) behavior, as well as private (or internal) events such as feelings and thoughts—are ultimately learned and controlled by the relationships between the situation that immediately precedes the behavior and the consequences that directly follow it. Although he believed that private behaviors are difficult to study, he acknowledged that we all have our own subjective experience of these behaviors. He did not, however, view internal events, such as thoughts and emotions, as causes of behavior but rather as part of the mix of environment and behavior that he was seeking to explain (see Schneider & Morris, 1987, for a detailed discussion of the term *radical behaviorism*).

To put Skinner's theory in basic terms, in any given situation, your behavior is likely to be followed by consequences. Some of these consequences, such as praise, receiving money, or the satisfaction of solving a problem, will make the behavior more likely to be repeated in the future, similar situations. These consequences are called reinforcers. Other consequences, such as injuring yourself or feeling embarrassed, will tend to make the behavior less likely to be repeated in similar situations. These consequences are called punishers. The effects of these *relationships* between behavior and the environment are called reinforcement and punishment, respectively (Edward K. Morris, personal communication, September 1987). Reinforcement and punishment are two of the most fundamental processes in what Skinner referred to as operant conditioning and may be diagrammed as follows:

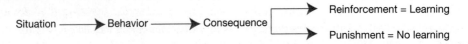

Within this conceptualization, Skinner also was able to explain how learned behaviors decrease and sometimes disappear entirely. When a behavior has been reinforced in a certain situation, and the reinforcement is then withdrawn, the likelihood of the behavior reoccurring will slowly decrease until the behavior is effectively suppressed. This process of behavior suppression is called *extinction*.

If you think about it, these ideas are not new to you. The process we use to train our pets follows these same rules. You tell a dog to sit, it sits, and you reward it with a treat. After a while, the dog will sit when told to, even without an immediate reward. You have applied the principles of operant conditioning. This is a very powerful form of learning and is effective with all animals, even old dogs learning new tricks and, yes, even cats! Also, if you want a pet to stop doing something, all you have to do for the behavior to stop is remove the reinforcement. For example, if your dog is begging at the dinner table, there is a reason for that (regardless of what you may think, dogs are not born to beg at the table). You, or someone, have conditioned this behavior in your dog through reinforcement. If you want to *put that behavior on extinction,* the reinforcement must be totally discontinued. Eventually, the dog will stop begging. By the way, if one member of the family cheats during extinction and secretly gives the canine beggar some food once in a while, extinction will never happen, but the dog will spend much more of its begging energy near that person's chair.

Beyond these fundamentals of learning, Skinner maintained that all human behavior is created and maintained in precisely the same way. It is just that with humans, the exact behaviors and consequences are not always easy to identify. Skinner was well-known for arguing that if a human behavior was interpreted by other theoretical approaches to be due to our highly evolved consciousness or intellectual capabilities, it was only because those theorists had been unable to pinpoint the reinforcers that had created and were maintaining the behavior. If this feels like a rather extreme position to you, remember that Skinner's position was called *radical behaviorism* and was always surrounded by controversy.

Skinner often met skepticism and defended his views by demonstrating experimentally that behaviors considered to be the sole property of humans could be learned by "lowly creatures" such as pigeons or rats. One of these demonstrations involved the contention by others that superstitious behavior is uniquely human. The argument was that superstition requires human *cognitive* activity (i.e., thinking, knowing, and reasoning). A superstition is a belief in something, and we do not usually attribute such beliefs to animals. Skinner said that superstitious behavior could be explained as easily as any other action by using the principles of operant conditioning. He performed this experiment to prove it.

Theoretical Propositions

Think back to a time when you have behaved superstitiously. Did you knock on wood, avoid walking under a ladder, avoid stepping on cracks, carry a lucky coin or other charm, shake the dice a certain way in a board game, or change your behavior because of your horoscope? It is probably safe to say that everyone has done something superstitious at some time, even if some of them might not want to admit it. Skinner said that the reason people do this is that they believe or presume a connection exists between the superstitious behavior in a certain setting and a reinforcing consequence even though—in reality—it does not. This connection exists because the behavior (such as shaking the dice that certain way) was accidentally reinforced (by something rewarding, such as a good roll) once, twice, or several times. Skinner called this *noncontingent* reinforcement—that is, a reward that is not contingent on any particular behavior. You *believe* that there is a *causal* relationship between the behavior and the reward when no such relationship exists. "If you think this is some exclusive human activity," Skinner might have said, "Oh, yeah? I'll create a superstitious pigeon!"

Method

To understand the method used in this experiment, a brief description of what has become known as the Skinner Box is necessary. The principle behind the Skinner Box (or *conditioning chamber,* as Skinner called it) is really simple. It consists of a cage or box that is empty except for a dish or tray into which food may be dispensed. This allows a researcher to have control over when the animal receives reinforcement, such as pellets of food. The early conditioning boxes also contained a lever, which, if pressed, would cause some food to be dispensed. If a rat (rats were used in Skinner's earliest work) was placed in one of these boxes, it would eventually, through trial and error and reinforcement, learn to press the lever for food. Alternatively, the experimenter could, if desired, take control of the food dispenser and reinforce a specific behavior. Later, Skinner and others found that pigeons also made ideal subjects in conditioning experiments, and conditioning chambers were designed with disks to be pecked with a beak instead of bars to be pressed with a nose.

These conditioning cages were used in the study discussed here, but with one important change. To study superstitious behavior, the food-dispensers were rigged to drop food pellets into the tray at intervals of 15 seconds, *regardless* of what the animal was doing at the time. The reward was *not contingent* on any particular behavior. This was "noncontingent" reinforcement: The animal received a reward every 15 seconds, no matter what it did.

Subjects in this study were eight pigeons. These birds were fed less than their normal daily amount for several days so that when tested they would be hungry and therefore motivated to perform behaviors for food (this increased the power of the reinforcement). Each pigeon was placed into the experimental cage for a few minutes each day and just left there to hang out and do whatever a pigeon does. During this time, reinforcement was being delivered automatically every 15 seconds. After several days of conditioning in this way, two independent observers recorded the birds' behavior in the cage.

Results

As Skinner reports,

> In six out of eight cases the resulting responses were so clearly defined that two observers could agree perfectly in counting instances. One bird was conditioned to turn counterclockwise about the cage, making two or three turns between reinforcements. Another repeatedly thrust its head into one of the upper corners of the cage. A third developed a tossing response as if placing its head beneath an invisible bar and lifting it repeatedly. Two birds developed a pendulum motion of the head and body in which the head was extended forward and swung from right to left with a sharp movement followed by a somewhat slower return. The body generally followed the movement and a few steps might be taken when it was extensive. Another bird was conditioned to make incomplete pecking or brushing movements directed toward but not touching the floor. (p. 168)

None of these behaviors had been observed in the birds prior to the conditioning procedure. The new behaviors had no effect on the delivery of food. Nevertheless, the pigeons behaved as if a certain action would produce the food—that is, they became superstitious.

Skinner next wanted to see what would happen if the time interval between reinforcements was extended. With one of the head-bobbing and hopping birds, the interval between each delivery of food pellets was slowly increased to 1 minute. When this occurred, the pigeon's movements became more energetic until finally the bobbing and hopping became so pronounced that it appeared the bird was performing a kind of dance during the minute between reinforcement (a *pigeon food dance*).

The birds' new behaviors were then put on extinction. This meant that the reinforcement in the test cage was discontinued. When this happened, the superstitious behaviors gradually decreased until they disappeared altogether. However, in the case of the *hopping* pigeon with a reinforcement interval that had been increased to a minute, over 10,000 responses were recorded before extinction occurred! A determined, tired pigeon.

Discussion

In this study, Skinner ended up with six superstitious pigeons. However, as a good scientist, he explained his findings more carefully and modestly: "The experiment might be said to demonstrate a sort of superstition. The bird behaves as if there were a causal relation between its behavior and the presentation of food, although such a relation is lacking" (p. 171).

The next step would be to apply these findings to humans. You can probably think of analogies in human behavior, and so did Skinner. He described "the bowler who has released a ball down the alley but continues to behave as if he were controlling it by twisting and turning his arm and shoulder as another case in point" (p. 171). You know, rationally, that behaviors such as these don't really have any effect on a bowling ball that is already halfway down the alley. However, due to past conditioning, you believe your antics may help, but the ball, in reality, will go wherever it is going to go regardless of your behavior after it has been released. As Skinner put it, the "bowler's behavior has no effect on the ball, but the behavior of the ball has an effect on the bowler" (p. 171). In other words, on some occasions, the ball might happen to move in the direction of the bowler's body movements. That movement of the ball, coupled with the consequence of a strike or a spare, is enough to accidentally reinforce the twisting and turning behavior and maintain the superstition. How different is that from Skinner's pigeons? Not very.

The reason that superstitions are so resistant to extinction was demonstrated by the pigeon that hopped 10,000 times before giving up the behavior. When any behavior is only reinforced once in a while in a given situation (called *partial reinforcement*), it becomes very difficult to extinguish. This is because the expectation stays high that the superstitious behavior *might* work to produce the reinforcing consequences. You can imagine that if the connection was present every time and then disappeared, the behavior would stop quickly. However, in real life, the instances of accidental reinforcement usually occur sporadically, so the superstitious behavior often may persist for a lifetime.

Criticisms and Subsequent Research

Skinner's behaviorist theories and research have always been the subject of great and sometimes heated controversy. Other prominent theoretical approaches to human behavior have argued that the strict behavioral view is unable to account for many of the psychological processes that are fundamental to humans. Carl Rogers, the founder of the *humanistic* school of psychology, and well-known for his debates with Skinner, summed up this criticism:

> In this world of inner meanings, humanistic psychology can investigate issues which are meaningless for the behaviorist: purposes, goals, values, choice, perceptions of self, perceptions of others, the personal constructs with which we build our world . . . the whole phenomenal world of the individual with its

connective tissue of meaning. Not one aspect of this world is open to the strict behaviorist. Yet that these elements have significance for man's behavior seems certainly true. (Rogers, 1964, p. 119)

Behaviorists would argue in turn that all of these human characteristics are open to behavioral analysis. The key to this analysis is a proper interpretation of the behaviors and consequences that constitute them. (See Skinner, 1974, for a complete discussion of these issues.)

On the specific issue of superstitions, however, there appears to be less controversy and a rather wide acceptance of the learning processes involved in their formation. An experiment performed by Bruner and Revuski (1961) demonstrated how easily superstitious behavior develops in humans. Four high school students each sat in front of four telegraph keys. They were told that each time they pressed the correct key, a bell would sound, a red light would flash, and they would earn 5 cents (worth about 50 cents today). The correct response was key number 3. However, as in Skinner's study, key number 3 would produce the desired reinforcement (the nickel) only after a delay interval of 10 seconds. During this interval, the students would try other keys in various combinations. Then, at some point following the delay, they would receive the reinforcement. The results were the same for all the students. After a while, they had each developed a pattern of key responses (such as 1, 2, 4, 3, 1, 2, 4, 3) that they repeated over and over between each reinforcement. Pressing the 3 key was the only reinforced behavior; the other presses in the sequence were completely superstitious. Not only did they behave superstitiously but also all the students believed that the other key presses were necessary to "set up" the reinforced key. They were completely unaware of their superstitious behavior.

Recent Applications

Skinner, as one of psychology's most influential figures, still has a far-reaching substantive impact on scientific literature in many fields. His 1948 article on superstitious behavior is cited in numerous studies every year. One of these studies, for example, compared two types of reinforcement in the development of superstitious behavior (Aeschleman, Rosen, & Williams, 2003). Positive reinforcement occurs when you receive something desirable as a consequence (such as money, food, or praise). Negative reinforcement, which is often confused with punishment, *rewards* you by *eliminating* something *undesirable* (such as not having to do homework or avoiding pain). The study found that greater levels of superstitious behavior (perceived control over noncontingent events) developed under conditions of negative reinforcement than under positive reinforcement. In the authors' words, "These findings . . . suggest that, relative to positive reinforcement, negative reinforcement operations may provide a more fertile condition for the development and maintenance of superstitious behaviors" (p. 37). In other words, the study suggested that you are more likely to employ superstitious tactics to prevent bad outcomes than to create good outcomes.

Another thought-provoking article citing Skinner's 1948 study (Sagvolden et al., 1998) examined the role of reinforcement in attention deficit hyperactivity disorder (ADHD). The researchers asked boys with and without a diagnosis of ADHD to participate in a game in which they would receive rewards of coins or small toys. Although the reinforcement was delivered at fixed 30-second intervals (noncontingent reinforcement), all the boys developed superstitious behaviors that they *believed* were related to the rewards. In the next phase of the study, the reinforcement was discontinued. You would expect this to cause a decrease and cessation of whatever behaviors had been conditioned (extinction). This is exactly what happened with the boys without ADHD. But the boys with ADHD, after a brief pause, became more active and began engaging impulsively in bursts of responses at an even faster pace, *as if* the reinforcement had been reestablished. The authors suggested that this overactivity and impulsiveness implied that the boys with ADHD possessed significantly less ability to cope with delays of reinforcement than did the comparison group of boys. Findings such as these are important additions to our understanding and our ability to treat ADHD effectively.

A recent simple yet elegant study relying on Skinner's research demonstrated strong superstitious behavior on a golf task (golfers are known to be among the most superstitious athletes). A total of 28 participants (who had never played golf) took part in a putting task, but with a twist. They had to do their best on a 15-foot putt toward a 7 × 7 grid of squares (this was on a carpeted surface), trying to place the ball as close to the center square as possible. However, a screen was set up that they had to putt under which blocked their view of the grid and where the ball ended up. This was so the experimenters could manipulate their "performance" by telling the participants where the ball stopped. (And they did not have to tell them the correct location!) In other words, the experimenters controlled the *perceived* performance of the amateur golfers. The subject was asked to use each of three totally identical putters. The performance feedback for each putter was unrelated to their actual performance and was scores were assigned to each putter *at random*. Then, the screen was removed and a friendly putting game was played by the participants (the winner would receive a small prize). Each player could select any of the three putters. You've already guessed the results, have n't you? Yes, all the participants were significantly more likely to select the putter for which they had been given the more positive feedback by the experimenters. Remember, the putters were identical and the performance feedback was random. The only explanation? Within minutes, the players had become superstitious about their choice of club—just like the pigeons and the food (Churchill, Taylor, & Parkes, 2015).

Conclusion

Superstitions are everywhere. You probably have some, and you surely know others who have them. Some superstitions are such a part of a culture that they produce society-wide effects. You may be aware that most high-rise buildings do not have a 13th floor. But that's not exactly true. Obviously, a 13th floor exists, but no floor is *labeled* "13." This is probably not because architects and builders are an overly superstitious bunch, but rather it is due to the difficulty of renting or selling space on the "unlucky" 13th floor. Another example is that Americans are so superstitious about the two-dollar bill (remember those?) that the U.S. Treasury prints fewer two-dollar notes than any other denomination (less than 1% of currency notes).

Are superstitions psychologically unhealthy? Most psychologists believe that even though superstitious behaviors, by definition, do not produce the consequences that you think they do, they can serve useful functions. Often such behaviors can produce a feeling of strength and control when a person is facing a difficult situation. It is interesting to note that people who are employed in dangerous occupations tend to have more superstitions than others. This feeling of increased power and control that is sometimes created by superstitious behavior can lead to reduced anxiety, greater confidence and assurance, and improved performance.

Aeschleman, S., Rosen, C., & Williams, M. (2003). The effect of non-contingent negative and positive reinforcement operations on the acquisition of superstitious behaviors. *Behavioural Processes, 61*, 37–45.

Bruner, A., & Revuski, S. (1961). Collateral behavior in humans. *Journal of the Experimental Analysis of Behavior, 4*, 349–350.

Churchill, A., Taylor, J. A., & Parkes, R. (2015). The creation of a superstitious belief regarding putters in a laboratory-based golfing task. *International Journal of Sport and Exercise Psychology, 13*(4), 335–343.

Rogers, C. R. (1964). Toward a science of the person. In F. W. Wann (Ed.), *Behaviorism and phenomenology: Contrasting bases for modern psychology*. Chicago: Phoenix Books.

Sagvolden, T., Aase, H., Zeiner, P., & Berger, D. (1998). Altered reinforcement mechanisms in attention-deficit/hyperactivity disorder. *Behavioral Brain Research, 94*(1), 61–71.

Schneider, S., & Morris, E. (1987). The history of the term *radical behaviorism:* From Watson to Skinner. *Behavior Analyst, 10*(1), 27–39.

Skinner, B. F. (1974). *About behaviorism.* New York: Knopf.

Reading 3.4: See Aggression . . . Do Aggression!

Bandura, A., Ross, D., & Ross, S. A. (1961). Transmission of aggression through-imitation of aggressive models. *Journal of Abnormal and Social Psychology, 63,* 575–582.

3.4   Explain how children learn to be aggressive according to social learning theory

Aggression, in its abundance of forms, is arguably the greatest social problem facing this country and the world today. It is also one of the most researched topics in the history of psychology. Over the years, the behavioral scientists who have been in the forefront of this research have been social psychologists, whose focus is on all types of human interaction. One goal of social psychologists has been to define and study aggression. This may, at first glance, seem like a relatively easy goal, but such a definition turns out to be rather elusive. For example, which of the following behaviors would you define as aggression: a boxing match? a cat killing a mouse? a soldier shooting an enemy? setting rat traps in your basement? a bullfight? The list of behaviors that may or may not be included in a definition of aggression is endless. As a result, if you were to consult 10 different social psychologists, you would probably hear 10 different definitions of aggression.

Many researchers have gone beyond trying to agree on a definition to the more important process of examining the sources of human aggression. The question they often pose is this: Why do people engage in acts of aggression? Throughout the history of psychology, many theoretical approaches have been proposed to explain the causes of aggression. Some of these contend that you are biologically preprogrammed to be aggressive because aggression in certain circumstances has been an evolutionary survival mechanism, so it has evolved into us. Other theories look to situational factors, such as repeated frustration or specific types of provocation, as the determinants of aggressive responses. A third view, and the one this study suggests is that aggression is learned.

One of the most famous and influential experiments ever conducted in the history of psychology demonstrated how children may *learn* to be aggressive. This study, by Albert Bandura and his associates Dorothea Ross and Sheila Ross, was carried out in 1961 at Stanford University. Bandura is considered to be one of the founders of a school of psychological thought called *social learning theory.* Social learning theorists propose that human interaction is the primary factor in the development of human personality. For example, as you are growing up, important people (such as your parents and teachers) reinforce certain behaviors and ignore or punish others. Even beyond direct rewards and punishments, however, Bandura believed that behavior can be shaped in important ways through simply observing and imitating the behavior of others—that is, through modeling.

As you can see from the title of this chapter's study, Bandura, D. Ross, and S. A. Ross were able to demonstrate this modeling effect for acts of aggression. This research has come to be known throughout the field of psychology as "the Bobo doll study," for reasons that will become clear shortly. The article began with a reference to earlier research findings demonstrating that children readily observed and imitated the behavior of adult models. One of the issues Bandura wanted to examine in this study was whether such imitative learning would generalize to settings in which the child was separated from the model *after* observing the model's behavior.

Theoretical Propositions

The researchers proposed to expose children to adult models who behaved in either aggressive or nonaggressive ways. The children would then be tested in a new situation without the model present to determine to what extent they would imitate the acts of aggression they had observed in the adult. Based on this experimental manipulation, Bandura and his associates offered four predictions:

1. Children who observed adult models performing acts of aggression would imitate the adult and engage in similar aggressive behaviors, even if the model was no longer present. Furthermore, this behavior would differ significantly from those children who observed nonaggressive models or no models at all.

2. Children who were exposed to the nonaggressive models would not only be less aggressive than those who observed the aggression but also significantly less aggressive than a control group of children who were exposed to no model at all. In other words, the nonaggressive models would have an aggression-inhibiting effect.

3. Because children tend to identify with parents and other adults of their same sex, participants would "imitate the behavior of the same-sex model to a greater degree than a model of the opposite sex" (p. 575).

4. "Since aggression is a highly masculine-typed behavior in society, boys should be more predisposed than girls toward imitating aggression, the difference being most marked for subjects exposed to the male model" (p. 575).

Method

This article outlined the methods used in the experiment with great organization and clarity. Although somewhat summarized and simplified here, these methodological steps were as follows.

PARTICIPANTS   The researchers enlisted the help of the director and head teacher of the Stanford University Nursery School in order to obtain participants for their study. A total of 36 boys and 36 girls, ranging in age from 3 years to almost 6 years, participated in the study. The average age of the children was 4 years, 4 months (parental permission was obtained, of course).

EXPERIMENTAL CONDITIONS   The control group, consisting of 24 children, was not exposed to any adult model. The remaining 48 children were first divided into two groups: one was exposed to aggressive models and the other exposed to nonaggressive models. These groups were divided again into males and females. Each of these groups was further divided so that half of the children were exposed to same-sex models and half to opposite-sex models. This created a total of eight experimental groups and one control group. A question you might be asking yourself is this: What if the children in some of the groups are already more aggressive than others? Due to the small number of participants in each group, Bandura guarded against this potential problem by obtaining ratings of each child's level of aggressiveness. The children were rated by an experimenter and a teacher (both of whom knew the children well) on their levels of physical aggression, verbal aggression, and aggression toward objects. These ratings allowed the researchers to match all the groups in terms of average aggression level.

THE EXPERIMENTAL PROCEDURE   Each child was exposed individually to the various experimental procedures. First, the experimenter brought the child to the playroom. On the way, they encountered the adult model who was invited by the experimenter to come and "join in the game." The child was seated in one corner of the playroom at a table containing highly interesting activities. There were potato prints (this was 1961, so for those of you who have grown up in our high-tech age, a potato print is a potato cut in half and carved so that, like a rubber stamp, it will reproduce geometric shapes when inked on a stamp pad) and stickers of brightly colored animals and flowers that could be pasted onto a poster. Next, the adult model was taken to a table in a different corner containing a Tinker Toy set (hopefully you know what that is!), a mallet, and an inflated 5-foot-tall Bobo doll (one of those large, inflatable clowns that are weighted at the bottom, so they pop back up when punched or kicked). The experimenter explained that these toys were for the model to play with and then left the room.

For both the aggressive and nonaggressive conditions, the model began assembling the tinker toys. However, in the aggressive condition, after a minute the model attacked the Bobo doll with violence. For all the children in the aggressive condition, the sequence of aggressive acts performed by the model was identical:

> The model laid Bobo on its side, sat on it, and punched it repeatedly in the nose. The model then raised the Bobo doll, picked up the mallet, and struck the doll on the head. Following the mallet aggression, the model tossed the doll up in the air aggressively and kicked it about the room. This sequence of physically aggressive acts was repeated three times, interspersed with verbally aggressive responses such as, "Sock him in the nose . . . , Hit him down . . . , Throw him in the air . . . , Kick him . . . , Pow . . . ," and two non-aggressive comments, "He keeps coming back for more" and "He sure is a tough fella." (p. 576)

All this took about 10 minutes, after which the experimenter came back into the room, said goodbye to the model, and took the child to another game room.

In the nonaggressive condition, the model simply played quietly with the Tinker Toys for the 10-minute period and completely ignored the Bobo doll. Bandura and his collaborators were careful to ensure that all experimental factors were identical for all the groups except for the factors being studied: the aggressive versus nonaggressive model and the sex of the model.

AROUSAL OF ANGER OR FRUSTRATION   Following the 10-minute play period, all children from the various conditions were taken to another room that contained very attractive toys, such as a fire engine; a jet fighter; and a complete doll set including wardrobe, doll carriage, and so on. The researchers believed that in order to test for aggressive responses, the children should be somewhat angered or frustrated, which would make such behaviors more likely to occur. To accomplish this, they allowed them to begin playing with the attractive toys, but after a short time told them that the toys in this room were reserved for other children. They also told the children, however, that they could play with some other toys in the next room.

TEST FOR IMITATION OF AGGRESSION   The final experimental room was filled with both aggressive and nonaggressive toys. Aggressive toys included a Bobo doll (of course), a mallet, two rubber dart guns, and a tether ball with a face painted on it. The nonaggressive toys included a tea set, crayons and paper, a ball, two dolls, cars and trucks, and plastic farm animals. Each child was allowed to play in this room for 20 minutes. During this period, judges behind a one-way mirror rated the child's behavior on several measures of aggression.

MEASURES OF AGGRESSION   A total of eight different responses were measured in the children's behavior. In the interest of clarity, only the four most revealing measures are summarized here. First, all acts that imitated the physical aggression of the model were recorded. These included sitting on the Bobo doll, punching it in the nose, hitting it with the mallet, kicking it, and throwing it into the air. Second, imitation of the models' verbal aggression was measured by counting the children's repetition of the phrases "Sock him," "Hit him down," "Pow," and so on. Third, other mallet aggression (e.g., hitting objects other than the doll with the mallet) were recorded. Fourth, nonimitative aggression was documented by tabulating all the children's acts of physical and verbal aggression that had not been performed by the adult model.

Results

The findings from these observations are summarized in Table 3.4.1. If you examine the results carefully, you will discover that three of the four hypotheses presented by Bandura, D. Ross, and S. A. Ross were supported.

The children who were exposed to the violent models tended to imitate the exact violent behaviors they observed. On average were 38.2 instances of imitative physical aggression for each of the boys, as well as 12.7 for the girls who had been exposed to the aggressive models. In addition, the models' verbally aggressive behaviors were imitated an average of 17 times by the boys and 15.7 times by the girls. These specific acts of physical and verbal aggression were virtually never observed in the participants exposed to the nonaggressive models or in the control group that was not exposed to any model.

As you will recall, Bandura and his associates predicted that nonaggressive models would have a violence-inhibiting effect on the children. For this hypothesis to be supported, the results should show that the children in the nonaggressive conditions averaged significantly fewer instances of violence than those in the no-model control group. In Table 3.4.1, if you compare the nonaggressive model columns with the control group averages, you will see that the findings were mixed. For example, boys and girls who observed the nonaggressive male exhibited far less nonimitative mallet aggression than controls, but boys who observed the nonaggressive female aggressed more with the mallet than did the boys in the control group. As the authors readily admit, these results were so inconsistent in relation to the aggression-inhibiting effect of nonaggressive models that they were inconclusive.

The predicted gender differences, however, were strongly supported by the data in Table 3.4.1. Clearly, boys' violent behavior was influenced more by the aggressive male model than by the aggressive female model. The average total number of aggressive behaviors by boys was 104 when they had observed a male aggressive model, compared with 48.4 when a female model had been observed. Girls, on the other hand, although their scores were less consistent, averaged 57.7 violent behaviors in the aggressive female model condition, compared with 36.3 when they observed the male model. The authors point out that in the same-sex aggressive conditions, girls were more likely to imitate verbal aggression, while boys were more inclined to imitate physical violence.

Table 3.4.1 Average Number of Aggressive Responses From Children in Various Treatment Conditions

Type of Aggression	Type of Model				
	Aggressive Male	Non-Aggressive Male	Aggressive Female	Non-Aggressive Female	Control Group
Imitative Physical Aggression					
Boys	25.8	1.5	12.4	0.2	1.2
Girls	7.2	0.0	5.5	2.5	2.0
Imitative Verbal Aggression					
Boys	12.7	0.0	4.3	1.1	1.7
Girls	2.0	0.0	13.7	0.3	0.7
Mallet Aggression					
Boys	28.8	6.7	15.5	18.7	13.5
Girls	18.7	0.5	17.2	0.5	13.1
Nonimitative Aggression					
Boys	36.7	22.3	16.2	26.1	24.6
Girls	8.4	1.4	21.3	7.2	6.1

Note: Based on data from p. 579.

Boys were significantly more physically aggressive than girls in nearly all the conditions. If all the instances of aggression in Table 3.4.1 are tallied, the boys committed 270 violent acts, compared with 128 committed by the girls.

Discussion

Bandura, D. Ross, and S. A. Ross claimed that they had demonstrated how specific behaviors—in this case, violent ones—could be learned through the process of observation and imitation without any reinforcement provided to either the models or the observers. They concluded that children's observation of adults engaging in these behaviors sends a message to the child that this form of violence is permissible, thus weakening the child's inhibitions against aggression. The consequence of this observed violence, they contended, is an increased probability that a child will respond to future frustrations with aggressive behavior.

The researchers also addressed the issue of why the influence of the male aggressive model on the boys was so much stronger than the female aggressive model was on the girls. They explained that in our culture, as in most, aggression is seen as more typical of males than females. In other words, it is a masculine-typed behavior. So, a man's modeling of aggression carried with it the weight of social acceptability and was, therefore, more powerful in its ability to influence the observer.

Subsequent Research

At the time this experiment was conducted, the researchers probably had no idea how influential it would become. By the early 1960s, television had grown into a powerful force in U.S. culture and consumers were becoming concerned about the effect of televised violence on children. This has been and continues to be hotly debated. In the past 30 years, no fewer than three congressional hearings have been held on the subject of television violence, and the work of Bandura and other psychologists has been included in these investigations.

These same three researchers conducted a follow-up study 2 years later that was intended to examine the power of aggressive models who are on film, or who are not even real people. Using a similar experimental method involving aggression toward a Bobo doll, Bandura, D. Ross, and S. A. Ross designed an experiment to compare the influence of a live adult model with the same model on film and to a cartoon version of the same aggressive modeling. The results demonstrated that the live adult model had a stronger influence than the filmed adult, who, in turn, was more influential than the cartoon. However, all three forms of aggressive models produced significantly more violent behaviors in the children than was observed in children exposed to nonaggressive models or controls (Bandura, D. Ross, & S. A. Ross, 1963).

On an optimistic note, Bandura found in a later study that the effect of modeled violence could be altered under certain conditions. You will recall that in his original study, no rewards were given for aggression to either the models or the children. But what do you suppose would happen if the model behaved violently and was then either reinforced or punished for the behavior while the child was observing? Bandura (1965) tested this idea and found that children imitated the violence more when they saw it rewarded but significantly less when the model was punished for aggressive behavior.

Critics of Bandura's research on aggression have pointed out that aggressing toward an inflated doll is not the same as attacking another person, and children know the difference. Building on the foundation laid by Bandura and his colleagues, other researchers have examined the effect of modeled violence on real aggression. In a study using Bandura's Bobo doll method (Hanratty, O'Neil, & Sulzer, 1972), children observed a violent adult model and were then exposed to high levels of frustration. When this occurred, they often aggressed against a live person (dressed like a clown), whether that person was the source of the frustration or not.

Recent Applications

Bandura's research discussed in this chapter made at least two fundamental contributions to psychology. First, it demonstrated dramatically how children can acquire new behaviors simply by observing adults, even when the adults are not physically present. Social learning theorists believe that many, if not most, of the behaviors that comprise human personality, are formed through this modeling process. Second, this research formed the foundation for hundreds of studies over the past 45 years on the effects on children of viewing violence in person or in the media. (For a summary of Bandura's life and contributions to psychology, see http://professoralbertbandura.com/index .html). Less than a decade ago, the U.S. Congress held new hearings on media violence focusing on the potential negative effects of children's exposure to violence on TV, movies, video games, computer games, and the Internet. Broadcasters and multimedia developers, feeling increased pressure to respond to public and legislative attacks, are working to reduce media violence or put in place parental advisory rating systems warning of particularly violent content.

Perhaps of even greater concern is scientific evidence demonstrating that the effects of violent media on children may continue into adulthood (e.g., Huesmann et al., 2003). One study found "that childhood exposure to media violence predicts young adult aggressive behavior for both males and females. Identification with aggressive TV characters and perceived realism of TV violence also predict later aggression. These relations persist even when the effects of socioeconomic status, intellectual ability, and a variety of parenting factors are controlled" (p. 201).

Conclusion

As children acquire easier access to quickly expanding media formats, concerns over the effects of violence embedded in these media are increasing as well. Blocking children's access to all violent media is probably an impossible task, but research is increasing on strategies for preventing media violence from translating into real-life aggression among children. These efforts have been stepped up considerably in the wake of deadly shootings by students at schools throughout the United States, and they are likely to continue on many research fronts for the foreseeable future. Recently, the California legislature passed a law banning the sale of "ultra-violent" video games to children under the age of 18 without parental permission and imposing a fine of $1,000 on retailers who fail to adhere to the law. What is "ultra-violent," you ask? According to the law, it is defined "as depicting serious injury to human beings in a manner that is especially heinous, atrocious or cruel" (Going after video game violence, 2006). If you find such a definition overly subjective, you would not be alone. The video game industry is suing to overturn this law as unconstitutional, and you can bet that Bandura's research will be part of that battle.

Bandura, A. (1965). Influence of models' reinforcement contingencies on the acquisition of imitative responses. *Journal of Personality and Social Psychology, 1,* 589–595.

Bandura, A., Ross, D., & Ross, S. A. (1963). Imitation of film mediated aggressive models. *Journal of Abnormal and Social Psychology, 66,* 3–11.

Going after video game violence. (2006). *State Legislatures 32*(1), 9.

Hanratty, M., O'Neil, E., & Sulzer, J. (1972). The effect of frustration on the imitation of aggression. *Journal of Personality and Social Psychology, 21,* 30–34. Retrieved from http://webspace.ship.edu/cgboer/bandura.html.

Albert Bandura, http://professoralbertbandura.com/index.html.

Huesmann, L. R., Moise, J., Podolski, C. P., & Eron, L. D. (2003). Longitudinal relations between childhood exposure to media violence and adult aggression and violence: 1977–1992. *Developmental Psychology, 39*(2), 201–221.

Chapter 4
Intelligence, Cognition, and Memory

 ## Learning Objectives

4.1 Relate the Pygmalion effect to school performance and experiences

4.2 Describe multiple intelligences according to Gardner

4.3 Explain how Tolman's experiments on latent learning and spatial orientation established theoretical pillars of cognitive-behaviorism

4.4 Describe the means by which Loftus developed her theory of memory and recall

The branch of psychology most concerned with the topics in this section is called *cognitive psychology*. Cognitive psychologists study human mental processes. Our intelligence, our ability to think and reason, and our ability to store and retrieve symbolic representations of our experiences all combine to help make humans different from other animals. And, of course, these mental processes greatly affect our behavior. However, studying these processes is often more difficult than studying outward, observable behaviors, so a great deal of research creativity and ingenuity have been necessary.

The studies included here have changed the way psychologists view our internal mental behavior. The first article discusses the famous "Pygmalion study," which demonstrated that not only performance in school but also actual intelligence scores of children can be influenced by the expectations of others, such as teachers. The second reading discusses a body of work that has transformed how we define human intelligence. In the early 1980s, Howard Gardner proposed that humans do not possess one general intelligence but rather seven distinct intelligences. His idea has become widely known as *Multiple Intelligence (MI) Theory*. Third, we encounter an early groundbreaking study in cognitive psychology that examined how animals and humans form *cognitive maps*, which are their mental images of the environment around them. Fourth, you will read about research that revealed how our memories are not nearly as accurate as we think they are, as well as the implications of this for eyewitness testimony in court and in psychotherapy.

Reading 4.1: What You Expect is What You Get

Rosenthal, R., & Jacobson, L. (1966). Teachers' expectancies: Determinates of pupils' IQ gains. *Psychological Reports, 19*, 115–118.

4.1 Relate the Pygmalion effect to school performance and experiences

We are all familiar with the idea of the self-fulfilling prophecy. One way of describing this concept is that if we *expect* something to happen in a certain way that expectation will tend to make it so. Whether self-fulfilling prophecies really do occur in a predictable way in everyday life is open to scientific study, but psychological research has demonstrated that in some situations they are a reality.

The question of the self-fulfilling prophecy in scientific research was first brought to the attention of psychologists in 1911 in the famous case of "Clever Hans," a horse owned by Wilhelm von Osten (Pfungst, 1911). Clever Hans was famous for, ostensibly, being able to read, spell, and solve math problems by stomping out answers with his front hoof. Naturally, many people were skeptical, but when Hans's abilities were tested by a committee of experts at the time, they were found to be genuine and seemed to occur without any prompting from von Osten. But how could any horse (except possibly Mr. Ed of the 1960s TV comedy) possess such a degree of *human* intelligence? A psychologist in the early 1900s, Oskar Pfungst, performed a series of careful experiments and found that Hans was not actually solving the problems but was receiving subtle, unintentional cues from his questioners. For example, after asking a question, people would look down at the horse's hoof for the answer. As the horse approached the correct number of hoofbeats, the questioners would raise their eyes or head slightly in anticipation of the horse's completing its answer. The horse had been conditioned to use these subtle movements from the observers as signs to stop stomping, and this usually resulted in the correct answer to the question.

You might ask, how is a trick horse related to psychological research? The Clever Hans findings pointed out the possibility that observers often have specific expectations or biases that may cause them to telegraph unintentional signals to a participant being studied. These signals then, may cause the participant to respond in ways that are consistent with the observers' bias and, consequently, confirm their expectations. What all this finally boils down to is that an experimenter may *think* a certain behavior results from his or her scientific treatment of one participant or one group of participants compared with another. Sometimes, though, the behavior may result from nothing more than the experimenter's own biased expectations. If this occurs, it renders the experiment invalid. This threat to the validity of a psychological experiment is called the *experimenter expectancy effect*.

Robert Rosenthal, a leading researcher on this methodological issue, demonstrated the experimenter expectancy effect in laboratory psychological experiments. In one study (Rosenthal & Fode, 1963), psychology students in a course about learning and conditioning unknowingly became participants themselves. Some of the students were told they would be working on conditioning rats that had been specially bred for high intelligence as measured by their ability to learn mazes quickly. The rest of the students were told that they would be working with rats bred to be poor maze-learners (called "maze-dull rats"). The students then proceeded to condition their rats to perform various skills, including maze learning. The students who had been assigned the maze-bright rats recorded significantly faster learning times than those reported by the students with the maze-dull rats. In reality, however, the rats given to the students were standard lab rats and were *randomly assigned*. These students were not cheating or purposefully slanting their results. The influences they exerted on their animals were apparently unintentional and unconscious.

As a result of this and other related research, the threat of experimenter expectancies to scientific research has been well established. Properly trained researchers, using careful procedures (such as the double-blind method, in which the experimenters who come in contact with the participants are unaware of the hypotheses of the study) are usually able to avoid most of these expectancy effects.

Beyond this, however, Rosenthal was concerned about how such biases and expectancies might occur outside the laboratory, in important, everyday settings, such as in school classrooms. Because teachers in public schools may not have had the opportunity to learn about the dangers of expectancies, how great an influence might this tendency have on their students' potential performance? After all, in the past, teachers have been aware of students' IQ scores beginning in 1st grade. Could this information set up biased expectancies in the teachers' minds and cause them to unintentionally treat "bright" students (as judged by high intelligence scores) differently from those seen as less bright? And if so, is this fair? Those questions formed the basis of Rosenthal and Jacobson's study.

Theoretical Propositions

Rosenthal labeled this expectancy effect, as it occurs in natural interpersonal settings outside the laboratory, the *Pygmalion effect*. In the Greek myth, a sculptor (Pygmalion) falls in love with his sculpted creation of a woman. Most people are more familiar with the modern George Bernard Shaw play *Pygmalion* (*My Fair Lady* is the musical version) about the blossoming of Eliza Doolittle because of the teaching, encouragement, and *expectations* of Henry Higgins. Rosenthal suspected that when an elementary school teacher is provided with information that creates certain expectancies about students' potential (such as intelligence scores), whether high or low, the teacher might unknowingly behave in ways that might subtly encourage or facilitate the performance of the students expected more likely to succeed. This, in turn, would create the self-fulfilling prophecy of actually *causing* those students to excel, perhaps at the expense of the students for whom lower expectations are created. To test these theoretical propositions, Rosenthal and his colleague Jacobson obtained the assistance of an elementary school (called Oak School) in a predominantly lower-middle-class neighborhood in a large town.

Method

With the cooperation of the Oak School administration, all the students in grades 1 through 6 were given an intelligence test (the Tests of General Ability, or TOGA) near the beginning of the academic year. This test was chosen because it was a nonverbal test for which a student's score did not depend primarily upon school-learned skills of reading, writing, and arithmetic. Also, it was a test with which the teachers in Oak School probably would not be familiar. The teachers were told that the students were being given the "Harvard Test of Inflected Acquisition." This deception was important in this case to create expectancies in the minds of the teachers, a necessary ingredient for the experiment. It was further explained to the teachers that the Harvard Test was designed to serve as a predictor of academic *blooming* or *spurting*. In other words, teachers believed that students who scored high on the test were ready to enter a period of increased learning abilities within the next year. This predictive ability of the test was also, in fact, not true.

Oak School offered three classes each of grades 1 through 6. All of the 18 teachers (16 women, 2 men) for these classes were given a list of names of students in their classes who had scored in the top 20% on the Harvard Test and were, therefore, identified as potential academic bloomers during the academic year. But here's the key to this study: the children on the teachers' top 10 lists had been assigned to this experimental condition purely at random. The only difference between these children and the others (the controls) was that they had been identified to their teachers as the ones who would show unusual intellectual gains. In reality, the average for the students in each group was the same.

Near the end of the school year, all children at the school were measured again with the same test (the TOGA), and the degree of change in IQ was calculated for each child. The differences in IQ changes between the experimental group and the controls could then be examined to see if the expectancy effect had been created in a real-world setting.

Figure 4.1.1 IQ score gains: grades 1 through 6.

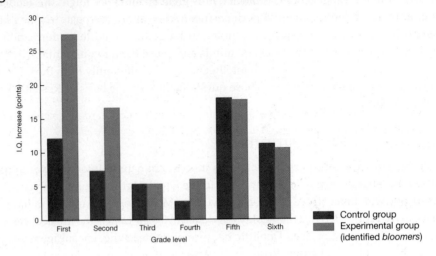

Results

Figure 4.1.1 summarizes the results of the comparisons of the IQ increases for the experimental versus the control groups. For the entire school, the children for whom the teachers had expected greater intellectual growth averaged significantly greater improvement than did the control children (12.2 and 8.2 points, respectively). However, if you examine Figure 4.1.1, it is clear that this difference was accounted for by the huge differences in grades 1 and 2. Possible reasons for this are discussed shortly. Rosenthal and Jacobson offered another useful and revealing way to organize the data for these 1st- and 2nd-grade students. Figure 4.1.2 illustrates the percentage of the children in each group who obtained increases in IQ of at least 10, 20, or 30 points.

Two major findings emerged from this study. First, the expectancy effect previously demonstrated in laboratory settings also appeared to function in less experimental, real-world situations. Second, the effect was very strong in the early grades, yet almost nonexistent for the older children. What does all this mean?

Discussion

As Rosenthal suspected from his past research, the teachers' expectations of their students' behavior became a self-fulfilling prophecy: "When teachers expected that certain children would show greater intellectual development, those children did show greater intellectual development" (Rosenthal & Jacobson, 1968, p. 85). Remember, the data are averages of three classes and three teachers for each grade level. It is difficult to think of explanations for the differences in IQ gains other than the teachers' expectations.

Figure 4.1.2 Percentage of 1st- and 2nd-grade students with major gains in IQ scores.

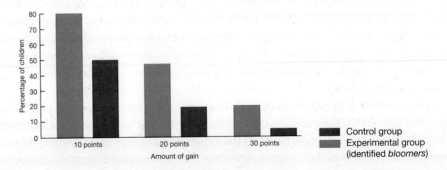

However, Rosenthal felt it was important to try to explain why the self-fulfilling prophecy was not demonstrated in the higher grade levels. Both in this article and in later writings, Rosenthal and Jacobson offered several possible reasons for their findings:

1. Younger children are generally thought of as more malleable or "transformable." If this is true, then the younger children in the study may have experienced greater change simply because they were easier than the older children to change. Related to this is the possibility that even if younger children are not more malleable, teachers may have *believed* that they were. This belief alone may have been enough to create differential treatment and produce the results.

2. Younger students in an elementary school tend to have less well-established reputations. In other words, if the teachers had not yet had a chance to form an opinion of a child's abilities, the expectancies created by the researchers could have carried more weight.

3. Younger children may be more easily influenced by and more susceptible to the subtle and unintentional processes that teachers use to communicate performance expectations to them:

   > Under this interpretation, it is possible that teachers react to children of all grade levels in the same way if they believe them to be capable of intellectual gain. But perhaps it is only the younger children whose performance is affected by the special things the teacher says to them; the special ways in which she says them; the way she looks, postures, and touches the children from whom she expects greater intellectual growth. (p. 83)

4. Teachers in lower grades may differ from upper-grade teachers in ways that produce greater communication of their expectations to the children. Rosenthal and Jacobson did not speculate as to exactly what these differences might be if indeed they exist.

Significance of Findings and Subsequent Research

The real importance of Rosenthal and Jacobson's findings at Oak School relates to the potential long-lasting effects of teachers' expectations on the scholastic performance of students. This, in turn, feeds directly into one of the most controversial topics in psychology's recent history: the question of the fairness of intelligence testing. Let's explore some later research that examined the specific ways in which teachers may unconsciously communicate their higher expectations to those students whom they believe possess greater potential.

A study conducted by Chaikin, Sigler, and Derlega (1974) involved videotaping teacher–student interactions in a classroom situation in which the teachers had been informed that certain children were extremely bright (these "bright" students had actually been chosen at random from all the students in the class). Careful examination of the videos indicated that teachers favored the identified "brighter" students in many subtle ways. They smiled at these students more often, made more eye contact, and had more favorable reactions to these students' comments in class. These researchers go on to report that students for whom these high expectations exist are more likely to enjoy school, receive more constructive comments from teachers on their mistakes, and work harder to try to improve. What this and other studies indicate is that teacher expectancies can affect more than just intelligence scores.

Imagine for a moment that you are an elementary school teacher with a class of 20 students. On the first day of class, you receive a class roster on which is printed the IQ scores for all your students. You notice that five of your pupils have IQ scores over 145, well into the genius range. Do you think that your treatment and expectations of those children during the school year would be the same as of your other students?

What about your expectations of those students compared with another five students with IQ scores in the low-to-normal range? If you answered that your treatment and expectations would be the same, Rosenthal would probably be willing to bet that you'd be wrong. As a matter of fact, they probably *shouldn't* be the same! The point is, if your expectations became self-fulfilling prophecies, then that could be unfair to some of the students. Now consider another, more crucial point. Suppose the intelligence scores you received on your class roster were *wrong*. If these erroneous scores created expectations that benefited some students over others, it would clearly be unfair and probably unethical. This is one of the major issues fueling the ongoing intelligence-testing controversy.

In recent decades, researchers have charged that many standard tests used to assess the intelligence of children contain a racial or cultural bias. The argument is that because the tests were originally designed primarily by white, upper-middle-class males, they contain ideas and information to which other ethnic groups are less exposed. Children from some ethnic minority groups in the United States have traditionally scored lower on these tests than white children. It would be ridiculous to assume that these nonwhite children possess less overall basic intelligence than white children, so the reason for these differences in scores must lie in the tests themselves. Traditionally, however, teachers in grades K through 12 were given this intelligence information on all their students. If you stop and think about this fact in relation to the research by Rosenthal and Jacobson, you'll see what a potentially precarious situation may have been created. In addition to the fact that children have been categorized and stratified in schools according to their test scores, teachers' unintended expectations, based on this possibly biased information, may have been creating systemic, unfair self-fulfilling prophecies in the students' academic performance. The arguments supporting this idea are convincing enough that many school districts have instituted a moratorium on routine intelligence testing and the use of intelligence test scores until new tests are developed (or old ones updated) to be valid and bias free. At the core of these arguments is the research addressed in this chapter.

Recent Applications

Due in large part to Rosenthal and Jacobson's research, the power of teachers' expectations on students' performance has become an integral part of our understanding of the educational process. Furthermore, Rosenthal's theory of interpersonal expectancies has exerted its influence in numerous areas other than education. In 2002, Rosenthal himself reviewed the literature on expectancy effects using meta-analysis techniques (this research technique is explained in the reading on Smith and Glass in Chapter IX). He demonstrated how "the expectations of psychological researchers, classroom teachers, judges in the courtroom, business executives, and health care providers can unintentionally affect the responses of their research participants, pupils, jurors, employees, and patients" (Rosenthal, 2002, p. 839).

An uncomfortably revealing article incorporating Rosenthal's expectancy research examined the criteria school teachers use to refer their students to school psychologists for assessment and counseling (Andrews, Wisniewski, & Mulick, 1997). The researchers found that teachers referred African American children for developmental handicap assessment at rates significantly higher than the rates of Caucasian students in their classrooms. In addition, boys were referred in equally disproportionate numbers over girls for classroom and playground behavior problems. The researchers suggested that the differences among the various student groups may have revealed more about teachers' expectancies than real individual differences.

Many educators (including Rosenthal) have suggested that because we know about the dangers of expectancies in education, we should be sure that teachers are trained to resist and avoid them. One study (Rubie-Davies & Rosenthal, 2016) developed an intervention protocol for teachers of mathematics. Teachers were randomly assigned to receive the intervention or to a control group. The intervention consisted of professional development workshops focusing on the issues of expectancies and trainings in class learning climate, strategies for forming learning groups, and the concepts of student goal-setting. Results were clear that student success rates for the intervention-trained teachers were significantly higher than for the control group (see also Rubie-Davies et al., 2016).

It should be noted that researchers in the fields of psychology and education are actively studying new ways of conceptualizing and measuring children's intellectual abilities. Several leading researchers have proposed methods of testing that focus on current theories of how the human brain works, and that go far beyond the old, limited idea of a single, general intelligence score expressed as IQ (see Benson, 2003).

One of these modern approaches is Robert Sternberg's Triarchic Abilities Test (1993), which is designed to measure three distinct aspects of intellectual ability: analytic intelligence, practical intelligence, and creative intelligence. Another leading researcher in the field of intelligence is Howard Gardner, who, in the early 1980s, developed his theory of *multiple intelligences*, which continues today to exert a powerful influence over the study and measurement of intelligence. As you will discover in the next reading, Gardner's theory contends that we have not one or three, but *eight* (and, perhaps nine or more!) *separate* intelligences, and each of us has differing amounts of each one (Gardner, 2006).

Andrews, T., Wisniewski, J., & Mulick, J. (1997). Variables influencing teachers' decisions to refer children for school psychological assessment services. *Psychology in Schools, 34*(3), 239–244.

Benson, E. (2003). Intelligent intelligence testing: Psychologists are broadening the concept of intelligence and how to test it [Electronic version]. *Monitor on Psychology, 34*(2), 48.

Chaikin, A., Sigler, E., & Derlega, V. (1974). Nonverbal mediators of teacher expectancy effects. *Journal of Personality and Social Psychology, 30*, 144–149.

Gardner, H. (2006). *Multiple intelligences: New horizons*. Jackson, TN: Perseus Books Group.

Pfungst, O. (1911). *Clever Hans (the horse of Mr. von Osten): A contribution to experimental, animal, and human psychology*. New York: Holt, Rinehart and Winston.

Rosenthal, R. (2002). Covert communication in classrooms, clinics, courtrooms, and cubicles. *American Psychologist, 57*, 839–849.

Rosenthal, R., & Fode, K. (1963). The effect of experimenter bias on the performance of the albino rat. *Behavioral Science, 8*, 183–189.

Rosenthal, R., & Jacobson, L. (1968). *Pygmalion in the classroom: Teacher expectations and pupils' intellectual development*. New York: Holt, Rinehart and Winston.

Rubie-Davies, C. M., & Rosenthal, R. (2016). Intervening in teachers' expectations: A random effects meta-analytic approach to examining the effectiveness of an intervention. *Learning and Individual Differences, 50*, 83–92.

Rubie-Davies, C. M., Peterson, E. R., Sibley, C. G., & Rosenthal, R. (2015). A teacher expectation intervention: Modelling the practices of high expectation teachers. *Contemporary Educational Psychology, 40*, 72–85.

Sternberg, R. J. (1993). *Sternberg Triarchic Abilities Test*. Unpublished test, Yale University.

Reading 4.2: Just *How* Are You Intelligent?

Gardner, H. (1983). *Frames of mind: The theory of multiple intelligences.* New York: Basic Books.

4.2 Describe multiple intelligences according to Gardner

The heading for this reading is an intentional play on words. The usual form of the question "Just how intelligent *are* you?" implies that you have a certain amount of intelligence. The question here, "Just *how are* you intelligent?" is unrelated to *amount* of overall intelligence and asks instead about the nature of your particular *type* of intelligence. This implies, of course that people are not simply more or less intelligent but that each of us possesses a unique combination of various forms of intellectual abilities.

Many of you probably have taken at least one intelligence test in your life (even if you don't remember it), and some of you may have taken several. For the most part, intelligence tests developed over the past hundred years or so have been designed to produce a single score. That score was usually called your *Intelligence Quotient* (IQ). If tests of intelligence are designed to produce a single score, a person's intelligence must also be conceptualized as a single, *general* mental ability. That is exactly how intelligence was interpreted throughout most of the 20th century. In fact, intelligence was often referred to as *g* for this general mental ability. People's IQ score, their *g*, was used widely to place, judge, categorize, and describe people in various life settings, including school, the workplace, and the military.

In the 1970s and 1980s, researchers began to question the validity of the unitary, *g*-theory approach to human intelligence. Many of the IQ tests themselves were shown to be biased toward certain economic classes and cultural groups. Moreover, children's educational opportunities were often dictated by their scores on these biased and potentially invalid scores (see the work of Robert Rosenthal in the previous reading for an example of the dangers of this bias).

As criticisms of the early conceptualization of intelligence grew in number and influence, IQ tests began to fade. At the same time, a new, and at the time radically different, view of intelligence was making its way into scientific and popular thinking about how our minds work. In stark contrast to the notion of a single, generalized intelligence, this emerging approach expanded the notion of intelligence into many *different* mental abilities, each possessing in itself the characteristics of a complete, "free-standing" intelligence. Howard Gardner, at Harvard University, introduced to the world this new view of *multiple intelligences* in his 1983 book *Frames of Mind*, which forms the basis of this reading.

Theoretical Propositions

Gardner's theory of multiple intelligences (*MI Theory*) was based on much more than simply observing the various, diverse mental skills people can demonstrate. His ideas stem from his research on the structure of the brain itself. Prior to launching his work on intelligence per se, Gardner had spent most of his career studying the biology and functioning of the brain. Gardner expanded on previous research that demonstrated that the human brain is not only diverse in its abilities but also extremely specialized in its functioning. In other words, different regions of your brain have evolved to carry out specific tasks related to thinking and knowing. This brain specialization may be demonstrated by observing, as Gardner has done, exactly what abilities are lost or diminished when a person experiences damage to a particular region of the brain. For example, language abilities reside, for most people, primarily in one section of the brain's left hemisphere, vision is centered in the occipital lobe of your cerebral cortex at the rear of the brain, and one specific brain structure located at the base of the visual cortex is responsible for your ability to recognize and discriminate among human faces (see Reading 1.1 on Michael Gazzaniga's split-brain research for more about brain specialization).

Carrying the theory of brain specialization a step further, Gardner contends that different parts of the human brain are responsible for different aspects of intelligence or, more correctly, different intelligences altogether. To defend scientifically his theory of multiple intelligences, Gardner drew upon evidence from many sources and developed criteria for defining a certain set of abilities as a unique intelligence. In developing his ideas on multiple intelligences, Gardner reviewed various sources including studies of child prodigies, gifted individuals, brain damaged patients, autistic individuals, normal children, normal adults, experts in different lines of work, and people from diverse cultures.

Method

Incorporating information from all these sources, Gardner then developed a set of eight indicators or "signs" that define an intelligence. Any intellectual ability or set of abilities, must map onto most of these criteria, if it is to be considered a separate, autonomous intelligence:

1. *Potential isolation of the intelligence by brain damage.* Gardner contended that if a specific mental ability can be destroyed through brain damage (such as injury or stroke), or if it remains relatively intact when other abilities have been destroyed, this provides convincing evidence that the ability may be a separate intelligence unto itself.

2. *The existence of savants, prodigies, and other exceptional individuals relating to the intelligence.* You may be aware that certain individuals possess an extreme level of intellectual skill in one particular ability. Some intellectually disabled and people on the Autism Spectrum demonstrate "strokes of genius," and some people with normal intelligence are *prodigies*, with abilities far beyond others of their age or experience. Gardner believes that the exceptional skills of these individuals lend significant support for considering an ability as a separate intelligence.

3. *A clear set of information-processing (thinking) operations linked to the intelligence.* This refers to mental abilities that are specific to the ability under consideration. To qualify as an intelligence, an ability must involve a specific set of mental processes, which Gardner calls *core operations* that exist in specific areas of the brain and are triggered by certain kinds of information. Table 4.2.1 lists the core operations for the various intelligences proposed by Gardner.

4. *A distinctive developmental history of the intelligence and the potential to reach high levels of expertise.* Gardner believes that an intelligence must include a developmental path that starts with simple and basic steps and progresses through incremental milestones of increased skill levels.

5. *Evidence that the intelligence has developed through evolutionary time.* Human intelligence has evolved over millions of years as one of many adaptive mechanisms that have allowed us to survive and excel as a species. If a particular set of abilities is to be defined as an intelligence, Gardner believes the skills involved should show evidence of evolutionary development, based on cross-cultural research and observations of similar types of abilities in nonhuman animals (such as the "mental maps" in the rats in Tolman's research discussed in Reading 4.3).

6. *Ability to study the intelligence with psychological experiments.* Gardner maintains that any ability proposed as an intelligence be confirmed using solid experimental techniques to be considered an intelligence. An example of this might be an experiment to determine a person's speed and accuracy in a *mental rotation task* as a sign of spatial relationships skills. Figure 4.2.1 contains a demonstration of this task. How fast can you figure it out?

7. *Ability to measure the intelligence with existing standardized tests.* Here, Gardner acknowledges the potential value of IQ and other intelligence tests of the past. However, the value he sees is not in the tests' ability to produce a single intelligence score but in the fact that some of the tests contain various subscales that may, in fact, measure different intelligences.

Table 4.2.1 Core Operations and Well-Known Individual Examples of Gardner's Eight Intelligences

Intelligence	Core Operations	Famous Examples
Linguistic	Syntax (word phrasing), phonology (the sounds of speech), semantics (the meaning of words), pragmatics (word usage)	Shakespeare, J. K. Rowling, Dr. Seuss, Woody Allen
Musical	Pitch (frequency of sounds), rhythm, timbre (quality of sounds)	Mozart, Gwen Stefani, Andrea Boccelli, Paul Simon
Logical-Mathematical	Numbers, quantities, categorization, causal relations	Albert Einstein, Carl Sagan, Marie Curie, B. F. Skinner
Spatial	Accurate visualization, mental rotation and transformation of images	Picasso, Frank Lloyd Wright, Leonardo da Vinci, Vincent van Gogh
Bodily-Kinesthetic	Control of one's own body, control in handling objects	Charlie Chaplin, LeBron James, Serena Williams and Venus Williams
Interpersonal	Awareness of others' feelings, emotions, goals, motivations	Mohandas Gandhi, Abraham Maslow, Oprah Winfrey
Intrapersonal	Awareness of one's own feelings, emotions, goals, motivations	Plato, Hermann Rorschach, Helen Keller
Naturalist	Recognition and classification of objects in the environment; sensitivity to the natural world	Charles Darwin, Jane Goodall, Rachel Carson
Existential*	Ability to engage in transcendental concerns, such as the fundamentals of human existence, the significance of life, and the meaning of death	Elie Wiesel; Martin Luther King, Jr.; Carl Rogers; Elizabeth Kübler-Ross

*Proposed.

8. *Aspects of the intelligence may be represented by a system of symbols.* Gardner proposes that any human intelligence should incorporate a system of symbols. The most obvious of these, of course, are human language and math. Other examples of symbol systems include notation for musical ability and pictures for spatial skills.

In the next section, we look at a summary of the intelligences Gardner proposed as part of his original theory in his 1983 book. Each intelligence included was analyzed using his eight criteria. If an intellectual ability failed to meet most of the criteria, it was rejected. Through this process of elimination, Gardner originally suggested seven distinct human intelligences, later added an eighth, and has recently proposed a ninth.

Results

Following, you will find brief descriptions of each intelligence, along with a quote from Gardner, to give you the "flavor" of the abilities described. In addition, Table 4.2.1

Figure 4.2.1 Example of Mental Rotation Task to Assess Spatial Intelligence. Are the two figures in each set the same or different?

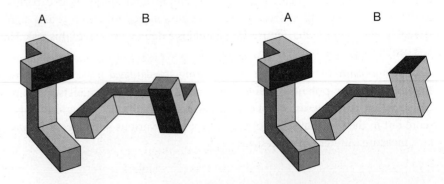

summarizes the core operations of each intelligence and provides examples of several well-known individuals who would be likely to score high on the abilities that comprise each intelligence. Although Gardner does not endorse any single test for measuring multiple intelligences, many have been developed. You can try some of these online simply by searching online for "tests of multiple intelligence," but keep in mind that a great deal of material on the Internet is of questionable validity.

LINGUISTIC INTELLIGENCE If you are strong in linguistic intelligence, you are able to use words in ways that are more skillful, useful, and creative than the average person. You are able to use language to convince others of your position, you can memorize and recall detailed or complex information, you are better than most at explaining and teaching concepts and ideas to others, and you enjoy using language to talk about language itself. Gardner suggested that talented poets are good examples of individuals possessing strong linguistic intelligence. For example, he pointed out that in the poet's struggling over the exact wording of a line or stanza can be seen some of the core aspects of linguistic intelligence. A poet must be extra sensitive to the minute meanings and nuances of words and work to preserve the as exactly as possible the exact intentions in the poem. This, Gardner contented, included the order in which the words fell, the true rules of grammar (to violate them on some occasions), and a feel for the rhythms inflections and meters of the words. This ability, he claimed, allow the poet to make a poem even in a foreign language beautiful to the ear.

MUSICAL INTELLIGENCE You are probably already guessing some of the components of musical intelligence: gifted abilities involving sound, especially pitch, timbre, and rhythm. Gardner claimed that this is the earliest of all intelligences to emerge. Musical child prodigies serve as examples of individuals who are "musical geniuses." Gardner points to the musical composer to illustrate musical intelligence: a composer, he contended, can be seen continually to have "tones in his head—that is, he is always near the top of his consciousness hearing the components of music: tones, harmonies, rhythms, and the overall composition of musical patterns."

LOGICAL-MATHEMATICAL INTELLIGENCE This intelligence enables you to think about, analyze, and compute various relationships among abstract objects, concepts, and ideas. High levels of this intelligence may be found among mathematicians, scientists, and philosophers, but they may also be present in those individuals who are obsessed with sports statistics, write computer code, develop or, perhaps, develop algorithms as a hobby. Gardener explained that individuals with logical-mathematical intelligence possess a love of abstractions and a deep-set skepticism; that is, no fact or truth may be accepted until and unless it has been proved using universal first steps. This person derives great pleasure from solving a mathematical problem that has always been considered to have no solution.

SPATIAL INTELLIGENCE You would score well in spatial intelligence if you are skilled in creating, visualizing, and manipulating mental images. These are abilities that come naturally and easily to those in various visually oriented professions or avocations, such as artists, sculptors, interior decorators, engineers, and architects. To be more specific, Gardner explained that spatial intelligence entails a unique ability to observe various instances of the same object; to be able to mentally transform or see a transformation of one object to another and mentally visualize that transformation. The person with spatial intelligence possesses the ability to produce graphic representations of spatial information.

The object rotation task in Figure 4.2.1 is an example of a skill with which someone strong in spatial intelligence would have very little difficulty.

BODILY-KINESTHETIC INTELLIGENCE These abilities also might be called "physical intelligence." If you possess strong bodily-kinesthetic intelligence, you are very aware of your own body and bodily movements and are skilled in using and controlling your body to achieve various goals or effects. As you might imagine, dancers, athletes, surgeons, potters, and many actors possess a high degree of bodily intelligence. Gardner further explains that signs of this intelligence are the skills to manipulate one's body in many different ways, to use the body for expression and practical purposes. Also present is the capacity to work with objects in skillful ways involving both fine motor movements of fingers as well as larger movements of the body.

The next two intelligences Gardner proposes, although separate, fall into a single category that Gardner called the *personal intelligences*. One type of personal intelligence is focused inward, while the other is focused outward. He referred to these as *intrapersonal intelligence* and *interpersonal intelligence*, respectively.

INTRAPERSONAL INTELLIGENCE   How well do you "know *yourself*"? Gardner proposed that the ability to be aware of and understand who you are, your emotions, your motivations, and the sources of your actions exist in varying degrees among humans. Gardner describes intrapersonal intelligence as the capacity to access one's *own* feelings, emotions, and then be capable of differentiating among those feelings; to be able to name them, to transform them into symbolic codes (i.e., pictures and words), and to use them to guide one's behavior toward others and toward the world.

INTERPERSONAL INTELLIGENCE   This intelligence is contrasted with intrapersonal intelligence by asking "How well do you know *others?*" Interpersonal intelligence involves skills similar to those of intrapersonal intelligence, but they are outward directed—focused on the feelings, motivations, desires, and behaviors of other people. The main abilities here are to notice and distinguish among *other* individuals and especially among their emotions, temperaments, motivations, and intentions. Interpersonal skill allows a person to predict the desires and intentions—even when hidden—of others and perhaps, where appropriate, to act on this knowledge.

These, then, are the seven sets of abilities that comprised Gardner's original conceptualization of multiple intelligences. He states very clearly in *Frames of Mind* that these formed a working, and somewhat preliminary, list and that through further study and research other intelligences might be added or a convincing argument might be made to remove one or more of the original seven. What has happened over the years is that these seven intelligences have maintained their positions in the theory, and, as discussed shortly, Gardner has added an eighth (and perhaps a ninth) intelligence.

Subsequent Research and Criticisms

Gardner's MI Theory was immediately seized upon by educators, parents, and society in general as proof of a belief they had always held: *People are smart in different ways.* Finally, here was an explanation for those children (and adults, too) who performed poorly on tests and in some subjects in school but were clearly exceptionally bright in other ways.

MI Theory mapped well onto growing concerns and research about learning disabilities and was largely responsible for the reformulation in education of "learning disabilities" into "learning differences." Indeed, MI Theory has exercised its greatest influence in the area of education, and Gardner's research following the publication of *Frames of Mind* focused on applying his ideas to enhancing the educational process for children and adults.

As Gardner was revisiting his original theory 10 years after its original publication, he considered the possibility of other sets of abilities that might qualify as intelligences. Several candidates had been suggested to him by colleagues in various fields, such as a "spiritual intelligence," a "sexual intelligence," and a "digital intelligence" (Gardner, 2003). Although Gardner concedes that selecting a certain set of skills that qualify as an intelligence is open to subjective interpretations, he believed that these and many other suggestions did not meet his eight criteria adequately to qualify as new intelligences.

Gardner did, however, find an additional set of abilities that he felt clearly met the criteria for an intelligence. Gardner was asked by a colleague to describe the abilities of history's most influential biologists, and when he attempted to do so, he realized that none of the other seven intelligences fit those individuals very well. This sparked the addition of an eighth ability that he called, *naturalist intelligence*. Gardner explains:

> The naturalist intelligence refers to the ability to recognize and classify plants, minerals, and animals, including rocks and grass and all variety of flora and fauna. Darwin is probably the most famous example of naturalist intelligence because he saw so deeply into the nature of living things. (quoted in Checkley, 1997)

Currently, the eight intelligences discussed here comprise Gardner's MI Theory. But Gardner is not yet finished with his theory. He sees the notion of multiple intelligences as fluid: always open to new, clearly defined sets of abilities. One skill he has suggested that might fit his criteria for an intelligence fairly well is *existential intelligence*. Because existential intelligence appears to be nearing the threshold for inclusion in MI Theory, it has been included here in Table 4.2.1. Gardner describes existential intelligence as follows:

> This candidate for intelligence is based on the human proclivity to ponder the most fundamental questions of existence. Why do we live? Why do we die? Where do we come from? What is going to happen to us? What is love? Why do we make war? I sometime say that these are questions that transcend perception; they concern issues that are too big or too small to be perceived by our five principle sensory systems. (Gardner, 2006, p. 20)

Since the 1983 release of *Frames of Mind*, Gardner has published numerous books and articles refining his theory and applying it in relevant settings. It is safe to say that MI Theory has been applied in educational settings, especially K–12, perhaps more than in any other learning or thinking environment. For example, only one year after the publication of *Frames of Mind*, a school district in Indianapolis began redesigning its curriculum completely around MI Theory. Today, virtually all schools in the United States and many other countries incorporate the theory to varying degrees.

Although MI Theory is an extremely popular approach to human intelligence and has found widespread support in various research and educational domains, it has certainly not gone uncriticized. New, influential theories that challenge long-standing views in any science are typically targets for intense controversy within the field. MI Theory has been no different.

One common objection to MI Theory suggests that Gardner's eight intelligences are not really separate intelligences but rather merely describe different "thinking styles," all of which may be seen as existing within earlier unified intelligence (*g*) views discussed at the beginning of this reading (Morgan, 1996). Another criticism contends that the theory contains embedded contradictions that make it too ambiguous to be valid (Klein, 1998). Moreover, because of its ambiguity, some contend that MI Theory can be molded "conveniently" to explain virtually any cognitive activity, rendering it impossible to prove or disprove. Moreover, some researchers have argued that not enough rigorous scientific research has been undertaken to demonstrate the validity of the intelligences and the effectiveness of applying MI Theory in real-world settings. These critics suggest—if future research finds that MI Theory is not a valid or an effective tool—that a great deal of time and effort will have been wasted and that learning thought to have been taking place, in reality, was not (Collins, 1998). These and other criticisms notwithstanding, MI Theory continues to influence strongly the field of human intelligence.

Recent Applications

Hundreds of scientific articles and books that rest on Howard Gardner's Theory of Multiple Intelligences, and that cite his 1983 book, appear every year. Dr. Gardner's work in this area continues to have a powerful and widespread impact on research and thinking about learning and intelligence. To give you an idea of the diverse applications of MI Theory, following is a brief description of just two of these recent applications.

A cross-cultural study of Gardner's seven intelligences compared British and Iranian students' self-ratings and their ratings of their parents' levels of each of Gardner's intelligences (Furnham et al., 2002). Some of the most interesting findings were that (a) Iranian students rated themselves lower in logical-mathematical intelligence but higher in spatial, musical, and intrapersonal intelligence than did the British students; (b) Iranians perceived their fathers' mathematical and spatial intelligence to be lower but their fathers' interpersonal and intrapersonal intelligence to be higher than did the British students; (c) the Iranian students rated their mothers' level of intelligence lower than did the British students on all but one (intrapersonal) of the seven intelligences; and (d) the Iranians rated their brothers higher than did the British students on all but one scale (mathematical).

Another fascinating study related Gardner's theory to Sandra Bem's research on androgyny (Bem's study is discussed in Reading 7.2). The authors found that people's estimates of their own intelligence were linked to their gender identity (Rammstedt & Rammsayer, 2002). Researchers asked participants to estimate their own level on various intelligences and also to complete the *Bem Sex Role Inventory* to measure their level of masculinity, femininity, and androgyny. Not only were gender differences found for the logical-mathematical intelligence (masculine) versus musical intelligence (feminine) but also the males' degree of self-perceived masculinity, femininity, or androgyny significantly influenced their estimates of their own levels of various intelligences.

Recently, a fascinating study (Tsai, 2016) compared junior high school students' intelligences based on age, sex, and type of student (general, special needs, or gifted). Moreover, to demonstrate the universality of Gardner's theory, these students were in Taiwan. Here are the differences the researchers found (many of them may not surprise you too much, see Tsai, p. 10):

1. Seventh grade students received the highest scores on *interpersonal intelligence*, and the lowest scores on *natural intelligence*. Eighth grade students scored highest on *interpersonal intelligence*, and lowest on *bodily-kinesthetic intelligences*.

2. General students and special needs students scored highest scores on *interpersonal intelligence*. However, the former scored the lowest scores on *natural intelligence*, and the latter scored the lowest scores on *logical-mathematical intelligence*. Gifted students received the highest scores on *logical-mathematical intelligence*, and the lowest on *bodily-kinesthetic intelligence*.

3. Seventh grade students received higher scores than eighth grade students *on spatial, music, bodily-kinesthetic,* and *natural intelligences*.

4. Girls outscored boys on *linguistic, spatial, music, interpersonal,* and *existential intelligences*. Boys only received higher scores than girls on *logical-mathematical intelligence*.

When you think about what your experience tells you about junior high aged boys and girls these findings confirm a lot of what you already suspected, don't they?

Conclusion

Gardner's MI Theory has survived over two decades and shows no signs of fading from view. Whether the ideas of the theory continue to grow in importance and influence or become overshadowed by new conceptualizations of intelligence remains to be seen. Whatever its future, however, one point is certain: MI Theory has changed forever how the world looks at learning, teaching, and intelligence. However, Gardner himself cautions that MI Theory is a means to an end and should not be seen as an end in itself:

> Educational goals should reflect one's own values, and these can never come simply or directly from a scientific theory. Once one reflects on one's educational values and states one's goals, however, then the putative existence of our

multiple intelligences can prove very helpful. And, in particular, if one's educational goals encompass disciplinary understanding, then it is possible to mobilize our several intelligences to help achieve that lofty goal. . . . I have come to realize that once one releases an idea into the world, one cannot completely control its behavior—anymore than one can control those products of our genes called children. Put succinctly, MI has and will have a life of its own, over and above what I might wish for it, my most widely known intellectual offspring. (Gardner, 2002)

Checkley, K. (1997). The first seven . . . and the eighth. *Educational Leadership, 55,* 8–13.

Collins, J. (1998). Seven kinds of smart. *Time, 152,* 94–96.

Furnham, A., Shahidi, S., & Baluch, B. (2002). Sex and cultural differences in perceptions of estimated multiple intelligence for self and family: A British-Iranian comparison. *Journal of Cross Cultural Psychology, 33,* 270–285.

Gardner, H. (2003). Multiple intelligences after twenty years. Paper presented at the American Educational Research Association, Chicago, IL, April 21, 2003.

Gardner, H. (2006). *Multiple intelligences: New horizons.* Jackson, TN: Perseus Books Group.

Klein, P. (1998). A response to Howard Gardner: Falsifiability, empirical evidence, and pedagogical usefulness in educational psychologies. *Canadian Journal of Education, 23,* 103–112.

Morgan, H. (1996). An analysis of Gardner's theory of multiple intelligence. *Roeper Review, 18,* 263–269.

Rammstedt, B., & Rammsayer, T. (2002). Gender differences in self-estimated intelligence and their relation to gender-role orientation. *European Journal of Personality, 16,* 369–382.

Min-Ying Tsai (2015). Research on multiple intelligences of junior high school students with different background variables. *Journal of Modern Education Review, 6,* 10–18, Doi: 10.15341/jmer(2155-7993)/01.06.2016/002.

Reading 4.3: Maps in Your Mind

Tolman, E. C. (1948). Cognitive maps in rats and men. *Psychological Review, 55,* 189–208.

4.3 Explain how Tolman's experiments on latent learning and spatial orientation established theoretical pillars of cognitive-behaviorism

Many of the studies in this book are included because the theoretical propositions underlying them and their findings contradicted the prevailing view and conventional wisdom of their time. Bouchard's revelations concerning genetic influences on personality (Reading 1.3), Watson's study of Little Albert (Reading 3.2), and Harlow's theory of infant attachment (Reading 5.1), among other research studies, all challenged the status quo of psychological thinking and thereby opened up new and often revolutionary interpretations of human behavior.

Edward C. Tolman's theories and studies of learning and cognition made just such a contribution. During the years when psychology was consumed with strict stimulus-response learning theories that dismissed unobservable, internal mental activity as "unknowable," Tolman, at the University of California at Berkeley, was doing experiments demonstrating that complex internal cognitive activity (the processes of thinking, analyzing, and knowing) could be studied not only in people, but also in rats, and that these mental processes could be studied without the necessity of observing them directly. Due to the significance of his work, Tolman is considered to be the one of the founders of a school of thought within the field of learning psychology that is called *cognitive-behaviorism.* He is among the top 50 most cited psychologists of the 20th century.

To experience some of what Tolman proposed in these studies, imagine for a moment that you want to make your way from your present location to the nearest post office or market. You probably already have an image in your mind of where these are located. Now think about the route you would take to get there. You know you have to take certain streets, make specific turns at the correct intersections, and eventually enter the building. This picture in your mind of your present location relative to the post office or market and the route you would follow to travel between them is called a *mental representation*. Tolman called these representations *cognitive maps*. Tolman maintained that not only do humans use cognitive maps, but also other animals, including rats, think about their world in similar ways. Why does anyone care how a rat thinks? Well, if you were a learning theorist in the 1930s and 1940s, the main research method being used was rats in mazes; people were very interested in how they *learned*.

Theoretical Propositions

In the first half of the 20th century, learning theorists were on the front lines of psychology. In addition to trying to explain the mechanisms involved in learning, they were invested in demonstrating the "respectability" of psychology as a true science. Because psychology had been emerging as a science, from its roots in philosophy, for only a few decades, many researchers felt that the best way to prove psychology's scientific potential was to emulate the so-called *hard* sciences, such as physics and chemistry. This notion led the learning theorists to propose that the only proper subjects for study were, as in physics and chemistry, observable, measurable events. In that light, a stimulus applied to an organism could be measured, and the organism's behavior in response to that stimulus could be measured. But, they contended that what went on *inside* the organism's brain, between these two events, was not observable or measurable, so it could not be studied and, no one really tried. According to this view, when a rat learned to run through a maze faster and faster and with fewer and fewer errors, the learning process consisted of a succession of stimuli to which a succession of correct responses led to the reward of food at the end of the maze. This focused, stimulus-response, connectionist view of all behavior formed the core of behaviorism and dominated the first 50 years or so of behavioral psychology's history.

Led by Tolman during the 1930s and 1940s, a small band of "renegades" appeared who maintained that much more was going on inside the learning organism than mere responses to stimuli. In fact, Tolman proposed two main modifications to the prevailing view. One was that the true nature and complexity of learning could not be fully understood without an examination of the internal mental processes that accompany the observable stimuli and responses. As Tolman stated in the famous 1948 article that is the subject of this discussion,

> We believe that in the course of learning something like a field map of the environment gets established in the rat's brain. We agree with the other [stimulus-response] school that the rat running a maze is exposed to stimuli and is finally led as a result of these stimuli to the responses which actually occur. We feel, however, that the intervening brain processes are more complicated, more patterned, and often . . . more autonomous than do the stimulus-response psychologists. (p. 192)

The second proposal made by Tolman was that even though internal cognitive processes could not be directly observed, they could be objectively and scientifically inferred from observable behavior.

Method and Results

Tolman presented numerous studies in his 1948 article to support his views, all of which involved maze learning by rats. Two of the studies that clearly and concisely demonstrated his theoretical position are included here.

The first was called the *latent learning* experiment. For this study, rats were divided into three groups. Group C (the control group) was exposed to a complex maze using the standard procedure of one run through the maze each day with a food reward at the end of the maze. Group N (no reward) was exposed to the maze for the same amount of time each day but found no food and received no reward for any behavior in the maze. Group D (delayed reward) was treated exactly like group N for the first 10 days of the study, but then on day 11 found food at the end of the maze and continued to find it each day thereafter.

Figure 4.3.1 summarizes the results for the three groups based on the average number of errors (running down blind alleys) made by each group of rats. As you can easily see in the figure, the rats in groups N and D did not learn much of anything about the maze when they were not receiving any reward for running through the maze. The control rats learned the maze to near perfection in about 2 weeks. However, when the rats in group D discovered a reason to run the maze (food!), they learned it to near perfection in only about 3 days (day 11 to day 13). The only possible explanation for these findings was that during those 10 days when the rats were wandering around in the maze without any reward, they were learning much more about the maze than they were showing. As Tolman explained, "Once . . . they knew they were to get food, they demonstrated that during the preceding nonreward trials, they had learned where many of the blinds were. They had been building up a mental 'map' and could utilize [it] as soon as they were motivated to do so" (p. 195).

The second study to be discussed here is called the *"spatial orientation"* experiment. Stimulus-response (S-R) theorists had maintained that a rat only "knows" where the food reward is by running the maze (and experiencing all the S-R connections) to get to it. This is very much like saying that you only know where your bedroom is by walking out of the kitchen, across the living room, down the hall, past the bathroom, and into your room. In reality, you have a mental representation of where your bedroom is in the house without having to "run the maze." Tolman's spatial orientation technique was designed to show that rats trained in a maze actually know the location in space of the food reward relative to their starting position even if the elements of the maze are radically changed, or even removed.

Figure 4.3.1 Latent learning experiment error rates in maze learning. (Based on data from p. 195.)

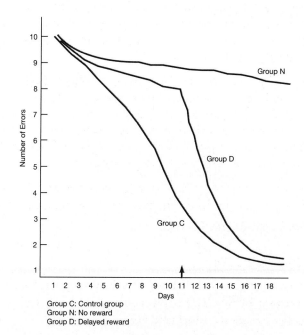

Group C: Control group
Group N: No reward
Group D: Delayed reward

Figure 4.3.2 Spatial orientation experiment: simple maze. (Based on data from p. 202.)

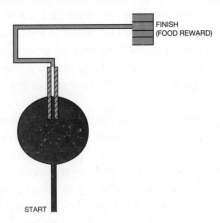

First, rats learned to run the simple maze shown in Figure 4.3.2. They would enter the maze at the start, and then run across a round table and into the path leading, in a somewhat circuitous route, to a food reward at the end. This was a relatively simple maze and no problem for the rats that learned it to near perfection in 12 trials.

Then the maze was changed to a sunburst pattern, similar to that shown in Figure 4.3.3. Now, when the trained rats tried to run their usual route, they found it blocked and had to return to the round table. There they had a choice of 12 possible alternate paths to try to get to where the food had been in the previous maze. Figure 4.3.4 shows the number of rats choosing each of the 12 possible paths.

As you can see, Path 6, which ran to about 4 inches from where the food reward box had been placed in the previous maze, was chosen by significantly more rats than any other possible route. S-R theory might have predicted that the rats would choose the path most closely in the direction of the first turn in the original maze (Path 11), but this was not the case: "The rats had, it would seem, acquired not merely a strip-map to the effect that the original specifically trained-on path led to food, but rather a wider,

Figure 4.3.3 Spatial orientation experiment: sunburst maze. (Based on data from p. 203.)

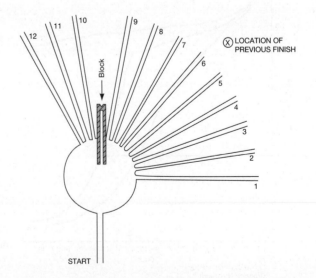

Figure 4.3.4 Spatial orientation experiment: number of rats choosing each path. (Based on data from p. 204.)

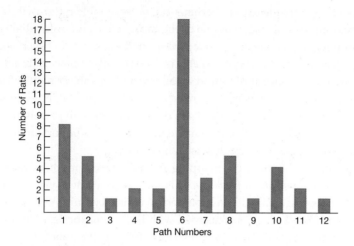

comprehensive map to the effect that food was located in such and such a direction in the room" (p. 204). Here, Tolman was expanding his theory beyond the notion that rats, and potentially other organisms including humans, produce cognitive maps of the route from point A to point Z. He was demonstrating that the maps that are produced are not mere *strip maps* represented as A to B to C and so on to Z, but are much broader, comprehensive or conceptual maps that give organisms a cognitive "lay of the land." Pretty smart rats.

Discussion

Tolman's concluding remarks in his 1948 article focused on this distinction between narrow strip maps and broader comprehensive maps. In applying his findings to humans, Tolman theorized that comprehensive maps of our social environment are advantageous to humans, although narrow, strip-like maps can lead to negative human conditions, such as mental illness or prejudice and discrimination. His reasoning was based on findings related to the studies described previously indicating that when rats were over-motivated (e.g., too hungry) or over-frustrated (e.g., too many blind alleys), they tended to develop very narrow maps and were less likely to acquire the comprehensive cognitive mapping skills of the rats described in his studies. Acknowledging that he was not a clinical or social psychologist, Tolman offered this as a possible explanation for some of society's social problems. In Tolman's words,

> Over and over again men are blinded by too violent motivations and too intense frustrations into blind . . . haters of outsiders. And the expression of their hates ranges all the way from discrimination against minorities to world conflagrations.
>
> What in the name of Heaven or Psychology can we do about it? My only answer is to preach again the virtue of reason—of, that is, broad cognitive maps. . . . We dare not let ourselves or others become so over-emotional, so hungry, so ill-clad, so over-motivated that only narrow strip-maps will be developed. All of us . . . must be made calm enough and well-fed enough to be able to develop truly comprehensive maps. . . . We must, in short, subject our children and ourselves (as the kindly experimenter would his rats) to the optimal conditions of moderate motivation and an absence of unnecessary frustrations, whenever we put them and ourselves before that great God-given maze which is our human world. (p. 208)

Subsequent Research and Recent Applications

Over the decades since Tolman's early studies, a great deal of research has supported his theories of cognitive learning. Perhaps the most notable outgrowth of Tolman's ideas and reasoning is the fact that one of the most active and influential subfields of the behavioral sciences today is *cognitive psychology*. This branch of psychology is in the business of studying internal, unobservable mental processes. Since only a few decades ago when the entire concept of "mind" was rejected as subject matter for scientific investigation, psychology has made a nearly complete reversal. Now it is generally accepted that the way a stimulus is processed mentally through perceiving, attending, thinking, expecting, remembering, and analyzing is at least as important in determining a behavioral response as the stimulus itself, if not more so.

Tolman's theory of cognitive mapping has influenced another area of psychology known as *environmental psychology*. This field is concerned with the relationship between human behavior and the environment in which it occurs. A key area of research in environmental psychology is concerned with how you experience and think about your life's various surroundings, such as your city, your neighborhood, your school campus, or the building in which you work. The study of your conceptualizations of these places is called *environmental cognition*, and your precise mental representations of them have been given Tolman's term, *cognitive maps*. Using Tolman's basic concepts, environmental psychologists have been influential not only in our understanding of how people understand their environments but also in how environments should be designed or adapted to create the optimal *fit* with our cognitive mapping processes.

One of the environmental psychologists who led in applying Tolman's ideas to humans was Lynch (1960). Lynch proposed five categories of environmental features that we make use of in forming our cognitive maps. *Paths* are perceived arteries that carry traffic, whether in cars, on foot, on bicycles, or in boats. *Edges* are boundaries we use in our cognitive mapping to divide one area from another, but they do not function as paths, such as a canyon, a wall, or the shore of a lake. *Nodes* are focal points, such as city parks, traffic circles, or a fountain, where paths or edges meet. *Districts* take up large spaces on our mental representations and are defined by some common characteristic, such as the theater district or restaurant row. *Landmarks* are structures that are used as points of reference within a map and are usually visible from a distance, such as a clock tower, a church steeple, or a tall or especially unusual building.

This early article by Tolman articulating his theory of cognitive mapping has been cited throughout the 50 years since its publication consistently and frequently in a wide array of diverse studies. For example, a recent study applied Tolman's model of cognitive maps to understanding how birds rely on the location of the sun to find landmarks and create cognitive maps for their remarkable migratory treks over hundreds or even thousands of miles each year (Bingman & Able, 2002). On a different track, a study from the field of tourism cited Tolman's ideas in an examination of how travelers in wilderness areas (*nature-based tourists*) develop their knowledge of the terrain they are exploring (Young, 1999). This study found that several factors influenced the quality of the participants' mental maps, including mode of transportation, whether they had visited the region before, number of days spent in the area, where they were from, their age, and their gender.

Today, much of our "traveling" does not require going anywhere at all, at least in a physical sense. We can now find our way to anywhere in the world on the Internet and even feel as if we are truly there through virtual reality. Tolman's conceptualization of cognitive maps has even influenced research on the psychology of the World Wide Web. Imagine for a moment what you do when you are on the Internet: You explore; you jump from place to place; you surf; you navigate; you Google. You don't really go anywhere geographically, yet you often feel as if you have been on a journey. And chances are, most of you could probably go there again using approximately the same route, right? If so, you have formed a mental map of a small part of the Web. A study in a journal devoted to research on human–computer relationships examined Internet search behavior and the strategies people use to navigate the Web (Hodkinson, Kiel, & McColl-Kennedy, 2000). The researchers were able to translate Web search behavior into graphic form, identify individual search strategies, and suggest possible methods for improving Internet search effectiveness.

Tolman's research was incorporated into a study that may have shed some light on that age-old gender stereotype, "Men never ask for directions." Research by Bell and Saucier (2004) explored the connection between people's gender and sex hormone levels with their ability to navigate along a specified route. Imagine for a moment that you are moving along a path from point A to point B. Along the way, you will pick up some mental images of your surroundings, such as notable landmarks in the distance and specific points of interest along your route, and you will probably have a general sense of the direction from which you began your journey. If asked to point to some of these mental representations, you would likely indicate the correct direction for some, but not for others. In other words, you would have developed a cognitive map of your route, but it would seldom be perfect. Bell and Saucier asked participants to do just this and found that greater levels of testosterone, the primary male sex hormone, were significantly related to increased accuracy in these pointing tasks, indicating a clearer understanding of the cognitive maps the participants formed during their environmental experiences. So, does this mean that men ask for directions less than women do because men already know where they are? No. As intriguing as these findings are, a great deal more research will be needed to answer *that* one!

Recent research, with the help of new, sophisticated brain scanning techniques, such as the functional MRI or fMRI (which is discussed in some detail in Reading 6.3, *Watching Your Emotions*), has allowed neuroscientists to observe the brain at work as it codes and creates your cognitive maps (e.g., E. Moser and M. B. Moser, 2014). These researchers liken these brain processes to the most advanced "surveillance system" ever created. Not only is your brain capable of monitoring your movements through the environment but also it appears to map and store every step you've ever taken. Beyond this, your cognitive mapping neurons do more than "simply" store these maps, but they attach to the maps what you did, what you sensed, and what you experienced while you were on the journey. As we discover more and more about the brain, the more astounding it becomes.

Bell, S., & Saucier, D (2004). Relationship among environmental pointing accuracy, mental rotation, sex, and hormones. *Environment and Behavior, 36*(2), 251–275.

Bingman, V., & Able, K. (2002). Maps in birds: Representational mechanisms and neural bases. *Current Opinion in Neurobiology, 12,* 745–750.

Hodkinson, C., Kiel, G., & McColl-Kennedy, J. (2000). Consumer Web search behavior: Diagrammatic illustration of wayfinding on the Web. *International Journal of Human-Computer Studies, 52*(5), 805–830.

Lynch, K. (1960). *The image of the city.* Cambridge, MA: MIT Press.

Moser, E., & Moser, M. B. (2014, March). Mapping your every move. In *Cerebrum: the Dana Forum on Brain Science, March-April, 2014*. Dana Foundation. Retrieved from https://www.ncbi.nlm.nih.gov/pmc/articles/PMC4087187.

Young, M. (1999). Cognitive maps of nature-based tourists. *Annals of Tourism Research, 26*(4), 817–839.

Reading 4.4: Thanks for the Memories!

Loftus, E. F. (1975). Leading questions and the eyewitness report. *Cognitive Psychology, 7,* 560–572.

4.4 Describe the means by which Loftus developed her theory of memory and recall

TV programs and movies focusing on law and courtroom dramas have, over the decades, portrayed eyewitness testimony as the surest route to a conviction (or acquittal). Most people would tell you that having an eyewitness (or two or three) constitutes the strongest evidence in a legal case. But, they would be wrong. Why do people believe that eyewitness reports provide such strong evidence in criminal cases? The reason is that we tend to believe that the way in which a person remembers an event must be the way it actually happened. In other words, memory is typically thought of as the *replaying* of an event, exactly as we saw it, like playing back a video. However, psychologists who study memory have drawn that notion into question, along with many other common beliefs about the reliability of human memory. Overall, our memory is actually quite poor.

One of the leading researchers in the area of memory is Elizabeth Loftus at the University of California at Irvine. She has found that when an event is recalled, it is not accurately recreated. Instead, what is actually recalled is a *reconstruction* of an event that is being remembered. Loftus's research has demonstrated that reconstructive memory is a result of our use of new and existing information to fill in the gaps in our recall of an experience. She maintains that memories are not stable, as we commonly believe, but that they are malleable and changeable over time. If you tell someone a story from your vacation 5 years ago, you *think* you are recreating the experience just as it happened, but you are not. Instead, you have reconstructed the memory using information from many sources, such as the previous times you've told it, other experiences from the same or later vacations, perhaps a movie you saw last year that was shot in a place similar to your vacation, and so on. All your experiences since the even come to bear on the recreation of the memory. You know this is true if you and a person who was with you at the time have ever recounted your shared experience. You are often surprised by how your stories can disagree about an event you both experienced simultaneously!

Usually, these alterations in memory are nothing more than interesting and harmless. However, in legal proceedings, when a defendant's fate may rest on the testimony of an eyewitness, memory reconstructions can be critical. For this reason, much of Loftus's research in the area of memory has been connected to eyewitness testimony within the legal system. In her early research, she found that very subtle influences in how a question is worded can alter a person's memory for an event. For example, if witnesses to an automobile accident are asked "Did you see a broken headlight?" or "Did you see the broken headlight?" the question using the word *the* produced more "yes" responses than the question using the word *a*, even when no headlight had been broken. The use of *the* presupposes (assumes) the presence of a broken headlight, and this, in turn, causes many witnesses to add one to their memories as they reconstruct the event they witnessed.

The article by Loftus about eyewitness testimony that is the focus of this discussion is one of the most often cited because it reports on four related studies that took her theories a major step forward. In these studies, she demonstrated that the mere wording of questions asked of eyewitnesses could alter their memories of events they witness when they were later asked questions about the events. This research influenced both memory theory and criminal law.

Theoretical Propositions

These studies focus on the power of questions containing presuppositions to alter a person's memory of an event. Loftus defines a presupposition as a condition that must be true for the question to make sense. For example, suppose you have witnessed an automobile accident, and I ask you "How many people were in the car that was speeding?" The question *presupposes* that the car was speeding. But what if the car was not actually speeding? You might answer the question anyway because it was not a question about the speed of the car—it was about its passengers. However, Loftus proposed that because of the way the question was worded, you might add the speeding information to your memory of the event. Consequently, if you are asked other questions later, you will be more likely to say the car was speeding. Loftus hypothesized that if eyewitnesses are asked questions that contain a false presupposition about the witnessed event, the new *false* information may be incorporated into the witness's memory of the event and appear subsequently in new testimony by the witness.

Method and Results

The methods and results for each of the four experiment reports are summarized in the following subsections.

EXPERIMENT 1   In the first study, 150 participants in small groups saw a film of a five-car chain-reaction accident that occurred when a driver ran through a stop sign into oncoming traffic. The accident took only 4 seconds and the entire film ran less than a minute. After the film, the participants were given a questionnaire containing 10 questions. For half of the participants, the first question was "How fast was Car A [the car that ran the stop sign] going when it ran the stop sign?" For the other half of the participants, the question was "How fast was Car A going when it turned right?" The remaining questions were of little interest to the researchers until the last one, which was the same for both groups: "Did you see a stop sign for Car A?"

In the group that had been asked about the stop sign, 40 participants (53%) said they saw a stop sign for Car A, while only 26 (35%) in the "turned-right" group claimed to have seen it. This difference was statistically significant.

EXPERIMENT 2   The second study Loftus reported was the first in this series to involve a delayed memory test and was the only one of the four not to use an automobile accident as the witnessed event. For this study, 40 participants were shown a 3-minute segment from the film *Diary of a Student Revolution*. The clip showed a class being disrupted by eight anti-war demonstrators. After they viewed the film, the participants were given questionnaires containing 20 questions relating to the film clip. Half of the participants were asked "Was the leader of the *four* demonstrators who entered the classroom a male?" The other half was asked "Was the leader of the *twelve* demonstrators who entered the classroom a male?" All remaining questions were identical for the two groups.

One week after this initial test, the participants from both groups returned and answered 20 new questions about the film (without seeing it again). The one question that provided the results of the study was "How many demonstrators did you see entering the classroom?" Remember, both groups of participants saw the same film and answered the same questions, except for the reference to 12 versus 4 demonstrators.

The group that had received the question presupposing 12 demonstrators reported seeing an average of 8.85. Those who had received the question asking about 4 demonstrators averaged 6.40. This was also a significant difference. This experiment showed that, on average, the wording of one question altered the way participants remembered the basic characteristics of a witnessed event.

EXPERIMENT 3   This third experiment was designed to see if a false presupposition inherent in a question could cause witnesses to reconstruct their memory of an event to include objects that, in reality, were not there. The participants (150 university students) watched a short video of an accident involving a white sports car and then answered 10 questions about the content of the video. One question included for only half the participants was "How fast was the white sports car going *when it passed the barn* while traveling along the country road?" The other half of the participants was asked "How fast was the white sports car going while traveling along the country road?" As in the previous study, the participants returned a week later and answered 10 new questions about the accident. The question under study was "Did you see a barn?"

Of those participants who had previously answered a question in which a barn was mentioned, 13 (17.3%) of them answered "yes" to the test question, compared with only 2 (2.7%) in the no-barn group. Once again, this was a statistically significant difference.

EXPERIMENT 4 The final experiment reported in this article was somewhat more elaborately designed to meet two goals. First, Loftus wanted to further demonstrate the memory reconstruction effects found in Experiment 3. Second, she wondered if perhaps just the mention of an object, even if it was not included as part of a false presupposition, might be enough to cause the object to be added to memory. For example, imagine you are asked directly "Did you see a barn?" when no barn was depicted in the film. You will probably answer "no." But if you are asked again a week later, might that barn have crept into your memory of the event? This is what Loftus tested in the fourth experiment.

Three groups of 50 participants viewed a 3-minute film shot from the inside of a car that ends with the car colliding with a baby carriage pushed by a man. The three groups then received booklets containing questions about the film. These booklets differed as follows:

> *Group D:* The direct question group received booklets containing 40 "filler" questions and 5 key questions directly asking about nonexistent objects—for example, "Did you see a barn in the film?" (See Table 4.4.1.)
>
> *Group F:* The false presupposition group received the same 40 filler questions and 5 key questions that contained presuppositions about the same nonexistent objects, such as, "Did you see a station wagon parked in front of the barn?"
>
> *Group C:* The control group received only the 40 filler questions.

One week later, all the participants returned and answered 20 new questions about the film. Of the questions, 5 were the exact same key questions as were asked of the direct-question group a week before. So, group D saw those 5 questions twice. The dependent measure (the result) was the percentage of participants in each group who claimed to remember the nonexistent objects.

Table 4.4.1 summarizes the findings for all three groups. Remember, the film included no school bus, truck, centerline on the road, woman pushing the carriage, or barn. Combining all the questions, the overall percentages of those participants answering "yes" to the direct questions 1 week later were 29.2% for the false-presupposition

Table 4.4.1 Appearance of Nonexistent Objects in Participants' Recall of Filmed Accident Following Direct Questions and False Presuppositions

Direct Question	False Presupposition	Percent of "Yes" Responses to Direct Question 1 Week Later by Group		
		D	C	F
Did you see a school bus in the film?	Did you see the children getting on the school bus?	12	6	26
Did you see a truck in the beginning of the film?	At the beginning of the film, was the truck parked beside the car?	8	0	22
Did you see a centerline on the country road?	Did another car cross the center line on the country road?	14	8	26
Did you see a woman pushing the carriage?	Did the woman pushing the carriage cross into the road?	36	26	54
Did you see a barn in the film?	Did you see a station wagon parked in front of the barn?	8	2	18

C = control group
D = direct-question group
F = false-presupposition group
(Based on information from p. 568.)

group, 15.6% for the direct-question group, and 8.4% for the control group. The differences between the direct-question group and the false-presupposition group for each item, as well as for all the items combined, were statistically significant.

Discussion

Based on these and other studies, Loftus argued that an accurate theory of memory and recall must include a process of reconstruction when new information is integrated into the original memory of an event. The findings of these studies cannot be explained by assuming that recall simply involves a mental replaying of an event, even with varying degrees of accuracy. To illustrate, Figure 4.4.1 compares the traditional view of recall with the reformulated process proposed by Loftus. As you can see, the extra step of integrating new information into memory has been added. This new information, in turn, causes your representation of the original memory to be altered or *reconstructed*. Later, if you are asked a question about the event, your recall will not be of the actual original event but, rather, your reconstruction of it. Loftus contended that this reconstruction process was the reason that barns, school busses, trucks, women pushing baby carriages, and center lines in roads were all conjured up in participants' memories when they were not part of the original experience. The false presupposition in the questions provided new information that was unintentionally integrated into the participants' memories of the event.

Applying this idea to eyewitnesses in criminal investigations, Loftus pointed out that witnesses to a crime are often questioned more than once. They might be asked questions by police at the scene of the crime, interviewed by the prosecuting

Figure 4.4.1 Recall of an event in response to a question.

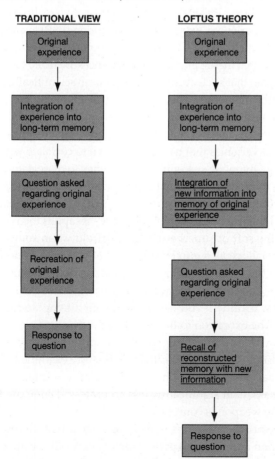

attorney assigned to the case, and again questioned in court. During these various question-and-answer sessions, it is not unlikely that false presuppositions will be made, possibly unintentionally, in numerous ways. Common, innocent-sounding questions such as "What did the guy's gun look like?" or "Where was the getaway car parked?" have been shown to increase the chances that witnesses will remember a gun or a getaway car whether or not those items were actually there (Smith & Ellsworth, 1987). Although the attorneys, the judge, and the jury are making the assumption that the witness is re-creating what was actually seen, Loftus contends that what is being remembered by the witness is a "regenerated image based on the altered memorial representation" (p. 571).

Recent Applications

Several studies represent the ongoing influence of Loftus's impressive body of work on eyewitness testimony. One study citing her 1975 article examined how lawyers' complicated questions negatively affect eyewitness accuracy and confidence (Kebbell & Giles, 2000). All participants watched identical videotaped events and were questioned a week later about what they saw. Half the participants were asked questions in confusing language (you know that lawyer-speak of "Is it not true that . . . ?"), while others were asked the same questions in simple language. The results were clear: The participants receiving the confusing form of the questions were less accurate in their eyewitness reports and were also less confident of their answers than those in the straightforward-question condition. Other research has demonstrated that when eyewitnesses are shown more than one photographic lineup of criminal suspects (a common event in law enforcement), their accuracy in identifying the correct perpetrator decreases significantly as they incorporate the newer faces into their reconstruction of the original event (Pezdek & Blandon-Gitlin, 2005).

Another intriguing study applied Loftus's work to reports of "fantastic memories," that is, memories that bear greater similarity to fantasy than reality, such as alien abductions, out-of-body experiences, extrasensory perception (ESP) events, encounters with ghosts, and so on (French, 2003). Clearly, if these reports of memories were true, they would provide proof that these paranormal occurrences are real. However, research tells us time and time again that such events have *never* been scientifically demonstrated. So, what accounts for the memories? The answer may lie in the fallibility and unreliability of human memory as discussed in this reading and, perhaps, the ability of our brains to *create* memories of events that never actually happened. As French points out, "A number of psychological variables that have been shown to correlate with susceptibility to false memories (e.g., hypnotic susceptibility, tendency to dissociate, etc.) also correlate with the tendency to report paranormal experiences" (French, p. 153).

Another factor in the accuracy (or lack of it) in eyewitness testimony is a well-known psychological phenomenon called the "weapons focus effect." Obviously, unless you are some sort of superhero, you are afraid when someone is threatening you with a weapon (such as a gun or knife). What you tend to do if this happens is turn your focus to the weapon and not to the person doing the threatening. Clearly, this is bound to have an effect on the accuracy of your memory of the characteristics of the person and how confident you would be in your attempt to identify the attacker. And, yes, it does. The exception to this, Is when the "victim" claims very high confidence in his or her ID. A recent study relying on Loftus's work, added an interesting twist to these findings (Carlson et al., 2017). This study examined the weapons effect first from the usual perspective of how seeing a gun pointed at you makes your description of the assailant significantly less accurate and compared those finding to the effect when the weapon is concealed.

The way this sort of research is done in to stage a mock crime using a weapon or without a weapon and then ask participants to pick out the attacker from a photo lineup. Sure enough, as predicted, the participants failed to pick out the assailant significantly more often in the visible weapon condition (obviously because they were more focused on the weapon than on the wielder of it). Then the researchers repeated the same procedure using a concealed weapon (i.e., a gun ostensibly in a coat pocket: you know, like on TV, "I've got a gun in my pocket, give me your money!"). Do you think this concealed weapon would produce the same weapons-effect? It did! The participants' confidence that they had picked the correct assailant was equal whether a weapon was visible or not. And, as expected, those participants with very high confidence in their ID were significantly more accurate. The researchers concluded that in light of these findings, police should be sure to take into account victims' degree of confidence in their identification regardless of whether a weapon was visible or not.

In addition to her ongoing work in the area of eyewitness testimony, Elizabeth Loftus is currently one of the leading experts in the heated controversy over repressed childhood memories. On one side of this debate are those people who claim to have been abused sexually sometime in their past but who have only recently, often with the help of a therapist, remembered the abuse. The usual explanation for the sudden recall of these victims assumes that the traumatic memories have been repressed in the unconscious and have only recently been revealed. On the other side are those who are suddenly accused of the abuse but who categorically deny it and claim that these memories are pure fantasy or have been somehow implanted during therapy (see Garry & Loftus, 1994, for a review of this controversy). This falls squarely into the area of Loftus's memory research.

Loftus's book *The Myth of Repressed Memories: False Memories and Allegations of Sexual Abuse* (Loftus & Ketcham, 1994) summarized her findings in this area and combined them into a cohesive argument. Loftus contends and appears to have demonstrated in numerous studies that repressed memories simply do not exist. In fact, she is at the forefront of psychologists who question the entire notion and existence of an unconscious. A main feature of Loftus's argument is that experimental evidence repeatedly demonstrates that especially traumatic memories tend to be the ones we remember *best*. And yet, clinicians often report these instances of repressed memories of sexual abuse that rise to the surface during specific and intense forms of therapy. How can these two seemingly opposing views be reconciled? Loftus suggests three possible memory distortions that might explain what clinicians see as repression (Loftus, Joslyn, & Polage, 1998). First, early sexual abuse may simply be forgotten, not repressed. She cites research demonstrating that when children do not understand the sexual nature of an abusive event, it tends to be remembered poorly. Second, it is possible that people in therapy *say* they had no memory of a traumatic event, but, in reality, they never actually forgot it. Avoiding thinking about something is different than forgetting it. And third, Loftus contends that some "people may *believe* that a particular traumatic event occurred and was repressed when, in fact, it did not happen in the first place. Under some circumstances, some combination of these distortions could lead to situations that are interpreted as repression" (p. 781).

You can imagine that Loftus's position on repressed and recovered memories is not without critics (e.g., Spitzer & Avis, 2006; Steinberg, 2000). After all, her rejection of the power of repression is opposed to commonly held beliefs about psychology and psychotherapy that have been around since Freud. Moreover, many therapists and victims have a very personal stake in their belief that memories of abuse can be repressed for years and later recovered. However, a careful reading of Loftus's thorough and careful scientific work should cause anyone to question this belief.

Conclusion

Elizabeth Loftus is considered by most to be the leading researcher in the areas of memory reconstruction and eyewitness inaccuracy. Her research in these areas continues.

Her findings over the years have held up quite well to challenges and have been supported by other researchers in the field.

Little doubt exists within the psychological and legal professions today that eyewitness reports are subject to many sources of error such as post-event information integration. Because of the body of research by Loftus and others, the power and reliability of eyewitnesses in judicial proceedings are now justifiably questioned. Loftus has been one of the most sought-after expert witnesses (usually for the defense) to demonstrate to juries the care they must use when evaluating the testimony of eyewitnesses.

As Loftus herself summarizes in her 1994 book, "I study memory and I am a skeptic" (Loftus & Ketcham, 1994, p. 7). Perhaps we all should be.

Carlson, C. A., Dias, J. L., Weatherford, D. R., & Carlson, M. A. (2017). An investigation of the weapon focus effect and the confidence–accuracy relationship for eyewitness identification. *Journal of Applied Research in Memory and Cognition, 6*(1), 82–92.

French, C. (2003). Fantastic memories: The relevance of research into eyewitness testimony and false memories for reports of anomalous experiences. *Journal of Con sciousness Studies, 10,* 153–174.

Garry, M., & Loftus, E. (1994). Repressed memories of childhood trauma: Could some of them be suggested? *USA Today Magazine, 122,* 82–85.

Kebbell, M. R., & Giles, D. C. (2000). Some experimental influences of lawyers' complicated questions on eyewitness confidence and accuracy. *Journal of Psychology, 134*(2), 129–139.

Loftus, E., Joslyn, S., & Polage, D. (1998). Repression: A mistaken impression? *Development and Psychopathology, 10*(4), 781–792.

Loftus, E., & Ketcham, K. (1994). *The myth of repressed memories: False memories and allegations of sexual abuse.* New York: St. Martin's Press.

Pezdek, K., & Blandon-Gitlin, I. (2005). When is an intervening line-up most likely to affect eyewitness identification accuracy? *Legal and Criminological Psychology, 10*(2), 247–263.

Smith, V., & Ellsworth, P. (1987). The social psychology of eyewitness accuracy: Leading questions and communicator expertise. *Journal of Applied Psychology, 72,* 294–300.

Spitzer, B., & Avis, J. M. (2006). Recounting graphic sexual abuse memories in therapy: The impact on women's healing. *Journal of Family Violence, 21*(3), 173–184.

Steinberg, M. (2000). The stranger in the mirror. *Psychology Today, 33,* 34.

Chapter 5
Human Development

 Learning Objectives

5.1 Determine the psychological, ethical, and cultural impacts of Harlow's attachment experiments

5.2 Analyze Piaget's influence on developmental psychology

5.3 Summarize how Kohlberg's experiments led to his theory of moral development

5.4 Explain how agency reduces anxiety

The human development branch of psychology is concerned with the complex set of developmental changes virtually everyone goes through from birth to death. It is one of the largest and most complex specialties in the behavioral sciences. Although we grow up to be unique individuals, a great deal of our development is similar and predictable and occurs according to certain relatively fixed schedules. Included among the most influential areas of research in developmental psychology are the processes of attachment or bonding between infant and mother, the development of intellectual abilities, and the changes relating to the aging process.

Some of the most famous and influential research ever conducted in psychology is discussed in this section. Harry Harlow's work with monkeys demonstrated the importance of early infant attachments in later psychological adjustment. The sweeping discoveries of Jean Piaget formed the foundation of what we know today about cognitive development; a small sample of his research is included here in detail so that you may glimpse the ingenuity of his methods and clarity of his reported findings. Next is a famous body of research by Lawrence Kohlberg focusing on how moral character develops and why some people appear to behave at a higher moral level than others. In addition, because human development is a lifelong process, a discussion of the well-known article by Ellen Langer and Judith Rodin (often referred to as "the plant study") is included to illustrate how everyone, no matter his or her stage in life, needs to feel in control of his or her own choices, activities, and destinies.

Reading 5.1: Discovering Love

Harlow, H. F. (1958). The nature of love. *American Psychologist, 13*, 673–685.

5.1 Determine the psychological, ethical, and cultural impacts of Harlow's attachment experiments

Sometimes you may think that research psychologists have gone too far. How can something such as love be studied scientifically? However you define love, you'll have to agree that it exerts a great deal of influence over human behavior. It follows then that psychologists would have to be interested in what love is, where it comes from, and how it works.

Harry Harlow (1906–1981), a developmental psychologist, is considered by many to have made the greatest contribution since Freud in studying how our early life experiences affect adulthood. Most psychologists agree that your experiences as an infant with closeness, touching, and attachment to your mother (or other primary caregiver) have an important influence on your abilities to love and be close to others later in life. If you think about it, what was your first experience with love? For most of you, it was the bond between you and your mother beginning at the moment of your birth. But what exactly was it about that connection that was so crucial? The Freudian interpretation was that it was the focus around the importance of the breasts and the instinctive oral feeding tendencies during the first year of life (Freud's *oral stage*). Later, the behavioral school countered that notion with the view that all human behavior is associated with the situation in which it occurs and its consequences. Because the mother can fill an infant's basic needs, the infant's closeness to her is constantly reinforced by the fact that she provides food and care for the infant. Consequently, the mother becomes associated in the infant's mind with pleasurable events and, therefore, this thing we call "love" develops. In both of these conceptualizations, love was seen as developing *from* other instinctive or survival needs. However, Harlow discovered that love and affection may be built-in basic needs that are just as strong as or even stronger than those of hunger or thirst.

One way to begin to uncover the components of the love between an infant and mother would be to place infants in situations where the mother does not provide for all of the infant's needs and where various components of the environment can be scientifically manipulated. According to previous theories, we should be able to prevent or change the quality and strength of the bond formed between the infant and mother by altering the mother's ability to meet the infant's primary needs. For ethical reasons, however, such research cannot be done on humans. Because Harlow had been working with rhesus monkeys for several years in his studies of learning, it was a simple process to begin his studies of love and attachment with these subjects. Biologically, rhesus monkeys are very similar to humans. Harlow also believed that the basic responses of the rhesus monkey relating to bonding and affection in infancy (such as nursing, contact, clinging, etc.) are the same for the two species. Whether such research with nonhuman subjects is ethical is addressed later in this section.

Theoretical Propositions

In Harlow's earlier studies, infant monkeys were raised carefully by humans in the laboratory so that they could receive well-balanced nutritional diets and be protected from disease more effectively than if they were raised by their monkey mothers. Harlow noticed that these infant monkeys became very attached to the cloth pads (cotton diapers) that were used to cover the bottoms of their cages. They would cling to these pads and would become extremely angry and agitated when the pads were removed for cleaning. This attachment was observed in the baby monkeys as young as 1 day old and became stronger over the monkeys' first several months of life. Apparently, as Harlow states, "The baby, human or monkey, if it is to survive, must clutch at more than a straw" (p. 675). If a baby monkey was in a cage without this soft covering, it would thrive very poorly even though it received complete nutritional and medical care. When the cloth was introduced, the infant would become healthier and seemingly content. Therefore, Harlow theorized that these infant monkeys must have some basic need for close contact with something soft and comforting in addition to primary biological needs such as hunger and thirst. To test this theory, Harlow and his associates decided to "build" different kinds of experimental, surrogate monkey mothers.

Method

The first surrogate mother they built consisted of a smooth wooden body covered in sponge rubber and terrycloth. It was equipped with a breastlike structure in the chest area that delivered milk, and the body contained a light bulb inside to give off warmth. They then constructed a different kind of surrogate mother that was less able to provide soft comfort. This mother was made of wire mesh shaped about the same as the wooden frame, so that an infant monkey could cling to it as to the cloth mother. This wire mother came equipped with a working nursing breast device and also was able to provide warmth. In other words, the wire mother was identical to the cloth mother in every way except for the ability to offer what Harlow called *contact comfort.*

These manufactured mothers were then placed in separate cubicles that were attached to the infant monkeys' living cage. Eight infant monkeys were randomly assigned to two groups. For one group, the cloth mother was equipped with the feeder (a nursing bottle) to provide milk, and for the other group, the wire mother was the milk provider. I'm sure you can already see what Harlow was testing here. He was attempting to separate the influence of feeding from the influence of contact comfort on the monkeys' behavior toward the mother. The monkeys were then placed in their cages and the amount of time they spent in direct contact with each mother was recorded for the first 5 months of their lives. The results were striking; we'll get to those shortly.

Following these preliminary studies, Harlow wanted to explore the effects of attachment and contact, comfort in greater detail. Common knowledge tells us that when children are afraid they will seek out the comfort of their mothers (or other primary caregivers). To find out how the young monkeys with the wire and cloth mothers would respond in such situations, Harlow placed in their cages objects that caused a fearful reaction, such as a wind-up-drum-playing toy bear (to a baby monkey, this bear, which is nearly as big as the monkey itself, was very frightening). The responses of the monkeys in these situations were observed and recorded carefully.

Another study Harlow developed was called the *open field test* and involved young monkeys placed in a small, unfamiliar room containing various objects such as wooden blocks, blankets, containers with lids, and a folded piece of paper. Under normal conditions, monkeys like to play with and manipulate these objects. The monkeys who were raised with both the cloth and wire mothers were placed in the room with either the cloth mother present, no mother present, or the wire mother present. The idea here was to examine the tendency of the young monkeys to adapt to and explore this strange situation with or without the presence of the mother.

Finally, Harlow wanted to find out if the attachments formed between the monkeys and their surrogate mothers would persist after periods of separation. When the monkeys reached 6 months of age and were on solid food diets, they were separated for short periods from the surrogate mother and then reunited in the open-field situation.

Results

In the original experiment, all the monkeys had access to both the cloth mother and the wire mother. For half the monkeys, the cloth mother provided the milk, and for the other half the wire mother did so. By now, you've probably guessed that the monkeys preferred the cloth mother (wouldn't *you*?), but what was so surprising was the intense strength of this preference even among those monkeys who received their milk from the wire mother. At the time of this research, the prevailing view was that fulfilling biological needs such as hunger and thirst was the primary motivator of animals' (and humans') behavior. However, in Harlow's studies, these needs appeared to exert a relatively insignificant influence on the monkeys' choice of a mother. Instead, a fundamental need for contact comfort was most significant in producing an attachment between infant and its mother. Figure 5.1.1 graphically illustrates this effect.

After the first few days of adjustment, all the monkeys, regardless of which mother had the milk, were spending nearly all their time each day on the cloth mother. Even those monkeys feeding from the wire mother would only leave the comfort of the cloth mother to nurse briefly and then return immediately to the cloth-covered surrogate.

Figure 5.1.1 Amount of time spent each day on the cloth and wire mothers.

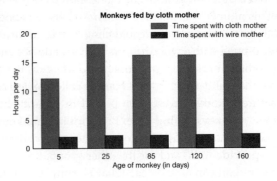

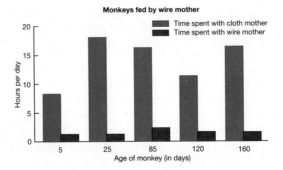

The two groups of monkeys that were raised with either a cloth or wire mother further demonstrated the importance of contact comfort. Although both groups of these infants ate the same amount and gained weight at the same rate, the infants feeding from the wire mother did not digest the milk as well and experienced frequent bouts of diarrhea. This suggests that the lack of the soft mother was psychologically stressful to these infants.

The results of the frightening object tests provided additional evidence of the young monkeys' attachment to the cloth mother. When the monkeys were faced with something frightening, they would run to the cloth mother and cling to it for comfort and protection. As the monkeys' age increased, this response became even stronger. Again, it made no difference whether a monkey had received its milk from the wire or the cloth mother; when afraid, they all sought the security of the soft, cloth-covered surrogate.

You may have noticed in humans that when children feel safe and secure because a parent is near, they are more curious and more willing to explore their environment. Often, they will investigate everything around them, provided they are still able to see the parent. Harlow's "strange-situation" and "open-field" tests were designed to simulate this behavior in the monkeys. When placed in the strange room, all the monkeys immediately rushed to the cloth mother, clutched it, rubbed their bodies against it, and manipulated its body and face. After a while these infants "began to use the mother surrogate as a source of security, a base of operations. . . . They would explore and manipulate a stimulus and then return to the mother before adventuring again into the strange new world" (p. 679).

However, when the infant monkeys were placed in the same room without the soft mother, their reactions were completely different. They would freeze with fear and engage in emotional behaviors such as crying, crouching, and thumb sucking. Sometimes they would run to the part of the room where the mother usually was and then run crying from object to object. When the wire mother was present, they behaved exactly the same as if no mother were present. This was once again true of all the monkeys, regardless of the nursing condition (cloth versus wire) in which they had been raised.

In the last part of this study, the monkeys were separated from the mother for various periods of time after they stopped nursing and were on solid food diets (at about 5 to 6 months of age). After the longest separation (30 days), when the monkeys were reunited with the cloth mother in the same open-field situation, the monkeys rushed to the mother, climbed on it, clutched it tightly, and rubbed their heads and faces on its body. They then played with the surrogate mother, which included biting and tearing at the cloth cover. The main difference was that the monkeys did not leave the mother to explore and play with the objects in the room as they had done before. Apparently, according to Harlow, the need for contact comfort was greater than the natural tendency for exploration. It should be pointed out, however, that these reunions were brief, and more exploration may have occurred if the sessions had been extended.

Discussion

As Harlow pointed out, these studies demonstrate the overwhelming importance of contact comfort in the development of the close attachment between infant monkeys and their mothers. This factor in bonding appears to be considerably more important than the mother's ability to provide life-sustaining milk to the infant.

One of the many reasons this research changed psychology is that the findings went against the grain of the popular beliefs of the behaviorists at that time who focused on the reinforcement qualities of feeding as the driving force behind the infant–mother bond. However, as Harlow stated, "the primary function of nursing as an affectional variable is that of ensuring frequent and intimate body contact of the infant with the mother. Certainly, man cannot live by milk alone" (p. 677).

Harlow and many others were convinced that his results could be applied to humans, an issue to be discussed shortly. In fact, he offered his findings' practical applications to humans. He contended that as socioeconomic demands on the family increased, women would begin to enter the workplace with increasing frequency. This was of concern to many at the time of Harlow's research because it was widely believed that the mother's presence and nursing were necessary for attachment and proper child development. He went on to state that, because the key to successful parenting is contact comfort and not the "mammary capabilities" of women, a man is capable of participating equally in the rearing of infants. This view may be generally accepted today, but when Harlow wrote this article in 1958, it was revolutionary.

Criticisms and Significance of the Findings

Harlow's claims notwithstanding, do you think it is appropriate to view humans as having the same attachment (or "love") processes as monkeys? Some research supports the view that the attachment of human babies to their caregivers does indeed go well beyond simply fulfilling biological needs. Studies have shown that greater skin-to-skin contact between a mother and her very young infant enhances attachment (e.g., Klaus & Kennell, 1976). However, the attachment process develops more slowly in humans: over the first 6 months compared with the first few days for monkeys. In addition, only approximately 70% of children appear to be securely attached to an adult caregiver at 1 year of age (Sroufe, 1985).

Many people, past and present, would criticize Harlow's work because of the ethics of performing such experiments on infant monkeys. The question raised is this: Do we as humans have the right to subject monkeys (or any animal) to potentially harmful situations for the sake of research? In the case of Harlow's research, rational arguments may be found on both sides of this issue. One of the ways science judges the ethics of research is by examining the potential benefits to people and society. Whether you feel that this study was ethical or not, the findings have affected humans in several positive ways. Some of these relate to institutionalized children, adoption, and child abuse.

Unfortunately, many children are forced to spend portions of their lives in institutional settings, either because their parents are unable to keep and care for them (orphanages) or because of various illnesses and other physical difficulties (hospital settings). Harlow's research has influenced the kind of care we try to provide for these children. Virtually all child development professionals accept that basic biological care in institutional settings is inadequate and that infants need physical contact with other humans. Institutionalized children need to be touched and held by staff members, nurses, and volunteers as much as possible. Also, when not precluded by medical conditions, these children are often placed in situations where they can see and touch each other, thereby gaining additional contact comfort. Although such attempts at filling attachment needs will never replace real loving parental care, they are clearly a vast improvement over simple custodial supervision.

In addition, Harlow's work has offered encouragement and optimism that nonmaternal caregivers are perfectly able to be effective parents. Because it appeared that nursing was secondary to contact comfort in the development and adjustment of infants, the actual mother of a child was no longer seen as the only person who could provide care. Now many fathers feel more comfortable assuming larger roles in the parenting process. But beyond this, other nonparental caregivers, such as babysitters or day-care-center workers, when necessary, can be acceptable options. Moreover, these discoveries greatly enhanced views about adoption because society began to recognize that an adoptive parent could offer a child just as much contact comfort as a biological parent.

Harlow's early studies shed light on the terrible problem of child abuse. One surprising aspect of such abusive relationships is that the abused child seems to love, and to be firmly attached, to the abusive parent in nearly all cases. According to a strict behaviorist interpretation, this is difficult to understand because the abuse should be perceived as punishment and the child should withdraw from any attachment. But if the attachment itself is our strongest basic need, as Harlow suggested, then this would far outweigh the effects of the abuse. Harlow actually tested this in later studies. He designed surrogate mother monkeys that were able to reject their infants. Some emitted strong jets of air, while others had blunt spikes that would pop out and force the baby monkeys away. The way the monkeys would respond to this treatment would be to move a small distance away until the rejection ended. They would then return and cling to the mother as tightly as ever (Rosenblum & Harlow, 1963).

Recent Applications

Harlow's research continues to be cited frequently in studies about touch, bonding, attachment, and the effects of human contact on humans' emotional and physical health. One such study examined the connection between social isolation (the lack of opportunities for close, meaningful, social contact with others) and physical health among adults who lived lonely lives (Cacioppo & Hawkley, 2003). Findings indicated that adults lacking in social contact experienced common, everyday life events as more stressful, were at greater risk of high blood pressure, healed from injuries more slowly, and slept more poorly than people whose lives contained healthy social connections.

Another study citing Harlow's work attempted the difficult task of understanding the concept of love, something psychologists have been working on for half a century (Berscheid, 2010). In this article, the author identified and described four distinct types of love: *romantic love, companionate love, compassionate love,* and *adult attachment love.*

Romantic love is characterized by passion, sexual attraction, psychological excitement, and physiological arousal. Companionate love is love that is felt deeply, but is more defined by a close, intimate friendship, accompanied by comfort, affection, and trust, accompanied by the enjoyment of interests and activities in common. Compassionate love has been defined by various researchers as a caring, giving, selfless love—focusing on caring, concern, and tenderness for another and overlooking his or her shortcomings (see also Sternberg, 1986). The fourth conceptualization of love, adult attachment love is based on the principle that love is based on a deep psychological attachment to another person who is viewed as unique and irreplaceable. This kind of love reveals great distress when forced to be separated and great grief if the separation is permanent.

Many psychologists have studied love over the decades, largely in response to Harlow's lead, because love is such a powerful force in how humans behave—probably at least as powerful as its opposite: hatred. But love, unfortunately been studied less.

Harlow's ideas have also been applied to psychotherapeutic settings. As humanistic and holistic approaches to counseling have developed over the past 40 years, the healing qualities of touch have played an increasingly central role. As one psychotherapist explains,

> I have found that when touch is focused and intentioned, particularly in touch therapies such as acupressure and therapeutic touch, it becomes an important aspect in the therapeutic interaction. It deepens awareness and supports change. Rather than creating confusion, touch therapies when used appropriately enhance the psychotherapeutic interaction instead of detracting from it. The key word here is *appropriate*. Touch is a very powerful tool and should not be used lightly. (LaTorre, 2000, p. 105)

Conclusion

It would be a mistake to assume that Harlow had a monopoly on the definition of "love." It is unmistakable, however, that his discoveries changed the way we view the connections between infant and mother. Perhaps, if this research has permeated, even a little, into society, some good has come from it. One small example indicating that this has happened is a story Harlow told in his own words about a woman who, after hearing Harlow present his research, came up to him and said, "Now I know what's wrong with me! I'm just a wire mother" (p. 677).

Berscheid, E. (2010). Love in the fourth dimension. *Annual Review of Psychology, 61,* 1–25.

Cacioppo, J., & Hawkley, L. (2003). Social isolation and health with an emphasis on underlying mechanisms. *Perspectives in Biology and Medicine, 46,* S39–S52.

Klaus, M. H., & Kennell, J. H. (1976). *Maternal infant bonding.* St. Louis, MO: Mosby.

LaTorre M. (2000). Integrative perspectives. Touch and psychotherapy. *Perspectives in Psychiatric Care, 36,* 105–106.

Rosenblum, L. A., & Harlow, H. (1963). Approach-avoidance conflict in the mother surrogate situation. *Psychological Reports, 12,* 83–85.

Sroufe, A. (1985). Attachment classification from the perspective of the infant-caregiver relationships and infant temperament. *Child Development, 56,* 1–14.

Sternberg, R. (1986). A triangular theory of love. *Psychological Review, 93,* 119–135.

Reading 5.2: Out of Sight, But *Not* Out of Mind

Piaget, J. (1954). The development of object concept. In J. Piaget, *The construction of reality in the child* (pp. 3–96). New York: Basic Books.

5.2   Analyze Piaget's influence on developmental psychology

How did you develop from an infant, with a few elementary thinking skills, to the adult you are now, with the ability to reason and analyze the world in many complex ways involving language, symbols, and logic? Your first reaction to this question may very likely be to say, "Well, I *learned* how to think from my experiences and from the teaching I received from adults throughout my life."

Although this explanation seems intuitively correct to most people, developmental psychologists believe that much more is involved in acquiring intellectual abilities than just learning. Intellectual development—the growth of our ability to think and know—is a process of maturation of our brains, much like the physical development of our bodies that occurs in a fairly predictable step-by-step fashion from birth through adulthood.

Do you look at an infant and see a person who, with enough learning, is capable of adult *physical* behaviors? Of course not. Instead, you know that the child's behavior will become increasingly complex over time through a process of physical maturation. You know that until the child achieves a certain level of development, all the learning in the world cannot produce certain behaviors. For example, consider the behavior of walking. You probably think of walking as a *learned* behavior. But imagine trying to teach a 6-month-old to walk. You could place the infant on an Olympic-level schedule of 8 hours of practice every day, but the child will not learn to walk. Why? Because the child has not yet reached the physical (or mental) maturity to perform the behaviors needed to walk.

Intellectual, or cognitive, development occurs in much the same way. Children simply cannot demonstrate certain thinking and reasoning abilities until they reach an appropriate level of cognitive (brain) development, no matter how much learning they may have experienced. Psychology owes much of its understanding of this conceptualization of cognitive development in to the work of one man: Swiss psychologist Jean Piaget (1896–1980).

Piaget is one of the most influential figures in the history of psychology. His work not only revolutionized developmental psychology but also formed the foundation for most subsequent investigations in the area of the formation of the intellect. Piaget was originally trained as a biologist and studied the inborn ability of animals to adapt to new environments. While Piaget was studying at the Sorbonne in Paris, he accepted a job (to earn extra money) at the Alfred Binet Laboratory, where the first human intelligence tests were being developed. He was hired to standardize a French version of a reasoning test that originally had been developed in English. It was during his employment in Paris that Piaget began to formulate his theories about cognitive development in children.

Theoretical Propositions

The work at the Binet Laboratory was tedious and not very interesting to Piaget at first. Then he began to detect some interesting patterns in the answers given by children at various ages to the questions on the test. Children at similar ages appeared to be making the same mistakes regardless of their individual experiences in life. That is, they appeared to be using similar reasoning strategies to reach similar answers. What fascinated Piaget were not the correct answers but the thinking processes that produced the similar *wrong* answers. Based on his observations, he theorized that older children had not just learned more than the younger ones but were *thinking differently* about the problems. This led him to question the prevailing definition of intelligence at the time (the IQ score), in favor of a model that involved a more complete understanding of the cognitive strategies used in common by children at various ages (Ginzburg & Opper, 1979).

Piaget devoted the next 50 years of his life and career to studying intellectual development in children. His work led to his famous theory of cognitive development, which for decades was a widely accepted explanation of how humans acquire their complex thinking skills. His theory holds that during childhood, humans progress through four stages of cognitive development that always occur in the same sequence and at approximately the same ages. These are summarized in Table 5.2.1.

Table 5.2.1 Piaget's Stages of Cognitive Development

Stage	Age Range	Major Characteristics
Sensorimotor	0–2 years	• All knowledge is acquired through senses and movement (such as looking and grasping). • Thinking is at the same speed as physical movement. • Object permanence develops.
Preoperational	2–7 years	• Thinking separates from movement and increases greatly in speed. • Ability to think in symbols develops. • Nonlogical, "magical" thinking occurs. • All objects have thoughts and feelings (animism). • Egocentric thinking (unable to see world from others' points of view) develops.
Concrete operations	7–11 years	• Logical thinking develops, including classifying objects and mathematical principles, but only as they apply to real, concrete objects. • Understanding of conservation of liquid, area, and volume develops. • Ability develops to infer what others may be feeling or thinking.
Formal operations	11 and up	• Logical thinking extends to hypothetical and abstract concepts. • Ability forms to reason using metaphors and analogies. • Ability forms to explore values, beliefs, and philosophies. • Ability forms to think about past and future. • Not everyone uses formal operations to the same degree, and some not at all.

Perhaps as important as his theory were the techniques Piaget used to study thinking abilities in children. At the Binet Laboratory, he realized that if he was to explore his new conceptualization of intelligence, he would also need to develop the methods to do so. Instead of the usual rigid, standardized intelligence tests, he proposed an interview technique that allowed the child's answers to influence the direction of the questioning. In this way, he would be able to explore the processes underlying the child's reasoning.

One of the most remarkable aspects of Piaget's research is that in reaching many of his conclusions, he studied his *own* children: Lucienne, Jacqueline, and Laurent. By today's scientific standards, this method would be highly suspect because of the rather likely possibility of bias and lack of objectivity. However, as rules always have exceptions, it turned out that Piaget's findings from his children could be applied quite well to all children, universally.

A single chapter in this text is far too little space to explore more than a small fraction of Piaget's work. Therefore, we will focus on his discovery of one key intellectual ability, *object permanence.* The cognitive skill of object permanence provides an excellent example of one of Piaget's most important findings, as well as ample opportunity to experience his methods of research.

Object permanence refers to your ability to know that an object exists even when it is hidden from your senses. If someone walks over to you now and takes this book out of your hands and runs into the next room, do you think that the book or the book snatcher has ceased to exist? Of course not. You have a *concept* of the book and of the person in your mind, even though you cannot see, hear, or touch him or her. However, according to Piaget, this was not always true for you. He demonstrated that your cognitive ability to conceive of objects as permanent and unchanging was something you, and everyone else, developed during your first 2 years of life. The reason this ability is of importance is that problem-solving and internal thinking are impossible without it. Therefore, before a child can leave the sensorimotor stage (0 to 2 years; see Table 5.2.1) and enter the preoperational period (2 to 7 years), object permanence *must* develop.

Method and Results

Piaget studied the development of object permanence using *unstructured evaluation methods:* Because infants cannot exactly be "interviewed," these techniques often took the form of games he would play with his children. Through observing problem-solving ability and the errors the infants made playing the games, Piaget identified six *substages* of development that occur during the sensorimotor period and that are involved in the formation of object permanence. For you to experience the flavor of his research, these six stages are summarized here with examples of Piaget's interactions with his children quoted from his actual observational journals:

- *STAGE 1 (Birth to 1 month).* This stage is concerned primarily with *reflexes* relating to feeding and touching. No evidence of object permanence is seen during this first month of life.

- *STAGE 2 (1 to 4 months).* During Stage 2, although no sign of an object concept is found, Piaget interprets some behaviors as preparing the infant for this ability. The child begins to repeat, on purpose, certain behaviors that center on the infant's own body. For example, if an infant's hand accidentally comes in contact with its foot, the child will "think," "Oh! That was interesting . . . let me see if I can do that again." [note: a baby does not really *think* that, but that's how it seems] So, it might reproduce the same movements over and over again to cause the event to be repeated. Piaget called these *primary circular reactions*. Also, at this stage, infants are able to follow moving objects with their eyes. If an object leaves the child's visual field and fails to reappear, the child will turn its attention to other visible objects and show no signs of looking for the "vanished" object. However, if the object repeatedly reappears in the same location, the infant will look longer at that point. Piaget called this behavior *passive expectation*. The following interaction between Piaget and his son, Laurent, illustrates this:

    > Observation 2. Laurent at 0;2 [0 years, 2 months]. Piaget looks at the child through the hood of his bassinet and every once in a while and disappears and then reappears at about the same location. The baby stares at the point Piaget leaves his sight obviously expecting him to reappear at approximately the same location. Remember this is only at 2 months of age.
    >
    > Each time, Laurent keeps his focus on the place where Piaget vanished. But if nothing reappears, the child gives up his focus quite readily. This demonstrates that the child does not yet possess the object concept because if he did, he would actively look for where Piaget went. But, in the child's mind, his father (or anything) is not yet established as a permanent object and when he disappears the child believes (according to Piaget) that he reentered the void when he vanishes and then suddenly emerges from it once again.

- *STAGE 3 (4 to 10 months).* During this stage, children begin to purposefully and repeatedly manipulate objects they encounter in their environment (called *secondary circular reactions*). The child begins to reach for and grasp things, to shake them, bring them closer to look at them or place them in the mouth, and to acquire the ability of rapid eye movements to follow quickly moving or falling objects. Late in this stage, the first signs of object permanence appear. For example, children begin to search for objects that are obscured from view if a small part of the object is visible.

    > Observation 23. At 0;9.
    > Here, Piaget hands Lucienne a plastic goose, which is a new object to her. She takes it and looks at it carefully. Piaget then covers the goose next to her either with it completely covered or with just its head showing. Two very clear and different responses were observed. When he covers the goose completely, Lucienne behaves as if the goose is simply gone (it has entered the void). However, when a part of the head, even just the beak is showing, she reaches for it and pulls it toward her or even raises the coverlet to reveal the entire object. She never does this with the goose is completely covered.

She does not search for it when it is out of her sight. Piaget explained this as proof that her ability to *reconstruct* the entire object in her mind is far easier that "knowing" that the object exists under the coverlet.

Still, however, Piaget maintains that the object concept is not fully formed. To the child at this stage, the object does not have an *independent* existence but is tied to the child's own actions and sensory perceptions. In other words, Piaget did not believe that the child perceives half the partially hidden object, but that it is *in the process* of disappearing.

- *STAGE 4 (10 to 12 months).* In the later weeks of Stage 3 and early in Stage 4, children have acquired the ability to know that objects continue to exist even when the objects are no longer visible. A child will search actively and creatively for an object that has been completely hidden from view. Although on the surface this may seem to indicate a fully developed object concept, Piaget found that this cognitive skill is still incomplete because the child lacks the ability to understand *visible displacements.* To understand what Piaget meant by this, consider the following example (with the parent's consent, you can try these yourself the next time you are around baby around 1 year old— it's OK, they enjoy the game). If you sit with an 11-month-old and hide a toy completely under a towel (call this place A), the child will search for and find it. However, if you then hide the toy, as the child watches, under a blanket (place B), the child will probably go back to searching for it where it was previously found, in place A. Furthermore, you can repeat this process over and over and the child will continue to make the same error, which Piaget called the *A-not-B effect.*

> Observation 40. At 0;10. In this observation, Jacqueline is sitting on a mattress playing with her toy parrot. Piaget takes the parrot from her and, right in front of her, as she watches, hides it twice under the mattress in what he called "place A" on the left. Jacqueline immediately looks for the parrot and retrieves it. Then he takes the parrot and hides in "place B" under the right side of the mattress, again, as she watches. As soon as the parrot is hidden, she looks for it. But not where it is now hidden, but in place A on the right, where it was before.

Piaget's interpretation of this error in Stage 4 was not that children are absent-minded but that the object concept is not the same for them as it is for you or me. To 10-month-old Jacqueline, her parrot is not a permanent, separate thing that exists independently of her actions. When it was hidden and then successfully found in A, it became a "parrot-in-A," a thing that was defined not only by its "parrotness" but also by its hiding place. In other words, the parrot is just a piece of the overall picture in the child's mind and not a separate object.

- *STAGE 5 (12 to 18 months).* Beginning around the end of the first year of life, the child gains the ability to follow visible sequential displacements and searches for an object where it was last visibly hidden. When this happens, Piaget claimed that the child had entered Stage 5 of the sensorimotor period.

> Observation 54. Laurent, at 0;11, is seated between two cushions, A and B. Piaget hides a watch under cushion A or cushion B and Laurent searches for it in the place where it was hidden each time. So now, the object is not "attached" to a specific place.

However, Piaget points out that true object permanence remains incomplete because the child is unable to understand what he called *invisible displacements.* Imagine the following example: You watch someone place a coin in a small box and then, with his or her back to you, the person walks over to the dresser and opens a drawer. When the person returns, you discover that the box is empty. This is an invisible displacement of the object because you could not see where it was placed but you know, logically, it's in the drawer (unless the person is purposely trying to trick you). Naturally, you would go to the dresser and look in the drawer. Piaget and Jacqueline demonstrated this as follows.

> Observation 55. At 1;6. Now, at a year-and-a-half, Jacqueline is playing with a potato, an object that is new to her and with which she is fascinated. She's putting the potato in an empty box and taking it out again repeatedly. Piaget takes the potato, places it in the box, and moves the box under the rug, all while she watches. But then, out of her field of vision, he flips the box over and pulls out an empty box for her to see. Then he says to her, "Give Papa the potato." She looks for the object in the box, looks at him, looks carefully in the box again, looks at the rug, but does not think to lift the rug to look for the object. This same sequence of events happened five times in succession. This was an invisible displacement because the child could not watch the potato being moved out of the box.

- *STAGE 6 (18 to 24 months).* As the child approaches the end of the sensorimotor period (refer back to Table 5.2.1), the concept of the permanent object becomes fully realized. Entry into this stage is determined by the child's ability to represent mentally objects that undergo invisible displacements.

> Observation 66. At 1;7. Only one month later, Piaget finds that Jacqueline has full object permanence. In this observation, he places a pencil in a box, wraps a piece of paper around it, then wraps a handkerchief around that, and finally covers all of this with a beret and a coverlet. Jacqueline removes the handkerchief and the beret, unwraps the handkerchief, sees the paper, unwraps it, opens the box, and finds the pencil!

Discussion

Piaget considered the cognitive skill of object permanence to be the beginning of true thought: the ability to use insight and mental symbolism to solve problems. This, then, prepares the child to move into the next full stage of cognitive development: the *pre-operational period*, during which thought separates from action, allowing the speed of mental operations to increase greatly. In other words, object permanence is the foundation for all subsequent advances in intellectual ability. As Piaget stated,

> The conservation of the object is, among other things, a function of its localization; that is, the child simultaneously learns that the object does not cease to exist when it disappears and he learns where it does go. This fact shows from the outset that the formation of the schema of the permanent object is closely related to the whole spatio-temporal and causal organization of the practical universe. (Piaget & Inhelder, 1969)

This method of exercises and observation of behavior formed the basis of Piaget's work throughout his formulation of all four stages of cognitive development. Piaget contended that all of his stages applied universally to *all* children, regardless of cultural or family background. In addition, he stressed several important aspects relating to the stages of development of the object concept during the sensorimotor period (see Ginzburg & Opper, 1979, for an elaboration of these points).

1. The ages associated with each stage are approximate. Because Piaget's early work only involved three children, it was difficult for him to predict age ranges with a great deal of confidence. For example, certain abilities he observed in Jacqueline at age 1;7 were present in Lucienne at 1;3.

2. Piaget maintained, however, that the sequence of the stages was invariant. All children must pass through each stage before going on to the next, and no stage can ever be skipped.

3. Changes from one stage to the next occur gradually over time so that the errors being made at one stage slowly begin to decrease as new intellectual abilities mature. Piaget believed that it is quite common and normal for children to be between stages and exhibit abilities from earlier and later stages at the same time.

4. As a child moves into the next higher stage, the behaviors associated with the lower stages do not necessarily disappear completely. It would not be unusual for a child in Stage 6 to apply intellectual strategies used in Stage 5. Then when these prove unsuccessful, the child will invoke new methods for solving the problem typical of Stage 6 reasoning.

Criticisms and Recent Applications

Although Piaget's conceptualization of cognitive development dominated the field of developmental psychology for several decades, his view has certainly not been without critics. Some of them have questioned Piaget's basic notion that cognitive development happens in discrete stages. Many learning theorists have disagreed with Piaget on this issue and contend that intellectual development is continuous, without any particular sequence built into the process. They believe that cognitive abilities, like all other behaviors, are a result of modeling and a person's learning and conditioning history.

Other critics of Piaget's ideas have claimed that the age ranges at which he asserted specific abilities appear are incorrect, and some even argue that certain cognitive skills may already be present at birth. Object permanence is one of those abilities that has been drawn into question. In a series of ingenious studies using research techniques known as *preference looking* (see Reading 2.1 on Fantz's discovery of this research methodology), developmental psychologist Renee Baillargeon and her associates have demonstrated that infants as young as 2½ months of age appear to possess early forms of object permanence (Aguilar & Baillargeon, 1999; Baillargeon, 1987). She and others have asserted that Piaget's methods were inadequate to measure accurately the abilities of very young infants because they required motor skills that infants do not possess.

Piaget's concepts and discoveries have influenced research in a wide variety of fields. This is evidenced by the fact that more than 50 scientific articles each year cite the book by Piaget that forms the basis for this discussion. For example, one study compared 6½-month-old infants' tendency to search for objects hidden by darkness to their tendency to search for objects hidden under a cloth in the light, as in Piaget's games with his children (Shinskey & Munakata, 2003). Interestingly, the researchers found that the infants were better at looking for objects in the dark compared to searching for them when the objects were covered by a cloth in the light. Why would this be true? One explanation may be that the appearance of the cloth interferes with the infants' new, fragile ability to represent the object mentally. An alternate explanation may be that our ability to think about, and search for, objects in (potentially dangerous) darkness was more adaptive from an evolutionary, survival perspective than doing so when items are merely hidden in the light.

Another fascinating study relating to Piaget's work found an association between infants' ability to differentiate among objects and their comprehension of the words for the objects (Rivera & Zawaydeh, 2007). Using preference-looking techniques, this study revealed that infants at only 10 or 11 months of age were able to differentiate between objects only if they understood the words for both objects. The authors propose that "These results suggest that comprehending the words for occluded/disoccluded [hidden and revealed] objects provides a kind of 'glue' which allows infants to bind the mental index of an object with its perceptual features (thus precipitating the formation of two mental indexes, rather than one)" (p. 146). That is, knowing the names for objects appears to help infants mentally store an image of an object as unique and recognizable in comparison with other objects.

An intriguing study citing Piaget's work on object permanence found an association between development of the object concept and sleep in 9-month-old infants (Scher, Amir, & Tirosh, 2000). These findings indicated that infants with a more advanced grasp of object permanence experienced significantly fewer sleep difficulties than those with lower levels of the object concept. This may make a certain intuitive sense, if you think about it. If you were not sure all your stuff would still exist in the morning, you probably wouldn't sleep very well either!

Conclusion

As methods have been refined for studying infants' cognitive abilities, such as preference-looking and habituation-dishabituation techniques, some of Piaget's discoveries are being drawn into question (for more information about these research methods, see Reading 2.1 on Fantz in this book; also, Craig & Dunn, 2007). In fact, numerous ongoing controversies surrounding Piaget's theory of cognitive development are swirling through the field of developmental psychology. Such controversy is healthy; it motivates discussion and research that will eventually lead to even greater understanding and knowledge about the sources and growth of human cognition.

Controversy notwithstanding, Piaget's theory remains the catalyst and foundation for all related research. His work continues to guide enlightened people's ideas about research with children, methods of education, and styles of parenting. Piaget's contribution was and is immeasurable.

Finally, lest we overestimate our special status in the animal kingdom, research has shown that object permanence can be demonstrated in *dogs* Zentall & Pattison, 2016). They are quite skilled at visible displacement tasks, not bad at invisible displacement tasks and demonstrate looking-time skills similar to those described in the study by Fantz (Number 5).

Aguilar, A., & Baillargeon, R. (1999). 2.5-month-old infants' reasoning about when objects should and should not be occluded. *Cognitive Psychology, 39*(2), 116–157.

Baillargeon, R. (1987). Object permanence in 3½- and 4½-month-old infants. *Developmental Psychology, 23,* 655–664.

Craig, G., & Dunn, W. (2007). *Understanding human development.* Upper Saddle River, NJ: Pearson Education/Prentice Hall.

Ginzburg, H., & Opper, S. (1979). *Piaget's theory of intellectual development.* Englewood Cliffs, NJ: Prentice Hall.

Piaget, J., & Inhelder, B. (1969). *The psychology of the child.* New York: Basic Books.

Rivera, S., & Zawaydeh, A. N. (2007). Word comprehension facilitates object individuation in 10- and 11-month-old infants. *Brain Research, 1146,* 146–157.

Scher, A., Amir, T., & Tirosh, E. (2000). Object concept and sleep regulation. *Perceptual and Motor Skills, 91*(2), 402–404.

Shinskey, J., & Munakata, Y. (2003). Are infants in the dark about hidden objects? *Developmental Science, 6,* 273–282.

Zentall, T. R., & Pattison, K. F. (2016). Now You See It, Now You Don't: Object Permanence in Dogs. *Current Directions in Psychological Science, 25*(5), 357–362.

Reading 5.3: How Moral are You?

Kohlberg, L. (1963). The development of children's orientations toward a moral order: Sequence in the development of moral thought. *Vita Humana, 6,* 11–33.

5.3 Summarize how Kohlberg's experiments led to his theory of moral development

Have you ever really thought about how moral you are compared to others? What are the moral principles guiding your decisions in life? Experience should tell you that people's level and type of morality varies a great deal. Psychologists generally define morals as those attitudes and beliefs that help people decide the difference between and degrees of right and wrong. Your concept of morality is determined by the rules and norms of conduct that are set forth by your parents, the culture in which you have been raised, and that have been internalized by you. Morality is not part of your standard equipment at birth: You were born without morals. As you developed through childhood into adolescence and adulthood, your ideas about right and wrong developed along with you. Every normal adult has a personal conception of morality. But where did your morality originate? How did it go from a set of cultural rules to part of who you are?

Probably the two most famous and influential figures in the history of research on the formation of morality were Jean Piaget (discussed in Reading 5.2) and Lawrence Kohlberg (1927–1987). Kohlberg's research at the University of Chicago incorporated and expanded upon many of Piaget's ideas about intellectual development and sparked a new wave of interest in this topic of study. Kohlberg was addressing this question: "How does the amoral infant become capable of moral reasoning?"

Using the work of Piaget as a starting point, Kohlberg theorized that the uniquely human ability to make moral judgments develops in a predictable way during childhood. He believed that specific, identifiable *stages* of moral development are related and similar in concept to Piaget's stages of intellectual development. As Kohlberg explained, "The child can internalize the moral values of his parents and culture and make them his own only as he comes to relate these values to a comprehended social order and to his own goals as a social self" (Kohlberg, 1964). In other words, a child must reach a certain stage of intellectual ability in order to develop a certain level of morality.

With these ideas in mind, Kohlberg set about formulating a method for studying children's abilities to make moral judgments. From that research, grew his widely recognized theory of moral development.

Theoretical Propositions

When Kohlberg asserted that morality is acquired in developmental stages, he was using the concept of *stage* in a precise and formal way. It is easy to think of nearly any ability as occurring in stages, but psychologists draw a clear distinction between changes that develop gradually, over time (such as a person's height) and those that develop in distinct and separate stages. So when Kohlberg referred to "structural moral stages in childhood and adolescence," he meant that (a) each stage is a uniquely different kind of moral thinking and not just an increased understanding of an adult concept of morality; (b) the stages always occur in the same step-by-step sequence so that no stage is ever skipped and there is rarely any backward progression; and (c) the stages are *prepotent*, meaning that children comprehend all the stages below their own and perhaps have some understanding of no more than one stage above. Children are incapable of understanding higher stages, regardless of encouragement, teaching, or learning (this understanding *develops* during childhood, it is not primarily learned). Furthermore, children tend to make decisions about what is right or wrong at the highest moral stage they have reached. Also implied in this stage formulation of moral development is the notion that the stages are universal and occur in the same order, regardless of individual differences in environment, experience, or culture.

Kohlberg believed that his theory of the formation of morality could be explored by giving children at various ages the opportunity to make moral judgments. If the reasoning they used to make moral decisions could be found to progress predictably at increasing ages, this would be evidence that his stage theory was essentially correct.

Method

Kohlberg's research methodology was really quite simple. He presented children of varying ages with 10 hypothetical moral dilemmas. Each child was interviewed for

2 hours and asked questions about the moral issues presented in the dilemmas. The interviews were tape-recorded for later analysis of the moral reasoning used. Two of Kohlberg's most widely cited moral dilemmas were as follows:

> *The Brother's Dilemma.* In this moral dilemma, Joe's father made a deal that Joe could go to camp if Joe worked and earned the $50 to pay for it. As the date of the camp arrived, Joe's father changed his mind and asked Joe for the money he had earned. Joe told his father he had only earned $10 and used the remaining $40 to go to the camp. Before he left for camp, he told his brother, Alex the story about the money and that he had lied to his father. The question was: should Alex tell this to the father?
>
> *The Heinz Dilemma* In this dilemma, Heinz's wife was dying of cancer and had only a short time to live. A new drug had been developed by a local pharmacist that might be able to save her. However, the drug was too expensive for Heinz to afford to purchase it. Heinz knew it cost the pharmacist $200 to make the drug, but he was selling it for $2000 for a small dose. Heinz tried to borrow the money for the drug, but could only gather about $1000. He explained his situation to the pharmacist, but the pharmacist refused to lower the price. Fearing for his wife's health, in desperation, Heinz broke into the pharmacy and stole the drug for his wife. The dilemma here was: Should Heinz have done this?

The participants in Kohlberg's original study were 72 boys living in the Chicago suburbs. The boys were in three different age groups: 10, 13, and 16 years. Half of each group of boys were from lower-middle-class socioeconomic brackets; the other half were from upper-middle-class brackets. During the course of the 2 hour interviews, the children expressed between 50 and 150 moral ideas or statements.

Following are four examples Kohlberg found, of responses made by children of different ages to these dilemmas:

> *Danny, age 10, The Brother's Dilemma.* Danny, at age 10 thought it might be OK for Alex to tell his father or the father might get mad at him (Alex) and spank him. But maybe it would be right not to tell because his brother (Joe) might beat him up.
>
> *Don, age 13, The Heinz Dilemma.* Don expressed that it was really the pharmacist's fault for being so unfair, overcharging, and letting someone die. It was a crime to break in, but Heinz cared so much for his wife and would do anything to save her. He would probably not go to jail because the judge would see that the pharmacist was charging too much for the drug.
>
> *Andy, age 13, The Brother's Dilemma.* Andy felt it was wrong because the father would never trust Alex again and his brother would not either. But he did not think it would be so bad if the brother didn't trust him.
>
> *George, age 16, The Heinz Dilemma.* George felt it was wrong to break in because the pharmacist had the right to set the price for the drug. But, anyone would do that to save his wife. Heinz would probably rather go to jail than for his wife to die. George felt that there was just cause for Joe to do it, but by law Joe would be wrong.

Based on such statements, Kohlberg and his associates defined six stages of moral development and assigned various statements to one of the six stages. In addition, six types of motives were used to justify the boys' reasoning, which corresponded to the six stages. It should be noted that each of the six stages of moral reasoning delineated by Kohlberg was intended to apply universally to any situation the child might encounter. The stages do not predict a specific action a child might take when faced with a real dilemma, but rather the *reasoning* the child would use in determining a course of action.

Results

Kohlberg grouped the six stages he had found into three moral levels, each with distinct stages as outlined in Table 5.3.1. The early stages of morality, which Kohlberg called

Table 5.3.1 Kohlberg's Six Stages of Moral Development

LEVEL 1. PREMORAL LEVEL

Stage 1.	Punishment and obedience orientation (Consequences for actions determine right and wrong.)
Stage 2.	Naive instrumental hedonism (Satisfaction of one's own needs defines what is good.)

LEVEL 2. MORALITY OF CONVENTIONAL ROLE CONFORMITY

Stage 3.	"Good boy–nice girl" orientation (What pleases others is good.)
Stage 4.	Authority maintaining morality (Maintaining law and order, doing one's duty are good.)

LEVEL 3. MORALITY OF SELF-ACCEPTED MORAL PRINCIPLES

Stage 5.	Morality of agreements and democratically determined law (Society's values and individual rights determine right and wrong.)
Stage 6.	Morality of individual principles of conscience (Right and wrong are matters of individual philosophy according to universal principles.)

(Based on data from p. 13.)

*Kohlberg notes that the data for this group of 7-year-old boys were acquired from an additional group of 12. (Figures based on data on p. 15.)

the "premoral" level, are characterized by egocentrism and personal interests. In Stage 1, the child fails to recognize the interests of others and behaves morally out of fear of punishment for *bad* behavior. In Stage 2, the child begins to recognize the interests and needs of others but behaves morally to get moral behavior back. Good behavior is, in essence, a manipulation of a situation to meet the child's own needs.

In Level 2, conventional morality that is a part of recognizing one's role in inter-personal relationships comes into play. In Stage 3, the child behaves morally in order to live up to the expectations of others and to maintain trust and loyalty in relationships. It is during this stage, according to Kohlberg, that "golden rule thinking" begins and the child becomes concerned about the feelings of others (similar to Piaget's notion of overcoming egocentric thinking). Stage 4 begins with the child's recognition of and respect for law and order. Here, an individual takes the viewpoint of the larger social system and sees good behavior in terms of being a law-abiding citizen. There is no questioning of the established social order but rather the belief that whatever upholds the law is good.

When a person enters Level 3, judgments about morality begin to transcend formal societal laws. In Stage 5, the child recognizes that some laws are better than others. Sometimes *what is moral may not be legal, and vice versa.* The individual still believes that laws should be obeyed to maintain social harmony but may seek to change laws through due process. At this stage, Kohlberg maintained, a person will experience con-flict in attempting to integrate morality with legality.

If a person reaches morality Stage 6 (*and not everyone does*), moral judgments will be based upon a belief in *universal* ethical principles. When laws violate these principles, the person behaves according to these ethical principles, regardless of the law. Moral-ity is determined by the individual's own conscience. Kohlberg was to find in this and later studies that very few individuals actually reach Stage 6. He eventually ascribed this level of reasoning to great leaders of conscience, such as Gandhi, Thoreau, and Martin Luther King, Jr.

Kohlberg claimed that there are six forces that drive or motivate a person's morality and vary with a person's developmental stage of morality:

1. Punishment by another;

2. Manipulation of goods or rewards by another;

3. Disapproval by others;

4. Censure by legitimate authorities followed by feelings of guilt;

Figure 5.3.1 Stages of moral reasoning by age.

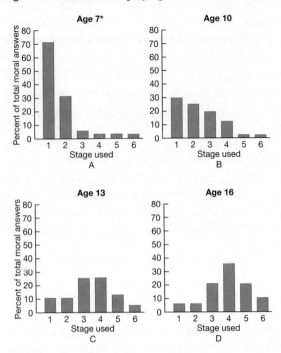

5. Community respect and disrespect;

6. Self-condemnation.

It was crucial to Kohlberg's stage theory that the different levels of moral reasoning are seen to advance with the age of a normally developing person. To test this idea, he analyzed the various stages corresponding to the children's answers according to the ages of the children. Figure 5.3.1 summarizes these findings: As the age of the subjects increased, the children used increasingly higher stages of moral reasoning to respond to the dilemmas. Other statistical analyses demonstrated that the ability to use each stage appeared to be a prerequisite to moving to the next higher level.

Discussion

In Kohlberg's discussion of the implications of his findings, he pointed out that this new conceptualization clarified how children actively organize the morality of the world around them in a series of predictable, sequential stages. For the child, this was not seen simply as an assimilation and internalization of adult moral teachings through verbal explanation and punishment but as an *emergence* of cognitive moral structures that developed as a result of the child's interaction with the social and cultural environment. In this view, children do not simply *learn* morality—they construct it. What this means is that a child is literally incapable of understanding or using Stage 3 moral reasoning before passing through Stages 1 and 2. And a person would not apply the moral concepts of basic human rights found in Stage 5 to solve a dilemma unless that person had already experienced and constructed the patterns of morality inherent in the first four stages. Further implications of this and later work of Kohlberg are discussed shortly.

Criticisms and Recent Applications

Kohlberg expanded and revised his stage theory of moral development over more than 30 years following this original study. As with most new, influential research, his views have been questioned from several perspectives. One of the most often cited criticisms is that even if Kohlberg was correct in his ideas about moral reasoning, this does not mean those ideas can be applied to moral *behavior*. In other words, what a person thinks or says is moral may not be reflected in the person's moral actions. Several studies have suggested a lack of correspondence between moral reasoning and moral behavior, although others have found evidence that such a relationship does exist. One interesting line of research related to this criticism focused on the importance of strong situational factors in determining whether someone will act according to his or her stage of moral reasoning (see Kurtines, 1986). Although this criticism may have some validity, Kohlberg acknowledged that his theory applied only to moral *reasoning*. The fact that situational forces may sometimes alter moral *behavior* does not negate the fact, according to Kohlberg that moral *reasoning* progresses through the stages he described.

Another criticism of Kohlberg's work has focused on his claim that the six stages of moral reasoning are universal. These critics claim that Kohlberg's stages represent an interpretation of morality that is found uniquely in Western individualistic societies and may not apply to the non-Western, collectivist cultures that make up most of the world's population (see Reading 7.4 on the research by Triandis for a discussion of the differences between these cultures). However, in defense of the universality of Kohlberg's ideas, 45 separate studies conducted in 27 different cultures were reviewed (Snarey, 1987). In every study examined, researchers found that all the participants passed through the stages in the same sequence, without reversals, and that stages 1 through 5 were present in all the cultures studied. Interestingly, however, in more collectivist cultures (e.g., Taiwan, Papua, New Guinea, and Israel), some of the moral judgments did not fit into *any* of Kohlberg's six stages. These were judgments based on the welfare of the entire community. Such reasoning was not found in the judgments made by U.S. participants (see Reading 7.4 on Triandis's research on individualistic and collectivist cultures later in this book).

A third area of criticism deals with the belief that Kohlberg's stages of moral development may not apply equally to males and females. The researcher who led this line of questioning was Carol Gilligan (1982). She maintained that girls and boys and women and men do not think about morality in the same way. In her research, she found that, in making moral decisions, women talked more than men about interpersonal relationships, the responsibility for others, the importance of avoiding hurting others, and the importance of the connections among people. She called this foundation upon which women's morality rests a *care orientation*. Based on this gender difference, Gilligan has argued that women will score lower on Kohlberg's scale because the lower stages deal more with these relationship issues (such as Stage 3, which is based primarily on building trust and loyalty in relationships). Men, on the other hand, Gilligan says, make moral decisions based on issues of justice, which fit more easily into Kohlberg's highest stages. She contends that neither of these approaches to morality is superior, and that if women are judged by Kohlberg to be at a lower moral level than men, it is because of an unintentional gender bias built into Kohlberg's theory.

Other researchers, for the most part, have failed to find support for Gilligan's assertion (see Walker, 2014). Several studies have found no significant gender differences in moral reasoning using Kohlberg's methods. Gilligan has responded to those negative findings by acknowledging that although women are *capable* of using all levels of moral reasoning, in their real lives they choose not to do so. Instead, women focus on the human relationship aspects discussed in the preceding paragraph. This has been demonstrated by research showing how girls are willing to make a greater effort to help another person in need and tend to score higher on tests of emotional empathy (see also Hoffman, 1977, for a more complete discussion of these gender issues).

Kohlberg's early work on the development of moral judgment continues to be cited in studies from a wide range of disciplines. One area of research that relied on Kohlberg's study examined the effects of women's alcohol abuse during pregnancy on their children's moral development (Schonfeld, Mattson, & Riley, 2005).

Although evidence is clear that alcohol abuse during pregnancy suppresses intelligence scores in exposed children, this study also found that "Children and adolescents with histories of prenatal alcohol exposure demonstrated lower overall moral maturity compared with the control group. According to Kohlberg's stages of moral development, the [alcohol exposed] group was primarily concerned with minimizing negative consequences to self (i.e., Stage 2), whereas the control group demonstrated concern for others and what is socially normative (i.e., Stage 3)" (pp. 550–551).

Another study citing Kohlberg's theory examined the accuracy of eyewitness testimony given by children (Bottoms et al., 2002). Children between the ages of three and six participated in a play session with their mothers. Half of the children were told not to play with certain toys in the room. However, when the researcher left, the children's mothers urged them to play with the "forbidden" toys but to "keep it a secret." Later the researchers interviewed the children and asked if they had played with the prohibited toys: "Results indicated that older children who were instructed to keep events secret withheld more information than did older children not told to keep events secret. Younger children's reports were not significantly affected by the secret manipulation" (p. 285). Often, children are told by adults to keep secrets about the adults' illegal or injurious activities. Understanding when their understanding of the use and meaning of secrecy may play an important role in the use of child eyewitness testimony in legal proceedings (see Reading 16 on Loftus's research on eyewitness testimony earlier in this book).

Conclusion

Dialogue and debate on Kohlberg's work has continued to the present (e.g., see Goodwin & Darley, 2010) and shows every sign of continuing into the future. Its ultimate validity and importance remain to be clearly defined. However, few new conceptualizations of human development have produced the amount of research, speculation, and debate that surrounds Kohlberg's theory of moral development. And its usefulness to society, in one sense, was predicted by Kohlberg in this quote from 1964:

> Although any conception of moral education must recognize that the parent cannot escape the direct imposition of behavior demands and moral judgments upon the child, it may be possible to define moral education primarily as a matter of stimulating the development of the child's own moral judgment and its control of action. . . . [I] have found teachers telling 13-year-olds not to cheat "because the person you copied from might have it wrong and so it won't do you any good." Most of these children were capable of advancing much more mature reasons for not cheating. . . . Children are almost as likely to reject moral reasoning beneath their level as to fail to assimilate reasoning too far above their level. (p. 425)

Bottoms, B., Goodman, G., Schwartz-Kenney, B., & Thomas, S. (2002). Children's use of secrecy in the context of eyewitness reports. *Law and Human Behavior, 26*, 285–313.

Gilligan, C. (1982). *In a different voice: Psychological theory and women's development.* Cambridge, MA: Harvard University Press.

Goodwin, G. P., & Darley, J. M. (2010). The perceived objectivity of ethical beliefs: Psychological findings and implications for public policy. *Review of Philosophical Psychology, 1*, 161–188.

Hoffman, M. L. (1977). Sex differences in empathy and related behavior. *Psychological Bulletin, 84*, 712–722.

Kohlberg, L. (1964). Development of moral character and moral ideology. In H. Hoffman & L. Hoffman (Eds.), *Review of child development research* (Vol. 1). New York: Russell-Sage Foundation.

Kurtines, W. (1986). Moral behavior as rule-governed behavior: Person and situation effect on moral decision making. *Journal of Personality and Social Psychology, 50,* 784–791.

Schonfeld, A., Mattson, S., & Riley, E. (2005). Moral maturity and delinquency after prenatal alcohol exposure. *Journal of Studies on Alcohol, 66*(4), 545–554.

Snarey, J. (1987). A question of morality. *Psychological Bulletin, 97,* 202–232.

Walker, L. J. (2014). Sex differences in moral reasoning. *Handbook of moral behavior and development, 2,* 333–364.

Reading 5.4: In Control and Glad of It!

Langer, E. J., & Rodin, J. (1976). The effects of choice and enhanced personal responsibility for the aged: A field experiment in an institutional setting. *Journal of Personality and Social Psychology, 34,* 191–198.

5.4 Explain how agency reduces anxiety

Control. This seemingly small psychological concept may be the single most important influence on all of human behavior. What we are talking about here is not your ability to control the actions of others but the personal power you possess over your *own* life and the events in it. Related to this ability are your feelings of competence and personal power and the availability of choices in any given situation. Most of us feel that we have at least some control over our individual destinies. You have made choices in your life— some good ones, and maybe some poor ones—and they have brought you to where you are today. And although you may not consciously think about it, you will make many more choices throughout your life. Each day you make choices and decisions about your behavior. If your choices are taken away, you will likely rebel against the forces that are taking that control away and will behave in ways to try to restore your perception of personal freedom. It's the well-worn idea that if someone tells you that you *have* to do something, you may respond by either refusing or by doing exactly the opposite. Or, conversely, try to forbid someone from doing something and he or she will find that activity more attractive than he or she did before it was forbidden (remember Romeo and Juliet?). This tendency to resist any attempt to limit our freedom is called *reactance*.

If our need to control our personal environment is as basic to human nature as it appears to be, what do you think would happen if that control were taken away from you and you were unable to get it back? You would very likely experience psychological distress that could take the form of anxiety, anger, outrage, depression, helplessness, and even physical illness. Studies have shown that when people are placed in stressful situations, the negative effects of the stress can be reduced if the participants believe they have some control over the stressful event. For example, people in a crowded elevator perceive the elevator to be less crowded and feel less anxiety if they are standing next to the control panel in the elevator car; they believe they have a greater sense of control over their environment regardless of whether they use the control to "escape" (Rodin, Solomon, & Metcalf, 1979). Another well-known line of research has demonstrated that when people perceive that they have control over a stressful situation, their stress is reduced (see Glass & Singer, 1972). For example, one study exposed participants to loud bursts of noise and then had them perform problem-solving tasks. One group had no control over the noise. Another group was told that it could press a button and stop the noise at any time. However, the participants were asked not to press the button if they could avoid it. Participants in the no-control group performed significantly worse on the tasks than the participants who believed they could exert control over the noise. By the way, none of the participants in this latter group actually pressed the button, so they were exposed to just as much noise as the group that had no perception of control.

What this all boils down to is that we are happier and more effective people when we have the power to choose. Unfortunately, in our society, many people's lives reach a stage when they lose this power and are no longer allowed to make even the simplest of choices for themselves. This life stage is called *old age.* Many of us have heard about or experienced firsthand the tragic sudden decline in alertness and physical health of an elderly person when he or she has been placed in a retirement or nursing home. Illnesses such as heart disease, depression, diabetes, and colitis have been linked to feelings of helplessness and loss of personal control. One of the most difficult transitions elderly people must endure when entering a nursing home is the loss of the personal power to make choices about their daily activities, to influence their life's destinies. Langer and Rodin, who had been studying these issues of power and control for some time prior to the study we consider here, decided to put these ideas to the test in an actual nursing home.

Theoretical Propositions

If the loss of personal responsibility for one's life causes a person to be less happy and healthy, then *increasing* control and power should have the opposite effect. Langer and Rodin wanted to test this theory directly by enhancing personal power and choice for a group of nursing home residents. Based on previous literature and their own earlier studies, they predicted that the patients given this control should demonstrate improvements in mental alertness, activity level, satisfaction with life, and other measures of behavior and attitude.

Method

PARTICIPANTS   Langer and Rodin obtained the cooperation of a Connecticut nursing home, Arden House. This facility was rated by the state as one of the finest care units in the area, offering high quality medical care, recreational facilities, and residential comforts. It was a large and modern home with four residential floors. The residents in the home were all of generally similar physical and psychological health and came from similar socioeconomic backgrounds. When a new resident entered the home, he or she was assigned to a room on the basis of availability, more or less at random. Consequently, the characteristics of the residents on all floors were, on average, equivalent. Two floors were randomly selected for the two treatment conditions. Fourth floor residents (8 men and 39 women) received the "increased-responsibility" treatment. The second floor was designated as the comparison group (9 men and 35 women); their level of personal responsibility was relatively unchanged. These 91 participants ranged in age from 65 to 90.

PROCEDURE   The nursing home administrator agreed to work with the researchers in implementing the two conditions. He was described as an outgoing and friendly 33-year-old who interacted with the residents daily. He called a meeting of the residents of the two floors where he gave them some new information about the home. The administrator's two messages informed the residents about the home's desire that their lives there be as comfortable and pleasant as possible and about several of the services that were available to them. However, some important differences for the two groups were integrated within these messages.

The residents in the responsibility-induced group (fourth floor) were told that they had the responsibility of caring for themselves and deciding how they should spend their time. The administrator went on to explain the following:

> You should be deciding how you want your room arranged—whether you want it to be as it is or whether you want the staff to help you rearrange the furniture. . . . It's your responsibility to make your complaints known to us, to tell us

what you would like to change, to tell us what you would like. Also, I wanted to take this opportunity to give each of you a present from Arden House. [A box of small plants was passed around and the patients were asked to make two decisions: first, whether or not they wanted a plant at all, and second, to choose which one they wanted. All residents selected a plant.] The plants are yours to keep and take care of as you'd like.

> One last thing: I wanted to tell you that we're showing a movie two nights next week, Thursday and Friday. You should decide which night you'd like to go, if you choose to see it at all. (p. 194)

The comparison group (second floor) was told how much the staff at the home wanted to make their lives fuller and more interesting. He explained the following to them:

> We want your rooms to be as nice as they can be and we've tried to make them that way for you. We want you to be happy here. We feel that it's our respon-sibility to make this a home you can be proud of and happy in and we'll do all we can to help you. . . . Also, I wanted to take this opportunity to give you each a present from Arden House. [The nurse walked around with a box of plants and handed one to each resident.] The plants are yours to keep. The nurses will water and care for them for you.

> One last thing: I wanted to tell you that we're showing a movie next week on Thursday and Friday. We'll let you know later which day you're scheduled to see it. (p. 194)

Three days later, the director went around to each resident's room and reiterated the same message.

It's not difficult to see what the important difference was between these two mes-sages. The fourth-floor group was given the opportunity to make choices and exercise control over their lives in various ways. The second-floor group, while other factors were basically the same, was given the message that most of their decisions would be made for them. These policies were then followed on these two floors for the next 3 weeks. (It is important to note that the level of control given to the fourth-floor resi-dents was always available to all residents at the home if they requested it. For this experiment, it was simply reiterated and made clearer to the experimental group.)

MEASURING OUTCOMES Several methods of measurement (dependent variables) were used in this study to determine if the responsibility conditions would make a dif-ference. Two questionnaires were administered: one week before the director's talk and again 3 weeks after. One questionnaire was given to the residents on both floors; it asked questions about how much control they felt they had and how active and happy they were at the home. The other questionnaire was given to nurses on each floor (who were not aware of the research being conducted), asking them to rate patients on 10-point scales for how happy, alert, dependent, sociable, and active they were, and about their sleeping and eating habits. Two measures of the residents' actual behavior were also recorded: (a) the staff kept a record of the attendance at the movie that was being shown the next week and (b) a contest was held for patients to guess the number of jelly beans in a large jar; if residents wished to enter the contest, they simply wrote their guess and their name on a slip of paper and placed it in a box next to the jar. This, seemingly silly game, was to measure the general participation in the home's activities.

Results

Table 5.4.1 summarizes the results of the two questionnaires. As you can see clearly, the differences between the groups were striking, and they supported Langer and Rodin's predictions about the positive effects of choice and personal power. The residents in the increased-responsibility group reported that they felt happier and more active than

Table 5.4.1 Summary of Questionnaire Responses

Difference Between First and Second Administration			
Questionnaire Item	Increased-responsibility Group	Comparison Group	Significant Difference?
RESIDENT'S SELF-REPORT			
• Happy	+0.28	0.12	YES
• Active	+0.20	1.28	YES
• Interviewer's rating of alertness	+0.29	0.37	YES
NURSES' RATINGS			
• General improvement	+3.97	2.39	YES
• Time spent			
—visiting other patients	+6.78	3.30	YES
—visiting others	+2.14	4.16	YES
—talking to staff	+8.21	+1.61	YES
—watching staff	2.14	+4.64	YES

SOURCE: Adapted from p. 195.

those in the comparison group. Also, the interview's rating of alertness was higher for the fourth-floor residents. All these differences were statistically significant. Even greater differences were seen on the nurses' ratings. Keep in mind that the nurses who rated the patients were "blind" (uninformed) as to the two treatment conditions to avoid any bias in their ratings. They determined that, overall, the increased-responsibility group's condition improved markedly over the 3 weeks of the study, while the comparison group in general was seen to decline. In fact, "ninety-three percent of the experimental group (all but one participant) were considered improved, whereas only 21% of the comparison group (six participants) showed this positive change" (p. 196). Fourth-floor residents took to visiting others more and spent considerably more time talking to various staff members. On the other hand, the increased-responsibility residents began to spend less time engaged in passive activities such as simply watching the staff or TV.

The behavioral measures added further support to the positive effects of personal control. Significantly more participants from the experimental group attended the movie. This level in attendance was not found for a movie shown one month previously. Although the jelly bean guessing contest may have seemed a somewhat silly measurement for a scientific study, the results were quite interesting. Among the fourth-floor residents, 10 participated in the game, but only 1 second-floor patient did so.

Discussion

Langer and Rodin pointed out that their study, combined with other previous research, demonstrated that when people who have been forced to give up their control and decision-making power are given a greater sense of personal responsibility, their lives and attitudes improve. As to the practical applications of this research, the authors are succinct and to the point:

> Mechanisms can and should be established for changing situational factors that reduce real or perceived responsibility in the elderly. Furthermore, this study adds to the body of literature suggesting that senility and diminished alertness are not an almost inevitable result of aging. In fact, it suggests that some of the negative consequences of aging may be retarded, reversed, or possibly prevented by returning to the aged the right to make decisions and a feeling of competence. (p. 197)

Significance of Findings and Subsequent Research

Probably the best example of the significance of the findings of this study was provided by the authors in a subsequent study of the same residents in the same nursing home (Rodin & Langer, 1977). Eighteen months after their first study, Langer and Rodin returned to Arden House for a follow-up to see if the increased-responsibility conditions had any long-term effects. For the patients still in residence, ratings were taken from doctors and nurses and a special talk on psychology and aging by one of the authors (J. Rodin) was given to the residents. The number of residents in each of the original conditions who attended the talk was recorded and the frequency and type of questions asked were noted.

Ratings from the nurses demonstrated continued superior condition of the increased-responsibility group. The average total ratings (derived by adding all their ratings together and averaging this total over all patients) for the experimental group was 352.33 versus 262.00 for the comparison group (a highly significant difference). The health ratings from doctors also indicated an increase in overall health status for the experimental group, compared with a slight decline in health for the control residents. Although no significant difference was noted in the number of residents attending the lecture, most of the questions were asked by the increased-responsibility participants and the content of the questions related to autonomy and independence. Probably the most important finding of all was that 30% of the participants in the comparison group had died during the 18-month interval. For the experimental group, only 15% had died during that time.

One important criticism of research such as this was pointed out by Langer and Rodin themselves. The consequences of intervention by researchers in any setting where the well-being of the participants is involved must be very carefully considered from an ethical perspective. Providing the elderly with new levels of power and control, only to have this responsibility taken away again when the research is completed, might be harmful or even dangerous to the participants. Indeed, a study by Schulz (1976) allowed nursing home residents varying amounts of control over when they would be visited by local college students. Those having the most control over when and for how long the visits would take place showed significantly improved functioning, just as Langer and Rodin found. However, when the study was completed and the students discontinued their visits, this (inadvertently on the part of the researchers) led to a greater decline in the health of the experimental group compared to those residents who were never exposed to the increased-control situation. In Langer and Rodin's study, this did not happen because feelings of general control over normal day-to-day decision-making were fostered among all the residents. This, then, was a positive change that was therefore continued over time with sustained positive results.

Recent Applications

As mentioned previously, personal power and control over one's life constitute key factors in a happy and productive life. Old age is a time when the potential exists for this power to be lost. Langer and Rodin's studies and the subsequent work of Judith Rodin (see Rodin, 1986) have made it clear that the greater our sense of control, the healthier, happier, and smoother our process of aging. Awareness of this is growing even today as nursing homes, state nursing home certification boards, hospitals, and other institutional settings encourage and require increased choice, personal power, and control for the elderly.

Many studies incorporating Langer and Rodin's 1976 research have continued to support the need for, and value of, personal control as we age. For example, a 2003 study of depression among elderly residents in senior citizen homes in Germany found that a lack of perceived freedom and personal choice were predictors of depressive symptoms, poor physical fitness, and a lack of social support (Krampe et al., 2003). The authors concluded that "therapy and prevention of depression among inhabitants of old people's residences should include both promotion of volitional self-regulation [personal choice] and improvement of perceived freedom because each of these factors contributes independently to the explanation of depression" (p. 117).

Research on the issues examined by Langer and Rodin continues to grow, using their early research as a foundation. A 2010 study called, "Born to Choose: The Origins and Value of the Need for Control," proposed that people's ability to exert control over their environment and to be able to perceive that they have personal choice over the outcomes of their actions is not only psychologically healthy but also may be biologically hardwired into us (Leotti, Iyengar, & Ochsner, 2010).

Interestingly, individualistic and collectivist cultures (see the studies by Trandis, "The One the Many," in Chapter VII) appear to differ in their desire for control. When group norms were manipulated, those in the individualistic groups (such as in the United States) those participants showed greater intrinsic motivation (Hagger, Rentzezels, & Chatzisarantis, 2014). This makes sense in that collectivist cultures focus more on the larger group and less on individual power and control. However, these groups place strong importance on the success and power of the group.

This biological imperative appears to be all about *choice* and our ability to make conscious decisions in a given situation. Increasing evidence from human, animal, and brain-scanning research models is demonstrating that control is a *survival mechanism* that has flowed down through evolution over millions of years to modern humans. In other words, early humans who were capable of making choices and exerting control over their environment were more likely to survive and pass their "control genes" on to the next generation. This transfer of those genes continued and exists in us even today. Findings have shown that when choice and control is removed, stress follows. As an extreme example, imagine that you are physically restrained (held down, tied up, etc.). Even though the restraint does not physically harm you, the restraint itself results in many of our strongest stress responses such as increased heart rate, higher blood pressure, and release of adrenaline. To further demonstrate this "natural" reaction to the loss of control, the exact same responses are shown by nonhuman animals subjected to the same kinds of restraints.

Conclusion

Personal power and control not only affect your happiness but they also can make you healthier, and the lack of them can make you unhappy and even sick. You can easily apply Langer and Rodin's ideas to your own life. Think for a moment about events, settings, and experiences in which you were allowed very little personal control over your behavior; the situation "forced" you to behave in specific ways. You probably remember those experiences as more uncomfortable, more unpleasant, and significantly less enjoyable than events where you could freely choose what to do and how to act. In most of life's situations, increasing your degree of behavioral choices, and those of others', is a goal clearly worth pursuing.

Glass, C., & Singer, J. (1972). *Urban stress: Experiments on noise and social stressors*. New York: Academic Press.

Hagger, M. S., Rentzelas, P., & Chatzisarantis, N. L. (2014). Effects of individualist and collectivist group norms and choice on intrinsic motivation. *Motivation and Emotion*, 38(2), 215–223.

Krampe, H., Hautzinger, M., Ehrenreich, H., & Kroner-Herwig, B. (2003). Depression among elderly living in senior citizen homes: Investigation of a multifactorial model of depression. *Zeitschrift fur klinische psychologie und psychotherapie*, 32, 117–128.

Leotti, L., Iyengar, S., & Ochsner, K. (2010). Born to choose: The origins and value of the need for control. *Trends in Cognitive Sciences, 14*, 457–463.

Rodin, J. (1986). Aging and health: Effects of the sense of control. *Science, 233*, 1271–1276.

Rodin, J., & Langer, E. J. (1977). Long term effects of a control relevant intervention with the institutionalized aged. *Journal of Personality and Social Psychology, 35*, 897–902.

Rodin, J., Solomon, S., & Metcalf, J. (1979). Role of control in mediating perceptions of density. *Journal of Personality and Social Psychology, 36*, 988–999.

Schulz, R. (1976). Effects of control and predictability on the psychological well being of the institutionalized aged. *Journal of Personality and Social Psychology, 33*, 563–573.

Chapter 6
Emotion and Motivation

 Learning Objectives

6.1 Summarize findings by Masters and Johnson in their study of human sexuality

6.2 Explain how Ekman and Friesen demonstrated the universality of facial expressions

6.3 Describe how fMRI scans show the difference between truth and lies

6.4 Analyze the impact of cognitive dissonance on decisions and behaviors

This section deals with our inner experiences of emotion and motivation. Many non-psychologists have trouble with the idea of researching these issues scientifically. A popular belief contends that our emotions and motivations just *happen*, that we don't have much control over them, and that they are part of our standard equipment from birth. However, psychologists have always been fascinated with the issues of where your emotions come from and how your feelings cause you to act as you do. Emotion and motivation are basic and powerful influences on behavior, and a great deal of research allows us to understand them better.

The first study in this section may surprise you in that it focuses on the sexual response studies begun by the famous research team of Masters and Johnson in the 1960s. It is included here because human sexual feelings and behaviors are strongly influenced by our emotions, which can also serve as powerful motivational forces. The second reading examines a famous and fascinating study about facial expressions of emotions and demonstrates that our facial expressions for basic emotions are the same for everyone in all cultures throughout the world. The third study in this section presents research about how *extreme* emotions, those that create stress, can affect your health. The fourth reading allows you to experience the process of one of the most, if not the most, famous experiments in the area of motivation: the original demonstration of a psychological event called *cognitive dissonance*.

Reading 6.1: A Sexual Motivation

Masters, W. H., & Johnson, V. E. (1966). *Human sexual response*. Boston: Little, Brown.

6.1   Summarize findings by Masters and Johnson in their study of human sexuality

You may not immediately realize this, but human sexuality is very psychological. Many people might logically place the study of sexual behavior into the disciplines of biology or physiology, and it is true that these fields certainly connect to the topic in various ways and are the central focus of sexual behavior of most nonhuman animals. For humans, however, sexual activity is just as much a *psychological* process. Think about it: sexual attraction, sexual desire, and sexual functioning are all dependent in many ways upon psychology. If you doubt this, just consider a couple of obvious facts. You know that most people engage in sexual behavior for many reasons other than reproduction. Those reasons are usually psychological. Also, as far as we know, humans are the only species on Earth to suffer from sexual problems such as hypoactive (low) sexual desire, problems with orgasm, erectile dysfunction, premature ejaculation, and so on. These problems often have psychological causes.

Having said that, however, you should be aware at the outset of this discussion that the full expression of ourselves as sexual beings, as well as the successful treatment of sexual problems, depends on a clear and thorough understanding of our sexual functioning: the *physiology* of human sexual response. This is what Masters and Johnson set out to study.

Prior to the 1960s, the definitive works on the sexual behavior of humans were the large-scale surveys of Americans' sexual activities published by Alfred Kinsey in the late 1940s and early 1950s. The famous Kinsey Reports, *Sexual Behavior in the Human Male* (1948) and *Sexual Behavior in the Human Female* (1953), asked thousands of men and women about their sexual behavior and attitudes, including topics ranging from frequency of intercourse to masturbation habits to homosexual experiences. With the publication of these reports, suddenly humans had a measure against which to compare their own sexual lifestyles and make relative judgments of their personal sexual behaviors. The Kinsey Reports offered a rare glimpse into the sexuality of humans, and the publications are still cited today as a source of statistical information about sexual behavior. The importance of Kinsey's work notwithstanding, his research only provided information about what people *say* they do sexually. However, a conspicuous gap yet remained in our knowledge about what happens to us physically when we engage in sexual behavior and what people should to do if they are experiencing some kind of sexual problem.

Enter William Masters and Virginia Johnson in the early 1960s. These are names that have become synonymous with human sexuality research and are recognized by millions throughout the world. As the 1960s began, the United States was launched into what has now become known as the "sexual revolution." The sweeping social changes that were taking place provided an opportunity for open and frank scientific exploration of our sexuality that would not have been possible previously. Until the 1960s, lingering Victorian messages that sexual behavior is something secretive, hidden, and certainly not a topic of discussion, much less a proper study, precluded virtually all support, social and financial, for Masters and Johnson's project. But as men and women began to acknowledge more openly the fact that we are sexual beings, with sexual feelings and desires, the social climate became one that was ready not only to accept the research of Masters and Johnson but also to demand it. Behavioral statistics were no longer enough. People were ready to learn about their physical responses to sexual stimulation.

It was within this social context that Masters and Johnson began to study human sexual response. Their early work culminated in the book that is the subject of this discussion. Although this work was carried out over five decades ago, it continues to serve as the definitive research to influence our knowledge of what our bodies do during sexual activity.

Theoretical Propositions

The most important proposition in Masters and Johnson's research was that to understand human sexuality, we must study actual sexual behaviors as they occur in response to sexual stimulation, rather than simply record what people perceive or believe their sexual experiences to be.

Their objective in proposing this theory was a therapeutic one: to help people overcome sexual problems that they might be experiencing. Masters and Johnson expressed this goal as follows:

> [The] fundamentals of human sexual behavior cannot be established until two questions are answered: What physical reactions develop as the human male and female respond to effective sexual stimulation? Why do men and women behave as they do when responding to effective sexual stimulation? If human sexual inadequacy ever is to be treated successfully, the medical and behavioral professions must provide answers to these basic questions. (p. 4)

Combined with this objective, Masters and Johnson also proposed that the only method by which such answers could be obtained was direct systematic observation and physiological measurements of men and women in all stages of sexual responding.

Method

PARTICIPANTS   As you might imagine, the first hurdle in a research project such as this is obtaining participants. The project required volunteers who would be willing to engage in sexual acts in a laboratory setting while being closely observed and monitored. Obviously, the researchers were concerned that such a requirement might create the impossibility of finding participants who would represent the general population. Another concern was that the strange and artificial environment of the research lab might cause participants who did volunteer for the study to be unable to respond in their usual ways.

During the early phases of their study, Masters and Johnson employed prostitutes as participants. This decision was based on their assumption that individuals from more average and typical lifestyles would refuse to participate. Prostitutes were studied extensively for nearly 2 years: eight females and three males. The researchers described the contributions of these first 11 participants as being crucial to the development of the methods and research techniques used throughout the entire study.

These participants, however, did not constitute an appropriate group on which to base an extensive study of human sexual response. This was because their lifestyle and sexual experiences did not even remotely represent the population at large. Therefore, the researchers knew that any findings based on this participant group could not be credibly applied to people in general. Think about it: would you accept Masters and Johnson's conclusions about you as if their studies were based solely on prostitutes? Most people would not. It was necessary, therefore, to obtain a sample of participants that would more accurately represent the population overall. Contrary to their earlier assumption, the researchers did not find this as difficult as they had anticipated.

Through their contacts in the academic, medical, and therapeutic communities in a large metropolitan area (St. Louis, MO; St. Louis University), Masters and Johnson were able to enlist a large group of volunteers from a wide range of socioeconomic and educational backgrounds. The age, gender, and educational demographics of the participants who were eventually chosen are summarized in Table 6.1.1. All volunteers were carefully interviewed to determine their suitability for participating and their ability to communicate on issues of sexual responsiveness. The prospective participants also agreed to a physical exam to ensure anatomical normalcy.

PROCEDURES   To study in detail, the physiological responses of the human body during sexual activity and stimulation, a wide variety of methods of measurement and observation were necessary. These included such standard measures of physiological response as pulse, blood pressure, and rate of respiration. In addition, specific sexual responses were to be observed and recorded. For this, the "sexual activity of study subjects included, at various times, manual and mechanical manipulation, natural coition

Table 6.1.1 Distribution of Participants by Age, Gender, and Educational Level

Age	Number of Males	Number of Females	High School	College	Graduate School
18–20	2	0	2	0	0
21–30	182	120	86	132	84
31–40	137	111	72	98	78
41–50	27	42	18	29	22
51–60	23	19	15	15	12
61–70	8	14	7	11	4
71–80	3	4	3	3	1
81–90	0	2	0	2	0
Total	382	312	203	290	201

(Based on data from pp. 13–15.)

[intercourse] with the female partner in supine, superior, or knee-chest position, and, for many female study subjects, artificial coition in the supine or knee-chest positions" (p. 21). What all that means is that sometimes participants were observed and measured while having intercourse in various positions, and other times they were observed and measured during masturbation either manually or with mechanical devices specially designed to allow for clear recording of response.

These special devices, designed by physicists, were, basically, clear plastic artificial penises with a film camera attached that allowed for internal observations and recording without distortion. These could be adjusted in size for the woman's comfort and were controlled completely by the woman for depth and rate of movement in the vagina throughout the response cycle.

Participant Orientation and Comfort

You can imagine that all these expectations, observations, and devices might create some real sexual/emotional difficulties for the participants, and Masters and Johnson were acutely aware of these potential difficulties. To help place participants at ease with the study's procedures, they ensured the following:

> Sexual activity was first encouraged in privacy in the research quarters and then continued with the investigative team present until the study subjects were quite at ease in their artificial surroundings. No attempt was made to record reactions . . . until the study subjects felt secure in their surroundings and confident of their ability to perform . . . . This period of training established a sense of security in the integrity of the research interest and in the absolute anonymity embodied in the program. (pp. 22–23)

Some participants were involved in only one recording session, while others participated actively for several years. For the research included in the book that is the topic of discussion here, Masters and Johnson estimated that they were able to study 10,000 complete sexual response cycles with female observation outnumbering male observation by a ratio of 3:1. In their words, "a minimum of 7,500 complete cycles of sexual response have been experienced by female study participants cooperating in various aspect of the research program, as opposed to a minimum total of 2,500 male orgasmic (ejaculatory) experiences" (p. 15).

Results

Masters and Johnson discovered a wealth of information about human sexual response, and some of their findings are summarized in the pages ahead. However, another aspect of their research to keep in mind is that much of what they found from their sample of participants is true of most people. Of course, some exceptions exist, but in general, everyone's basic physiological responses to sexual stimulation are similar. You must remember, though, as you read about their early findings, that Masters and Johnson's research did *not* address sexual attitudes, emotions, morals, values, preferences, orientations, or likes or dislikes. These matters clearly are *not* similar for everyone, and it is our individual variations in these issues that create the vast and wondrous diversity that exists in human sexuality. Let's look at some of Masters and Johnson's most influential findings.

THE SEXUAL RESPONSE CYCLE   After studying approximately 10,000 sexual events, Masters and Johnson found that human sexual response could be divided into four stages, which they termed the *human sexual response cycle.* These stages are excitement, plateau, orgasm, and resolution (Table 6.1.2). Although they acknowledged in their book that the stages were somewhat arbitrarily defined, these divisions made the discussion of sexual response easier and clearer. Today, human sexual response is rarely discussed in academic or professional settings without reference to these four stages.

SEXUAL ANATOMY   One of the great contributions made by Masters and Johnson in their research on sexual response was the dispelling of sexual myths. And one area of widespread misunderstanding that the researchers attempted to correct relates to sexual anatomy—specifically, the penis and the vagina. Throughout history, one of the most common sexual concerns expressed by men has related to penis size. Masters and Johnson studied a lot of penises and could finally shed some scientific light on these concerns. They called them "phallic fallacies." The two worries men have expressed are (a) larger penises are more effective in providing satisfying sexual stimulation for the woman, and (b) their own penises are too small. Masters and Johnson demonstrated that both concerns are misguided by revealing actual average penis sizes found in their research and explaining the functioning of the penis and vagina during heterosexual intercourse.

   The researchers found that the normal range for flaccid penile length in this study population was between 2.8 inches and 4.3 inches, with an average length of about 3 inches. For erect penises, the average length ranged from about 5.5 inches to just under 7 inches, with an average of about 6 inches. These numbers were significantly smaller than the commonly held beliefs about what constitutes a large versus a small penis. But what was even more surprising was that when they measured the size of erect penises, the researchers found that a larger flaccid penis does not predict a larger erect penis.

Table 6.1.2 Masters and Johnson's Stages of the Sexual Response Cycle

Stage	Female Response Summary	Male Response Summary
Excitement	First sign: vaginal lubrication. Clitoral glans becomes erect. Nipples become erect; breasts enlarge. Vagina increases in length, and inner two-thirds of vagina expands.	First sign: erection of penis. Time to erection varies (with person, age, alcohol/drug use, fatigue, stress, etc.). Skin of scrotum pulls up toward body; testes rise. Erection may be lost if distracted but usually regained readily.
Plateau	Outer one-third of vagina swells, reducing opening by up to 50%. Inner two-thirds of vagina continues to balloon or "tent." Clitoris retracts toward body and under hood. Lubrication decreases. Minor lips engorge with blood and darken in color, indicating orgasm is near. Muscle tension and blood pressure increase.	Full erection attained; not lost easily if distracted. Corona enlarges further. Cowper's gland secretes pre-ejaculate fluid. Testes elevate further, rotate, and enlarge, indicating orgasm is near. Muscle tension and blood pressure increase.
Orgasm	Begins with rhythmic contractions in pelvic area at intervals of 0.8 second, especially in muscles behind the lower vaginal walls. Uterus contracts rhythmically as well. Muscle tension increased throughout body. Duration recorded from 7.4 to 104.6 seconds. Length does not equal-perceived intensity.	Begins with pelvic contractions 0.8 second apart. Ejaculation, the expelling of semen, occurs in two phases: (1) emission (semen builds up in urethral bulb, producing sensation of ejaculatory inevitability); (2) expulsion (genital muscles contract, forcing semen out through urethra).
Resolution	Clitoris, uterus, vagina, nipples, etc., return to unaroused state in less than 1 minute. Clitoris often remains very sensitive to touch for 5–10 minutes. This process may take several hours if woman has not experienced anorgasm.	Approximately 50% loss of erection within 1 minute; more gradual return to fully unaroused state. Testes reduce in size and descend. Scrotum relaxes.

In fact, they discovered overall that smaller flaccid penises tend to enlarge more upon sexual excitement than do penises that are larger in their flaccid state. Looking at averages, a flaccid penis of 3 inches increased to a length of 6 inches, but a 4-inch flaccid penis only added about 2.5 inches to reach a length of 6.5 inches. To further illustrate this finding, Masters and Johnson reported the largest and smallest observed change from flaccid to erect state. One male participant was found to have a flaccid penile length of 2.8 inches. The increase that was observed in this participant upon erection was 3.3 inches, to an erect length of 6.1 inches. Another participant who was measured flaccid at 4 inches increased only 2.1 inches, for an identical erect length of 6.1 inches.

More important than all these measurements of penises is the notion that a woman's sexual enjoyment and satisfaction depend on penis size. Masters and Johnson's research, as explained in a section titled "Vagina Fallacies," found that idea to be totally without merit. In their careful observations using the artificial penis technique described earlier, they determined that the vagina is an extremely elastic structure capable of accommodating penises of varying size: "Full accommodation usually is accomplished with the first few thrusts of the penis regardless of penile size" (p. 194). Furthermore, they found that during the plateau stage of the response cycle (see Table 6.1.2), the walls of the vaginal opening swell to envelop a penis of virtually any size. Therefore, as the authors conclude, "It becomes obvious that penile size usually is a minor factor in sexual stimulation of the female partner" (p. 195).

FEMALE AND MALE DIFFERENCES IN SEXUAL RESPONSE   Although Masters and Johnson demonstrated many similarities in the sexual response cycles of men and women, they also pointed out some important differences. Their most famous and revolutionary finding concerned the orgasm and resolution stages of the cycle. Following orgasm, both men and women enter the resolution stage, when sexual tension decreases rapidly and sexual structures return to their unaroused states (this is also known as *detumescence*). Masters and Johnson found that during this time, a man experiences a *refractory period,* during which he is physically incapable of experiencing another orgasm regardless of the type or amount of stimulation he receives. This refractory period may last from several minutes to several hours or even a day, and it tends to lengthen as a man ages.

Masters and Johnson found that many women do not appear to have a refractory period and with continued, effective stimulation are capable of experiencing one or more additional orgasms following the first, an experience referred to as *multiple orgasms.* The researchers reported that women, unlike men, are "capable of maintaining an orgasmic experience for a relatively long period of time" (p. 131).

While this multiorgasmic capacity was not news to many women, it was not widely known. Prior to Masters and Johnson's work, it was commonly believed that men had the greater orgasmic capabilities. Consequently, this finding, as well as many others in Masters and Johnson's research, had a far-reaching impact on cultural and societal attitudes about male and female sexuality. It should be noted here that although most women are physiologically capable of multiple orgasms, not all women seek or even desire them. Indeed, many women have never experienced multiple orgasms and are completely satisfied with their sexual lives. Also, many women who have had multiple orgasms find that they also are usually satisfied with a single orgasm. The important point is that individuals vary greatly in terms of what is physically and emotionally satisfying sexually. Masters and Johnson were attempting to address the full range of physiological possibilities.

Criticisms

Most of the criticisms of Masters and Johnson's early research focus either on the arbitrary nature of their four stages of sexual response or on the fact that they spent little time discussing the cognitive and emotional aspects of sexuality. However, Masters and Johnson addressed these criticisms in their early writings.

As mentioned previously, the authors were fully aware that their four sexual response phases were purely arbitrary but that the divisions were helpful in researching and explaining the complex process of sexual response in humans. Other researchers, over the years, have suggested different stage theories. For example, Helen Singer Kaplan (Kaplan, 1974) proposed a three-stage model that includes desire, vasocongestion (engorgement of the genitals with blood), and muscle contractions (orgasm). These stages reflect Kaplan's belief that an analysis of sexual response should begin with sexual desire before any sexual stimulation begins, and she suggests that no distinction can or needs be drawn between excitement and plateau. Her focus on the desire aspect of sexuality leads into the other main criticism of Masters and Johnson's original work: the lack of attention to psychological factors.

Masters and Johnson acknowledged that an examination of psychological and emotional factors was not the goal of the project. They did believe, however, that a complete understanding of the *physiological* side of sexual behavior was a necessary prerequisite for a satisfying and fulfilling sex life. And they demonstrated this belief in subsequent books dealing with the psychological and emotional aspects of our sexuality.

Over the 30 years since Masters and Johnson's first book appeared, some research has questioned some of their findings as they apply to all humans. For example, research has demonstrated that some women may experience a refractory period during which time they are incapable of experiencing additional orgasms, and a small percentage of men may be capable of multiple orgasms with little or no refractory period between them. Also, although ejaculation was thought to be entirely the domain of men, recent research proposes that some women may, under some circumstances, ejaculate a fluid that is similar in composition to semen (without semen) at orgasm (see Zaviacic, 2002, for a discussion of this research).

Recent Applications

It would be impossible to list here even a representative sample of the numerous articles and books published each year that refer substantively to Masters and Johnson's early work on human sexual response. These publications range from basic core texts in human sexuality (e.g., Hock, 2016; King & Regan, 2013) to very specific, cutting-edge articles in psychology and sexuality journals.

One study carried out in 2014 compared the most intense stage of sexual activity—orgasm—between individuals of differing sexual orientations (Garcia and Lloyd, 2014). The study sampled 1,497 single men and 1,353 women who had sexual activity during the preceding 12 months with a familiar partner. The data showed that men did not differ by sexual orientation, with heterosexual men having an orgasm 85.5% of the time, homosexual men, 84.7%, and bisexual men 77.6 (not statistically different). For women, it was a different story: Heterosexual women had an orgasm (at least one) 61.6% of the time, lesbian women 74.7%, and bisexual women, 58.0%. Why would this be? The most likely explanation is that it is the sexual behaviors of the six groups are varied. The behaviors men engage in, whether gay, straight, or bisexual, all provide strong sensations to the penis and increase the likelihood of having an orgasm. For heterosexual women, the activity of intercourse often does not provide the stimulation that a woman needs for orgasm without additional stimulation before, during, or after intercourse. For gay women, intercourse is not commonly part of their sexual repertoire; they typically have oral or manual sexual stimulation which is far more stimulating than penile-vaginal intercourse, so they are more orgasmic than either straight or bisexual women. They also tend to spend more time than others on the sexual encounter. For the bisexual women, it may be that some are less comfortable with their partners and/or do not spend as much time as the other woman groups.

Masters and Johnson's model of sexual responding has generated controversy for over 60 years and still does so today. Probably the liveliest debate today revolves around whether their four-phase model can be applied to both men and women more or less equally, as the researchers suggested.

One study in this vein incorporated Masters and Johnson's pioneering work in designing, administering, and analyzing responses to a national survey of sexual satisfaction among nearly 1,000 women, ages 20 to 65 years, in heterosexual relationships (Bancroft et al., 2003). The goal of the study was to examine whether women's sexual problems may be viewed as similar to men's sexual problems and to what extent pharmacological treatments might be helpful for women, in the way that erectile disorder drugs (Viagra, Levitra, Cialis) have helped many men. The study found that problems with the physical side of sexual response (arousal, vaginal lubrication, and orgasm) were *not* strongly related to sexual distress among the respondents: "The overall picture is that lack of emotional well-being and negative emotional feelings during sexual interaction with the partner are more important determinants of sexual distress than impairment of the more physiological aspects of female sexual response. Although we do not have directly comparable data for men, we can predict that the pattern would be different, with greater importance attached to genital response" (Bancroft et al., 2003, p. 202). In other words, women's most common sexual problems may be far too complex to be solved with just a "little *pink* pill."

Indeed, in 2000, a new approach to understanding female sexual problems was developed by a collaborative group of 12 women scientists, researchers, and clinicians who argued that, sexually, men and women are more different than they are similar and that Masters and Johnson's four-phase model is invalid in describing, explaining, or treating sexual problems in women (see Tiefer, 2001). This "new view of women's sexual problems" contends that "women's accounts do not fit neatly into the Masters and Johnson model; for example, women generally do not separate 'desire' from 'arousal,' [and] women care less about physical than [about] subjective arousal" (Tiefer, 2001, p. 93). The researchers propose that Masters and Johnson's model—which, for the most part, equates male and female sexual response—fails to take into account some important factors that are necessary to understand women's sexual problems. These include the context of the relationship in which the sexual responding is occurring and individual differences among women in their sexual response patterns. More specifically, they suggest that women's sexual difficulties require a classification system that takes into account cultural, political, and economic factors (e.g., lack of sexuality education or access to contraception); a woman's partner and issues in the relationship (e.g., fear of abuse, imbalance of power, and overall discord); psychological factors (e.g., past sexual trauma, depression, and anxiety); and medical factors (e.g., hormonal imbalances, sexually transmitted infections, and medication side effects).

Thanks in large part to the work of Masters and Johnson, our understanding of the physical processes involved in human sexual pleasure and response is quite advanced compared to a half century ago, but we still have a great deal to learn. Undoubtedly, with Masters and Johnson's groundbreaking studies as a backdrop, research will continue and our insights into human sexual response will expand.

Conclusions

In 1971, Masters and Johnson were married. Over the following two decades, they continued to work and publish as a team. In 1992, due to increasing differences between them about the direction of their research and retirement, the couple divorced and Johnson went into retirement. Masters continued as director of the *Masters and Johnson Institute* in St. Louis until his retirement in 1994. He died from complications of Parkinson's disease on February 16, 2001, at the age of 85.

You'll recall from the beginning of this discussion that the main goal of Masters and Johnson's research was to address problems of sexual inadequacy—to help people solve their sexual problems. Almost without question they have done that. Virtually all sex therapy, whether for erectile problems, orgasm difficulties, rapid ejaculation, inhibited arousal issues, or any other sexual problem rests on a basic foundation of Masters and Johnson's research. It is impossible to overestimate the contributions of Masters and Johnson in our understanding and study of human sexuality. An examination of any recent sexuality textbook will reveal more citations for and more space devoted to the work of Masters and Johnson than to any other researchers. But beyond this, William Masters and Virginia Johnson, over the decades following the publication of *Human Sexual Response* (which forms the basis of this reading), continued researching and applying their findings to help people attain sexual fulfilment. Four years after the publication *Human Sexual Response*, they released *Human Sexual Inadequacy* (1970), which applied their earlier research directly to solutions for sexual problems. Their continuous attention to their chosen field is demonstrated by a list of their subsequent books: *The Pleasure Bond* (1970); *Homosexuality in Perspective* (1979); *Human Sexuality* (1997); *Crisis: Heterosexual Behavior in the Age of AIDS* (1988); *Masters and Johnson on Sex and Human Loving* (1986); and *Heterosexuality* (1998).

Bancroft, J., Loftus, J., & Long, J. (2003). Distress about sex: A national survey of women in heterosexual relationships. *Archives of Sexual Behavior, 32*, 193–208.

Garcia, J. R., Lloyd, E. A., Wallen, K., & Fisher, H. E. (2014). Variation in orgasm occurrence by sexual orientation in a sample of US singles. *The Journal of Sexual Medicine, 11*(11), 2645–2652.

Hock, R. R. (2016). *Human sexuality*. New York, NY: Pearson.

Kaplan, H. S. (1974). *The new sex therapy*. New York: Brunner/Mazel.

King, B. M., & Regan, P. (2013). *Human Sexuality Today*. Hoboken, NJ, Pearson.

Kinsey, A. C., Pomeroy, W. B., Martin, C. E. (1948). *Sexual behavior in the human male*. Philadelphia: W. B. Saunders.

Kinsey, A. C., Pomeroy, W. B., Martin, C. E., & Gebhard, P. H. (1953). *Sexual behavior in the human female*. Philadelphia: W. B. Saunders.

Tiefer, L. (2001). A new view of women's sexual problems: Why new? Why now? *Journal of Sex Research, 38*, 89–96.

Zaviacic, Milan (2002). Female urethral expulsions evoked by local digital stimulation of the G-spot: Differences in the response patterns. *Journal of Sex Research, 24*, 311–318.

Reading 6.2: I Can See It All Over Your Face!

Ekman, P., & Friesen, W. V. (1971). Constants across cultures in the face and emotion. *Journal of Personality and Social Psychology, 17*, 124–129.

6.2 Explain how Ekman and Friesen demonstrated the universality of facial expressions

Think of something funny. What is the expression on your face? Now think of something in your past that made you sad. Did your face change? Chances are it did. Undoubtedly, you are aware that certain facial expressions coincide with specific emotions. And, most of the time, you can probably tell how people are feeling emotionally from the expressions on their faces. Now, consider this: Could you be equally successful in determining someone's emotional state based on facial expression if that person is from a different culture—say, Romania, Sumatra, or Mongolia? In other words, do you believe facial expressions of emotion are universal? Most people believe that they are, until they stop and consider how radically different other cultures are from their own. Think of the multitude of cultural differences in styles of dress, gestures, personal space, rules of etiquette, religious beliefs, humor, attitudes, and so on. With all these differences influencing behavior, it would be rather amazing if any human characteristics, including emotional expressions, were identical across all cultures.

Paul Ekman is considered the leading researcher in the area of the facial expression of emotion. The TV show, "Lie to Me" was based on him and his research. This article details his early research, which was designed to demonstrate the universality of these expressions. Although the authors acknowledged in their introduction that previous researchers had found some evidence that facial behaviors are determined by culturally variable learning, they argued that previous studies were poorly done and, in reality, expressions for basic emotions are equivalent in all cultures.

Several years prior to this study, Ekman and Friesen had conducted research in which they showed photographs of faces to college-educated people in Argentina, Brazil, Chile, Japan, and the United States. All the participants from every country correctly identified the same facial expressions as corresponding to the same emotions regardless of the nationality of the person in the photo. The researchers presented their findings as evidence of the universality of emotional expressions. However, as Ekman and Friesen themselves pointed out, these findings were open to criticism because members of the cultures that were studied had all been exposed to international mass media (movies, magazines, and television), which are full of facial expressions that might have been transmitted to all these countries and influenced by that media. What was needed to prove the universality of emotional expression was to study a culture that had not been exposed to any of these influences. Imagine how difficult (perhaps impossible) it would be to find such a culture given today's mass media. Well, even in 1971, it wasn't easy.

Ekman and Friesen traveled to the southeast Highlands of New Guinea to find participants for their study among the Fore people who still existed as an isolated Stone Age society as late as 1971. Many of the members of this group had experienced little or no contact with modern cultures. Therefore, they had not been exposed to emotional facial expressions other than those of their own people.

Theoretical Propositions

The theory underlying Ekman and Friesen's study was that specific facial expressions corresponding to basic emotions are universal. Ekman and Friesen stated it quite simply:

> The purpose of this paper was to test the hypothesis that members of a preliterate culture who had been selected to ensure maximum visual isolation from literate cultures will identify the same emotion concepts with the same faces as do members of literate Western and Eastern cultures. (p. 125)

Method

The most isolated subgroup of the Fore was that group referred to as the South Fore. The individuals selected to participate in the study had seen no movies, did not speak English or Pidgin, had never worked for a Westerner, and had never lived in any of the Western settlements in the area. A total of 189 adults and 130 children were chosen to participate, out of a total South Fore population of about 11,000. For comparison, 23 adults were chosen who had experienced a great deal of contact with Western society through watching movies, living in the settlements, and attending missionary schools.

Through trial and error, the researchers found that the most effective method of asking the participants to identify emotions was to present them with three photographs of different facial expressions and to read a brief description of an emotion-producing scene or story that corresponded to one of the photographs. The participant could then simply point to the expression that best matched the story. The stories used were selected very carefully to be sure that each scene was related to only one emotion and that it was recognizable to the Fore people. Table 6.2.1 lists the six stories developed by Ekman and Friesen. The authors explained that the fear story had to be longer to prevent the participants from confusing it with surprise or anger.

Table 6.2.1 Ekman and Friesen's Stories Corresponding to Six Emotions

Emotion	Story
1. Happiness	His (her) friends have come and he (she) is happy.
2. Sadness	His (her) child (mother) has died and he (she) feels very sad.
3. Anger	He (she) is angry and about to fight.
4. Surprise	He (she) is just now looking at something new and unexpected.
5. Disgust	He (she) is looking at something he (she) dislikes; or he (she) is looking at something that smells bad.
6. Fear	He (she) is sitting in his (her) house all alone and there is no one else in the village. There is no knife, axe, or bow and arrow in the house. A wild pig is standing in the door of the house and the man (woman) is looking at the pig and is very afraid of it. The pig has been standing in the doorway for a few minutes, and the person is looking at it very afraid, and the pig won't move away from the door, and he (she) is afraid the pig will bite him (her).

(Based on information on p. 126.)

A total of 40 photographs of 24 different people, including men, women, boys, and girls, were used as examples of the six emotional expressions. These photographs had been validated previously by showing them to members of various other cultures. Each photograph had been judged by at least 70% of observers in at least two literate Western or Eastern cultures to represent the emotion being expressed.

The actual experiment was conducted by teams consisting of one member of the research group and one member of the South Fore tribe, who explained the task and translated the stories. Each adult participant was shown three photographs (one correct and two incorrect), told the story that corresponded to one of them, and asked to choose the expression that best matched the story. The procedure was the same for the children, except that they only had to choose between two photographs, one correct and one incorrect. Each participant was presented with various sets of photographs so that no single photograph ever appeared twice in the comparison.

The translators received careful training to ensure that they would not influence the participants. They were told that no responses were absolutely right or wrong and were asked not to prompt the participants. Also, they were taught how to translate the stories exactly the same way each time and to resist the temptation to elaborate and embellish them. To avoid unintentional bias, the Western member of the research team avoided looking at the participant and simply recorded the answers given.

Remember that these were photographs of expressions of emotions on the faces of Westerners. Could the Fore people correctly identify the emotions in the photographs, even though they never had seen a Western face before?

Results

First, analyses were conducted to determine if any responses differed between males and females or between adults and children. The adult women tended to be more hesitant to participate and had experienced less contact with Westerners than the men had. However, no significant differences in ability to correctly identify the emotions in the photographs were found among any of the groups.

Tables 6.2.2 and 6.2.3 summarize the percentage of correct responses for the six emotions by the least Westernized adults and the children, respectively. Not all participants were exposed to all emotions, and sometimes participants were exposed to the same emotion more than once. Therefore, the number of participants in the tables does not equal the overall total number of participants. All the differences were statistically significant except when participants were asked to distinguish fear from surprise. In this situation, many errors were made, and, for one group, surprise was actually selected 67% of the time when the story described fear.

Table 6.2.2 Percentage of Adults Correctly Identifying Emotional Expression in Photographs

Emotion in Story	Number of Participants	Percent Choosing Correct Photograph (%)
Happiness	220	92.3
Anger	98	85.3
Sadness	191	79.0
Disgust	101	83.0
Surprise	62	68.0
Fear	184	80.5
Fear (with surprise)	153	42.7

Table 6.2.3 Percentage of Children Correctly Identifying Emotional Expressions in Photographs

Emotion in Story	Number of Participants	Percent Choosing Correct Photograph (%)
Happiness	135	92.8
Anger	69	85.3
Sadness	145	81.5
Disgust	46	86.5
Surprise	47	98.3
Fear	64	93.3

SOURCE: Adapted from p. 127.

The researchers also compared the Westernized and non-Westernized adults. No significant differences between these two groups were found on the number who chose the correct photographs. Also, no differences were found between younger and older children. As you can see in Table 6.2.3, the children appeared to perform better than the adults, but Ekman and Friesen attributed this to the fact that they had to choose between only two photographs instead of three.

Discussion

Ekman and Friesen did not hesitate to draw a confident conclusion from their data: "The results for both adults and children clearly support our hypothesis that particular facial behaviors are universally associated with particular emotions" (p. 128). They based their conclusion on the fact that the South Fore group had no opportunity to learn anything about Western expressions and, thus, had no way of identifying them, unless the expressions were universal.

As a way of double-checking their findings, the researchers videotaped members of the isolated Fore culture portraying the same six facial expressions. Later, when these tapes were shown to college students in the United States, the students correctly identified the expressions corresponding to each of the emotions:

> The evidence from both studies contradicts the view that all facial behavior associated with emotion is culture-specific, and that posed facial behavior is a unique set of culture-bound conventions not understandable to members of another culture. (p. 128)

The one exception to their consistent findings—that of the confusion participants seemed to experience in distinguishing between expressions of fear and surprise—Ekman and Friesen explained by acknowledging that certainly some cultural differences are seen in emotional expression, but that this did not detract from the preponderance of evidence that nearly all the other expressions were correctly interpreted across the cultures. They speculated that fear and surprise may have been confused "because in this culture fearful events are almost always also surprising; that is, the sudden appearance of a hostile member of another village, the unexpected meeting of a ghost or sorcerer, etc." (p. 129).

Implications of the Research

This study by Ekman and Friesen served to demonstrate scientifically what you already suspected: Facial expressions of emotions are universal. However, you might still be asking yourself "What is the significance of this information?" Well, part of the answer to that question relates to the nature–nurture debate over whether human behaviors are present at birth or are acquired through learning. Because facial expressions for the six emotions used in this study appear to be influenced very little by cultural differences, it is possible to conclude that they must be innate, that is, biologically *hardwired* into the brain at birth.

Another reason behavioral scientists find the notion of universal emotional expressions important is that it addresses issues about how humans evolved. In 1872, Darwin published his famous book *The Expression of Emotion in Man and Animals*. He maintained that facial expressions were survival mechanisms that assisted animals in adapting to their environment, thereby enhancing their ability to survive. The idea behind this was that if certain messages could be communicated within and across species of animals through facial expressions, the odds of surviving and reproducing would be increased. For example, an expression of fear would provide a silent warning of imminent danger from predators, an expression of anger would warn less dominant members of the group to stay away from more powerful ones, and an expression of disgust would communicate a message of "Yuck! Don't eat that, whatever you do" and prevent a potential poisoning. These expressions, however, would do the animals no good if they were not universally recognized among all the individuals making up the species. Even though these expressions may now be less important to humans in terms of their survival value, the fact that they are universal among us would indicate that they have been passed on to us genetically over millions of years from our evolutionary ancestors which, along with many adaptations, played a role in reaching our present position on the evolutionary ladder.

A fascinating study demonstrated this *leftover* survival value of facial expressions in humans. The researchers (Hansen & Hansen, 1988) reasoned that if facial expressions could warn of impending danger, then humans should be able to recognize certain expressions, such as anger, more easily than other, less threatening expressions. To test this, they presented participants with photographs of large crowds of people with different facial expressions. In some of the photographs, all the people's expressions were happy except for one that was angry. In other photographs, all the expressions were angry, except for one that was happy. The participants' task was to pick out the face that was different. The amount of time it took the participants to find a single happy face in a crowd of angry faces was significantly longer than when they searched a crowd of happy faces for a single angry face. Furthermore, as the size of the crowds in the photographs increased, the time for participants to find the happy face also increased, but finding the angry face did not take significantly longer. This and other similar findings have indicated that humans may be biologically programmed to respond to the information provided by certain expressions better than others because those expressions offered more survival information.

Recent Applications

Other more recent studies in various areas of research have relied on Ekman's early findings in attempting to improve our understanding of children and adults with developmental or learning disabilities. One such study found that children diagnosed with autism (a pervasive developmental disorder marked by language deficits, sensory sensitivities, social withdrawal, and repetitive self-stimulation behaviors) appear to have difficulty recognizing the facial expressions that correspond to basic emotions (Bolte & Poustka, 2003). This difficulty was even more pronounced in families with more than one autistic child and may help explain why many autistic individuals show difficulty interpreting emotional responses from others.

The influence of Ekman's research, however, is not limited to humans. Ekman's 1971 study has been cited in research on the emotions of, believe it or not, *farm animals* (Desire, Boissy, & Veissier, 2002). These researchers suggest that the welfare of farm animals depends, in part, on their emotional reactions to their environment. When individual animals feel in harmony with their environment, their welfare is maximized; however, "any marked deviation from the state, if perceived by the individual, results in a welfare deficit due to negative emotional experiences" (p. 165). And this deficit can be observed from the animals' "facial" expressions.

A study citing Ekman's 1971 article attempted to shed light on exactly how one, specific facial feature—the human eyebrows—contributes to facial recognition (Sadr, Jarudi, & Sinha, 2003). Previous research had centered more on the eyes and mouth, but these researchers found that the eyebrows may be more important than the eyes themselves. The authors concluded "that the absence of eyebrows in familiar faces leads to a very large and significant disruption in recognition performance. In fact, a significantly greater decrement in face recognition is observed in the absence of eyebrows than in the absence of eyes" (p. 285). So, if you are ever in need of an effective disguise, be sure to cover your eyebrows!

A fascinating 2015 study analyzed the facial expression recognition of 478 children from 6 to 16 years of age, specifically looking at age, sex, and puberty (Lawrence, Cambell, & Skuse, 2015). Using Ekman and Friesen's facial expression photos, the researchers found that for happiness, surprise, fear, and disgust, the recognition skill was linear, that is, it improved with higher age. However, for the recognition of sad and angry expressions there was little change over the age range—children's abilities were at near adult levels (this could be interpreted as an adaptive mechanism similar to that discussed above). Girl's recognition was slightly better than boys at all ages, especially for happiness, surprise, disgust, and anger. Also, an improved recognition of anger and disgust only was evident with advancing puberty for both boys and girls unrelated to chronological age. What all this means is that the recognition of emotional expression may be a development process similar to the stages in Piaget's and Kohlberg's theories in the Development chapter in this book.

Conclusion

Over the past three decades following his early cross-cultural studies on emotional expressions, Ekman has continued his research individually and in collaboration with Friesen and several other researchers. Within this body of work, many fascinating discoveries have been made. One further example of Ekman's research involves what is called the *facial feedback theory* of emotional expressions. The theory states that the expression on your face actually feeds information back to your brain to assist you in interpreting the emotion you are experiencing. Ekman tested this idea by identifying the exact facial muscles involved in each of the six basic emotions. He then instructed participants to tense these muscles into expressions resembling the various emotions. When they did this, Ekman was able to measure physiological responses in the participants that corresponded to the appropriate emotion resulting from the facial expression alone, and not from the actual presence of the emotion itself (Ekman, Levensen, & Friesen, 1983).

Ekman has also extended his research into the area of deception and how the face and the body *leak* information to others about whether someone is telling the truth.

In general, his findings have indicated that people are able to detect when others are lying at a slightly better than chance level when observing just their facial expressions. However, when allowed to observe another's entire body, participants were much more successful in detecting lies, indicating that the body may provide better clues to certain states of mind than the face alone (see Ekman, 1985, for a complete discussion of this issue). Most recently, Ekman has distilled his extensive research in a book titled, *Emotions Revealed: Recognizing Faces and Feelings to Improve Communication and Emotional Life*, written to help all of us apply his work on the recognition of the meaning of facial expressions to improving our communication and interactions with romantic partners, children, coworkers, and even strangers (Ekman, 2007).

Ekman and his associates have provided us with a large literature on the nonverbal communication provided by facial expressions (see Ekman, 2003). And research in this area continues. It is likely that studies will continue as we become increasingly skilled at the process that was the title of Ekman and Friesen's 1975 book, *Unmasking the Face.*

Bolte, S., & Poustka, F. (2003). The recognition of facial affect in autistic and schizophrenia subjects and their first-degree relatives. *Psychological Medicine, 33,* 907–915.

Darwin, C. R. (1872). *The expression of the emotions in man and animals.* London: John Murray.

Desire, L., Boissy, A., & Veissier, I. (2002). Emotions in farm animals: A new approach to animal welfare in applied ethology. *Behavioural Processes, 60,* 165–180.

Ekman, P. (1985). *Telling lies.* New York: Norton.

Ekman, P. (2003). *Emotions revealed: Recognizing faces and feelings to improve communication and emotional life.* New York: Times Books.

Ekman, P. (2007). *Emotions revealed: Recognizing faces and feelings to improve communication and emotional life.* New York: Henry Holt.

Ekman, P., & Friesen, W. (1975). *Unmasking the face.* Englewood Cliffs, NJ: Prentice-Hall.

Ekman, P., Levensen, R., & Friesen, W. (1983). Autonomic nervous system activity distinguishes between emotions. *Science, 164,* 86–88.

Hansen, C., & Hansen, R. (1988). Finding the face in the crowd: An anger superiority effect. *Journal of Personality and Social Psychology, 54,* 917–924.

Lawrence, K., Campbell, R., & Skuse, D. (2015). Age, gender, and puberty influence the devel opment of facial emotion recognition. *Frontiers in psychology, 6,* 761.

Sadr, J., Jarudi, I., & Sinha, P. (2003). The role of eyebrows in face recognition. *Perception, 32,* 285–293.

Reading 6.3: *Watching* Your Emotions?

Ross, P. (2003, August 11). Mind readers. *Scientific American, 289*(3), 74–77.

6.3 Describe how fMRI scans show the difference between truth and lies

This research report is a bit of a departure from the other studies in this book, but it seems very appropriate to include it. As you know, this is a book about the major *classic* studies that changed the field of psychology in significant ways. The study discussed in this section is one that has done that, but, as you may have noticed, it's relatively recent. So this study is representative of research that is in the *process* of changing psychology in potentially compelling ways, right now, as we speak. This research concerns new, highly technical methods of actually peering into your brain (noninvasively) and "seeing" what is happening in your brain and how your brain functions including your emotions, your thoughts, your experiences, etc. OK, that may not be true "mind reading" as you usually think of it, but what psychology and neuroscience is capable of today is nothing short of astounding.

Most of you have heard of magnetic resonance imaging (MRI); probably, many of you have experienced the procedure on some part of your body or brain. The MRI is a major advance compared to the X-ray or CT scan because it does not emit radiation (so it's harmless to the body) and can show soft tissue abnormalities clearer (often three-dimensional) than the CT scan (this is especially important in visualizing the structures of the brain). That's why, if you injure your knee, and a CT scan doesn't show any obvious damage, your next diagnostic step might very well be to have an MRI to see more exactingly if cartilage or other tissue damage has occurred, so that proper treatment may be prescribed.

MRI scanners have been in medical use since the 1970s, but the technology has evolved considerably over the past 40 years. The pioneers in the development of MRI imaging were Paul Lauterbur of the University of Illinois and Peter Mansfield of the University of Nottingham, England (Lauterbur, 1973; Mansfield, 2007). In 2003, they jointly received the Nobel Prize in medicine for their work on this technology.

The article examined here by Philip Ross is an early report on how the MRI might be employed for uses beyond medicine such as detecting the brain structures involved in human thinking, emotions, motivations, and behaviors. Specifically, Ross examines a study that tests the potential of the MRI to determine if a person is telling the truth—if it might be a high-tech lie detector!

The fundamental basis for using the MRI for "reading" the brain is that it can reveal which parts of the brain are *functioning* at any particular time during a scan. This use of the MRI to detect brain functioning rather than a purely a diagnostic tool, is referred to as the *fMRI* (the *functional* MRI). In other words, while someone's brain is being scanned using an MRI, the person can be asked questions, shown pictures, asked to read short text fragments, etc. Researchers can then see exactly what parts of the brain are involved in these activities. How can they tell? Your brain functions can be seen when the MRI detects changes in the amount of oxygen in the blood flow around the active areas as well as glucose utilization. When researchers observe changes in these activities in certain parts of the brain on the monitors connected to the scanners, they can literally see which parts of the brain are activated during a task. In a way, those brain areas "light up."

Theoretical Propositions

Would you say that when you are telling the truth or when you are lying (and everybody lies; some more than others!), the truth or the lie "comes from" different parts of your brain? The answer is, that based on your personal experience, you don't know. Nothing *feels* different in your brain. But if we could *watch* your brain functioning while telling the truth and/or while lying and observe which areas are active for each activity, we could answer that question.

The fMRI can do this. And it's far superior to a polygraph (lie detector) because polygraphs fundamentally measure responses separated from the brain that create anxiety and people may become anxious for a variety of reasons other than telling a lie, which is why polygraphs are not considered scientifically valid and are not allowed as evidence in a court of law. The fMRI's brain imaging does not track anxiety, but rather reveals *thinking* processes.

The basic idea discussed in this article is that when the brain is being observed and the subject tells the truth, one part of the person's brain will "light up": the part containing the truthful statement. However, if the person lies, two parts of the brain will show up: the part that is creating the lie and the part holding the truth that the lie is covering up. In other words, a lie cannot exist unless it is hiding a truth and these two processes exist in different parts of your brain (see Langleben et al., 2002). These brain regions should be detectable using the fMRI.

Method

The research described in this article involved lying and truth telling when the participants and the researchers knew which was which. In other words, this was not a test of using the fMRI to detect a lie from a person, say, accused of a crime or being questioned about unethical misconduct. Instead, this was an exploratory study to test the theory (Langleben et al., 2002).

The method was fundamentally simple. Participants were asked to select one of three envelopes, all of which contained the five of clubs and a $20 bill (they did not know the contents were all the same). They were then asked to memorize the card and return it and the money to the envelope and conceal it in their pocket. They were told that if they could successfully keep the card a secret from a "computer" that could analyze their thoughts, they could keep the $20 (no actual computer was involved, other than the fMRI). Other participants received the two of hearts about which they were instructed to tell the truth and not conceal what card they had.

Each participant was then placed in the fMRI scanner with access to a YES or a NO button. They were then asked, "Do you have this card?" The researchers were aware of which card the participants possessed, but the participants did not know this (which did not really matter as "tricking" the researchers was not the point of the study!).

Results

Findings from the fMRI scans were clear. As you can see in Figure 6.3.1, those participants who told the truth about their 2 of hearts utilized only one brain region (the *anterior cingulate gyrus*). In the lie condition, however, two regions (the *anterior cingulate gyrus* and the *dorsolateral prefrontal cortex*) went into action.

Significance of the Findings

These findings were significant for two primary reasons. First, they demonstrated that MRI scanning may have important uses beyond medical diagnoses (which it does; to be discussed shortly) and perhaps could become a "foolproof" lie detector, the results of which might eventually be allowed in court, in much the same way as DNA evidence has become an accepted way of proving or disproving certain crimes.

Second, this study broadened our understanding of the amazing specialization of the human brain. If you look (directly) at a human brain, it appears to be no more than a mushy mass of cells and tissue. But in reality, you brain is extremely specialized, reserving specific regions for specific tasks. Your brain has a multitude of specialized regions that are "assigned" specific jobs from recognizing faces to speaking to planning and problem solving, and so on. In this particular study, you saw one region dedicated to truth telling, and another dedicated to lying.

Recent Applications

How has psychological science progressed in "brain reading" since the early 2000s when this article was published? Can we now use the fMRI as a lie detector? What else is the fMRI allowing us to do? As for the first question, the answer appears to be a resounding "maybe." One study found fMRI lie detection to be significantly more reliable than the conventional polygraph tests. However, critics argue that the court's ability to peer inside someone's head may raise serious ethical concerns (Simpson, 2008).

Another study important to note applied similar methodology to the playing card study discussed here, but used actual line-ups of human faces (Bhatt et al., 2008). Participants were shown groups of photos of faces and later, under the fMRI scanner, were

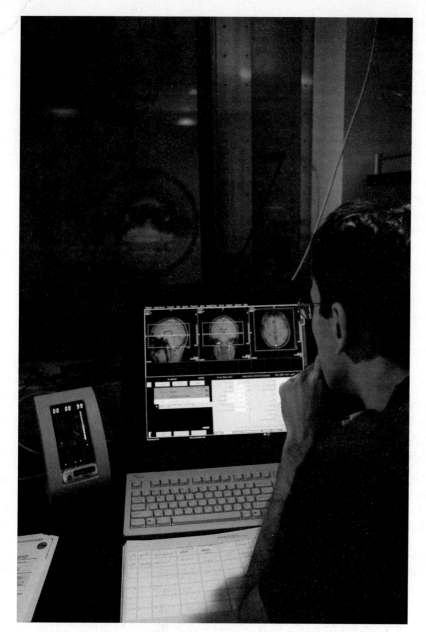

A patient about to enter the fMRI unit. (Juan Manuel Silva/Glow Images, Inc.)

Figure 6.3.1 fMRI scan results for truth-telling and lying participants. Top: Brain scan of participants telling the truth (2 of hearts). Bottom: Brain scans of participants lying (5 of clubs).

(Based on: Langleben et al., 2002.)

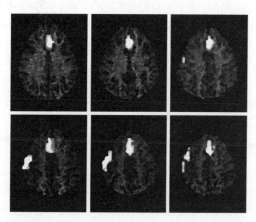

shown faces selected from the ones they had seen. They were told either to tell the truth about having seen them before or to lie. The findings were essentially the same as the playing card study. Two brain regions became active when they lied, but only one lit up when they told the truth.

One example of a new use for the fMRI that is outside the "lie detector" area relates to psychological disorders. The fMRI has been a great assistance to neuropsychological medicine in identifying the regions in the brains of schizophrenics that appear to be responsible for the characteristic loss of clear and rational thinking (Libby & Ragland, 2011). This knowledge may help researchers to zero in on one of schizophrenia's most devastating symptoms in the development of new treatments.

Another important improvement in neuropsychology involving the fMRI is an increased understanding in the brain functioning of individuals with autism spectrum disorders (Philipa et al., 2012). These disorders are often marked most clearly by social deficits, the inability or difficulty in relating appropriately to others. An fMRI study of autism patients revealed abnormal activity in the regions of the brain that are thought to be responsible for socialization and may indicate that it is not an inability to socialize that affects those with autism disorders, but rather a *preference* to avoid socialization. Additionally, the study revealed abnormalities in how the brain modulates in response to changes in routine tasks, which may help explain why those diagnosed with autism-related disorders become very distraught when routines to which they are accustomed are altered.

Perhaps, as of 2012, the most surprising fMRI results came to us from the Gallant FMRI Laboratory at U.C. Berkeley, California. Participants were shown movie clips while in the fMRI unit. Using new computer software, researchers were able to reconstruct fuzzy, but remarkably representative reproductions of the movie images watched by the participants, purely from their fMRI scans. In the sample images from the movies, presented in Figure 6.3.2, you can see just how close the technology comes to literally *reading your mind*.

Conclusion

The applications and utility of the fMRI to help us understand how the brain works—whether it be relating to lie detection, psychological brain disorders and injuries, or revealing variations in how the brains of people or groups of people (e.g., men and women) are "wired"—are still largely unrealized. However, prior to the technology of noninvasive scanning devices, such as the MRI, our methodology for researching the brain directly was limited to surgery or autopsy. Now neuroscientists have the fMRI and other noninvasive tools to study, diagnose, treat, and cure brain-related disorders far more effectively than ever before and, perhaps, even record your thoughts. Whether

---

Figure 6.3.2 Images from movies and their fMRI scan reproductions.

(Top and bottom left: AF archive/Alamy; top and bottom right: Dean Drobot/Shutterstock)

this technology will be put to good or "evil" purposes will depend on the ethics and values of those who control it.

Bhatt, S., Mbwana, J., Adeyemo, A., Sawyer, A., Hailu, A., & VanMeter, J. (2009). Lying about facial recognition: An fMRI study. *Brain and Cognition, 69*, 382–390.

Langleben, D., Schroeder, L., Maldjian, J., Gur, R., McDonald, S., Ragland, J., O'Brien, C., & Childress, R. (2002). Brain activity during simulated deception: An event-related functional magnetic resonance study. *NeuroImage, 15*, 727–732.

Lauterbur, P. (1973). Image formation by induced local interactions: Examples employing nuclear magnetic resonance. *Nature 242*, 190–191.

Libby, L., & Ragland, J. (2011). fMRI as a measure of cognition related brain circuitry in schizophrenia. *Current Topics in Behavioral Neurosciences.* Retrieved from www.biomedsearch.com/nih/fMRI-as-Measure-Cognition-Related/22105156.html.

Mansfield, P. (1973). A personal view of my involvement in the development of NMR and the conception and development of MRI. *Nature, 242*, 190–191.

Philipa, R., Dauvermanna, M., Whalleya, H., Baynhama, K., Lawrie, S., & Stanfield, A. (2012). A systematic review and meta-analysis of the fMRI investigation of autism spectrum disorders. *Neuroscience & Biobehavioral Reviews, 36*, 901–942.

Simpson, J. (2008). Functional MRI lie detection: Too good to be true? *Journal of the American Academy of Psychiatry and Law, 36*, 491–498.

Reading 6.4: Thoughts Out of Tune

Festinger, L., & Carlsmith, J. M. (1959). Cognitive consequences of forced compliance. *Journal of Abnormal and Social Psychology*, 58, 203–210.

6.4 Analyze the impact of cognitive dissonance on decisions and behaviors

Have you ever been in a position of having to do or say something that was contrary to your attitudes or private opinions? Chances are you have; everyone has at some time. When you behaved that way, what happened to your attitude or opinion? Nothing? Well, maybe nothing. However, studies have shown that in some cases, when your behavior is contrary to your attitude, your attitude will change a bit (or a lot) to bring it into alignment with your behavior. For example, if a person is forced (say, by the demands of an experiment) to deliver a speech in support of a viewpoint or position opposed to his or her personal opinion, the speaker's attitudes will tend to shift toward those given in the speech.

In the early 1950s, various studies tried to explain this opinion shift as a result of (a) mentally rehearsing the speech, and (b) the process of trying to think of arguments in favor of the forced position. In performing those mental tasks, the early theories argued that participants convinced themselves of the position they were about to take. In pursuing this line of reasoning further, additional studies were conducted that offered monetary rewards to participants for giving convincing speeches contrary to their own views. It was expected that the greater the reward, the greater would be the resulting opinion change in the speaker. It seems logical, doesn't it? You get paid a lot of money, your attitudes are more likely to shift, right? However, as one of many examples of how common sense is a poor predictor of human behavior, just the opposite was found to be true. Larger rewards produced *less* attitude change than smaller rewards. Based on behavioral theories of psychology that were popular at the time (e.g., operant conditioning, reinforcement theory, etc.), such findings were difficult for researchers to explain.

A few years later, Leon Festinger (1919–1989), a research psychologist at Stanford University, proposed the highly influential and now famous theory of *cognitive dissonance,* which could account for these seemingly discrepant findings. The word *cognitive* refers to mental processes, such as thoughts, ideas, attitudes, or beliefs; the word *dissonance* simply means "out of tune." Therefore, Festinger suggested, you will experience cognitive dissonance when you simultaneously hold two or more cognitions that are psychologically inconsistent. When this condition exists, it creates discomfort and stress to varying degrees, depending on the importance of the dissonant attitude. This discomfort then motivates you to change something to reduce the dissonance. Because you cannot change your behavior (because you have already done it or because the situational pressures are too great), you change your attitudes. You may not think you would change your attitudes, but it appears that such changes are a basic tenant of human behavior.

Festinger's theory grew out of a historical event involving rumors that spread throughout India following a 1934 earthquake there. In the areas outside the disaster zone, the rumors predicted that people should expect additional earthquakes of even greater proportions and throughout an even greater portion of the country. These rumors were untrue and lacked any rational, geological foundation. Festinger wondered why people would spread such catastrophic and anxiety-increasing ideas. It occurred to him over time that perhaps the rumors were not anxiety increasing, but *anxiety justifying.* That is, these people were very frightened, even though they lived outside the danger area. This created *cognitive dissonance:* Their cognition of intense fear was out of tune with the fact that they were, in reality, safe. Therefore, the people spread rumors of greater disasters to justify their fears and reduce their dissonance. Without realizing it, they made their view of the world (greater earthquakes) fit with what they were feeling and how they were behaving.

Theoretical Propositions

Festinger theorized that normally what you publicly state will be substantially the same as your private opinion or belief. Therefore, if you believe "X" but publicly state "not X," you will experience the discomfort of cognitive dissonance. However, if you know that the reasons for your statement of "not X" were clearly justified by pressures, promises of rewards, or threats of punishment, then your dissonance will be reduced or eliminated. Therefore—and this is the key—the more you view your inconsistent behavior to be *of your own choosing*, the greater will be your dissonance.

One way for you to reduce this unpleasant dissonance is to alter your opinion to bring it into agreement, or consonance, with your behavior. Festinger contended that changes in attitudes and opinions will be greatest when dissonance is large. Think about it for a moment. Suppose someone offers you a great deal of money to state, in public, specific views that are the opposite of your true views, and you agree to do so. Then suppose someone else makes the same request but offers you just a little money, and even though it hardly seems worth, you agree anyway. In which case will your dissonance be the greatest? Logically, you would experience more dissonance in the less-money situation because you would feel *insufficient justification* for your attitude-discrepant behavior. Therefore, according to Festinger's theory, your private opinion would shift more in the little-money condition. Let's see how Festinger (with the help of his associate James Carlsmith) set about testing this theory.

Method

Imagine you are a university student enrolled in an introductory psychology course. One of your course requirements is to participate for 3 hours during the semester as a participant in psychology experiments. You check the bulletin board that posts the various studies being carried out by professors and graduate students, and you sign up for one that lasts 2 hours and deals with "measures of performance." In Festinger and Carlsmith's study, as in many psychology experiments, the true purpose of the study cannot be revealed to the participants because this could bias their responses and invalidate the results. The group of participants in the original study consisted of 71 males, lower-division psychology students. [When this study was conducted in 1959, most psychology students; indeed, most *college* students were male. Therefore, most participants in studies were male as well—rightly or wrongly.]

Imagine you arrive at the laboratory at the appointed time (here, the laboratory is nothing more than a room with chairs). You are told that this experiment takes a little over an hour, so it had to be scheduled for 2 hours. Because extra time will be available, the experimenter informs you that some people from the psychology department are interviewing participants about their experiences as participants, and he asks you to talk to them after participating. Then you are given your first task.

A tray containing 12 spools is placed in front of you. You are told to empty the tray onto the table, refill the tray with the spools, empty it again, and refill it, and so on. You are to work with one hand and at your own speed. While the experimenter looks on with a stopwatch and takes notes, you do this over and over for 30 minutes. Then the tray is removed, and you are given a board with 48 square pegs. Your task now is to turn each peg a quarter of a turn clockwise and to repeat this over and over for 30 minutes more! If this sounds incredibly boring to you, that was precisely the intention of the researchers. This part of the study was, in the authors' words, "intended to provide, for each participant uniformly, an experience about which he would have a somewhat negative opinion" (p. 205). Undoubtedly, you would agree that this objective was accomplished. Following completion of these boring tasks, the experiment really began.

The participants were randomly assigned to one of three conditions. In the control condition, the participants, after completing the tasks, were taken to another room where they were interviewed about their reactions to the experiment they had just completed. The rest of the participants were lured a little further into the experimental manipulations. Following the tasks, the experimenter spoke to them as if to explain the purpose of the study. He told each of them that they were among the participants in "group A," who performed the tasks with no prior information, while participants in "group B" always received descriptive information about the tasks prior to entering the lab. He went on to state that the information received by group B participants was that the tasks were fun and interesting. This message was delivered by an undergraduate student posing as a participant who had already completed the tasks. It is important to keep in mind that none of this was true; it was a fabrication intended to make the next, crucial part of the study realistic and believable. This was, in other words, a cover story.

The experimenter then left the room for a few minutes. Upon returning, he continued to speak but now appeared somewhat confused and uncertain. He explained, a little embarrassed, that the undergraduate who usually gives the information to group B participants had called in sick, that a participant from group B was waiting, and that they were having trouble finding someone to fill in for him. He then very politely asked the participant if he would be willing to join the experiment and be the one to inform the waiting participant.

The experimenter offered some of the participants a dollar each for their help, while others were offered $20 (a sizable amount of money in 1959). After a participant agreed, he was given a sheet of paper marked "For Group B" on which was written, "It was very enjoyable, I had a lot of fun, I enjoyed myself, it was intriguing, it was exciting." The participant was then paid either $1 or $20 and taken into the waiting room to meet the incoming "participant." Participants were left alone in the waiting room for 2 minutes, after which time the experimenter returned, thanked them for their help, and led them to the interview room where they were asked their opinions of the tasks exactly as had been asked of the participants in the control condition.

If this whole procedure seems a bit complicated, it really is not. The bottom line is that there were three groups of 20 participants each. One group received $1 each to lie about the tasks, one group was paid $20 each to lie about the tasks, and the control group did not lie at all.

Results

The results of the study were reflected in how each of the participants actually felt about the boring tasks in the final interview phase of the study. They were asked to rate the experiment as follows:

1. *Were the tasks interesting and enjoyable?* This was measured on a scale of −5 (extremely dull and boring) to +5 (extremely interesting and enjoyable). The 0 point indicated that the tasks were neutral: neither interesting nor uninteresting.

2. *How much did you learn about your ability to perform such tasks?* Measured on a 0 to 10 scale, where 0 meant nothing learned and 10 meant a great deal learned.

3. *Do you believe the experiment and tasks were measuring anything important?* Measured on a 0 to 10 scale, where 0 meant no scientific value and 10 meant great scientific value.

4. *Would you have any desire to participate in another similar experiment?* Measured on a scale of −5 (definitely dislike to participate) to +5 (definitely like to participate), with 0 indicating neutral feelings.

The averages of the answers to the interview questions are presented in Table 6.4.1. Questions 1 and 4 were designed to address Festinger's theory of cognitive dissonance, and the differences indicated are clearly significant. Contrary to previous research in the field, and contrary to what most of us might expect using common sense, those participants who were paid $1 for lying about the tasks were the ones who later reported liking the tasks more, compared to both those paid $20 to lie and those who did not lie. This finding is reflected both in the first direct question and also in the $1 group's greater willingness to participate in another similar experiment (question 4).

Discussion

The theory of cognitive dissonance states the following, in Festinger's words:

1. If a person is induced to do or say something that is contrary to his private opinion, there will be a tendency for him to change his opinion to bring it into correspondence with what he has said or done.

2. The larger the pressure used to elicit the overt behavior, the weaker will be the above-mentioned tendency. (pp. 209–210)

Festinger and Carlsmith's findings clearly support this theory. Festinger's explanation for this was that when people engage in attitude-discrepant behavior (the lie) but have strong justification for doing so ($20), they will experience only a small amount of dissonance and, therefore, will not feel particularly motivated to make a change in their opinion. On the other hand, people who have insufficient justification ($1) for their attitude-discrepant behavior will experience greater levels of dissonance

Table 6.4.1 Average Ratings on Interview Questions for Each Experimental Condition

Question	Control Group	$1 Group	$20 Group
1. How enjoyable tasks were (from −5 to +5)*	0.45	+1.35	0.05
2. How much learned (from 0 to 10)	3.08	2.80	3.15
3. Scientific importance (from 0 to 10)	5.60	6.45	5.18
4. Participate in similar experiences (from −5 to +5)*	0.62	+1.20	0.25

*Questions relevant to Festinger and Carlsmith's hypothesis (Data from p. 207)

and will, therefore, alter their opinions more radically in order to reduce the resultant discomfort. The theory may be presented graphically as follows:

Attitude-discrepant behavior → *Sufficient justification for behavior ($20)* →
Dissonance small → *Attitude change small*

Attitude-discrepant behavior → *Insufficient justification for behavior ($1)* →
Dissonance large → *Attitude change large*

Questions and Criticisms

Festinger himself anticipated that previous researchers whose theories were threatened by this new idea would attempt to criticize the findings and offer alternate explanations for them (such as mental rehearsal and thinking up better arguments, as discussed previously). To counter these criticisms, the sessions in which the participant lied to the incoming participant were recorded and rated by two independent judges who had no knowledge of which condition ($1 versus $20) they were rating. Statistical analyses of these ratings showed no differences in the content or persuasiveness of the lies between the two groups. Therefore, the only apparent explanation remaining for the findings is what Festinger termed *cognitive dissonance.*

Over the decades since cognitive dissonance was demonstrated by Festinger and Carlsmith, other researchers have refined—but not rejected—the theory. Many of these refinements were summarized by Cooper and Fazio (1984), who outlined four necessary steps for an attitude change to occur through cognitive dissonance. The first step is that the attitude-discrepant behavior must produce unwanted negative consequences. Festinger and Carlsmith's participants had to lie to fellow students and convince them to participate in a very boring experiment. This produced the required negative consequences. This also explains why, when you compliment someone on their clothes even though you can't stand them, your attitude toward the clothes probably doesn't change. In other words, cognitive dissonance does not always occur following your attitude discrepant behaviour.

The second step is that participants must feel personal responsibility for the negative consequences. This usually involves a choice. If you choose to behave in an attitude-discrepant way that results in negative consequences, you will experience dissonance. However, if someone forces or coerces you to behave in that way, you will not feel personally responsible, and you will experience little or no cognitive dissonance. Although Festinger and Carlsmith used the term *forced compliance* in the title of their article, the participants actually *believed* that their actions were voluntary.

Physiological arousal (the third step) is also a necessary component of the process of cognitive dissonance. Festinger believed that dissonance is an uncomfortable state of tension that motivates us to change our attitudes. Studies have shown that, indeed, when participants freely behave in attitude-discrepant ways, they experience physiological arousal. Festinger and Carlsmith did not measure this with their participants, but it is safe to assume that physiological arousal (increased heart rate, raised BP, etc.) was present.

The fourth step requires that a person be aware that the arousal he or she is experiencing is caused by the attitude-discrepant behavior. The discomfort the participants felt in Festinger and Carlsmith's study would have been easily and clearly attributed to the fact that they knew they were lying about the experiment to a fellow student.

Festinger and Carlsmith's conceptualization of cognitive dissonance has become a widely accepted and well-documented psychological phenomenon. Most psychologists agree that two fundamental processes are responsible for changes in our opinions and attitudes. One is persuasion—when other people actively work to convince us to change our views—and the other is cognitive dissonance.

Recent Applications

Social science research continues to rely on, demonstrate, and confirm Festinger and Carlsmith's theory and findings. One interesting study found that you may experience cognitive dissonance and change your attitude about an issue simply by *observing* people whom you like and respect engaging in attitude-discrepant behavior, without any personal participation on your part at all (Norton et al., 2003). The authors referred to this process as *vicarious dissonance.* In Norton's study, college students heard speeches disagreeing with their attitudes on a controversial issue (a college fee increase). For some, the speech in favor of the increase was given by a member of their own college (their "ingroup"), while for others, the speech was made by a member of another college (their "outgroup"). When an ingroup member delivered the speech, the participants experienced cognitive dissonance and decreased their negative attitudes toward the increase. In an even stronger demonstration of vicarious dissonance, the researchers found that the participants did not even have to hear the speech itself; simply *knowing* that the ingroup member agreed to make the speech created enough dissonance to cause the attitude change.

A fascinating study in a different vein used the theory of cognitive dissonance to explain why some cigarette smokers refuse to quit even though they know (as does nearly everyone) the negative health effects of smoking (Peretti-Watel et al., 2007). If you smoke cigarettes, knowing the risk to your health, and feel unable to quit, you will likely experience cognitive dissonance. Because this is an unpleasant state, you will develop strategies that will reduce your dissonance. In this 2007 study, the researchers found that smokers often expressed "self-exempting" beliefs along the lines of "Smoking is dangerous to people's health but not to me because I don't smoke very much" or "The way I smoke cigarettes will protect me from disease." The researchers suggest that "Future tobacco control messages and interventions should specifically address these self-exempting beliefs that reduce smokers' cognitive dissonance and then inhibit their willingness to quit" (p. 377).

Very important research based on Festinger's theory of cognitive dissonance, conducted by the psychologist Elliot Aronson at the University of California, Santa Cruz, focused on changing students' risky sexual behaviors (Shea, 1997). Sexually active students were asked to make videotapes about how condom use can reduce the risk of STD infection. After making the tapes, half of the students were divided into groups and encouraged to discuss why college students resist using condoms and to reveal their own experiences of not using condoms. In other words, these participants had to admit that they did not always adhere to the message they had just promoted in the videos; they had to face their own hypocrisy. The other students who engaged in making the videos did not participate in the follow-up discussions. When all the students were then given the opportunity to buy condoms, a significantly higher proportion of those in the hypocrisy group purchased them compared to the video-only group. More importantly, 3 months later, when the participants were interviewed about their sexual practices, 92% of the students in the hypocrisy group said they had been using condoms every time they had intercourse compared to only 55% of those who participated in making the videotapes but were not required to publicly admit their attitude-discrepant behavior. This is a clear example of cognitive dissonance at work.

Conclusion

When you are forced to confront the discrepancy between your beliefs and your behavior, you will usually experience cognitive dissonance that will motivate you to change either your behavior or your beliefs to bring them more "in tune" with each other. Elliot Aronson, a strong proponent of the importance of cognitive dissonance in bringing about real-life behavioral change, explains that "Most of us engage in hypocritical behavior all the time, because we can blind ourselves to it. But if someone comes along and forces you to look at it, you can no longer shrug it off" (Shea, 1997, p. A15).

Cooper, J., & Fazio, R. (1984). A new look at dissonance theory. In L. Berkowitz (Ed.), *Advances in experimental social psychology*. New York: Academic Press.

Norton, M. I., Monin, B., Cooper, J., & Hogg, M. A. (2003). Vicarious dissonance: Attitude change from the inconsistency of others. *Journal of Personality and Social Psychology, 85*, 47–62.

Peretti-Watel, P., Halfen, S., & Gremy, I. (2007). Risk denial about smoking hazards and readiness to quit among French smokers: An exploratory study. *Addictive Behaviors, 32*, 377–383.

Shea, C. (1997). A University of California psychologist investigates new approaches to changing human behavior. *Chronicle of Higher Education, 43*(41), A15.

Chapter 7
Personality

 Learning Objectives

7.1 Compare the impacts of using an internal or external locus of control

7.2 Evaluate Bem's research on gender expression

7.3 Describe the relationship between personality and health

7.4 Analyze how living in a collectivist or individualist culture influences behavior

If you ask yourself the question "Who am I?" you are asking the same basic question posed by personality psychologists. Personality psychologists seek to reveal the human characteristics that combine to make each person unique and to determine the origins of those characteristics. When behavioral scientists speak of personality, they are usually referring to human qualities that are relatively stable across situations and consistent over time. Who you are does not change each day, each week, or, usually, even each year or decade. Instead, certain basic characteristics about you are constant and predictable. Psychologists have proposed hundreds of personality theories over psychology's history. Most of these models have been debated and argued so much that it is often unclear whether they truly measure meaningful differences among individuals. However, a few factors have been repeatedly shown to predict specific behaviors reliably. These are the focus of this section.

The first reading discusses Julian Rotter's famous research into how people view the location of "control" in their lives. Some believe that their lives are controlled by external factors, such as fate or luck, but others feel the control is internal—in their own hands. This quality of a person's belief in external versus internal control has been shown to be a consistent and important factor in defining who you are. Second, you will read about research from the 1970s by Sandra Bem, who literally revolutionized the way we view a fundamental and powerful component of personal identity: gender. Third is the highly influential study that first identified what many of you now know as Type A and Type B personalities and how these two types of people are fundamentally different. These differences are not minor or unimportant for many reasons especially that Type A individuals may be more prone to heart attacks. You'll also read about a study that has influenced virtually all branches of psychology by reminding us that human behavior must always be considered within a cultural context. This reading discusses the work of Harry Triandis, who, over the past 40 years, has carefully and convincingly developed his theory that most human societies fall within one of two overarching categories: *collectivist* cultures and *individualistic* cultures. This single (though certainly not simple) dimension may explain a great deal about how the culture in which you are raised has a profound effect on who you are.

Reading 7.1: Are You the Master of Your Fate?

Rotter, J. B. (1966). Generalized expectancies for internal versus external control of reinforcement. *Psychological Monographs, 80*, 1–28.

7.1 Compare the impacts of using an internal or external locus of control

This groundbreaking study by Rotter relates in some important ways to the study in Chapter 4 by Langer and Rodin about nursing home residents given greater control over their lives in the home (known as the "plant study"). Again, the crucial topic of personal control over our lives is the subject of this research.

Are the consequences of your individual behavior under your personal control or are they determined by forces outside of yourself? Think about it for a moment: When something good happens to you, do you take credit for it or do you think how lucky you were? When something negative occurs, is it usually due to your actions or do you chalk it up to fate? The same question may be posed in more formal psychological language: Do you believe that a causal relationship exists between your behavioral choices in your life and their consequences?

Julian Rotter, one of the most influential behaviorists in psychology's history, proposed that individuals differ a great deal in terms of where they place the causes—the "location"—for what happens to them. When people interpret the consequences of their behavior to be controlled by luck, fate, or powerful others, this indicates a belief in what Rotter called an *external locus of control* (locus meaning location). Conversely, he maintained that if people interpret their own choices and personality as responsible for their behavioral consequences, they believe in an *internal locus of control*. In his 1966 article, Rotter explained that a person's tendency to view events from an internal, versus an external, locus of control is fundamental to who we are and can be explained from a social learning theory perspective.

In this view, as a person develops from infancy through childhood, behaviors in a given situation are learned because they are followed by some form of _reward_ or *reinforcement*. This reinforcement increases the child's expectation that a particular behavior will produce the desired reward. Once this expectancy is established, the removal of reinforcement will cause the expectancy of such a relationship between behavior and reinforcement to fade. Therefore, reinforcement is sometimes seen as contingent upon behavior, and sometimes it is not (see the discussion of contingencies in Reading 3.3 in the work of B. F. Skinner). As children develop, some will have frequent experiences in which their behavior directly influences consequences, while for others, reinforcement will appear to result from actions outside of themselves. Rotter claimed that the totality of your individual learning experiences creates in you a generalized expectancy about whether reinforcement is internally or externally controlled.

"These generalized expectancies," Rotter wrote, "will result in characteristic differences in behavior in a situation culturally categorized as chance-determined versus skill-determined, and may act to produce individual differences within a specific condition" (p. 2). In other words, you have developed an internal or external interpretation of the consequences for your behavior that will influence your future behavior in almost all situations. Rotter believed that your locus of control, whether internal or external, is a chief part of your personality—who you are.

Look back at the questions posed at the beginning of this reading. Which do you think you are: an internal or an external locus-of-control person? Rotter wanted to study differences among people on this dimension and, rather than simply ask them, he developed a test that measured a person's locus of control. Once he was able to measure this characteristic in people, he could then study how an external versus an internal locus influenced their behavior.

Theoretical Propositions

Rotter proposed to demonstrate two main points in his research. First, he predicted that a test could be developed to measure reliably the extent to which individuals possess an internal or an external locus-of-control orientation toward life. Second, he hypothesized that people will display stable individual differences in their interpretations of the causes of reinforcement in the same situations. He proposed to demonstrate his hypothesis by presenting research comparing behavior of "internals" with that of "externals" in various contexts.

Method

Rotter designed a scale containing a series of many pairs of statements. Each pair consisted of one statement reflecting an internal locus of control and one reflecting an external locus of control. Those taking the test were instructed to select "the one statement of each pair (and only one) which you more strongly believe to be the case as far as you're concerned. Be sure to select the one you actually believe to be more true rather than the one you think you should choose or the one you would like to be true. This is a measure of personal belief: Obviously, there are no right or wrong answers" (p. 26). The test was designed so that participants had to choose one statement or the other and could not designate *neither* or *both*.

Rotter's measuring scale endured many revisions and alterations. In its earliest form, it contained 60 pairs of statements, but by using various tests for reliability and validity, it was eventually refined and streamlined down to 23 items. Added to these were six "filler items," which were designed to disguise the true purpose of the test. Such filler items are often used in psychological tests because if participants were able to guess what the test is trying to measure, they might alter their answers in some way in an attempt to "perform better."

Rotter called his test the *I-E Scale* (for Internal and External), which is the name it is known by today. Table 7.1.1 includes examples of typical items from the I-E Scale, plus samples of the filler items. If you examine the items, you can see quite clearly which statements reflect an internal or an external orientation. Rotter contended that his test was a measure of the extent to which a person possesses the personality characteristic of internal or external locus of control.

Rotter's next, and most important, step was to demonstrate that he could actually use this characteristic to predict people's behavior in specific situations. To do this, he reported on several studies (conducted by himself and others) in which scores on the I-E Scale were examined in relation to individuals' interactions with various events in their lives. These studies revealed significant correlations between I-E scores and people's behavior in many diverse situations, such as gambling, political activism, persuasion, smoking, achievement motivation, and conformity.

Results

Following is a brief summary of the findings reported by Rotter of his research in the areas mentioned in the previous paragraph. (See pp. 19–24 of the original study for a complete discussion and citation of specific references.)

Table 7.1.1 Sample Items and Filler Items from Rotter's I-E Scale

Item Number	Statements
2a.	Many of the unhappy things in people's lives are partly due to bad luck.
2b.	People's misfortunes result from the mistakes they make.
11a.	Becoming a success is a matter of hard work; luck has little or nothing to do with it.
11b.	Getting a good job depends mainly on being in the right place at the right time.
18a.	Most people don't realize the extent to which their lives are controlled by accidental happenings.
18b.	There is really no such thing as "luck."
23a.	Sometimes I can't understand how teachers arrive at the grades I get.
23b.	There is a direct connection between how hard I study and the grades I get.
	Filler Items
1a.	Children get into trouble because their parents punish them too much.
1b.	The trouble with most children nowadays is that their parents are too easy with them.
14a.	There are certain people who are just no good.
14b.	There is some good in everybody.

SOURCE: Adapted from pp. 13–14.

GAMBLING   Rotter reported on studies that looked at betting behavior in relation to locus of control. These studies found that individuals identified as internals by the I-E Scale tended to prefer betting on "sure things" and liked moderate odds over the long shots. Externals, on the other hand, would wager more money on risky bets. In addition, externals would tend to engage in more unusual shifts in betting, called the "gambler's fallacy" (such as betting more on a number that has not come up for a while on the basis that it is "due," when the true odds of it occurring are unchanged).

PERSUASION   An interesting study cited by Rotter used the I-E Scale to select two groups of students, one highly internal and the other highly external. Both groups shared similar attitudes, on average, about the fraternity and sorority system on campus. Both groups were asked to try to persuade other students to change their attitudes about these organizations. The internals were found to be significantly more successful than externals in altering the attitudes of others. Conversely, other studies demonstrated that internals were more resistant to manipulation of their attitudes by others.

SMOKING   An internal locus of control appeared to relate to self-control as well. Two studies discussed by Rotter found that (a) smokers tended to be significantly more external than nonsmokers and (b) individuals who were able to quit smoking after the original surgeon general's warning appeared on cigarette packs in 1966 were more internally oriented, even though both internals and externals believed the warning was true.

ACHIEVEMENT MOTIVATION   If you believe your own actions are responsible for your successes, it is logical to assume that you would be more motivated to achieve success than someone who believes success is more a matter of fate. Rotter pointed to a study of 1,000 high school students that found a positive relationship between a high internal score on the I-E Scale and achievement motivation. The indicators of achievement included plans to attend college, amount of time spent on homework, and how interested the parents were in the students' school work. Each of these achievement-oriented factors was more likely to be found in those students who demonstrated an internal locus of control.

CONFORMITY   One study was cited that exposed participants to the conformity test developed by Solomon Asch, in which a participant's willingness to agree with a majority's incorrect judgment was evidence for conforming behavior (see Reading 10.2 on Asch's conformity study). Participants were allowed to bet (with money provided by the experimenters) on the correctness of their judgments. Under this betting condition, those found to be internals conformed significantly less to the majority opinion and bet more money on themselves when making contrary judgments than did the externals.

Discussion

As part of his discussion, Rotter posed possible sources for the individual differences he found on the dimension of internal–external locus of control. Citing various studies, he suggested three potential sources for the development of an internal or external orientation: cultural differences, socioeconomic differences, and variations in styles of parenting.

One study he cited found differences in locus of control among various cultures. In one rather isolated community in the United States, three distinct groups could be compared: Ute Indians, Mexican Americans, and Caucasians. The researchers found that those individuals of Ute heritage were, on average, the most external, while Caucasians were the most internal. The Mexican Americans scored between the other two groups on the I-E Scale. These findings, which appeared to be independent of socioeconomic level, suggested ethnic differences in locus of control.

Rotter also referred to some early and tentative findings indicating that socioeconomic levels within a particular culture may relate to locus of control. These studies suggested that a lower socioeconomic position predicts greater externality.

Styles of parenting were implicated by Rotter as an obvious source for our learning to be internal or external. Although he did not offer supportive research evidence at the time, he suggested that parents who administer rewards and punishments to their children in ways that are unpredictable and inconsistent would likely encourage the development of an external locus of control (this is discussed in greater detail shortly).

Rotter summarized his findings by pointing out that the consistency of the results leads to the conclusion that locus of control is a defining characteristic of individuals that operates fairly consistently across various situations. Furthermore, the influences on behavior produced by the internal–external dimension are such that it will influence different people to behave differently when faced with the same situation. In addition, Rotter contended that locus of control can be measured, and that the I-E Scale is an effective tool for doing so.

Rotter hypothesized that those with an internal locus of control (i.e., those who have a strong belief that they can control their own destiny) are more likely than externals to (a) gain information from the situations in their lives in order to improve their future behavior in similar situations, (b) take the initiative to change and improve their condition in life, (c) place greater value on inner skill and achievement of goals, and (d) be more able to resist manipulation by others.

Subsequent Research

Since Rotter developed his I-E Scale, hundreds of studies have examined the relationship between locus of control and various behaviors. Following is a brief sampling of a few of those as they relate to rather diverse human behaviors.

In his 1966 article, Rotter touched on how locus of control might relate to health behaviors. Since then, other studies have examined this relationship. In a review of locus-of-control research, Strickland (1977) found that individuals with an internal focus generally take more responsibility for their own health. They are more likely to engage in more healthy behaviors (such as not smoking and adopting better nutritional habits) and practice greater care in avoiding accidents. In addition, studies have found that internals generally have lower levels of stress and are less likely to suffer from stress-related illnesses.

Rotter's hypotheses regarding the relationship between parenting styles and locus of control have been at least partially confirmed. Research has shown that parents of children who are internals tend to be more affectionate, more consistent and fair with discipline, and more concerned with teaching children to take responsibility for their actions. Parents of externally oriented children have been found to be more authoritarian and restrictive and do not allow their children much opportunity for personal control (see Davis & Phares, 1969, for a discussion of those findings).

A fascinating study demonstrated how the concept of locus of control may have sociological and even catastrophic implications. Sims and Baumann (1972) applied Rotter's theory to explain why more people have died in tornados in Alabama than in Illinois. These researchers noticed that the death rate from tornados was five times greater in the South than in the Midwest, and they set out to determine the reason for this. One by one they eliminated all the explanations related to the physical locations, such as storm strength and severity (the storms are actually stronger in Illinois), time of day of the storms (an equal number occur at night in both regions), type of business and residence construction (both areas used similar construction techniques), and the quality of warning systems (even before warning systems existed in either area, Alabama had a higher death rate).

With all the obvious environmental reasons ruled out, Sims and Baumann suggested that the difference might be due to psychological variables and proposed the locus-of-control concept as a likely possibility. Questionnaires containing a modified version of Rotter's I-E Scale were administered to residents of four counties in Illinois and Alabama that had experienced a similar incidence of tornado-caused deaths. They found that the respondents from Alabama demonstrated a significantly greater external locus of control than did those from Illinois. From this finding, as well as from responses to other items on the questionnaire relating to tornado behavior, the researchers concluded that an internal orientation promotes behaviors that are more likely to save lives in the event of a tornado (such as paying attention to the news media or alerting others). This stems directly from the internals' *belief* that their behavior will be effective in changing the outcome of the event. In this study, Alabamians were seen as "less confident in themselves as causal agents; less convinced of their ability to engage in effective action. . . . The data constitute a suggestive illustration of how people's personality is active in determining the quality of their interaction with nature" (Sims & Baumann, 1972, p. 1391).

Recent Applications

To say that hundreds of studies have incorporated Rotter's locus-of-control theory since his article appeared in 1966 may have been a serious understatement. In reality, there have been thousands! Such a great reliance on Rotter's theory speaks clearly to the broad acceptance of the impact and validity of the internal–external personality dimension. Following are a few representative examples from the great variety of recent studies citing his pioneering work.

When people discuss Rotter's research on locus of control, the subject of religious faith often arises. Many devoutly religious people believe that it is desirable and proper at times to place their fate in God's hands, yet within Rotter's theory, this would indicate an external locus of control and its potential negative connotations. A fascinating study in the *Journal of Psychology and Religion* addressed this very issue (Welton et al., 1996). Using various locus-of-control scales and subscales, participants were assessed on their degree of internal locus of control, perceived control by powerful others, belief in chance, and belief in "God control." The advantages associated with an internal locus of control were also found in the participants scoring high on the God-control dimension. The authors contend that if a person has an external locus of control, as measured by Rotter's scale, but the external power is perceived as a strong faith in a supreme being, he or she will be less subject to the typical problems associated with externals (e.g., powerlessness, depression, low achievement, and low motivation for change).

The concept of locus of control is theorized to be closely related to the perception that you have choices in your life. In fact, having choices allows people (especially those with an internal focus) to exert their personal control. One study examined various studies employing animal research, human clinical studies, and neuroimaging (e.g., fMRI studies; see Reading 6.3). This study suggested that the human desire for control is not learned, but is an evolutionary, survival mechanism, passed down to us genetically (Leotti et al., 2010). The authors proposed that without the belief in your ability to make choices you perceive as producing the best outcome for you, there would be little motivation to face any challenge in your life at all, including choices that help to keep you healthy and safe from danger. This explains why, when your freedom to choose—your ability to control events—is taken away from you, the results often approach pathological results, ranging from profound depression to extreme anger and aggression.

On another front, a great deal of important cross-cultural research has relied heavily on Rotter's conceptualization of the internal–external locus of control dimension of personality. For example, one study from Russian researchers examined locus-of-control and right-wing authoritarian attitudes in Russian and American college students (D'yakonova & Yurtaikin, 2000). Results indicated that among the U.S. students, greater internal locus of control was correlated with higher levels of authoritarianism, while no such connection was found for the Russian participants. Another cross-cultural study relied on Rotter's I-E Scale to examine the psychological adjustment to the diagnosis of cancer in a highly superstitious, collectivist culture (Sun & Stewart, 2000) [see the study by Triandis on collectivist and individualistic cultures later in this chapter]. Interestingly, findings from this study indicated that "even in a culture where supernatural beliefs are widespread, an [internal locus of control] relates positively and 'chance' beliefs relate negatively with adjustment [to a serious illness such as cancer]" (p. 177).

A 2016 study using Rotter's research examined the personality variables of parents of Autistic children (Frantzen et al., 2016). The researchers found that the most important predictors in parents' skills in successful parenting of these children was *parental self-perception,* which includes locus of control, self-efficacy, and feelings of competence.

Research areas other than those discussed previously that have cited Rotter's study include post-traumatic stress disorder, issues of control and aging, childbirth methods, coping with anticipatory stress, the effects of environmental noise, academic performance, white-collar crime, adult children of alcoholics, child molestation, mental health following natural disasters, contraceptive use, and HIV and AIDS prevention research.

Conclusion

This dimension of internal–external locus of control has been generally accepted as a relatively stable and robust component of human personality that has meaningful implications for predicting behavior across a wide variety of situations. The descriptor *relatively stable* is used because a person's locus of control can change under certain circumstances. Those who are externally oriented often will become more internal when their profession places them in positions of greater authority and responsibility. People who are highly internally oriented may shift toward a more external focus during times of extreme stress and uncertainty. Moreover, it is possible for individuals to learn to be more internal, if given the opportunity.

Implicit in Rotter's concept of locus of control is the assumption that internals are better adjusted and more effective in life. Although most of the research confirms this assumption, Rotter, in his later writings, sounded a note of caution (see Rotter, 1975). Everyone, especially internals, must be attentive to the environment around them. If a person sets out to change a situation that is not changeable, frustration, disappointment, and depression are the potential outcomes. When forces outside of the individual are *actually* in control of behavioral consequences, the most realistic and healthy approach to take is probably one of an external orientation.

Davis, W. L., & Phares, E. J. (1969). Parental antecedents of internal–external control of reinforcement. *Psychological Reports, 24*, 427–436.

D'yakonova, N., & Yurtaikin, V. (2000). An authoritarian personality in Russia and in the USA: Value orientation and locus of control. *Voprosy Psikhologii, 4*, 51–61.

Frantzen, K. K., Lauritsen, M. B., Jørgensen, M., Tanggaard, L., Fetters, M. D., Aikens, J. E., & Bjerrum, M. (2016). Parental self-perception in the autism spectrum disorder literature: a systematic mixed studies review. *Review Journal of Autism and Developmental Disorders, 3*(1), 18–36.

Leotti, L., Iyengar, S., & Ochsner, K. (2010). Born to choose: The origins and value of the need for control. *Trends in Cognitive Science, 14*(10), 457–463.

Rotter, J. (1975). Some problems and misconceptions related to the construct of internal versus external reinforcement. *Journal of Consulting and Clinical Psychology, 43*, 56–67.

Sims, J., & Baumann, D. (1972). The tornado threat: Coping styles in the North and South. *Science, 176*, 1386–1392.

Strickland, B. (1977). Internal–external control of reinforcement. In T. Blass (Ed.), *Personality variables in social behavior*. Hillsdale, NJ: Erlbaum.

Sun, L., & Stewart, S. (2000). Psychological adjustment to cancer in a collective culture. *International Journal of Psychology, 35*(5), 177–185.

Welton, G., Adkins, A., Ingle, S., & Dixon, W. (1996). God control: The 4th dimension. *Journal of Psychology and Theology, 24*(1), 13–25.

Reading 7.2: Masculine or Feminine . . . or Both?

Bem, S. L. (1974). The measurement of psychological androgyny. *Journal of Consulting and Clinical Psychology, 42*, 155–162.

7.2 Evaluate Bem's research on gender expression

Are you male or female? Are you a man or a woman? Are you masculine or feminine? These are three seemingly similar questions, yet the range of possible answers may surprise you. As for the first question, the answer is usually fairly clear: It is a biological answer based on a person's chromosomes, hormones, and sexual anatomical structures. Most people also have little trouble answering the second question with confidence. Virtually, all of you are quite sure about which sex you perceive yourself to be, and you've been sure since you were about 4 years old. Odds are good you did not have to stop for even a split second to think about whether you *perceive* yourself to be a man or a woman.

However, the third question might not be quite so easy to answer. Different people possess varying amounts of "maleness" and "femaleness," or masculinity and femininity. If you think about people you know, you can probably place some on the extremely feminine side of this dimension (they are *more likely* to be women), others fit best on the extremely masculine side (they are *more likely* to be men), and still others seem to fall somewhere between the two, possessing both masculine and feminine characteristics (they may be *either* men or women). These "categories" are not intended to be judgmental; they simply define variations in one important personality characteristic among people. This masculinity–femininity dimension forms the basis of what psychologists usually refer to as *gender,* and your perception of your own maleness and femaleness is simply put your *gender identity.* Your gender identity is one of the most basic and most powerful components comprising your personality: your own and others' perceptions about who you are.

Prior to the 1970s, behavioral scientists (and most nonscientists as well) usually assumed a mutually exclusive view of gender: that people's gender identity was either primarily masculine or primarily feminine. Masculinity and femininity were seen as opposite ends of a one-dimensional gender scale. If you were to complete a test measuring your gender identity based on this view, your score would place you somewhere along a single scale, either more toward the masculine or more toward the feminine side of the scale. Furthermore, researchers and clinicians presumed that psychological adjustment was, in part, related to how well a person "fit" into one gender category or the other, based on their biological sex. In other words, the thinking was that for optimal psychological health, men should be as masculine as possible and women should be as feminine as possible.

Then, in the early 1970s, this one-dimensional view of gender was challenged in an article by Anne Constantinople (1973) claiming that masculinity and femininity are not two ends of a single scale but, rather, are best described as two *separate* dimensions on which individuals could be measured. In other words, a person could be either high or low in masculinity and either high or low in femininity *at the same time*. Figure 7.2.1 illustrates the comparison of a one-dimensional and a two-dimensional concept of gender.

This idea may not seem particularly surprising to you, but it was revolutionary when first presented. The two-dimensional view of gender was seized upon at the time by Sandra Bem (1944–2014) of Cornell University. Bem challenged the prevailing notion that healthy gender identity is represented by behaving predominantly according to society's expectations for one's biological sex. She proposed that a more balanced person, who is able to incorporate both masculine and feminine behaviors, may actually be happier and better adjusted than someone who is strongly sex-typed as either masculine or feminine. Bem took the research a step further and set out to develop a method for measuring gender on a two-dimensional scale (high/low masculine and high/low feminine). In the article that forms the basis for this reading, Bem coined the term *androgynous* (from *andro* meaning "male" and *gyn* referring to "female") to describe individuals who embrace both masculine and feminine characteristics, depending on which behaviors best fit a particular situation. Moreover, Bem contended that not only are some people androgynous, but androgyny offers an *advantage* of greater behavioral flexibility as a person moves from situation to situation in life. Bem explained it in this way:

> The highly sex-typed individual is motivated to keep [his or her] behavior consistent with an internalized sex-role standard, a goal that [he or she] presumably accomplishes by suppressing any behavior that might be considered undesirable or inappropriate for [his or her] sex. Thus, whereas a narrowly masculine self-concept might inhibit behaviors that are stereotyped as feminine, and a narrowly feminine self-concept might inhibit behaviors that are stereotyped as masculine, a mixed, or androgynous, self-concept might allow an individual to engage freely in both "masculine" and "feminine" behaviors. (p. 155)

Figure 7.2.1 Comparison of the traditional one-dimensional and the more recent two-dimensional models of gender.

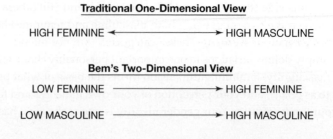

For example, you may know a woman who is gentle, sensitive, and soft-spoken (traditional feminine characteristics), but she is also ambitious, self-reliant, and athletic (traditional masculine characteristics). On the other hand, a male friend of yours may be competitive, dominant, and a risk taker (masculine traits), but he displays traditional feminine characteristics as well, such as affection, sympathy, and cheerfulness. Bem would describe such individuals as *androgynous*. This article explains the theories and processes Bem used to develop a scale for assessing gender, the *Bem Sex-Role Inventory* (BSRI).

Theoretical Propositions

Whenever scientists propose new and novel theories that challenge the prevailing views of the time, they must bear the responsibility of demonstrating the validity of their revolutionary ideas. If Bem wanted to explore the notion of androgyny and demonstrate differences between androgynous people and those who are highly masculine or feminine, she needed to find a way to establish the existence of androgynous individuals. In other words, she had to *measure it*.

Bem contended that measuring androgyny would require a scale that was fundamentally different from masculinity–femininity scales that had been used previously. With this goal in mind, her scale contained the following innovations:

1. Bem's first concern was to develop a gender scale that did not assume a one-dimensional view: that masculinity and femininity were opposite ends of a single dimension. Her test incorporated two separate scales, one measuring masculinity and another measuring femininity (see Table 7.2.1).

Table 7.2.1 Sample Sex Role Inventory Items

Rating	Feminine Items	Rating	Masculine Items	Rating	Neutral Items
_____	Affectionate	_____	Acts as a leader	_____	Adaptable
_____	Yielding	_____	Willing to take risks	_____	Conceited
_____	Cheerful	_____	Ambitious	_____	Unpredictable
_____	Flatterable	_____	Will take a stand	_____	Truthful
_____	Compassionate	_____	Analytical	_____	Inefficient
_____	Understanding	_____	Strong personality	_____	Tactful
_____	Gentle	_____	Assertive	_____	Jealous
_____	Feminine	_____	Self-sufficient	_____	Sincere
_____	Loves children	_____	Masculine	_____	Moody
_____	Soft spoken	_____	Independent	_____	Reliable

(Modified, based on Table 1, p. 156.)

Rate items using the following scale as they apply to you:
1 = Never or almost never true
2 = Usually not true
3 = Sometimes, but infrequently, true
4 = Occasionally true
5 = Often true
6 = Usually true
7 = Always or almost always true

Scoring Key
Femininity Score: Total of Feminine ratings ÷ 10 = _____
Masculinity Score: Total of Masculine ratings ÷ 10 = _____
Androgyny Score: Subtract Masculine from Feminine = _____

Interpretation:
Feminine = 1.00 or greater
Near Feminine = .50 to .99
Androgynous = −.50 to .49
Near Masculine = −1.00 to −.49
Masculine = less than −1.00

2. Her scale was based on masculine and feminine traits that were *perceived* as desirable for men and women, respectively. Previous gender scales were based on the behaviors most commonly *observed* in men and women, rather than those judged by U.S. society to be more desirable:

> A characteristic qualified as masculine if it was judged to be more desirable for a man than for a woman, and it qualified as feminine if it was judged to be more desirable for a woman than for a man. (pp. 155–156)

3. The BSRI was designed to differentiate among masculine, feminine, and androgynous individuals by looking at the *difference* in the score on the feminine section of the scale and the score on the masculine section. In other words, when a person's feminine trait score is subtracted from his or her masculine trait score, the difference would determine the degree of masculinity, femininity, or androgyny.

Bem decided that her scale would be composed of a list of personality characteristics or traits. To arrive at a gender score, each characteristic could simply be rated on a scale of 1–7 indicating the degree to which respondents perceived that a particular trait described them. Let's take a look at how the scale was developed.

Method

ITEM SELECTION   Remember, Bem's idea was to use masculine and feminine characteristics that are seen by society as desirable in one sex or the other. To arrive at her final scale, she began with long lists of positively valued characteristics that seemed to her and several of her psychology students to be either masculine, feminine, or neither masculine nor feminine. Each of these three lists of traits contained about 200 items. She then asked 100 undergraduate students (half male and half female) at Stanford University to serve as judges and rate whether the characteristics were more desirable for a man or for a woman on a 7-point scale from 1 ("not at all desirable") to 7 ("extremely desirable") in U.S. society.

Using these ratings from the student judges, Bem selected the "top 20" highest-rated characteristics for the masculinity scale and for the femininity scale. She also selected items that were rated no more desirable for men than for women but were equally desirable for *anyone* to possess regardless of sex (these are not androgynous items but simply gender neutral). She selected 10 positive items and 10 negative gender-neutral items. These items were included in the final scale to ensure that respondents would not be overly influenced by seeing all masculine and feminine descriptors or all desirable items. The final scale consisted of 60 items. A sampling of the final selection of traits on the BSRI is shown in Table 7.2.1. Note that in the actual scale, the items are not divided according to sex-type but are mixed up in random order.

As mentioned previously, a person completing the BSRI simply needs to respond to each item using a 7-point scale indicating how well the descriptor describes himself or herself. The response scale is as follows: 1 = Never or almost never true; 2 = Usually not true; 3 = Sometimes, but infrequently, true; 4 = Occasionally true; 5 = Often true; 6 = Usually true; 7 = Always or almost always true. After respondents complete the scale, they receive three scores: a masculinity score, a femininity score, and, most important for this article, an androgyny score. The masculinity score is determined by adding up all the scores on the masculine items and dividing by 20 to obtain the average rating on those items. The femininity score is likewise determined. The average score on each of these scales may be anywhere from 1.0 to 7.0. Have you figured out how an androgyny score might be calculated from these averages? Remember, the scale taps into masculinity and femininity independently, but it does not contain androgynous items per se. If you are thinking androgyny could be determined by looking at the degree of *difference* between a person's masculine and feminine scores, you are right: That is exactly what Bem did. Androgyny was determined by subtracting the masculinity score from the femininity score. Androgyny scores, then, could range from −6 to +6. It's simple, really. Following are three rather extreme examples to illustrate a masculine sex-typed person, a feminine sex-typed person, and an androgynous person.

Jennifer's masculinity score is 1.5, and her femininity score is 6.4. Subtracting 1.5 from 6.4 gives Jennifer an androgyny score of 4.9. Richard's masculinity score is 5.8, and his femininity score is 2.1. So, Richard's androgyny score is −3.7. Dana receives a masculinity score of 3.9 and a femininity score of 4.3. Dana's androgyny score, then, is 0.4.

Jennifer: Femininity score = 6.4
Minus Masculinity score = −1.5
Androgyny score = 4.90

Richard: Femininity score = 2.1
Minus Masculinity score = −5.8
Androgyny score = −3.70

Dana: Femininity score = 4.3
Minus Masculinity score = −3.9
Androgyny score = 0.40

Looking at the numbers, which of our three examples scored the *highest* in androgyny? The answer is Dana because Dana's scores for masculine and feminine characteristics were about the same (the score was closest to zero) and did not show much bias in either direction, unlike Jennifer and Richard. Therefore, Dana's score reflected a *lack* of sex-typed self-perception and more of a balance between masculine and feminine, which is the *definition* of androgyny.

The scoring on the BSRI is interpreted like this: Scores closest to zero (whether positive or negative) indicate androgyny. As scores move farther away from zero in the plus direction, greater femininity is indicated; as scores move farther away from zero in the minus direction, greater masculinity is indicated.

You may want to try completing the scale for yourself. Of course, at this point, you are *not* the ideal respondent because you now know too much about how the scale works! Also, you will be rating feminine, masculine, and neutral traits separately, rather than all mixed up as they would be in the actual scale. Nevertheless, with those cautions in mind, you should feel free to give it a try. Table 7.2.1 provides simplified scoring and interpretation guidelines.

Results

Any measuring device must be both reliable and valid. *Reliability* refers to a scale's consistency of measurement—that is, how well the various items tap into the same characteristic being measured, and the scale's ability to produce similar results over repeated administrations. *Validity* refers to how well the scale truly measures what it is intended to measure—in the case of the BSRI, that is masculinity and femininity.

RELIABILITY OF THE BSRI Statistical analyses on the scores from the student samples demonstrated that the internal consistency of the BSRI was very high for both scales. This implies that the 20 masculine items were all measuring a single trait (presumably masculinity), and the 20 feminine items were measuring a single trait (presumably femininity). To determine the scale's consistency of measurement over time, Bem administered the BSRI a second time to about 60 of the original respondents 4 weeks later. Their scores for the first and second administrations correlated very highly, thereby suggesting a high level of "test–retest" reliability.

VALIDITY OF THE BSRI To ensure that the BSRI was valid, the masculinity and femininity scales must be analyzed to ensure that they are not measuring the *same* trait. This was important because a basic theoretical proposition of Bem's study was that masculinity and femininity are *independent* dimensions of gender and should be able to be measured separately. Bem demonstrated this by correlating scores on the masculine scale and the feminine scale of the BSRI. The correlations showed that the scales were clearly *unrelated* and functioned independently from each other.

Next, Bem needed to verify that the scale was indeed measuring masculine and feminine gender characteristics. To confirm this, Bem analyzed average scores on the masculine and feminine scales for men and women separately. You would expect such an analysis should show that men scored higher on the masculine items and women scored higher on the feminine items. This is exactly what Bem found for respondents from both colleges, and the difference was highly statistically significant.

Bem divided her sample of respondents into the gender categories listed previously in this discussion: masculine, feminine, and androgynous. She found a large number of people who had very small differences in their feminine and masculine scores. In other words, they were androgynous. Table 7.2.2 shows the percentages of masculine, feminine, and androgynous respondents in Bem's study.

Discussion

The discussion section of Bem's article is short, succinct, and cogent. The best way to represent it is to quote it here:

> It is hoped that the development of the BSRI will encourage investigators in the areas of sex differences and sex roles to question the traditional assumption that it is the sex-typed individual who typifies mental health and to begin focusing on the behavioral and societal consequences of the more flexible sex-role concepts. In a society where rigid sex-role differentiation has already outlived its utility, perhaps the androgynous person will come to define a more human standard of psychological health. (p. 162)

This statement from Bem illustrates how this study changed psychology. Over the decades since Bem's article, Western cultures have become increasingly accepting of the idea that some people are more androgynous than others, and that possessing some characteristics of both traditionally masculine and feminine characteristics is not only acceptable but may provide certain advantages. More men and women than ever before are choosing to engage in vocations, avocations, sports activities, and family activities that have traditionally been seen as "limited" to their opposite gender. From women corporate executives to stay-at-home dads, from female firefighters and soldiers to male nurses and schoolteachers, and from women taking charge to men exploring their sensitive sides, the social changes in gender roles and expectations are everywhere you look.

Table 7.2.2 Percentages of Feminine, Masculine, and Androgynous Respondents

Category	Males (%)	Females (%)
Feminine	7	35
Near Feminine	6	17
Androgynous	35	29
Near Masculine	19	11
Masculine	33	8

Number of respondents = 917
SOURCE: Adapted from Table 7, p. 161, samples combined.

This is not to say, by any means, that the culture has become "gender-blind." On the contrary, sex-role expectations still exert powerful influences over our choices of behaviors and attitudes, and discrimination based on gender continues to be a significant social problem. In general, rightly or wrongly males are still expected to be more assertive and women more emotionally expressive; the vast majority of airline pilots still are men (94%), and nearly all dental hygienists still are women (98%); but the degree of *cultural* differentiation along gender lines has decreased and is continuing to do so.

A great deal of research was generated by Bem's new conceptualization of gender. As discussed previously, prior to the 1970s, the prevailing belief was that people would be most well adjusted in life if their "gender matched their sex"—that is, boys and men should display masculine attitudes and behaviors, and girls and women should display feminine attitudes and behaviors. However, the "discovery" of androgyny shifted this focus, and studies began to explore gender differences among masculine, feminine, *and* androgynous individuals.

Criticisms and Subsequent Research

Research has shown that androgynous children and adults tend to have higher levels of self-esteem and are more adaptable in diverse settings (Taylor & Hall, 1982). Other research has suggested that androgynous individuals have greater success in heterosexually intimate relationships, probably due to their greater ability to understand and accept each other's differences (Coleman & Ganong, 1985). More recent research has even revealed that people with the most positive traits of androgyny are psychologically healthier and happier (Woodhill & Samuels, 2003). However, the basic theory of androgyny as developed by Bem and others has undergone various changes and refinements over the years.

Numerous researchers have suggested that the psychological advantages experienced by people who score high in androgyny may be due more to the presence of masculine traits rather than a balance between male and female characteristics (Whitley, 1983). If you think about it, this makes sense. Clearly, many traditional feminine traits, such as those termed dependent, self-critical, and overly emotional, are seen by society as undesirable. So, it stands to reason that people who possess more masculine than feminine characteristics will receive more favorable treatment by others, which in turn creates greater levels of self-confidence and self-esteem in the individual. However, not all masculine qualities are positive, and not all feminine qualities are negative. Positive and negative traits exist for both genders.

This has led researchers to propose a further refinement of the androgyny concept to include *four* dimensions: desirable femininity, undesirable femininity, desirable masculinity, and undesirable masculinity (see Ricciardelli & Williams, 1995). Qualities such as firm, confident, and strong are seen as desirable masculine traits, while bossy, noisy, and sarcastic are undesirable masculine traits. On the feminine side, patient, sensitive, and responsible are desirable traits, and nervous, timid, and weak are undesirable traits. Depending on how someone's set of personality traits lines up, a person could be seen as *positive masculine, negative masculine, positive feminine, negative feminine, positive androgynous,* or *negative androgynous.*

When gender characteristics are more carefully defined to consider both positive and negative traits, the advantages for positive androgynous individuals become even more pronounced (i.e., Woodhill & Samuels, 2003). People who possess the best of male and female gender qualities are more likely to be more well-rounded, happier, more popular, better liked, more flexible and adaptable, and more self-loving than those who are able to draw on only one set of gender traits or than those who combine negative aspects of both genders. Just imagine someone (male or female) who is patient, sensitive, responsible, firm, confident, and strong (positive androgyny) compared to someone who is nervous, timid, weak, bossy, noisy, and sarcastic (negative androgyny) to get the idea behind this enhancement of Bem's theory.

Sandra Bem was a leading researcher in the field of gender and sex roles. She applied her theories and research findings to ongoing debates about gender inequality and discrimination, which she discusses at length in her 1993 book, *The Lenses of Gender*. She also mapped her ideas onto the complexities of marriage, family, and child rearing in her book, *An Unconventional Family* (1998). In this book, Bem drew from her own experiences with her former husband, Daryl Bem (the noted Cornell psychologist), to explore how a couple might attempt to avoid gender-stereotyped expectations, function as two truly equal partners, and raise their children as "gender-liberated," positive-androgynous individuals.

Recent Applications

One question that may have occurred to you as you read this chapter was whether or not the items used to measure masculinity and femininity are still valid—that is, do they still discriminate accurately between people who are masculine and feminine? In fact, you may have disagreed with some or many of them. After all, this study is several decades old and society's expectations of sex-typed behaviors are bound to change over time, right? The answer to that question is a resounding "Maybe!" One study from the late 1990s reexamined all the items on the BSRI with a sample of students from a midsize U.S. university in the South. The researchers were able to demonstrate that all but two items from Bem's scale still distinguished masculinity and femininity to a statistically significantly degree (Holt & Ellis, 1998). The two exceptions—"childlike" and "loyal"—were both feminine descriptors on the BSRI but were not rated as more desirable for women than for men in the 1998 study.

Another study, however, found strikingly conflicting results. When students from an urban U.S. university in the Northeast were asked to validate the BSRI's descriptors, results were quite different (Konrad & Harris, 2002). These researchers found that (a) women rated only *one* masculine item out of 20 ("masculine") more desirable for men than for women, (b) men rated only 13 out of the 20 masculine items more desirable for men than for women, (c) women rated only 2 of the feminine items more desirable for women than for men ("feminine" and "soft spoken"), and (d) men rated just 7 feminine items more desirable for women than for men.

How can we reconcile these discrepancies? One possibility is that people's views of gender vary significantly according to geographic region. Holt and Ellis's data were from the southern United States (and a relatively small town), while Konrad and Harris's participants were from the northeastern United States (and a large city). Alternatively, the authors acknowledge that the participants in their study may have "guessed" the purpose of the study and slanted their answers accordingly:

> Specifically, despite the fact that respondents were asked to rate only one sex or the other, merely specifying the sex of the target could have cued respondents to the study's purpose. Given this possibility, respondents might have provided more egalitarian responses than they actually had in order to present a positive self-image. (Konrad and Harris, 2002, p. 270)

Bem's research and findings have exerted a powerful influence on studies involving sexuality and gender. In fact, they have formed the foundation for hundreds of gender-related studies on a wide range of topics. For example, one study examined how gender characteristics affect the perceptions of men and women in leadership positions (Ayman & Korabik, 2010). Among many effects, the researchers found that gender, in part, determines who become leaders. Men continue to make up the vast majority of leadership positions. Why? Traditionally, higher levels of masculine characteristics and social dominance were perceived in those who emerged as leaders. Also, people greater in task orientation and lower in emotional expressivity were more likely to attain leadership positions, and this trait combination is more common in men. More recent research, however, has indicated that when the gender composition of the group and the specific leadership task were taken into account, those individuals who displayed greater androgyny were the ones most likely to become leaders. This appears to be because androgynous people are more comfortable *combining* a task-focused approach with emotional expressivity, and this approach appears very effective in many leadership roles.

In contrast, a 2016 study found that K-12 student teachers were significantly more likely to enter the teaching profession (Moses, Admiraal, and Berry, 2016)). Researchers administered a comprehensive questionnaire to university-based education students examining commitment to teaching, gender, and items from the BSRI. Analysis of the responses found three clusters of students' characteristics: (1) Highly androgynous students (2) medium androgynous students with moderate scores on both masculine and feminine scales and (3) low androgynous students with low scores compared to masculine and feminine scores in the other 2 groups. Highly androgynous students were found to be most committed to teaching and most highly committed to entering the teaching world than either of the other two groups. Gender was not related to this level of commitment and the desire to teach was only related to degree of androgyny.

Conclusion

This study by Sandra Bem changed psychology because her studies altered the way psychologists, individuals, and entire societies view one of the most basic human characteristics: gender identity. Bem's research has played a pivotal role in broadening our view of what is truly meant to be male or female, masculine or feminine and, in doing so, has allowed everyone the opportunity to expand their range of activities, choices, and life goals.

Ayman, R., & Korabik, K. (2010). Leadership: Why gender and culture matter. *American Psychologist, 157,* 157–170.

Bem, S. L. (1994). *The lenses of gender: Transforming the debate on sexual inequality.* New Haven, CT: Yale University Press.

Bem, S. L. (1998). *An unconventional family.* New Haven, CT: Yale University Press.

Coleman, M., & Ganong, L. (1985). Love and sex role stereotypes: Do macho men and feminine women make better lovers? *Journal of Personality and Social Psychology, 49,* 170–176.

Constantinople, A. (1973). Masculinity-femininity: An exception to a famous dictum? *Psychological Bulletin, 80,* 389–407.

Holt, C., & Ellis, J. (1998). Assessing the current validity of the Bem Sex Role Inventory. *Sex Roles: A Journal of Research, 39,* 929–941.

Konrad, A., & Harris, C. (2002). Desirability of the Bem Sex-Role Inventory for women and men: A comparison between African Americans and European Americans. *Sex Roles: A Journal of Research, 47,* 259–271.

Moses, I., Admiraal, W. F., & Berry, A. K. (2016). Gender and gender role differences in student-teachers' commitment to teaching. *Social Psychology of Education, 19*(3), 475– 492.

Ricciardelli, L., & Williams, R. (1995). Desirable and undesirable gender traits in three behavioral domains. *Sex Roles, 33,* 637–655.

Taylor, M., & Hall, J. (1982). Psychological androgyny: Theories, methods and conclusions. *Psychological Bulletin, 92,* 347–366.

Whitley, B. (1983). Sex role orientation and self esteem: A critical meta-analytic review. *Journal of Personality and Social Psychology, 44,* 773–786.

Woodhill, B., & Samuels, C. (2003). Positive and negative androgyny and their relationship with psychological health and well-being. *Sex Roles, 48,* 555–565.

Reading 7.3: Racing Against Your Heart

Friedman, M., & Rosenman, R. H. (1959). Association of specific overt behavior pattern with blood and cardiovascular findings. *Journal of the American Medical Association*, *169*, 1286–1296.

7.3 **Describe the relationship between personality and health**

As mentioned in the introduction to this chapter, we are focusing on the branch of psychology called *personality*. So, we are asking the question: Who are you? If someone were to ask you that question, you would probably respond by describing some of your more obvious or dominant characteristics. Such characteristics, often referred to as traits, are important in making you the unique person that you are. Traits are assumed to be fairly consistent across situations and over time (throughout your life). Psychologists who have supported the trait theory of personality (and not all have) have proposed that personality consists of various groups of traits, such as androgyny or locus of control, that exist in varying amounts in all of us; that is, some have more or less of certain traits that do others of us, but all of us have basically the same traits. Most interesting to psychologists (and everyone, really) is the ability of a person's traits to predict his or her behavior in given situations and over time. In other words, trait theorists believe that insight into your unique profile of traits will allow us to predict various behavioral outcomes for you now and in the future. Therefore, it is easy to imagine how dramatically this interest would increase if certain personality characteristics were found to predict how healthy you will be or even your chances of dying from a serious illness.

You are probably aware of one group of personality characteristics related to health, popularly known as the *Type A Personality*. To be precise, *Type A* refers to a specific *pattern* of behaviors rather than the overall personality of an individual. This behavior pattern was first reported in the late 1950s by two cardiologists, Meyer Friedman (1910–2001) and Ray Rosenman (1920–2013). Their theory and findings exerted a huge influence on linking psychology and health and on our understanding of the role of personality in the development and prevention of illness.

Theoretical Propositions

The story about how these doctors first realized the idea for their research demonstrates how careful observation of small, seemingly unimportant details can lead to major scientific breakthroughs. Dr. Friedman was having the furniture in his office waiting room reupholstered. The upholsterer pointed out how the material on the couches and chairs had worn out in an odd way. The front edges of the seat cushions had worn away faster than the rest. It was as if Dr. Friedman's cardiac patients were literally "sitting on the edge of their seats." This observation prompted Friedman to wonder if his patients (people with heart disease) were different in some important characteristic, compared to those of doctors in other specialties.

Through surveys of executives and physicians, Friedman and Rosenman found a common belief that people exposed over long periods of time to chronic stress stemming from excessive drive, pressure to meet deadlines, competitive situations, and economic frustration are more likely to develop heart disease. They decided to put these ideas to a scientific test.

Method

Using their earlier research and clinical observations, the two cardiologists developed a *model*, or set of characteristics, for a specific overt (observable) behavior pattern that they believed was related to increased levels of cholesterol and consequently to coronary heart disease (CHD). This pattern, which he labeled *Pattern A*, consisted of the following characteristics: (1) an intense, sustained drive to achieve one's personal goals; (2) a profound tendency and eagerness to compete in all situations; (3) a persistent desire for recognition and advancement; (4) continuous involvement in multiple activities that are constantly subject to deadlines; (5) habitual tendency to rush to finish activities; and (6) extraordinary mental and physical alertness (p. 1286). This set of behaviour patterns was often referred to as the "hurry-up" disease.

The researchers then developed a second set of overt behaviors, labeled *Pattern B*. Pattern B was described as essentially the opposite of pattern A and was characterized by a relative absence of the following: drive, ambition, sense of time urgency, desire to compete, or involvement in deadlines. Perhaps we could call this the "laid-back" personality.

Friedman and Rosenman next needed to find participants for their research who fit the descriptions of patterns A and B. To do this, they contacted managers and supervisors of various large companies and corporations. They explained the behavior patterns and asked the managers to select from among their associates those who most closely fit the particular patterns. The groups that were finally selected consisted of various levels of executives and nonexecutives, all males. Each group consisted of 83 men, with an average age of 45 years in group A and 43 years in group B. All participants were given several tests relating to the goals of the study.

First, the researchers designed interviews to assess the history of CHD in the participants' parents; the participants' own history of heart trouble; the number of hours of work, sleep, and exercise each week; and smoking, alcohol, and dietary habits. Also, during these interviews, the researchers determined if a participant had a fully or only partially developed behavior pattern in his group (either A or B), based on body movements, tone of conversation, teeth clenching, gesturing, general air of impatience, and the participant's own admission of drive, competitiveness, and time urgency. They determined that 69 of the 83 men in group A exhibited this fully developed pattern, while 58 of the 83 participants in group B were judged to be of the fully developed Type B.

Second, all participants were asked to keep a diary of everything they ate or drank over one week's time. Code numbers were assigned to the participants so that they would not feel reluctant to report alcohol consumption honestly. The diets of the participants were then broken down and analyzed by a hospital dietician who was not aware of the participants' identities or to which group they belonged.

Third, research assistants took blood samples from all participants to measure cholesterol levels and clotting time. Instances of coronary heart disease were determined through careful questioning of the participants about past coronary health and through standard electrocardiogram readings. Rosenman and a cardiologist not involved in the study interpreted these findings independently (to avoid bias). With one exception, their interpretations agreed for all participants. The researchers also determined the number of participants with *arcus senilis* (the formation of an opaque ring around the cornea of the eye caused by the breakdown of fatty deposits in the bloodstream) through illuminated inspection of the participants' eyes.

Now, let's sum up Friedman and Rosenman's data and see what they found.

Results

The interviews indicated that the men chosen for each group fit the profiles developed by the researchers. Group A participants were found to be chronically harassed by commitments, ambitions, and drives. Also, they were clearly eager to compete in all their activities, both professional and recreational. In addition, they also admitted a strong desire to win. The men in group B were found to be strikingly different from those in group A, especially in their lack of the sense of time urgency. The men in group B appeared to be satisfied with their present positions in life and avoided pursuing multiple goals and competitive situations. They were much less concerned about advancement and typically spent more time with their families and in noncompetitive recreational activities.

Table 7.3.1 is a summary of the most relevant comparisons for the two groups on the characteristics from the tests and surveys. Table 7.3.2 summarizes the outcome measurements relating to blood levels and illnesses. In Table 7.3.1, you can see that the two groups were similar on every measured characteristic. Although the men in group A tended to be a little higher on most of the measurements, the only differences that were statistically significant were the number of cigarettes smoked each day and the percentage of men whose parents had a history of coronary heart disease.

However, if you take a look at the cholesterol and illness levels in Table 7.3.2, some very convincing differences emerge. First, though, considering the overall results in the table, it appears that no meaningful difference in blood clotting time was found for the two groups. The speed at which your blood coagulates relates to your potential for heart disease and other vascular illness. The slower your clotting time, the less your risk. To examine this statistic more closely, Friedman and Rosenman compared the clotting times for those participants who exhibited a *fully developed* Type A pattern (6.8 minutes) with those judged as *fully developed* Type B (7.2 minutes). This difference in clotting time was statistically significant.

The other findings in Table 7.3.2 are unambiguous. Cholesterol levels were clearly and significantly higher for group A participants. This difference was even greater if the participants with the fully developed patterns were compared. The incidence of arcus senilis was three times greater for group A and five times greater in the fully developed comparison groups.

The key finding of the entire study, and the one that secured its place in history, was the striking difference in the incidence of clinical CHD found in the two groups. In group A, 23 of the participants (28%) exhibited clear evidence of CHD, compared with 3 men (4%) in group B. When the researchers examined these findings in terms of the fully developed subgroups, the evidence became even stronger. All 23 of the CHD cases in group A came from those men with the fully developed Type A pattern. For group B, all three of the cases were from those participants exhibiting the incomplete Type B pattern.

Table 7.3.1 Comparison of Characteristics for Group A and Group B (Averages)

	Weight	Work Hours/ Week	Exercise Hours/ Week	Number of Smokers	Ciga- rettes/ Day	Alcohol Calories/ Day	Total Calories	Fat Calories	Parents with Children
Group A	176	51	10	67	23	194	2,049	944	36
Group B	172	45	7	56	15	149	2,134	978	27

(Compiled from data on pp. 1289–1293.)

Table 7.3.2 Comparisons of Blood and Illness for Group A and Group B

	Average Clotting Time (Minutes)	Average Serum Cholesterol	Arcus Senilis (Percent)	Coronary Heart Disease (Percent)
Group A	6.9	253	38	28
Group B	7.0	215	11	4

(Compiled from data on p. 1293.)

Discussion of Findings

The conclusion suggested by the authors was that the Type A behavior pattern was a major cause of CHD and related blood abnormalities. However, if you carefully examine the data in the tables, you will notice a couple of possible alternative explanations for these results. One was that group A men reported a greater incidence of CHD in their parents. Therefore, maybe something *genetic* rather than the behavior pattern accounted for the differences found. The other rather glaring difference was the greater number of cigarettes smoked per day by group A participants. Today, we *know* that smoking contributes to CHD. Perhaps it was not the Type A behavior pattern that produced the results but rather the heavier smoking.

Friedman and Rosenman responded to both of those potential criticisms in their discussion of the findings. First, they found that an equal number of light smokers (10 cigarettes or fewer per day) within group A had CHD as did heavy smokers (more than 10 cigarettes per day). Second, group B included 46 men who smoked heavily, yet only two exhibited CHD. These findings led the authors to suggest that cigarette smoking may have been a characteristic of the Type A behavior pattern but not a direct cause of the CHD that was found. It is important to remember that this study was done *over 40 years ago,* before the link between smoking and CHD was as firmly established as it is today.

As for the possibility of parental history creating the differences, "The data also revealed that of the 30 group A men having a positive parental history, only eight (27%) had heart disease and of 53 men without a parental history, 15 (28%) had heart disease. None of the 23 group B men with a positive parental history exhibited clinical heart disease" (p. 1293). Again, more recent research that controlled carefully for this factor has demonstrated a family link in CHD. However, it is not clear whether it is a tendency toward heart disease or toward a certain behavior pattern (such as Type A) that is inherited.

Significance of the Research and Subsequent Findings

This study by Friedman and Rosenman was of crucial importance to the history of psychological research for three basic reasons. First, this was one of the earliest systematic studies to establish clearly that specific behavior patterns characteristic of some individuals can contribute in dramatic ways to serious illness. This sent a message to physicians that to consider only the physiological aspects of illnesses may be wholly inadequate for successful prognosis, treatment, intervention, and prevention. Second, this study began a new line of scientific inquiry into the relationship between human *behavior* and CHD that has produced scores of research articles. The concept of the *Type A personality* and its connection to CHD has been refined to the point that it may be possible to prevent heart attacks in high-risk individuals before the first one occurs.

The third long-range outcome of Friedman and Rosenman's research is that it has played an important role in the creation and growth of *health psychology*, a relatively new branch of the behavioral sciences. Health psychologists study all aspects of health and medicine in terms of the psychological (behavioral) influences that exist in health promotion and maintenance, the prevention and treatment of illness, the causes of illness, and the health care system.

One subsequent study is especially important to report here. In 1976, Rosenman and Friedman published the results of a major 8-year study of over 3,000 men who were diagnosed at the beginning of the study as being free of heart disease and who fit the Type A behavior pattern. Compared with the participants with the Type B behavior pattern, these men were twice as likely to develop CHD, suffered significantly more fatal heart attacks, and they reported five times more coronary problems. What was perhaps even more important, however, was that the Type A pattern predicted *who* would develop CHD independently of such other predictors as age, cholesterol level, blood pressure, or smoking habits (Rosenman et al., 1976).

One question you might be asking yourself by now is *why?* What is it about this Type A pattern that causes CHD? The most widely accepted theory answers that Type As respond to stressful events with far greater physiological arousal than do non-Type As. This extreme arousal causes the body to produce more hormones, such as adrenaline, and also increases heart rate and blood pressure. Over time, these exaggerated reactions tend to damage the arteries, which, in turn, lead to heart disease (Matthews, 1982).

Recent Applications

Both Friedman and Rosenman, together and separately, continued in their roles as leading researchers in the field of personality and behavioral variables in CHD for many decades. Their research along with many others' has spawned a new research niche referred to as *cardiopsychology*, which focuses on the psychological factors involved in the development, course, rehabilitation, and coping mechanisms of CHD (Jordan, Barde, & Zeiher, 2001). Their original article, discussed here, as well as more recent research, is cited in a broad range of studies published in many countries. The Type A concept has been refined, strengthened, and applied to numerous research areas, some of which follow quite logically, while others might surprise you.

For example, one study examined the relationship between Type A behavior and driving (Perry & Baldwin, 2000). The results left little doubt that "Friends should not let Type A friends drive!" The study found a clear association between Type A personality and an increase in driving-related incidents: more traffic accidents, more tickets, greater impatience on the road, more displays of road rage, and overall riskier driving behaviors. You might want to respond to the Type A assessment items at the end of this reading before you get behind the wheel next time.

Just when you thought your main worry was being a Type A person, researchers have continued to explore the link between personality factors and health, especially CHD, and they have now identified a new syndrome: the *Type D* personality (see Denollet et al., 2010). The "D" stands for "distressed." Characteristics of those with Type D personality include negative emotions that are present most of the time, a pessimistic view of the world ("nothing will be OK"), and social inhibition (discomfort being around other people). This particular constellation of symptoms has been associated with an increased risk of various negative health events including artery disease, angioplasty or heart bypass procedures, heart failure, heart transplantation, heart attack, and heart-related death. Researchers have found that Type D people are anxious when they are around other people, and they show elevated levels of anxiety and depression. Also, they avoid talking to anyone about their discomfort because they are intensely afraid of the disapproval of others. Type D is considered by some to be a refinement of Type A, but others see it as a separate and distinct condition.

Type A personality (and possibly Type D, as well) has also been found to affect the relationships between parents and their adolescent children (Forgays, 1996). In that study, Type A characteristics and family environments of over 900 participants were analyzed. Results indicated that teenage children of Type A parents tend to be Type As themselves. That is not surprising, but, once again, it brings up the nature–nurture question. Do kids inherit a genetic tendency toward Type A behavior, or do they learn it from being raised by Type A parents? Forgays addressed this in his study: "Further analyses indicated an *independent* contribution of perceived family environment to the development of TABP [Type A Behavior Pattern] in adolescents" (p. 841, emphasis added). However, it would not be particularly surprising in light of recent research trends, if adoption, twin, and brain-scan studies reveal a significant inherited, genetic influence on the Type A and Type B personality dimension (see the study by Bouchard in Reading 1.3 for a discussion of genetic influences on personality).

Conclusion

Do you have a Type A personality? How would you know? As with your level of introversion or extroversion, mentioned at the beginning of this reading, your *Type A-ness* versus your *Type B-ness* is a part of who you are. Tests have been developed to assess people's Type A or Type B behavior patterns. You can get a rough idea by examining the following list of Type A characteristics to see how many apply to you:

1. Frequently doing more than one thing at a time
2. Urging others to hurry up and finish what they are saying
3. Becoming very irritated when traffic is blocked or when you are waiting in line
4. Gesturing a lot while talking
5. Having a hard time sitting with nothing to do
6. Speaking explosively and using obscenities often
7. Playing to win all the time, even in games with children
8. Becoming impatient when watching others carry out a task

If you suspect that you are a Type A, you may want to consider a more careful evaluation by a trained physician or a psychologist. Several successful programs to intervene in the connection between Type A behavior and serious illness have been developed, largely in response to the work of Friedman and Rosenman (e.g., George et al., 1998).

Denollet, J., Schiffer, A., & Spek, V. (2010). General propensity to psychological distress affects cardiovascular outcomes: Evidence from research on the type D (distressed) personality profile. *Circulation: Cardiovascular Quality and Outcomes, 3*, 546–557.

Forgays, D. (1996). The relationship between Type-A parenting and adolescent perceptions of family environment. *Adolescence, 34*(124), 841–862.

George, I., Prasadaro, P., Kumaraiah, V., & Yavagal, S. (1998). Modification of Type A behavior pattern in coronary heart disease: A cognitive-behavioral intervention program. *NIMHANS Journal, 16*(1), 29–35.

Jordan, J., Barde, B., & Zeiher, A. (2001). Cardiopsychology today. *Herz, 26*, 335–344.

Matthews, K. A. (1982). Psychological perspectives on the Type A behavior pattern. *Psychological Bulletin, 91*, 293–323.

Perry, A., & Baldwin, D. (2000). Further evidence of associations of Type A personality scores and driving-related attitudes and behaviors. *Perceptual and Motor Skills, 91*(1), 147–154.

Rosenman, R. H., Brond, R., Sholtz, R., & Friedman, M. (1976). Multivariate prediction of CHD during 8.5-year follow-up in the Western Collaborative Group Study. *American Journal of Cardiology, 37*, 903–910.

Reading 7.4: The One, the Many

Triandis, H., Bontempo, R., Villareal, M., Asai, M., & Lucca, N. (1988). Individualism and collectivism: Cross-cultural perspectives on self-ingroup relationships. *Journal of Personality and Social Psychology, 54*, 323–338.

7.4 Analyze how living in a collectivist or individualist culture influences behavior

If one characteristic of human nature could be agreed upon by virtually all psychologists, it is that *behavior never occurs in a vacuum.* Even those who place the greatest emphasis on internal motivations, dispositional demands, and genetic drives make allowances for various external, environmental forces to enter the equation that ultimately leads to what you do and who you are. Over the past 30 to 40 years, the field of psychology has increasingly embraced the belief that one very powerful environmental influence on humans is the culture in which they grow up. In fact, researchers *rarely* find observable patterns of human behavior that are consistent and stable in all, or even most, cultures (see the discussion of Ekman's research on facial expressions in Reading 6.2 for an extended analysis of cross-cultural consistency). This is especially true of behaviors relating to human interactions and relationships. Interpersonal attraction, sex, touching, personal space, friendship, family dynamics, parenting styles, childhood behavior expectations, courtship rituals, marriage, divorce, cooperation versus competition, crime, love, and hate are all subject to profound cultural influences. We can say with confidence that an individual cannot be understood with any degree of completeness or precision, without careful consideration of the impact of his or her culture.

Conceptually, that's all well and good, but in practice, culture is a tough nut. Think about it. How would you go about unraveling all the cultural factors that have combined to influence who you have become? Most cultures are far too complex to draw many valid conclusions. For example, colon cancer rates in Japan are a fraction of rates in the United States. Japan and the United States are diverse cultures, so what cultural factors might account for this difference? Differences in amount of fish consumed? Amount of rice? Amount of alcohol? What about differences in stress levels and the pace of life? Perhaps differences in religious practices of the two countries have effects on health? Could variations in the support of family relations and friendships contribute to health and wellness? Or, as is more likely, does the answer lie in a combination of two or three or all these factors, plus many others? The point is that you will need reliable and valid ways of defining cultural differences if you are going to include culture in a complete understanding of human nature. This is where Harry Triandis enters psychology's recent history.

Since the 1960s, and throughout his career in the psychology department at the University of Illinois, Urbana-Champaign, Triandis has worked to develop and refine fundamental attributes of cultures and their members that allow them to be differentiated and studied in meaningful ways. The article referenced here, published in 1988, explains and demonstrates his most influential contribution to cross-cultural psychology: the delineation of *individualistic* versus *collectivist* cultures. Today, this dimension of fundamental cultural variation forms the basis for literally hundreds of studies each year in psychology, sociology, anthropology, and several other fields. In this article, Triandis proposes that the degree to which a particular culture can be defined as individualistic or collectivist determines the behavior and personalities of its members in complex and pervasive ways.

In very basic terms, a collectivist culture is one in which the individual's needs, desires, and outcomes are *secondary* to the needs, desires, and goals of the *ingroup,* the larger group to which the individual belongs. Ingroups may include a family, a tribe, a village, a professional organization, or even an entire country, depending on the situation. In these cultures, a great deal of the behavior of individuals is motivated by what is good for the larger group as a whole, rather than that which provides maximum personal achievement for the individual. The ingroups to which people belong tend to remain stable over time, and individual commitment to the group is often extremely high even when a person's role in the group becomes difficult or unpleasant for him or her. Individuals look to their ingroup to help meet their emotional, psychological, and practical needs.

Individualistic cultures, on the other hand, place a higher value on the welfare and accomplishments of the individual than on the needs and goals of the larger ingroups. In these cultures, the influence of the ingroup on a member's individual behavior is likely to be small. Individuals feel less emotional attachment to the group and are willing to leave an ingroup if it becomes too demanding and to join or to form a new ingroup. Because of this minimal commitment of individuals to groups in individualistic cultures, it is quite common for a person to assume membership in numerous ingroups, while no single group exerts more than a little influence on his or her behavior. In this article, Triandis and his associates from several diverse cultures describe a multitude of distinguishing characteristics of collectivist and individualistic cultures. These are summarized in Table 7.4.1. Such distinctions are, of course, broad generalizations, and exceptions are always found in any culture, whether individualistic or collectivist.

In general, according to Triandis, individualistic cultures tend to be in Northern and Western Europe and in those countries that historically have been influenced by northern Europeans. In addition, highly individualistic cultures appear to share several characteristics: possessing a frontier, large numbers of immigrants, and rapid social and geographical mobility, "all of which tend to make the control of ingroups less certain. The high levels of individualism . . . in the United States, Australia, and Canada are consistent with this point" (p. 324). Most other regions of the world, he maintains, are collectivistic cultures.

Theoretical Propositions

Triandis stated the following at the beginning of this article:

> Culture is a fuzzy construct. If we are to understand the way culture relates to social psychological phenomena, we must analyze it by determining dimensions of cultural variation. One of the most promising such dimensions is individualism-collectivism. (p. 323)

Table 7.4.1 Differences Between Collectivist and Individualistic Cultures

Collectivist Cultures	Individualistic Cultures
• Sacrifice: emphasize personal goals over ingroup goals	• Hedonism: focus on personally satisfying goals over ingroup goals
• Interpret self as extension of group	• Interpret self as distinct from group
• Concern for group is paramount	• Self-reliance is paramount
• Rewards for achievement of group	• Rewards for personal achievement
• Less personal and cultural affluence	• Greater personal and cultural affluence
• Greater conformity to clear group norms	• Less conformity to group norms
• Greater value on love, status, and service	• Greater value on money and possessions
• Greater cooperation within group, but less with outgroup members	• Greater cooperation with members of ingroup and members of various outgroups
• Higher value on "vertical relationships" (child–parent, employer–employee)	• Higher value on "horizontal relationships" (friend–friend, husband–wife)
• Parenting through frequent consultation and intrusion into child's private life	• Parenting through detachment, independence, and privacy for the child
• More people oriented in reaching goals	• More task oriented in reaching goals
• Prefer to hide interpersonal conflicts	• Prefer to confront interpersonal conflicts
• Many individual obligations to the ingroup, but high level of social support, resources, and security in return	• Many individual rights with few obligations to the group, but less support, resources, and security from the group in return
• Fewer friends, but deeper and lifelong friendships with many obligations	• Make friends easily, but friends are less intimate acquaintances
• Few ingroups and everyone else is perceived as one large outgroup	• Many ingroups, but less perception of all others as outgroup members
• Great harmony within groups, but potential for major conflict with members of outgroups	• Ingroups tend to be larger, and interpersonal conflicts more likely to occur within the ingroup
• Shame (external) used more as punishment	• Guilt (internal) used more as punishment
• Slower economic development and industrialization	• Faster economic development and industrialization
• Less social pathology (crime, suicide, child abuse, domestic violence, mental illness)	• Greater levels of all categories of social pathology
• Less illness	• Higher illness rates
• Happier marriages, lower divorce rate	• Less happy marriages, higher divorce rate
• Less competition	• More competition
• Focus on family group rather than larger public good	• Greater concern for greater public good

(Summarized from Triandis, 1988, pp. 323–335.)

His assumption underlying this and many of his studies and publications is that when cultures are defined and interpreted according to the individualism–collectivism model, we can explain a large portion of the variation we see in human behavior, social interaction, and personality. In this article, Triandis was attempting to summarize the extensive potential uses of his theory (see Table 7.4.1) and to report on three scientific studies he undertook to test and demonstrate his individualism–collectivism theory.

Method

As mentioned previously, this article reported on three separate studies. The first study employed only participants from the United States and was designed to define the concept of individualism more clearly as it applies to the United States. The second study's goal was to begin to compare an individualistic culture, the United States, with cultures assumed to be fundamentally collectivist, specifically Japan and Puerto Rico. In Study 2, the focus was on comparing the relationships of individuals to their ingroups in the two types of cultures. The third study was undertaken to test the hypothesis that members of collectivist cultures perceive that they receive better social support and enjoy more consistently satisfying relationships with others, whereas those in individualistic cultures report that they are often lonely. All the studies gathered data from participants through the use of questionnaires. Each study and its findings are summarized briefly here.

STUDY 1 Participants in Study 1 were 300 undergraduate psychology students at the University of Chicago, where Triandis is a professor (now, Emeritus) of psychology. Each student was given a questionnaire consisting of 158 items structured to measure his or her tendency toward collectivist versus individualistic behaviors and beliefs. Agreement with a statement such as "Only those who depend on themselves get ahead in life" represented an individualistic stance, while support for an item such as "When my colleagues tell me personal things about themselves, we are drawn closer together" was evidence for a more collectivist perspective. Also included in the questionnaire were five scenarios that placed participants in hypothetical social situations and asked them to predict their behavior. The example provided in the article was for the participants to imagine they wanted to go on a long trip that various ingroups opposed. The participants were asked how likely they were to consider the opinions and wishes of parents, spouses, close relations, close friends, acquaintances, neighbors, and coworkers in deciding whether to take the trip.

When the response data were analyzed, nearly 50% of the variation in the participants' responses could be explained by three factors: "self-reliance," "competition," and "distance from ingroups." Only 14% of the variation was explained by the factor called "concern for ingroup." More specifically, Triandis summed up the results of Study 1 as follows:

> These data suggest that U.S. [individualism] is a multifaceted concept. The ingredients include more concern for one's own goals than the ingroup goals, less attention to the views of ingroups, self-reliance combined with competition, detachment from ingroups, deciding on one's own rather than asking for the views of others, and less general concern for the ingroup. (p. 331)

He also suggested that the items comprising the questionnaire and the scenarios are effective measures for determining the degree of individualism in one individualistic culture, the United States, but that this scale may or may not produce equally valid results in other cultural settings.

STUDY 2 The question asked in this study was "Do people in collectivist cultures indicate more willingness to subordinate their personal needs to the needs of the group?" The participants were 91 University of Chicago students, 97 Puerto Rican and 150 Japanese university students, and 106 older Japanese individuals. A 144-item questionnaire designed to measure collectivist characteristics was translated into Spanish and Japanese and completed by all participants. Items from the scale had been shown in previous research to tap into three collectivist-related tendencies: "concern for ingroup," "closeness of self to ingroup," and "subordination of own goals to ingroup goals."

In this study, the findings were a fascinating mixed bag, with some results supporting the individualistic–collectivist theory and others seeming to refute it. For example, the Japanese students were significantly more concerned with the views of coworkers and friends than were the Illinois students, but this difference was not observed for the Puerto Rican students. Also, the Japanese participants expressed feeling personally honored when their ingroups are honored, but they paid attention to the views of and sacrificed their personal goals to only *some* ingroups in their lives and not others. And, while conformity is a common attribute of collectivist cultures, very little conformity was found among the Japanese participants—less, in fact, than among the U.S. students. One finding suggested that as collectivist cultures become more affluent and Westernized, they may undergo a shift to greater individualism. As evidence of this, the older Japanese participants perceived themselves to be more similar to their ingroups than did the Japanese university students.

At this point, you might be asking how the findings of the second study figure into Triandis's theory. Triandis interpreted them as a warning that conclusions about collectivist and individualistic cultures should not be overly sweeping and must be carefully applied to selective, specific behaviors, situations, and cultures. He stated this idea as follows:

> The data of this study tell us to restrict and sharpen our definition of collectivism . . . that we must consider each domain of social behavior separately, and collectivism, defined as subordination to the ingroup's norms, needs, views, and emotional closeness to ingroups is very specific to ingroup and to domain. . . . Collectivism takes different forms . . . that are specific to each culture. (p. 334)

STUDY 3   The third reported study attempted to do exactly what Triandis suggested in the preceding quote: restrict and sharpen the research focus. This study extended previous findings that collectivist societies provide high levels of social support to their members, while those in individualistic cultures tend to experience greater loneliness. Here, a 72-item collectivist–individualist questionnaire was completed by 100 participants, equally divided by sex, at the University of Chicago and at the University of Puerto Rico. Participants also filled out questionnaires measuring their perceived degree of social support and perceived amount of loneliness.

The results of this study clearly indicated that collectivism correlated positively with social support, meaning that as the degree of collectivism increased, the level of social support also increased. Moreover, collectivism was negatively associated with loneliness, implying that as the effect of collectivism increased, participants' perceived level of loneliness diminished. As further evidence for Triandis's model, the most important factor in this study for the U.S. students (accounting for the most variance) was "self-reliance with competition," while the most influential factor for the Puerto Rican students was "affiliation" (interacting with others). These results are exactly what you would expect from the individualistic–collectivist theory.

Discussion

Overall, Triandis explained, the studies described in this article supported, but also modified, his definitions of collectivism and individualism. Looking back at the characteristics of each type of culture in Table 7.4.1, the picture that emerges is one of opposition—that is, individualistic and collectivist cultures appear to be nearly exact opposites of each other. This article, however, seems to demonstrate that these cultural descriptions fall at two ends of a continuum and that a particular society will be best described as falling somewhere between the two but usually clearly closer to one end than the other. In addition, within any single culture will be found specific individuals, groups, subcultures, and situations that may violate that culture's overall placement on the continuum by fitting better toward the opposite end. A graphical, hypothetical representation of this interpretation is shown in Figure 7.4.1. "In short," Triandis states, "The empirical studies suggest that we need to consider individualism and collectivism as multidimensional constructs . . . [each of which] depends very much on which ingroup is present, in what context, and what behavior was studied" (p. 336).

Significance of the Findings and Related Research

Over a relatively short period of historical time, Triandis's work has found its way into the fundamental core of how psychologists view human behavior. You would be hard pressed, for example, to open any recent text in most subfields of psychology—introductory psychology, social psychology, developmental psychology, personality psychology, human sexuality, abnormal psychology, cognitive psychology, to name a few—without finding multiple references to this and many other of his individualism–collectivism studies. Arguably, the individualistic–collectivistic cultural dimension, as articulated, clarified, and refined by Triandis, is the most reliable, valid, and influential factor seen in current studies on the role culture plays in determining the personalities and social behaviors of humans. Moreover, the range of research areas to which this dimension has been applied is remarkably broad. Following are just two examples.

In the article that is the subject of this discussion, Triandis offers evidence that the psychosocial concepts of collectivism and individualism may play a significant part in the physical health of the members of a given culture. A case in point relates to coronary heart disease. In general, heart attack rates tend to be lower in collectivist societies than in individualistic ones. Triandis suggests that unpleasant and stressful life events often related to heart disease are more common in individualistic cultures where pressures are intense on solitary individuals to compete and achieve on their own. Along with these negative life events, individualistic social structures inherently offer less social cohesion and social support, which have been clearly demonstrated to reduce the effects of stress on health. Of course, many factors might account for cultural differences in heart attack rates or any other disease, as discussed at the beginning of this reading. However, numerous studies have shown that members of collectivist cultures who move to countries that are individualistic become increasingly prone to various illnesses, including heart disease.

Perhaps even more convincing are studies of two different subgroups within the same culture. As Triandis points out (p. 327), one study of 3,000 Japanese Americans compared those who had acculturated—that is, had adapted their lifestyle and attitudes to U.S. norms—to those who still maintained a traditional Japanese way of life *within* the United States. Heart attack rates among the acculturated participants were *five times*

Figure 7.4.1 Collectivist–individualistic cultural continuum (culture and subculture placements are approximate).

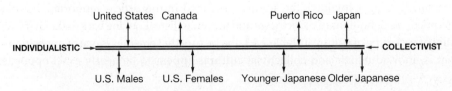

greater than among the nonacculturated participants even when cholesterol levels, exercise, cigarette smoking, and weight were statistically equalized for the two groups.

Of course, you would expect that the individualism–collectivism dimension would affect how children are raised in a particular culture and, indeed, it does. Parents in collectivist societies place a great deal of emphasis on developing the child's "collective self" characterized by conformity to group norms, obedience to those in authority within the group, and reliability or consistency of behavior over time and across situations. Children are rewarded in both overt and subtle ways for behavior patterns and attitudes that support and correspond to the goals of the ingroup (Triandis, 1989). In this context, refusing to do something that the group expects of you, just because you don't enjoy doing it, is unacceptable and rarely seen. Yet in highly individualistic cultures, such as the United States, such refusal is a very common response and is often valued and respected! That happens because parenting practices in individualistic cultures emphasize development of the child's "private self." This focus rewards children for behaviors and attitudes leading to self-reliance, independence, self-knowledge, and reaching their maximum potential as an individual. Another way to look at this distinction is that rebellion (within certain socially acceptable limits) and an independent streak in individualistic cultures are seen as personality *assets,* whereas in collectivist societies, they are seen as *liabilities.* The messages from the culture to the children, via the parents, about these assets or liabilities are loud and clear and exert a potent influence upon the kids' development into adulthood.

Recent Applications

Triandis's work has impacted a wide variety of research fields. One article applied Triandis's ideas to a study about the attitudes of college football fans in two cultures (Snibbe et al., 2003). Students at important football games in the United States (Rose Bowl) and in Japan (Flash Bowl) were asked to rate their own and their opponent's universities and students before and after the big game. In both games, the university with the better academic reputation lost the Game. However, the reactions of the students in the two cultures were markedly different: "American students from both universities evaluated their in-groups more positively than out-groups on all measures before and after the game. In contrast, Japanese students' ratings offered *no evidence* of in-group bias. . . . Instead, Japanese students' ratings reflected each university's status in the larger society and the students' status in the immediate situation" (p. 581).

Another study employed Triandis's model to examine the experience of loneliness across cultures (Rokach et al., 2002). Over 1,000 participants from North America and Spain completed questionnaires about the various causes of their loneliness, including personal inadequacies, developmental difficulties, unfulfilling intimate relationships, relocations and separations, and feeling marginalized by society: "Results indicated that cultural background indeed affects the causes of loneliness. North Americans scored higher on *all five factors*" (p. 70, emphasis added).

One study highlighted a particularly important aspect of Triandis's work. When collectivist and individualistic cultures are studied and compared, this is not, by any means, limited to comparisons *between* countries. Many countries contain *within* their borders pockets of widely varying levels of collectivism and individualism. Nowhere on earth is this truer than in the United States. An engaging study by Vandello and Cohen (1999) charted the United States on the basis of Triandis's model. Before you read the following, stop and think for a moment about which states you would predict to find the strongest collectivist and individualistic tendencies. The researchers reported that states in the Deep South were most collectivist and those in the Plains and Rocky Mountain regions were highest on individualism. However, even within these divergent areas of the United States, smaller, subcultural groups of individualistic and collectivist individuals may be found.

Conclusion

Triandis has provided all the social sciences a new lens through which we can view fundamental cultural differences. The diversity we all experience first hand as the world becomes smaller and societies increasingly intertwine often creates the potential for misunderstandings, breakdowns in communication, friction, and frustration. Perhaps an awareness and appreciation of collectivist and individualistic cultural differences provide us with a small, yet meaningful, step forward toward the positive goal of easing intercultural discord and enhancing world harmony.

Rokach, A., Orzeck, T., Moya, M., & Exposido, F. (2002). Causes of loneliness in North America and Spain. *European Psychologist, 7,* 70–79.

Snibbe, A., Kitayama, S., Markus, H., & Suzuki, T. (2003). They saw a game: A Japanese and American (football) field study. *Journal of Cross-Cultural Psychology, 34,* 581–595.

Triandis, H. (1989). The self and social behavior in differing cultural contexts. *Psychological Review, 96*(3), 506–520.

Vandello, J., & Cohen, D. (1999). Patterns of individualism and collectivism across the United States. *Journal of Personality and Social Psychology, 77*(2), 279–292.

Chapter 8
Psychopathology

 Learning Objectives

8.1 Explain how context influences the process by which psychologists determine abnormal behavior

8.2 Describe defense mechanisms according to Freud

8.3 Explain how research into the development and display of learned helplessness has impacted the field of psychology

8.4 Relate Calhoun's rat crowding experiments to human psychology in high population density areas

Most people who have never studied psychology have the impression that the field is primarily concerned with analyzing and treating mental illnesses (the branch of psychology called *abnormal psychology*). However, as you may have noticed, nearly all the research discussed in this book has focused on *normal* behavior. Overall, psychologists are more interested in normal behavior than in abnormal behavior because the vast majority of human behavior is not pathological; it is normal. Consequently, we would not know very much about human nature if we only studied the small percentage of it that is abnormal. Nevertheless, mental illness is to many people one of the most fascinating areas of study in all of psychology. A variety of studies essential to the history of psychology are included here.

First is a study that has kept the mental health profession talking for over 40 years. In this study, normally healthy people *pretending* to be mental patients entered psychiatric facilities to see if the doctors and staff could distinguish them from those who were actually mentally ill. Second, no book about the history of psychological research would be complete without reference to Sigmund Freud. Therefore, a discussion of his most enduring concept, *ego defense mechanisms,* is discussed through the writings of his daughter, Anna Freud. The third study examined is an experiment with dogs as subjects that demonstrated a phenomenon called *learned helplessness.* This condition relates to psychopathology in that it led to a widely held theory explaining clinical depression in humans. And fourth, an intriguing and well-known experiment is presented involving overcrowded rats and their resulting deviant behavior, which may have offered some important implications for humans.

Reading 8.1: Who's Crazy Here, Anyway?

Rosenhan, D. L. (1973). On being sane in insane places. *Science, 179,* 250–258.

8.1 Explain how context influences the process by which psychologists determine abnormal behavior

The task of distinguishing who is "normal" from those whose behavior may be considered "abnormal" is fundamental in psychology. The definition of *abnormality* plays a key role in determining whether someone is diagnosed as mentally ill, and the diagnosis largely determines the treatment a patient receives. The line that divides normal from abnormal is not as clear as you may think. Rather, all behavior lies on a continuum with normal, or what might be called *effective psychological functioning,* at one end, and abnormal, indicating a *psychological disorder,* at the other.

It is often up to mental health professionals to determine where on this continuum a particular person's behavior falls. To make this determination, clinical psychologists, psychiatrists, and other behavioral scientists and clinicians may use one or more of the following criteria:

- *Context of the Behavior.* This is a subjective judgment, but you know that some behaviors are clearly bizarre in a given situation, whereas they may be unremarkable in another. For example, nothing is strange about standing outside watering your lawn, unless you are doing it in your pyjamas during a pouring rainstorm! A judgment about abnormality must carefully consider the context in which a behavior occurs.

- *Persistence of Behavior.* We all have our "crazy" moments. A person may exhibit abnormal behavior on occasion without necessarily demonstrating the presence of mental illness. For instance, you might have just received some great news and, as you are walking along a busy downtown sidewalk, you dance for half a block or so. This behavior, although somewhat odd, would not indicate mental illness, unless you began to dance down that sidewalk on, say, a weekly or daily basis. This criterion for mental illness requires that a bizarre, an antisocial, or a disruptive behavior pattern persists over time.

- *Social Deviance.* When a person's behavior radically violates society's expectations and norms, it may meet the criteria for social deviance. When deviant behavior is extreme and persistent, such as auditory or visual hallucinations, it is evidence of mental illness.

- *Subjective Distress.* Frequently, we are aware of our own psychological difficulties and the suffering they are causing us. When a person is so afraid of enclosed spaces that he or she cannot ride in an elevator, or when someone finds it impossible to form meaningful relationships with others, they often do not need a professional to tell them they are in psychological pain. This subjective distress is an important sign that mental health professionals use in making psychological diagnoses.

- *Psychological Handicap.* When a person has great difficulty being satisfied with life due to psychological problems, this is considered to be a psychological handicap. A person who fears success, for example, and therefore sabotages each new endeavor in life, is suffering from a psychological handicap.

- *Effect on Functioning.* The extent to which the behaviors in question interfere with a person's ability to live the life that he or she desires, and that society will accept, may be the most important factor in diagnosing psychological problems. A behavior could be bizarre and persistent, but if it does not impair your ability to function in life, pathology may not be indicated. For example, suppose you have an uncontrollable need to stand on your bed and sing the national anthem every night before going to sleep. This is certainly bizarre and persistent, but unless you are waking up the neighbors, disturbing other household members, or feeling terrible about it, your behavior may have little effect on your general functioning and, therefore, may not be classified as a clinical problem.

These symptoms and characteristics of mental illness all involve *judgments* on the part of psychologists, psychiatrists, and other mental health professionals. Therefore, the foregoing guidelines notwithstanding, two questions remain: Are mental health professionals truly able to distinguish between the mentally ill and the mentally healthy? And what are the consequences of mistakes? These are the questions addressed by David Rosenhan in his provocative study of mental hospitals.

Theoretical Propositions

Rosenhan questioned whether the characteristics that lead to psychological diagnoses reside in the patients themselves or in the situations and contexts in which the observers (those who do the diagnosing) find the patients. He reasoned that if the established criteria and the training mental health professionals have received for diagnosing mental illness are adequate, then those professionals should be able to distinguish between the insane and the sane. (Technically, the words *sane* and *insane* are legal terms and are not usually used in psychological contexts. They are used here because they have a commonly understood meaning and Rosenhan incorporated them into his research.) Rosenhan proposed that one way to test mental health professionals' ability to categorize prospective patients correctly would be to have *normal* people seek admittance to psychiatric facilities to see if those charged with diagnosing them would see that, in reality, they were psychologically healthy. If these "pseudopatients" behaved normally in the hospital, just as they would in their daily lives outside the facility, and if the doctors and staff failed to recognize that they were indeed normal, this would provide evidence that diagnoses of the mentally ill are tied more to the situation than to the patient.

Method

Rosenhan recruited eight participants (including himself) to serve as pseudopatients. The eight participants (three women and five men) consisted of one graduate student, three psychologists, one pediatrician, one psychiatrist, one painter, and one homemaker. The participants' mission was to present themselves for admission to 12 psychological hospitals, in five states on both the East and West Coasts of the United States.

All the pseudopatients followed the same instructions. They called the hospital and made an appointment. Upon arrival at the hospital, they complained of hearing voices that said "empty," "hollow," and "thud." Other than this single symptom, all participants acted completely normally and gave truthful information to the interviewer (other than changing their names and occupations to conceal the study's purpose and to protect themselves). Upon completion of the intake interview, all eight participants were admitted to the hospitals, and all but one was admitted with a diagnosis of *schizophrenia*.

Once inside the hospital, the pseudopatients dropped their pretend symptoms and behaved normally. The participants had no idea when they would be allowed to leave the hospital. It was up to them to gain their release by convincing the hospital staff that they were mentally healthy enough to be discharged. All the participants took notes of their experiences. At first, they tried to conceal this activity, but soon, it was clear that this secrecy was unnecessary because hospital staff interpreted their "note-taking behavior" as just another symptom of their illness. The goal of all the pseudopatients was to be released as soon as possible, so they behaved as model patients, cooperating with the staff and accepting all medications (which they did not swallow but rather flushed down the toilet).

Results

The length of the hospital stays for the pseudopatients ranged from 7 to 52 days, with an average of 19 days. The key finding in this study was that not one of the pseudopatients was detected by anyone on the hospital staff. When they were released, their mental health status was recorded in their files as "schizophrenia in remission." That's very different than *cured*. They recorded other interesting findings and observations, as well.

Although the hospitals' staffs of doctors, nurses, and attendants failed to detect the participants, the other patients could not be fooled so easily. In three of the pseudopatients' hospitalizations, 35 out of 118 real patients voiced suspicions that the participants were not actually mentally ill. They would make comments such as these: "You're not crazy!" "You're a journalist or a reporter." "You're checking up on the hospital!"

Contacts among the patients (whether participants or not) and the staff were minimal and often bizarre. One of the tests the pseudopatients initiated in the study was to approach various staff members and attempt to make verbal contact by asking common, normal questions (e.g., "When will I be allowed grounds privileges?" or "When am I likely to be discharged?"). Often these questions were ignored or the responses from doctors and staff were unrelated to the specific questions asked, such as "Good morning. How are you today?" and continuing to walk away without waiting for a response.

In contrast to the severe lack of personal contact in the hospitals studied, the patients received no shortage of medications. The eight pseudopatients in this study were given a total of 2,100 pills that, as mentioned previously, were not swallowed. The participants noted that many of the real patients also secretly disposed of their pills down the toilet.

Another anecdote from one of the pseudopatients tells of a nurse who unbuttoned her uniform to adjust her bra in front of a dayroom full of male patients. It was not her intention to be provocative, according to the participant's report, but she simply did not consider the patients to be "real people."

Discussion

Rosenhan's study demonstrated that even trained professionals often cannot distinguish the normal from the mentally ill in a hospital setting. According to Rosenhan, this is because of the overwhelming influence of the psychiatric hospital setting on the staff's judgment of an individual's behavior. Once patients are admitted to such a facility, the doctors and staff tend to view them in ways that ignore them as individual people. The attitude created is "If they are here, they must be crazy." More important was what Rosenhan referred to as the "stickiness of the diagnostic label." That is, when a patient is labeled as "schizophrenic," that diagnosis becomes his or her central characteristic or personality trait. From the moment the label is given and the staff members know it, they perceive all of the patient's behavior as stemming from the diagnosis—thus, the lack of concern or suspicion over the pseudopatients' note taking, which was perceived as just another behavioral manifestation of the psychological label.

The hospital staff tended to ignore the situational pressures on patients and saw all behavior as relevant to the pathology assigned to the patients. This was demonstrated by the following observation of one of the participants:

> One psychiatrist pointed to a group of patients who were sitting outside the cafeteria entrance half an hour before lunchtime. To a group of young resident psychiatrists, he indicated that such behavior was characteristic of the "oral-acquisitive" nature of the [schizophrenic] syndrome. It seemed not to occur to him that there were simply very few things to do in a psychiatric hospital besides eating. (p. 253)

Beyond this, the sticky diagnostic label even colored how a pseudopatient's *history* would be interpreted. Remember, all the participants gave honest accounts of their pasts and families. Following is an example from Rosenhan's research of a pseudopatient's stated history, followed by its interpretation by the staff doctor in a report after the participant was discharged. The participant's *true* history was as follows:

> The pseudopatient had a close relationship with his mother but was rather remote with his father during his early childhood. During adolescence and beyond, however, his father became a very close friend while his relationship with his mother cooled. His present relationship with his wife was characteristically close and warm. Apart from occasional angry exchanges, friction was minimal. The children had rarely been spanked. (p. 253)

The doctor's interpretation of this rather normal and innocuous history was as follows:

> This white 39-year-old male manifests a long history of considerable ambivalence in close relationships which begins in early childhood. A warm relationship with his mother cools during his adolescence. A distant relationship with his father is described as becoming very intense. Affective [emotional] stability is absent. His attempts to control emotionality with his wife and children are punctuated by angry outbursts and, in the case of the children, spankings. And although he says he has several good friends, one senses considerable ambivalence embedded in those relationships also. (p. 253)

Nothing indicates that any of the doctor's distortions was intentional. He believed in the diagnosis (in this case, schizophrenia) and interpreted a patient's history and behavior in ways that were consistent with that diagnosis.

Significance of Findings

Rosenhan's study shook the mental health profession. The results pointed out two crucial factors. First, it appeared that the "sane" could not be distinguished from the "insane" in mental hospital settings. As Rosenhan himself stated in his article, "The hospital itself imposes a special environment in which the meaning of behavior can be easily misunderstood. The consequences to patients hospitalized in such an environment seem undoubtedly countertherapeutic" (p. 257). Second, Rosenhan demonstrated the danger of diagnostic labels. Once a person is labeled as having a certain psychological condition (such as schizophrenia, depression, etc.), that label eclipses any and all of his or her other characteristics. All behavior and personality characteristics are then seen as stemming from the disorder. The worst part of this sort of treatment is that it can become self-confirming. That is, if a person is treated in a certain way consistently over time, he or she may begin to behave that way.

Out of Rosenhan's work grew greater care in diagnostic procedures and increased awareness of the dangers of applying labels to patients. The problems this study addressed began to decline with the decrease in patients confined to mental hospitals. This decrease in hospital populations was brought about by the discovery in the 1950s and increased use of antipsychotic medications, which can reduce symptoms in most patients enough for them to live outside a hospital and in many cases lead relatively normal lives. Concurrent to this was the growth of community mental health facilities, crisis intervention centers, and behavior therapies that focus on specific problems and behaviors and tend to avoid diagnostic labels altogether.

This does not imply by any means that the mental health profession has eliminated labels. However, largely because of Rosenhan's research and other research in the same vein, psychiatric labels are now used more carefully and treated with the respect their power demands.

Questions and Criticisms

One research and teaching hospital whose staff members had heard about Rosenhan's findings before they were published doubted that such mistakes in diagnosis could be made in their hospital. To test this, Rosenhan informed the hospital staff members that during the next 3 months, one or more pseudopatients would try to be admitted to their psychiatric unit. Each staff member was asked to rate each presenting patient on a 10-point scale as to the likelihood that he or she was a pseudopatient. At the end of 3 months, 193 patients had been admitted. Of those, 41 were considered, with high confidence, to be pseudopatients by at least one staff member. At least one psychiatrist suspected 23, and one psychiatrist and one other staff member identified 19. Rosenhan (the tricky devil) had not sent any pseudopatients to the hospital during the 3-month period! "The experiment is instructive," states Rosenhan:

> It indicates that the tendency to designate sane people as insane can be reversed when the stakes (in this case prestige and diagnostic ability) are high. But one thing is certain: Any diagnostic process that lends itself so readily to massive errors of this sort cannot be a very reliable one. (p. 252)

Rosenhan replicated this study several times in 12 hospitals between 1973 and 1975. Each time, he found similar results (see Greenberg, 1981; Rosenhan, 1975). However, other researchers dispute the conclusions Rosenhan drew from this research. Spitzer (1976) argued that although the methods used by Rosenhan appeared to invalidate psychological diagnostic systems, in reality, they did not. For example, it should not be difficult for pseudopatients to lie their way into a mental hospital because many such admissions are based on verbal reports (and who would ever suspect someone of using trickery to get *into* such a place?). The reasoning here is that you could walk into a medical emergency room complaining of severe intestinal pain, and you might get yourself admitted to the hospital with a diagnosis of gastritis, appendicitis, or an ulcer. Even though the doctor was tricked, Spitzer contended, the diagnostic methods were not invalid. In addition, Spitzer has pointed out that although the pseudopatients behaved normally once admitted to the hospital, such symptom variation in psychiatric disorders is common and does not mean that the staff was incompetent in failing to detect the deception.

The controversy over the validity of psychological diagnosis that began with Rosenhan's 1973 article continues. Regardless of the ongoing debate, we can have little doubt that Rosenhan's study remains one of the most influential in the history of psychology.

Recent Applications

As an indication of this continuing controversy, we can consider two of many studies that have used Rosenhan's research in challenging the validity of diagnoses made by mental health professionals. One of these was conducted by Thomas Szasz, a psychiatrist who has been a well-known critic of the overall concept of mental illness since the early 1970s. His contention is that mental illnesses are not diseases and cannot be properly understood as such but rather must be seen as "problems in living" that have social and environmental causes. In one article, Szasz makes the case that the *crazy talk* exhibited by some who have been diagnosed with a mental illness "is not a valid reason for concluding that a person is insane" simply because one person (the mental health professional) cannot comprehend the other (the patient) (Szasz, 1993, p. 61).

Another study building on Rosenhan's 1973 article examined how, in some real-life situations, people may indeed purposely fabricate symptoms of mental illness (Broughton & Chesterman, 2001). The case study discussed in the article involved a man accused of sexually assaulting a teenage boy. When the perpetrator was evaluated for psychiatric problems, he displayed various psychotic behaviors. Upon further examination, clinicians found that he had faked all his symptoms. The authors point out that mental health professionals traditionally have assumed the accuracy of patient statements in diagnosing psychological disorders (as they did with Rosenhan's pseudopatients). However, they suggest that inventing symptoms "is a fundamental issue for all psychiatrists, especially [when] . . . complicated by external socio-legal issues which could possibly serve as motivation for the fabrication of psychopathology" (p. 407). In other words, we have to be careful that criminals are not able to fake mental illness as a "get-out-of-jail-free card."

How do the people themselves feel who have been given a psychiatric diagnostic label? In a survey of more than 1,300 mental health patients, Wahl (1999) asked participants about their experiences of being discriminated against and stigmatized. The majority of respondents reported feeling the effects of the stigma surrounding mental illness from various sources, including community members in general, family, church members, coworkers, and even mental health professionals. In addition, the author reported, "The majority of respondents tended to try to conceal their disorders and worried a great deal that others would find out about their psychiatric status and treat them unfavorably. They reported discouragement, hurt, anger, and lowered self-esteem as a result of their experiences and urged public education as a means for reducing stigma" (p. 467).

The authors of a related study entitled "Listen to My Madness" (Lester & Tritter, 2005) suggested that one possible approach to help us understand the experience of those with mental illness is to interpret their impairment in society similar to our perception of those with other types of defined disabilities. These authors propose that seriously mentally ill individuals' interaction with society is often very similar to people with other disabilities in terms of receiving care. By applying a disability model to the mentally ill, they will have an easier time gaining access to and receiving the services and help they need.

An even more radical suggestion has been proposed by Timimi (2014): That psychiatric labeling systems should be abolished altogether. Timimi argues that these labels are not useful or valid and that the stigma stemming from them is so harmful that they should not even be used to aid in diagnosis or treatment. He argues that the current diagnostic system imposes western cultural beliefs about mental distress on other cultures even when we know that mental illness symptomology is interpreted differently in diverse societies. Timimi goes so far as to suggest that the International Classification of Diseases (ICD-10) and the Diagnostic and Statistical Manual of Mental Disorders (DSM-5) be eliminated. This is an interesting idea in principle for helping to prevent stigma and discrimination, but in practice, it is probably not the solution and would not be realistic. The mental health profession requires diagnostic codes and schemes for reliability of psychiatric condition identification, consistency of treatments and medications, and someway (however imperfect) for insurance providers to cover psychological disorders.

Conclusion

Mental health professionals and others hope that we, as a culture, will increase our tolerance and understanding of psychological disorders. As we do, our ability to diagnose these disorders will continue to improve, although, in many cases, it continues to be as much art as science. Chances are we will never do away with psychiatric labels; they are an important part of effective treatment of psychological disorders, just as names of diseases are part of diagnosing and treating physical illnesses. However, if we are stuck with labels (no pun intended), we must continue to work to take the stigma, embarrassment, and shame out of them.

Broughton, N., & Chesterman, P. (2001). Malingered psychosis. *Journal of Forensic Psychiatry, 12,* 407–422.

Greenberg, J. (1981, June/July). An interview with David Rosenhan. *APA Monitor,* 4–5.

Lester, H., & Tritter, J. (2005) "Listen to my madness": Understanding the experiences of people with serious mental illness. *Sociology of Health & Illness, 27*(5), 649–669.

Rosenhan, D. L. (1975). The contextual nature of psychiatric diagnosis. *Journal of Abnormal Psychology, 84,* 442–452.

Spitzer, R. L. (1976). More on pseudoscience in science and the case of the psychiatric diagnosis: A critique of D. L. Rosenhan's "On being sane in insane places" and "The contextual nature of psychiatric diagnosis." *Archives of General Psychiatry, 33,* 459–470.

Szasz, T. (1993). Crazy talk: Thought disorder or psychiatric arrogance? *British Journal of Medical Psychology, 66,* 61–67.

Timimi, S. (2014). No more psychiatric labels: Why formal psychiatric diagnostic systems should be abolished. *International Journal of Clinical and Health Psychology, 14*(3), 208-215.

Wahl, O. (1999). Mental health consumers' experience of stigma. *Schizophrenia Bulletin, 25*(3), 467–478.

Reading 8.2: You're Getting Defensive Again!

Freud, A. (1946). *The ego and the mechanisms of defense.* New York: International Universities Press.

8.2 Describe defense mechanisms according to Freud

In a book about the history of research that changed psychology, one imposing figure would be extremely difficult to omit: Sigmund Freud (1856–1939). Psychology as we know it would probably not exist today without Freud's contributions. He was largely responsible for elevating our interpretations of human behavior (especially maladaptive behavior) from irrational superstitions of demonic possession and evil spirits to the rational approaches of reason and nascent psychological science. Without an examination of his work, this book would be incomplete. Now, you may be asking yourself, if Sigmund Freud is so important, why does this discussion focus on a book written by his daughter, *Anna* Freud (1895–1982)? The answer to that question requires a bit of explanation.

Although Sigmund Freud was integral to psychology's history and, therefore, is a necessary part of this book, the task of including his research here along with all the other researchers is a difficult one because Freud did not reach his discoveries through a clearly defined scientific methodology. It is not possible to choose a single study or series of experiments to represent his work, as has been done for other major researchers in this book. Freud's theories grew out of his detailed observations of his patients over decades of clinical analysis. Consequently, his writings are abundant, to say the least. The English translation of his collected published writings (Freud, 1953 to 1974) totals 24 volumes! Obviously, only a very small piece of his work can be discussed here. In choosing what to include, consideration was given to the portions of Freud's theories that have stood the test of time relatively unscathed. Over the past century, a great deal of criticism has been focused on Freud's ideas, and in the last 50 years especially, his work has been drawn into serious question from a scientific perspective. Critics have argued that many of his theories either cannot be tested scientifically; or if they are tested, they prove to be invalid. Therefore, although few would doubt the historical importance of Freud's work, many of his theories about the structure of personality, the development of personality through five psychosexual stages, and the sources of people's psychological problems have been rejected by most psychologists today. However, some aspects of his work have received more positive reviews through the years and now enjoy relatively wide acceptance. One of these is his concept of the *ego defense mechanisms:* psychological "weapons" that your ego uses to protect you from your various manifestations of anxiety. This element from Freud's work dealing with the defense mechanisms has been selected to represent Freud in this book.

Sigmund Freud's discovery of ego defense mechanisms occurred gradually over 30 or more years as his experiences in dealing with psychological problems grew. A cohesive, self-contained discussion of this topic does not appear anywhere in Sigmund Freud's many volumes. In fact, he passed that job on to his daughter, who was an important psychoanalyst in her own right, specializing in helping children. Freud acknowledged this fact in 1936 just before Anna's book *The Ego and the Mechanisms of Defense* was originally published in German: "There are an extremely large number of methods (or mechanisms, as we say) used by the ego in the discharge of its defensive functions. My daughter, the child analyst, is writing a book about them" (S. Freud, 1936). Because it was Anna Freud who synthesized her father's theories regarding the defense mechanisms into a single work, her book has been chosen for our discussion of the work of Sigmund Freud.

Theoretical Propositions

To examine Freud's notion of defense mechanisms, we should discuss briefly his theory of the structure of personality. Freud proposed that personality consists of three components: the *id, ego,* and *superego.*

In Freud's view, the id (which is simply Latin for "it") is present at birth and contains your basic human biological urges and instincts such as hunger, thirst, and sexual impulses. Whenever these needs are not met, the id generates strong signals that demand the person find a way to satisfy them—and to do so immediately! The id operates on what Freud called the *pleasure principle,* meaning it insists upon instantaneous gratification of all desires, regardless of reason, logic, safety, or morality. Freud believed that dark, antisocial, and dangerous instinctual urges (especially sexual ones) are present in everyone's id and that these constantly seek expression. You are not usually aware of them because Freud contended, the id operates on the unconscious level. However, if you were lacking the other parts of your personality and only had an id, Freud would expect your behavior to be amoral, shockingly deviant, and even potentially fatal to you and others.

In Freud's view, the reason you do not behave in these dangerous and deviant ways is that your ego develops to place limits and controls on the impulses of your id. According to Freud, the *ego* (*ego* means "the self") operates on the *reality principle,* which means it is alert to the real world and the consequences of behavior. The ego is conscious, and its job is to satisfy your id's urges, but to do so using means that are rational and reasonably safe. However, the ego also has limits placed upon it by the *superego* (meaning "above the ego"). Your superego, in essence, requires that the ego finds solutions to the id's demands that are moral and ethical, according to your own internalized set of rules about what is good or bad, right or wrong. These moral rules, Freud contended, were instilled in you by your parents, and if you behave in ways that violate them your superego will punish you with its own very effective weapon: guilt. Do you recognize the superego? It is commonly referred to as your *conscience.* Freud believed that your superego operates on both conscious and unconscious levels.

Freud's conceptualization of your personality was a dynamic one in which your ego is constantly trying to balance the needs and urges of your id with the moral requirements of the superego in determining your behavior. Following is an example of how this might work. Imagine a young man strolling down the street in a small town. It is 10:00 PM, and he is on his way home. Suddenly, he realizes he is hungry. He passes a grocery store and sees food on the other side of the large windows, but the store is closed. His id might say, "Look! Food! Jump through the glass and get some!" (Remember, the id wants immediate satisfaction, regardless of the consequences.) He would probably not be aware of the id's suggestion because it would be at a level below his consciousness. The ego would "hear" it, though, and because its job is to protect the boy from danger, it might respond, "No, that would be dangerous. Let's go around back, break into the store, and steal some food!" At this, his superego would remark indignantly, "You can't do that! It's immoral, and if you do it, I will punish you!" Therefore, the young man's ego reconsiders and makes a new suggestion that is acceptable to both the id and the superego: "You know, there's an all-night fast-food place four blocks over. Let's go there and buy some food." This solution, assuming that the boy is psychologically healthy, is finally the (normal) one that is reflected in his behavior.

According to Freud, the reason most people do not behave in antisocial or deviant ways is because of this system of checks and balances among the three parts of the personality. But what would happen if the system malfunctioned—if this balance were lost? One way this could happen would be if the demands of the id became too strong to be controlled adequately by the ego. What if the unacceptable urges of the id edged their way into your consciousness (into what Freud called the *preconscious*) and began to overpower the ego? Freud contended that if this happens, you will experience a very unpleasant condition called *anxiety*. Specifically, he called it *free-floating anxiety*, because although you feel anxious and afraid, the causes are not fully conscious, so you are not sure why you feel this way.

When this state of anxiety exists, it is uncomfortable, and we are motivated to change it. To do this, the ego will bring on its "big guns," the *ego defense mechanisms*. The purpose of the defense mechanisms is to prevent the id's forbidden impulse from entering consciousness. If this is successful, the discomfort of the anxiety associated with the impulse is decreased or even eliminated. The defense mechanisms ward off anxiety through self-deception and the distortion of reality so that the id's unacceptable urges will not have to be acknowledged.

Method

Freud claimed to have discovered the defense mechanisms gradually over many years of clinical interactions with his patients. In the years since Sigmund Freud's death and since the publication of Anna Freud's book, many refinements have been made in the interpretation of the defense mechanisms. The next section summarizes a selection of only those mechanisms identified by Sigmund Freud and elaborated on by his daughter.

Results and Discussion

Anna Freud (p. 44) identified 10 defense mechanisms that had been described by her father. Five of the original mechanisms that are commonly used and widely recognized today are discussed here: *repression, regression, projection, reaction formation*, and *sublimation*. Keep in mind that the primary function of your defense mechanisms is to alter reality in order to protect you against anxiety.

REPRESSION *Repression* is probably the most basic and most common mechanism we use in defending the ego. In his early writings, Freud used the terms *repression* and *defense* interchangeably and interpreted repression to be virtually the only defense mechanism. Later, however, he acknowledged that repression was only one of many psychological processes available to protect a person from anxiety. Freud believed that a person's use of repression forces disturbing thoughts completely out of consciousness. Consequently, the anxiety associated with the "forbidden" thoughts is avoided because the person is unaware of their existence. In Freud's view, repression is often employed to defend against the anxiety caused by unacceptable sexual desires. For example, a woman who has sexual feelings about her father would probably experience intense anxiety if these impulses were to become conscious. To avoid that anxiety, she might repress her unacceptable desires, forcing them fully into her unconscious. This would not mean that her urges are gone, but because they are repressed, they cannot produce anxiety.

You might be wondering how such thoughts are ever discovered if they remain in the unconscious. According to Freud, these hidden conflicts may be revealed through slips of the tongue, through dreams, or through the various techniques used in psychoanalysis, such as free association or hypnosis. Furthermore, repressed desires, in the Freudian view, can create psychological problems that are expressed in the form of *neuroses*. For instance, consider again the woman who has repressed sexual desires for her father. She might express these impulses by becoming involved in successive failed relationships with men in an unconscious attempt to resolve her conflicts about her father.

REGRESSION   *Regression* is a defense used by the ego to guard against anxiety by causing the person to retreat to the behaviors of an earlier stage of development that was less demanding and safer. Often when a second child is born into a family, the older sibling will regress, using younger speech patterns, wanting a bottle, and even bed-wetting. Adults can use regression as well. Consider a man experiencing a "midlife crisis" who is afraid of growing old and dying. To avoid the anxiety associated with these unconscious fears, he might regress to an adolescent stage by becoming irresponsible, cruising around in a sports car, trying to date younger women, and even eating the foods associated with his teenage years. Another example of regression is the married adult who goes home to mother whenever a problem in the marriage arises.

PROJECTION   Imagine for a moment that your ego is being challenged by your id. You're not sure why, but you are experiencing a lot of anxiety. If your ego uses the defense mechanism of *projection* to eliminate the anxiety, you will begin to see *your* unconscious urges in *other* people's behavior. That is, you will *project* your impulses onto them. In theory, this externalizes the anxiety-provoking feelings and reduces the anxiety. You will not be aware that you're doing this, and the people onto whom you project may not be guilty of your accusations. An example of this offered by Anna Freud involves a husband who is experiencing impulses to be unfaithful to his wife (p. 120). He may not even be conscious of these urges, but they are creeping up from his id and creating anxiety. To ward off the anxiety, he projects his desires onto his wife, becomes intensely jealous, and accuses her of having affairs, even though no evidence supports his claims. Another example is the woman who is afraid of aging and begins to point out how old her friends and acquaintances are looking. The individuals in these examples are not acting or lying; they truly believe their projections. If they did not, the defense against anxiety would fail.

REACTION FORMATION   The defense identified by Freud as a *reaction formation* is exemplified by a line from Shakespeare's *Hamlet,* when Hamlet's mother, after watching a scene in a play, remarks to Hamlet, "The lady doth protest too much, me thinks." When a person is experiencing unacceptable, unconscious "evil" impulses, the anxiety caused by them might be avoided by engaging in behaviors that are the exact *opposite* of the id's real urges. Anna Freud pointed out that these behaviors are usually exaggerated or even obsessive. By adopting attitudes and behaviors that demonstrate outwardly a complete rejection of the id's true desires, anxiety is blocked. Reaction formations tend to become a permanent part of an individual's personality unless the id–ego conflict is somehow resolved. As an example of this, reconsider the husband who unconsciously desires other women. If he employs a reaction formation rather than projection to prevent his anxiety, he may become obsessively devoted to his wife and shower her with gifts and pronouncements of his unwavering love. Another example comes from many disturbing news reports of the violent crime referred to as *gay bashing*. In a Freudian interpretation, a man who is experiencing unconscious homosexual desires (which he fears, due to much of society's disapproval of nonheterosexual orientations) might engage in the extreme opposite behavior of attacking and beating up gay men to hide his true desires and the anxiety associated with them (this concept is discussed further in this reading).

SUBLIMATION   Both Sigmund Freud and Anna Freud considered most of the defense mechanisms, including the four previously described, as indicating problems in psychological adjustment (*neuroses*). Conversely, they saw the defense of *sublimation* as not only normal but also desirable. When people invoke sublimation, they are finding socially acceptable ways of discharging anxious energy that is the result of unconscious forbidden desires. Sigmund Freud maintained that because everyone's id contains these desires, sublimation is a necessary part of a productive and healthy life. Furthermore, he believed that most strong desires can be sublimated in various ways. Someone who has intense aggressive impulses might sublimate them by engaging in contact sports or becoming a surgeon. A teenage girl's passion for horseback riding might be interpreted as sublimated unacceptable sexual desires. A man who has an erotic fixation on the human body might sublimate his feelings by becoming a painter or a sculptor of nudes.

Freud proposed that all of what we call "civilization" has been made possible through the mechanism of sublimation. In his view, humans have been able to sublimate their primitive biological urges and impulses, channeling them instead into building civilized societies. However, Freud suggested, sometimes humans' unconscious forces overpower our *collective egos* and these primitive, animalistic urges may burst out in barbaric, uncivilized expressions, such as war. Overall, however, Freud believed it is only through sublimation that civilization can exist at all (S. Freud, 1936).

Implications and Recent Applications

Although Anna Freud stated clearly in her book that the use of defense mechanisms is often associated with neurotic behavior, this is not always the case. Nearly everyone uses various defense mechanisms occasionally in their lives, sometimes to help them cope with periods of increased stress. They help us reduce our anxiety and maintain a positive self-image. Use of certain defense mechanisms has even been shown to reduce unhealthy physiological activity. For example, use of projection has been found to be associated with lower blood pressure (Cramer, 2003). Nevertheless, defense mechanisms involve self-deception and distortions of reality that can produce negative consequences if they are overused. For example, those who use regression every time life's problems become overwhelming might never develop the strategies necessary to deal with their problems and solve them. Consequently, the person's development as a whole person may be inhibited. Moreover, Freud and many other psychologists have contended that when anxiety caused by specific conflicts is repressed, it is sometimes manifested in other ways, such as phobias, anxiety attacks, or obsessive-compulsive disorders.

Most researchers today question the majority of Freud's theories, including his notion of ego defense mechanisms (especially the <u>reasons</u> Freud contended that people use them). Do defense mechanisms really exist? Do they actually function "unconsciously" to block anxiety created by forbidden impulses of the id? Probably, the most often cited criticism of all of Freud's work is that to test it scientifically is difficult at best—and usually impossible. Many studies have tried to demonstrate the existence of various Freudian concepts. The results have been mixed. A few of his ideas have found some scientific support (see Cramer, 2007), others have been clearly disproved, and still others simply cannot be studied (see Fisher & Greenberg, 1977; 1995). Studies about his defense mechanisms have been the most common.

One interesting study looked at the association between medical students' ego defense mechanisms and anxiety and depression (Waqas et al., 2015). Surveys of over 400 medical students found, of the defense mechanisms discussed in this reading, direct or indirect correlations between reaction formation and projection, with academic performance, anxiety, and depression. That is to say that there was a link between students engaging in these defense mechanisms and differences in academic performance either directly or indirectly (via anxiety or depression). The directions of these defense mechanisms were projection related negatively to academic performance, and reaction formation related positively to anxiety. This may possibly be explained by projection being employed by those students who are concerned by their ability to succeed in med school and so choose to see others as subpar academically. Students who see themselves as less able to complete assignments on time or complete clinical tasks adequately may work extra hard which places extra pressure leading to anxiety.

A fascinating study may have found supporting scientific evidence that *homophobia*—an irrational fear, avoidance, and prejudice toward gay and lesbian individuals—may be a reaction formation used to ward off the extreme anxiety caused by a person's own repressed homosexual tendencies (Adams, Wright, & Lohr, 1996). In this study, a group of men were given a written test to determine their level of homophobia and then divided into two groups: homophobic and nonhomophobic. Then, participants were exposed to videos depicting explicit heterosexual, gay, or lesbian sexual scenes, and while they viewed these videos they were monitored for physiological signs of sexual arousal. The only difference found between the groups was when they viewed the videos of gay males. In this condition, "The results indicate that the homophobic men showed a significant increase in [arousal], but that the [non-homophobic] men did not" (p. 443). In fact, 66% of the nonhomophobic group showed no significant signs of arousal while viewing the homosexual video, but only 20% of the homophobic group showed little or no evidence of arousal. Furthermore, when asked to rate their level of arousal, the homophobic men *underestimated* their degree of arousal in response to the homosexual video. This study's results are clearly consistent with Anna Freud's description of the defense mechanism of reaction formation and lend support for a possible explanation of violence targeted against gay individuals.

Conclusion

As evidenced by studies discussed in this reading, scientific interest in the defense mechanisms appears to be on the upswing among psychologists in various subfields, including cognition, human development, personality, and social psychology (see Cramer, 2007). Through an awareness and understanding of the defense mechanisms, your ability to obtain important insights into the causes of people's actions is clearly enhanced. If you keep a list of the defense mechanisms handy in your "brain's back pocket," you may begin to notice them in others or even in yourself. By the way, if you think someone is using a defense mechanism, remember this: He or she is doing so to avoid unpleasant anxiety. Therefore, it is probably not a great idea to bring it to his or her attention. Knowledge of the defense mechanisms can be a powerful tool in your interactions with others, but that knowledge must be used carefully and responsibly. Knowledge is power.

You can easily experience for yourself the continuing influence of Anna Freud's synthesis and analysis of her father's concept of defense mechanisms by picking up virtually any recent academic or scholarly work that discusses psychoanalytic theory in detail. Most of the Freud citations you will encounter will be referring to Sigmund, and rightly so. But when the discussion turns to the defense mechanisms, it is Anna Freud's 1946 book and its various revisions that serve as the authoritative work on the topic.

Adams, H., Wright, L., & Lohr, B. (1996). Is homophobia associated with homosexual arousal? *Journal of Abnormal Psychology, 105*(3), 440–445.

Cramer, P. (2003). Defense mechanisms and physiological reactivity to stress. *Journal of Personality, 71,* 221–244.

Cramer, P. (2007). *Protecting the self: Defense mechanisms in action.* New York: Guilford Press.

Fisher, S., & Greenberg, R. (1977). *The scientific credibility of Freud's theories and therapy.* New York: Basic Books.

Fisher, S., & Greenberg, R. (1995). *Freud scientifically reappraised: Testing the theories and therapy.* New York: Wiley.

Freud, S. (1936). *A disturbance of memory on the Acropolis.* London: Hogarth Press.

Freud, S. (1953 to 1974). *The standard edition of the complete psychological works of Sigmund Freud.* London: Hogarth Press.

Waqas, A., Rehman, A., Malik, A., Muhammad, U., Khan, S., & Mahmood, N. (2015). Association of ego defense mechanisms with academic performance, anxiety and depression in medical students: a mixed methods study. *Cureus, 7*(9).

Reading 8.3: Learning to Be Depressed

Seligman, M. E. P., & Maier, S. F. (1967). Failure to escape traumatic shock. *Journal of Experimental Psychology, 74*, 1–9.

8.3 **Explain how research into the development and display of learned helplessness has impacted the field of psychology**

If you are like most people, you expect that your actions will produce certain consequences. Your expectations cause you to behave in ways that will produce desirable consequences *and* to avoid behaviors that will lead to undesirable consequences. In other words, your actions are determined, at least in part, by your belief that they will bring about a certain result; they are *contingent* upon a certain consequence.

Let's assume for a moment that you are unhappy in your present job, so you begin the process of making a change. You make contacts with others in your field, read publications that advertise positions in which you are interested, begin training in the evening to acquire new skills, and so on. All those actions are motivated by your belief that your effort will eventually lead to the outcome of a better job and a happier life. The same is true of interpersonal relationships. If you are in a relationship that is wrong for you because it is abusive or it otherwise makes you unhappy, you will, hopefully, take the necessary actions to change it or end it because most people expect to succeed in making the desired changes.

All these are issues of power and control. Most people believe they are personally powerful and able to control what happens to them, at least part of the time, because they have exerted control in the past and have been successful. They believe they are able to help themselves achieve their goals. If this perception of power and control is lacking, all that is left is helplessness and hopelessness. If you feel you are stuck in an unsatisfying job and you are unable to find another job or learn new skills to improve your professional life, you will be unlikely to make the effort needed to change. If you are too dependent on, or afraid of the person with whom you have a damaging relationship and you feel powerless to fix it or end it, you may simply remain in the relationship and endure the pain. Or, as Henry Ford said, "Whether you believe you can do a thing or not, you are right."

Perceptions of power and control are crucial for psychological and physical health (refer to Reading 5.4 on the research by Langer and Rodin regarding issues of control for the elderly in nursing homes). Imagine how you would feel if you suddenly found that you no longer had the power or control to make changes in your life—that what happened to you was independent of your actions. You would probably feel helpless and hopeless, and you would give up trying altogether. In other words, you would become depressed.

Martin Seligman, a well-known and influential behavioral psychologist, proposed that our perceptions of power and control are learned from experience. He believes that when a person's efforts at controlling certain life events fail repeatedly, the person may stop attempting to exercise control altogether. If these failures happen often enough, the person may generalize the perception of lack of control to all situations, *even when* control may actually be possible. This person then begins to feel like a pawn of fate and becomes helpless and depressed; Seligman termed this cause of depression *learned helplessness*. He developed his theory at the University of Pennsylvania, in a series of now classic experiments that used dogs as subjects. The research discussed here, which Seligman conducted with Steven Maier, is considered to be the definitive original demonstration of his theory.

Theoretical Propositions

Seligman had found in an earlier experiment on learning that when dogs were exposed to electrical shocks they could neither control nor escape, they later failed to learn to escape from shocks when such escape was easily available. You have to imagine how odd this looked to a behaviorist. In the laboratory, dogs had experienced shocks that were designed to be punishing but not harmful. Later, they were placed in a shuttle box, which is a large box with two halves divided by a partition. An electrical current could be activated in the floor on either side of the box. When a dog was on one side and felt the electricity, it simply had to jump over the partition to the other side to escape the shock. Normally, dogs and other animals learn this escape behavior very quickly (it's not difficult to see why!). When a signal (such as a flashing light or a buzzer) was later added to warn the dog of the impending electrical current, the animal will learn to jump over the partition before the shock and thus avoid it completely. However, in Seligman's experiment, when the dogs that had already experienced electrical shocks from which they could not escape were placed in the shuttle box, they did not learn this escape-avoidance behavior even when the light or the buzzer warned them.

Seligman theorized that something in what the animals had learned about their ability (or lack of ability) to *control* the unpleasant stimulus determined the later learning. In other words, these dogs had learned from previous experience with electrical shocks that their actions were ineffective in changing the consequence of the shocks. Then, when they were in a new situation where they *did* have the power to escape—to exercise control—they just gave up. They had *learned to be helpless.*

To test this theory, Seligman and Maier proposed to study the effect of controllable versus uncontrollable shock on later ability to learn to avoid shock.

Method

This is one of several classic studies in this book that used animals as subjects. However, this one, probably more than any of the others, raises questions about the ethics of animal research. Dogs received electrical shocks that were designed to be painful (though not physically harmful) in order to test a psychological theory. Whether such treatment was (or is) ethically justifiable is an issue that must be faced by every researcher and student of psychology. (This issue is addressed again in this reading after a discussion of the results of Seligman's research.)

Subjects for this experiment were 24 "mongrel dogs, 15 to 19 inches high at the shoulder and weighing between 25 and 29 pounds" (p. 2). They were divided into three groups of eight subjects each. One group was the *escape group*, another the *no-escape group*, and the third was the *no-harness control group.*

The dogs in the escape and no-escape groups were placed individually in a harness similar to that developed by Pavlov (see the discussion of Pavlov's methods in Reading 3.1); they were restrained but not completely unable to move. On either side of the dog's head was a panel to keep the head facing forward. A subject dog could press the panel on either side by moving its head. When an electrical shock was delivered to a dog in the escape group, it could terminate the shock by pressing either panel with its head. For the no-escape group, each dog was paired with a dog in the escape group (this is an experimental procedure called *yoking*). Identical shocks were delivered to each pair of dogs at the same time, but the no-escape group had no control over the shock. No matter what those dogs did, the shock continued until it was terminated by the panel press of the dog in the escape group. This ensured that both groups of dogs received exactly the same duration and intensity of shock, the only difference being that one group had the power to stop it and the other did not. The eight dogs in the no-harness control group received no shocks at this stage of the experiment.

The subjects in the escape and no-escape groups received 64 shocks at about 90-second intervals. The escape group quickly learned to press the side panels and terminate the shocks (for themselves and for the no-escape group). Then, 24 hours later, all the dogs were tested in a shuttle box similar to the one already described. Lights were attached on both sides of the box. When the lights were turned off on one side, an electrical current would pass through the floor of the box 10 seconds later. If a dog jumped the barrier within those 10 seconds, it escaped the shock completely. If not, it would continue to feel the shock until it jumped over the barrier or until 60 seconds of shock passed, at which time the shock was discontinued. Each dog was given 10 trials in the shuttle box.

Learning was measured by the following: (a) how much time it took, on average, from the time the light in the box went out until the dog jumped the barrier and (b) the percentage of dogs in each group that failed entirely to learn to escape the shocks. Also, the dogs in the no-escape group received 10 additional trials in the shuttle box 7 days later to assess the lasting effects of the experimental treatment.

Results

In the escape group, the time it took for the dogs to press the panel and stop the shock quickly decreased over the 64 shocks. In the no-escape group, panel pressing completely stopped after 30 trials.

Figure 8.3.1 shows the average time until escape for the three groups of subjects over all the trials in the shuttle box. Remember, this was the time between when the lights were turned off and when the animal jumped over the barrier. The difference between the no-escape group and the other two groups was statistically significant, but the small difference between the escape group and the no-harness group was insignificant. Figure 8.3.2 illustrates the percentage of subjects from each group that failed to jump over the barrier and escape the shock in the shuttle box in at least 9 of the 10 trials. This difference between the escape and no-escape groups was also highly significant. In the no-escape group, six failed entirely to escape on either 9 or all 10 of the trials. Those six dogs were tested again in the shuttle box 7 days later. In this delayed test, five of the six failed to escape on every trial.

Discussion

Because the only difference between the escape and the no-escape groups was the dogs' ability to terminate the shock, Seligman and Maier concluded that it must have been this control factor that accounted for the clear difference in the two groups' later learning to escape the shock in the shuttle box. In other words, the reason the escape group dogs performed normally in the shuttle box was that they had learned in the harness phase that their *behavior* was correlated with the termination of the shock. Therefore, they were motivated to jump the barrier and escape from the shock. For the no-escape group, the termination of shock in the harness was independent of their behavior. Thus, because they had no expectation that their behavior in the shuttle box would terminate the shock; they had no incentive to attempt to escape. They had, as Seligman and Maier had predicted, learned to be helpless.

Figure 8.3.1 Average time to escape in shuttle box. (From p. 3.)

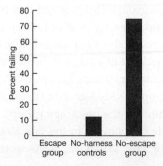

Figure 8.3.2 Percent of subjects failing to learn to escape shock in shuttle box. (From p. 3.)

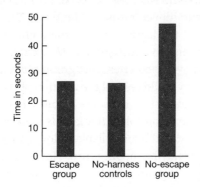

Occasionally, a dog from the no-escape group made a successful escape in the shuttle box. Following this, however, it reverted to helplessness on the next trial. Seligman and Maier interpreted this to mean that the animal's previous ineffective behavior in the harness prevented the formation of a new behavior (jumping the barrier) to terminate shock in a new situation (the shuttle box), *even after a successful experience.*

In their article, Seligman and Maier reported the results of a subsequent experiment that offered some interesting additional findings. In this second study, dogs were first placed in the harness-escape condition where the panel press would terminate the shock. They were then switched to the no-escape harness condition before receiving 10 trials in the shuttle box. These subjects continued to attempt to press the panel throughout all the trials in the no-escape harness and did not give up as quickly as did those in the first study. Moreover, they all successfully learned to escape and avoid shock in the shuttle box. This indicated that once the animals had learned that their behavior could be effective, later experiences with failure were not adequate to extinguish their motivation to change their fate.

Subsequent Research

Of course, Seligman wanted to do what you are probably already doing in your mind: apply these findings to humans. In later research, he asserted that the development of depression in humans involves processes similar to those of learned helplessness in animals. In both situations, there is passivity, giving up and *just sitting there,* lack of aggression, slowness to learn that a certain behavior is successful, weight loss, and social withdrawal. Both the helpless dog and the depressed human have learned from specific past experiences that their actions are fundamentally useless. The dog was unable to escape the shocks, no matter what it did, while the human had no control over events such as the death of a loved one, an abusive parent, the loss of a job, or a serious illness (Seligman, 1975).

The learned helplessness that leads to depression in humans can have serious consequences beyond the depression itself. Research has demonstrated that the elderly who, for various reasons such as nursing-home living, are forced to relinquish control over their daily activities have poorer health and a greater chance of dying sooner than those who are able to maintain a sense of personal power. In addition, several studies have demonstrated that uncontrollable stressful events can play a role in such serious diseases as cancer. One such study found an increased risk of cancer in individuals who in previous years had suffered the loss of a spouse, the loss of a profession, or the loss of prestige (Horn & Picard, 1979). In hospitals, patients are expected by the doctors and staff to be cooperative, quiet, and willing to place their fates in the hands of the medical authorities. Patients believe that to recover as quickly as possible they must follow doctors' and nurses' instructions without question. A prominent health psychologist has suggested that being a "good hospital patient" implies that one must be passive and give up all expectations of control. This actually may create a condition of learned helplessness in the patients whereby they fail to exert control later when control is both possible and desirable for continued recovery (Taylor, 1979).

As further evidence of the learned helplessness effect, consider the following remarkable study by Finkelstein and Ramey (1977). Groups of human infants had rotating mobiles mounted over their cribs. One group of infants had special pressure-sensitive pillows so that they could control the rotation of the mobile by moving their heads. Another group of infants had the same mobiles, but these were programmed to turn randomly without any control by the infants. After a 2-week exposure to the mobiles for 10 minutes each day, the controllable-pillow group had become very skilled at moving their heads to make the mobiles turn. However, the most important finding came when the no-control group of infants was later given the same controllable pillows and an even greater amount of learning time than the first group. The infants failed entirely to learn to control the rotation of the mobiles. Their experience in the first situation had taught them that their behavior was meaningless, and this knowledge transferred to the new situation where control *was* possible. Here, in terms of moving mobiles, the infants had learned to be helpless.

Recent Applications

Seligman's study of learned helplessness continues to influence current research and stimulate debate in many fields. His ideas dovetail with those of other researchers working to increase our understanding of the importance of personal control over events in our lives.

One terrible example of this broad influence relates to the widespread fear of terrorist attacks and the professed "War on Terror." Following the attacks on the World Trade Center and Pentagon on September 11, 2001, the psychological reverberations of that horrific event echoed across the United States and throughout the world. Symptoms included increased anxiety, anger, nervousness, increased alcohol use, feelings of a loss of control over external events, and helplessness (Centers for Disease Control, 2002). Indeed, one of the goals of terrorists is to make people feel vulnerable and helpless. One clinical psychologist summarized the effects of the attack like this:

> The threat of terrorism creates the textbook psychological setup for anxiety and depression. Psychologists call this "anticipatory anxiety"—waiting for the proverbial shoe to drop or, in this case, the terrorist bomb to go off. Add the element of "learned helplessness"—the perception that there is nothing or very little you can do to stop the terrorism—and depression, vulnerability, and a profound sense of loss of control will develop. These are precisely the conditions to which we have all been exposed since the September 11 attacks. They define the "New Normalcy" and the "September 11 Syndrome." (Braiker, 2002)

Interestingly, a more recent study suggested that indirectly experiencing a traumatic event, may, after some time passes, lead to some psychological *benefits* (Swickert et al., 2006). Although the authors do not deny or seek to diminish the profoundly painful psychological effects of witnessing the September 11 attacks, they point to a paradoxical result in some individuals that they refer to as *posttraumatic growth*. They point out past research, which postulated that "posttraumatic growth occurs when fundamental assumptions about the self, others, and the future are challenged. In response to this challenge, traumatized individuals may try to find meaning from their experience. Thus, individuals often discover that they have benefited from the traumatic event" (p. 566). You may ask, what possible benefits could come from such an experience? These authors reported that other research has found a wide variety of positive characteristics that strengthened in the aftermath of the 9/11 tragedy, including gratitude, hope, kindness, leadership, love, spirituality, and teamwork. They reported that individuals who indirectly witnessed the attacks reported similar benefits soon after the event, but these effects appeared to diminish over time.

A 2017 study looked at learned helplessness and acute myocardial infarction (sudden heart attack) in the development of depression in heart patients (Smallheer, Vollman, & Dietrich, 2017). Scales assessing learned helplessness and depression were administered to patients who experienced a heart attack within the last 12 months. The direct relationship between scores on the two scales was statistically significant. The reason for this link is probably quite obvious to you. These patients had no idea they were going to have a heart attack and probably felt there was little they could do to prevent another. In one event, they had learned to be helpless and, consequently, depressed. This study suggested that clinicians should be focusing on the psychological condition of learned helplessness and depression to the same degree as physiological treatments for these patients.

Conclusion

We return now to the issue of experimental ethics. Most of us have difficulty reading about animals, especially dogs or other animals that we often keep as pets, being subjected to painful shocks in a psychology laboratory. Over the years, strict standards have been developed to ensure that laboratory animals are treated humanely (see the discussion of these standards in this book's Preface). However, many, both within and outside the scientific professions, believe these standards to be inadequate. Some advocate the complete elimination of animal research in psychology, medicine, and all the sciences. Whatever your personal stand on this issue, the question you should be asking is this: Do the findings from the research extend our knowledge, reduce human suffering, and improve the quality of life sufficiently to justify the methods used to carry out the study?

Ask yourself that question about this study by Seligman and Maier, who discovered the beginnings of a theory to explain why some people become helpless, hopeless, and depressed. Seligman went on to develop a widely accepted model of the origins of and treatments for depression. Over the years, his theory has been refined and detailed so that it applies more accurately to types of depression that occur under well-defined conditions, from the death of a loved one to massive natural and human-caused disasters.

Through Seligman's research, for example, we now understand that individuals are most likely to become depressed if they attribute their lack of control to causes that are (a) permanent rather than temporary, (b) related to factors within their own personality (instead of situational factors), and (c) pervasive across many areas of their life (see Abramson, Seligman, & Teasdale, 1978). Through this understanding, therapists and counselors have become better able to diagnose, intervene in, and treat serious depression.

Does this body of knowledge justify the methods used in this early research on learned helplessness? Each of you must decide that thorny issue for yourself.

Abramson, L., Seligman, M., & Teasdale, J. (1978). Learned helplessness in humans: Critique and reformulation. *Journal of Abnormal Psychology, 87*, 49–74.

Braiker, H. (2002). "The September 11 syndrome"—A nation still on edge. Retrieved September 15, 2003, from www.harrietbraiker.com/OpEd.htm

Centers for Disease Control (CDC) (2002). Psychological and emotional effects of the September 11 attacks on the World Trade Center—Connecticut, New Jersey, and New York, 2001. *Centers for Disease Control and Prevention: Morbidity and Mortality Weekly Report, 51*, 784–786.

Finkelstein, N., & Ramey, C. (1977). Learning to control the environment in infancy. *Child Development, 48*, 806–819.

Horn, R., & Picard, R. (1979). Psychosocial risk factors for lung cancer. *Psychosomatic Medicine, 41*, 503–514.

Seligman, M. (1975). *Helplessness: On depression, development, and death.* San Francisco, CA: Freeman.

Smallheer, B. A., Vollman, M., & Dietrich, M. S. (2017). Learned helplessness and depressive symptoms following myocardial infarction. *Clinical Nursing Research,* https://doi.org/10.1177/1054773816689752.

Swickert, R., Hittner, J., DeRoma, V., & Saylor, C. (2006). Responses to the September 11, 2001, terrorist attacks: Experience of an indirect traumatic event and its relationship with perceived benefits. *The Journal of Psychology, 140*(6), 565–577.

Taylor, S. (1979). Hospital patient behavior: Reactance, helplessness, or control? *Journal of Social Issues, 35,* 156–184.

Reading 8.4: Crowding Into the Behavioral Sink

Calhoun, J. B. (1962). Population density and social pathology. *Scientific American, 206*(3), 139–148.

8.4   Relate Calhoun's rat crowding experiments to human psychology in high population density areas

The effect of overcrowding on human behavior has interested psychologists for decades. You have probably noticed how your emotions and behaviors change when you are in a situation that you perceive as overly crowded. You may withdraw into yourself and try to become invisible, you may look for an escape, or you may find yourself becoming irritable and aggressive.

The title of the article in this chapter uses the phrase *population density* rather than *crowding.* Although these may seem very similar, psychologists draw a clear distinction between them. *Density* refers to the number of individuals in a given amount of space. If 20 people occupy a 12-by-12-foot room, the room would probably be seen as densely populated. *Crowding,* however, refers to your subjective *experience* that results from various degrees of density. If you are trying to concentrate on a difficult task in that small room with 20 people, you may feel extremely crowded. Conversely, if you are at a party with 20 friends in that same room, you might not feel very crowded at all.

One way behavioral scientists study the effects of density and crowding is to observe places where crowding already exists, such as Manhattan, Mexico City, some housing projects, prisons, and so on. The problem with this method is that all these places contain many factors other than population density that may influence behavior. For example, if we find high crime rates in a crowded inner-city neighborhood, we cannot know for sure that crowding is the cause of the crime. Maybe the cause is the fact that people there are poor, or that there is a higher rate of drug abuse; or perhaps all these factors and others combine with crowded conditions to produce the high crime rates.

Another way to study crowding is to place human participants into high-density conditions for relatively short periods of time and study their reactions (it would not be ethical to leave them there for very long). Although this method offers more control and allows us to isolate crowding as a cause of behavior, it is not very realistic in terms of real-life crowded environments because they typically exist over extended periods of time. Nevertheless, both of these research methods have yielded some interesting findings about crowding that will be discussed later in this reading.

Because it would be ethically impossible (due to the stress and other potential damaging effects) to place humans in crowded conditions over long periods of time simply to do research on them, researchers have employed a third approach to address the effects of density: Do research using animal subjects (see the Preface for a discussion of animal research). One of the earliest and most pivotal series of studies of this type was conducted by John B. Calhoun (1917–1995) in the early 1960s. Calhoun allowed groups of white rats to increase in population (on their own) to twice the number that would be normal for the breed in a small space, and then he observed their "social" interactions for 16 months.

Theoretical Propositions

Calhoun especially wanted to explore the effects of high-density population on social behavior. It may seem strange to you to think of rats as social animals, but they interact in many social ways in their natural environment.

To appreciate what led Calhoun to the study discussed in this chapter, it is necessary to back up several years to an earlier project he conducted. Calhoun had confined a population of rats to a quarter acre of enclosed, protected, outdoor space. The rats were given plenty of food; they had ideal, protected nesting areas; predators were absent; and all disease was kept to a minimum. In other words, this was a rat's paradise. The point of Calhoun's early study was simply to study the population growth rate of the rats in a setting free from the usual natural controls on overpopulation (e.g., predators, disease, etc.). After 27 months, the population consisted of only 150 adult rats. This was very surprising because with the low mortality rate of adult rats in this ideal setting, and considering the usual rate of reproduction, Calhoun should have seen about 5,000 adult rats accumulate in this period of time! Calhoun learned that the reason for this limited rat population was an extremely high infant mortality rate. Apparently, reproductive and maternal behavior had been severely altered by the stress of social interaction among the 150 rats, and very few young rats survived to reach adulthood. Even though 150 rats living in a quarter acre does not seem to be particularly *dense*, it was obviously *crowded* enough for the rats to produce extreme behavioral changes.

These findings prompted Calhoun to design a more controlled and observable situation inside the lab to study more closely what sorts of changes occur in rats when they are faced with high population density. In other words, he had observed *what* happened, and now he wanted to find out *why*.

Method

In a series of three studies, adult rats were placed in a 10-by-14-foot laboratory room that was divided into four sections or pens (see Figure 8.4.1). The rats had ramps that allowed them to cross from pen 1 to pen 2, from pen 2 to pen 3, and from pen 3 to pen 4, but it was not possible for the rats to cross directly between pen 1 and pen 4. Therefore, 1 and 4 were "end-pens." If a rat wanted to go from 1 to 4, it would have to go through 2 and 3. The partitions dividing the pens were electrified, so the rats quickly learned that they could not climb over them.

These pens consisted of feeders and waterers and enclosures for nests. The rats were supplied with plenty of food, water, and materials for building nests. A viewing window in the ceiling of the room allowed the research team to observe and record the rats' behavior.

From his years of studying rats, Calhoun was aware that this particular breed is normally found in colonies of 12 adults. Therefore, the observation room was of a size to accommodate 12 rats per pen, or a total of 48. After the groups were placed in the observation room, they were allowed to multiply until their normal density was nearly doubled, to 80. Once the population level of 80 was reached, young rats that survived past weaning were removed so that the number of rats remained constant and dense.

With this arrangement in place, all that was left was to observe these crowded animals for an extended time and record their behavior. These observations went on for 16 months.

Figure 8.4.1 Diagram of laboratory room as arranged in Calhoun's study of crowding.

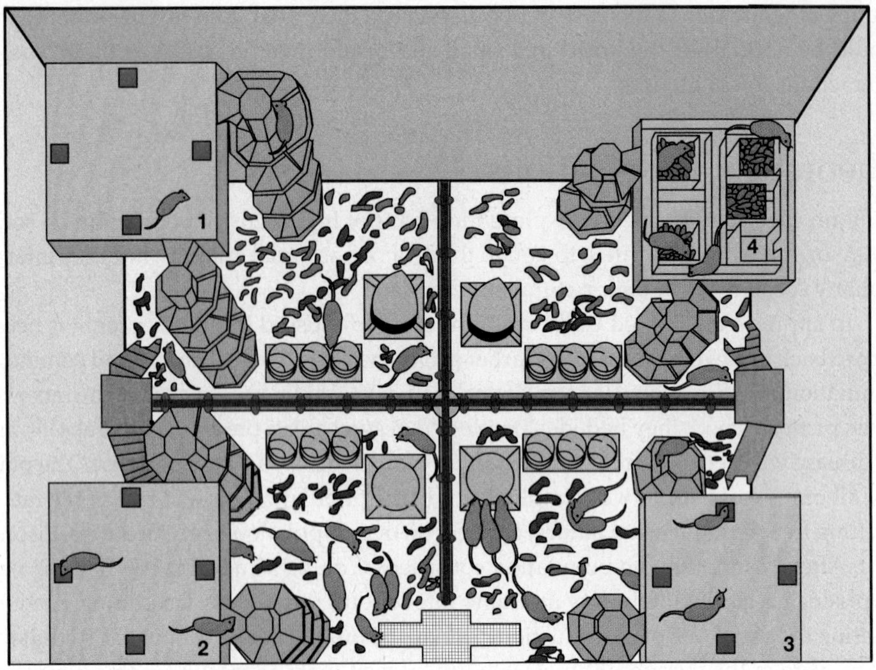

Results

This level of population density was not extreme for the rats; in fact, it was quite moderate. If the rats wanted to spread out, each pen would hold 20 or so with room left over, but that did not happen. When the male rats reached maturity, they began to fight with each other for social status, as they do naturally. These fights took place in all the pens, but the outcome was not the same for all of them. If you think about the arrangement of the room, the two end-pens had only one way in and one way out. When a male rat won a battle for dominance in one of these pens, he could hold his position and his territory (the whole pen) simply by guarding the single entrance and attacking any other male that ventured over the ramp. As it turned out, only one male rat ended up in charge of each of the end-pens. However, he was not in there alone. The female rats distributed themselves more or less equally over all four pens. Therefore, the "masters" of pens 1 and 4 each had a harem of 8 to 12 females that they could keep all to themselves. And they didn't take any chances. To prevent infiltration, the males took to sleeping directly at the foot of the ramp and were always on guard.

On occasion, a few other male rats entered the end-pens, but they were extremely submissive. They spent most of their time asleep in the nesting burrows with the females and only came out to feed. They did not attempt to mate with the females. The females in these pens functioned well as mothers. They built comfortable nests and nurtured and protected their offspring. In other words, life for the rats in these end-pens was relatively normal, and reproductive behavior was successful. About half the infant rats in those pens survived to adulthood, which is close to normal.

The rest of the 60 or so rats crowded into the middle two pens. Because these two pens each had central feeding and watering devices, they had many opportunities to come in contact with each other. The kinds of behaviors observed among the rats in pens 2 and 3 demonstrate a phenomenon that Calhoun termed the *behavioral sink*—"the outcome of any behavioral process that collects animals together in unusually great numbers. The unhealthy connotations of the term are not accidental: A behavioral sink does act to aggravate all forms of pathology that can be found within a group" (p. 144). Let's examine some of the extreme and pathological behaviors he observed:

1. *Aggression.* In the wild, normal male rats will fight other male rats for dominant positions in the social hierarchy. These fights were observed among the more aggressive rats in this study as well. The difference was that in the end-pens, unlike in their natural environments, top-ranking males were required to fight frequently to maintain their positions, and often the fights involved several rats in a general brawl. Nevertheless, the strongest males were observed to be the most normal within the center pens. However, even those animals would sometimes exhibit "signs of pathology; going berserk; attacking females, juveniles, and less active males; and showing a particular predilection—which rats do not normally display—for biting other rats on the tail" (p. 146).

2. *Submissiveness.* Contrary to this extreme aggression, other groups of male rats ignored and avoided battles for dominance. One of these groups consisted of the most healthy-looking rats in the pens. They were fat, and their fur was full without the usual bare spots from fighting. However, these rats were complete social misfits. They moved through the pens as if asleep or in some sort of hypnotic trance, ignoring all others, and were, in turn, ignored by the rest. They were completely uninterested in sexual activity and made no advances, even toward females in heat.

   Another group of rats engaged in extreme activity and were always on the prowl for receptive females. Calhoun termed them *probers.* Often, they were attacked by the more dominant males, but they were never interested in fighting for status. They were hypersexual, and many of them even became cannibalistic!

3. *Sexual deviance.* These probers also refused to participate in the natural rituals of mating. Normally, a male rat will pursue a female in heat until she escapes into her burrow. Then, the male will wait patiently and even perform a courtship dance directly outside her *door.* Eventually, the female emerges from the burrow and the mating takes place. In Calhoun's study, this ritual was adhered to by most of the sexually active males, except the probers, which completely refused to wait and followed the female right into her burrow. Sometimes the nests inside the burrow contained young that had failed to survive, and it was here that late in the study the probers turned cannibalistic.

   Certain groups of male rats were termed *pansexuals* because they attempted to mate with any and all other rats indiscriminately. They sexually approached other males, juveniles, and females that were not in heat. This was a submissive group that was often attacked by the more dominant male rats but did not fight for dominance.

4. *Reproductive abnormalities.* Rats have a natural instinct for nest building. In this study, small strips of paper were provided in unlimited quantities as nest material. The females are normally extremely active in the process of building nests as the time for giving birth approaches. They gather the material and pile it up so that it forms a cushion. Then, they arrange the nest so that it has a small indentation in the middle to hold the young. However, the females in the behavioral sink gradually lost their ability (or inclination) to build adequate nests. At first, they failed to form the indentation in the middle. Then, as time passed, they collected fewer and fewer strips of paper so that eventually the infants were born directly on the sawdust that covered the pen's floor.

   The mother rats also lost their maternal ability to transport their young from one place to another if they felt the presence of danger. They would move some of the litter and forget the rest, or simply drop them onto the floor as they were moving them. Usually, these infants were abandoned and died where they were dropped. They were then eaten by the adults.

The infant mortality rate in the middle pens was extremely high, ranging from 80% to 96%. In addition to these maternal deficits, the female rats in the middle pens, when in heat, were chased by large groups of males until they were finally unable to escape. These females experienced high rates of complications in pregnancy and delivery, and they became extremely unhealthy.

Discussion

You might expect that a logical extension of these findings would be to apply them to humans in high-density environments. However, for reasons to be discussed next, Calhoun did not draw any such conclusions. In fact, he discussed his findings very little—probably assuming, and logically so, that his results spoke volumes for themselves. He did comment on one clear result: that the natural social and survival behaviors of the rats were severely altered by the stresses associated with living in a high-population-density environment. In addition, he noted that through additional research, with improved methods and refined interpretation of the findings, his studies and others like them may contribute to our understanding of similar issues facing human beings.

Significance of Findings

As with many of the studies in this book, one of the most important aspects of Calhoun's studies was that they sparked a great deal of related research on the effects on humans of high-density living. It would be impossible to examine this large body of research in detail here, but perhaps a few examples should be mentioned. One environment where the equivalent of a behavioral sink might exist for humans is in extremely overcrowded prisons. A study funded by the National Institute of Justice examined prisons where inmates averaged only 50 square feet each (or an area about 7-by-7 feet), compared with less crowded prisons. It was found that significantly higher rates of mortality, homicide, suicide, illness, and disciplinary problems occurred in the crowded prisons (McCain, Cox, & Paulus, 1980). Again, however, remember that other factors besides crowding could be influencing these behaviors (e.g., see Reading 10.1 on Zimbardo's prison study).

Another interesting finding has been that crowding produces negative effects on problem-solving abilities. One study placed people in small, extremely crowded rooms (only 3 square feet per person) or in larger, less crowded rooms. The participants were asked to complete rather complex tasks, such as placing various shapes into various categories while listening to a story on which they were to be tested later. Those in the crowded conditions performed significantly worse than those who were not crowded (Evans, 1979).

What do you suppose happens to you physiologically in crowded circumstances? Research has determined that your blood pressure and heart rate increase. Along with those effects, you tend to feel that other people are more hostile and that time seems to pass more slowly as density increases (Evans, 1979).

Criticisms

Calhoun's results with animals have been supported by later animal research (see Marsden, 1972). However, as has been mentioned before in this book, we must always be careful in applying animal research to humans. Just as substances that may be shown to cause illness in rats may not have the same effect on human physical health, environmental factors influencing rats' social behaviors may not be directly applicable to people. At best, animals can only represent certain aspects of humans. Sometimes animal research can be very useful and revealing and lead the way for more definitive research with people. At other times, it can be a dead end.

In 1975, researchers undertook a study in New York City that attempted to replicate with people some of Calhoun's findings (Freedman, Heshka, & Levy, 1975). The researchers collected data from areas of varying population density on death rates, fertility rates (birth rates), aggressive behavior (court records), psychopathology (admissions to mental hospitals), and so on. When all the data were analyzed, no significant relationships were found between population density and any form of social pathology.

Nevertheless, Calhoun's work in the early 1960s focused a great deal of attention on the psychological and behavioral effects of crowding. This line of research, as it relates to humans, continues today.

Recent Applications

John Calhoun left behind a legacy of insightful and historically meaningful research. The kinds of social problems he discussed in his 1962 article are increasingly relevant to the human condition. Consequently, when scientists undertake research to better understand and intervene in such problems as aggression, infertility, mental illness, or various forms of social conflict, it is not unusual for them to make reference to Calhoun's research on crowding and behavioral pathology.

An interesting study citing Calhoun's work examined changes in animal behavior that accompany domestication (Price, 1999). Price contended that species of animals that are domesticated—that is, kept as pets—have undergone genetic and developmental changes over many generations that have altered their behaviors in ways that allow them to share a common living environment with humans. Basically, what Price suggested is that as wild animals have become domesticated over centuries, they have had to adapt to human settings that are very different from their original habitats. This usually includes living in peaceful harmony (most of the time, at least) with others of their own species, other animal species, and humans, usually in relatively crowded conditions (compared to the animals' conditions in the wild). This is accomplished, the author contends, through the evolution of increased response thresholds, meaning it takes a lot more provocation for a domesticated animal to become territorial and aggressive. In other words, dogs, cats, and humans are all able to live together in a relatively small space without running away or tearing each other to pieces, as would occur among undomesticated animals in the wild.

A related study found a possible key difference in human reactions to population density compared to animals. In animal studies, pathology appears to increase in a linear way as a direct result of increased density: as one increases the other increases. However, a study by Regoeczi (2002) found for humans that the effect of household population density on increased social withdrawal and aggression actually *decreased* as the number of people in a single household increased. However, this effect was only observed until the number of people exceeded the total number of rooms; very much beyond that, the antisocial effects begin to appear with increasing density. In other words, when living conditions are such that, say, five people occupy a three-room apartment or seven people are squeezed into a four-room house, the tendency for people to withdraw or display more aggression increases. Two possible causes may be at work here. Either density is causing the pathology, or people who are more withdrawn or more aggressive end up in less crowded living situations, by choice or by ostracism, respectively.

Calhoun's research has also contributed to the literature on psychotherapy. As the world becomes more populated, mobile, and diverse, the need for increased specialization among psychotherapists is becoming necessary (see Dumont & Torbit, 2012). For example, as the various cultures increasingly interact, the need for counselors specializing in cross-cultural relations will also increase. As people are living longer, the need for counselors who specialize in issues of transitioning from work to retirement and problems surrounding chronic illness and death are needed. Calhoun's work is most relevant as cities grow larger, become more crowded (more and larger pockets of high density), inner-city populations grow, crime rates rise, and many cities become increasingly toxic in general. As this all occurs, counselors who have the skills to focus on a wide variety of urban dysfunctions will be in greater demand.

Conclusion

These and many other studies demonstrate how social scientists are continuing to explore and refine the effects of density and crowding. Although the causes of social pathology are many and complex, the impact of population density, first brought to our attention by Calhoun over 45 years ago, is only one—but a very crucial—piece of the puzzle.

Dumont, F., & Torbit, G. (2012). The expanding role of the counselor: Fitting means to ends. *Canadian Journal of Counseling and Psychotherapy, North America,* February 11, 2012. Retrieved from http://cjc.synergiesprairies.ca/cjc/index.php/rcc/article/view/1776

Evans, G. W. (1979). Behavioral and psychological consequences of crowding in humans. *Journal of Applied Social Psychology, 9,* 27–46.

Freedman, J. L., Heshka, S., & Levy, A. (1975). Population density and social pathology: Is there a relationship? *Journal of Experimental Social Psychology, 11,* 539–552.

Marsden, H. M. (1972). Crowding and animal behavior. In J. F. Wohlhill & D. H. Carson (Eds.), *Environment and the social sciences.* Washington, DC: American Psychological Association.

McCain, G., Cox, V. C., & Paulus, P. B. (1980). The relationship between illness, complaints, and degree of crowding in a prison environment. *Environment and Behavior, 8,* 283–290.

Price, E. (1999). Behavioral development in animals undergoing domestication. *Applied Animal Behavior Research, 65*(3), 245–271.

Regoeczi, W. (2002). The impact of density: The importance of nonlinearity and selection on flight and fight responses. *Social Forces, 81,* 505–530.

Chapter 9
Psychotherapy

 Learning Objectives

9.1 Determine the usefulness of psychotherapy

9.2 Describe the process and applications of systematic desensitization

9.3 Explain the use and criticisms of the Rorschach assessment scale

9.4 Evaluate the TAT interview as a diagnostic tool

Psychotherapy simply means "therapy for psychological problems." Therapy typically involves a close and caring relationship between a therapist and a client. The branch of psychology that focuses on researching, diagnosing, and treating psychological problems is *clinical psychology*. The history of psychotherapy consists primarily of a long series of various therapeutic techniques, each one considered to be "the best" by those who developed it and at various times in the history of psychology. The research demonstrating the effectiveness of all those methods has been generally weak and not very scientific. However, some important and influential research breakthroughs have occurred.

One question people often raise about psychotherapy is "Which method is best?" The first study in this section addressed this question using an innovative (at that time) statistical analysis and demonstrated that, in general, various forms of therapy are equally effective. Another line of research discussed in the second study in this chapter, however, suggested one exception to this idea. If you have a *phobia* (an intense and irrational fear of some thing or some situation), a form of behavior therapy called *systematic desensitization* has been shown to be a superior method of treatment. The study included here was conducted by Joseph Wolpe, the psychologist who is generally credited with developing systematic desensitization. Both the third and the fourth studies in this section involved the development of two related therapeutic and diagnostic tools: the *Rorschach Inkblot Method* and the *Thematic Apperception Test* (TAT). These tests are commonly used by therapists to try to diagnose mental problems or to help their clients discuss sensitive, traumatic, or concealed psychological problems.

Reading 9.1: Choosing Your Psychotherapist

Smith, M. L., & Glass, G. V. (1977). Meta-analysis of psychotherapy outcome studies. *American Psychologist, 32,* 752–760.

9.1   Determine the usefulness of psychotherapy

You do *not* have to be "crazy" to need psychotherapy. The vast majority of people treated by counselors and psychotherapists are not mentally ill but are simply having problems in life that they are unable to resolve through their usual coping mechanisms and support networks.

Imagine for a moment that you are experiencing a difficult, emotional time in your life. You consult with your usual group of close friends and family members, but you just cannot seem to work things out. Eventually, when you have endured the pain long enough, you decide to seek some professional help. Because you are an informed, intelligent person, you do some reading on psychotherapy and discover that many different approaches are available. You read about various types of therapy, such as *behavior therapies* (including *systematic desensitization*, discussed in Reading 9.2 on Wolpe's work), *humanistic therapy, cognitive therapies, cognitive behavioral therapy*, and various Freudian-based *psychodynamic therapies*. These assorted styles of psychotherapy, although they stem from different theories and employ different techniques, all share the same basic goal: to help you change your life in ways that make you a happier, more productive, and more effective person. (See Wood, 2007, for more about various forms of psychotherapy.)

Now you may be totally confused. Which one should you choose if you need help? Here is basically what you need to know: (a) Does psychotherapy really work? (b) If it does work, which type works best? It may (or may not) help you to know that over the past 40 years, psychologists have been asking the same questions. Although researchers have conducted many comparison studies, most of them tend to support the method used by the psychologists conducting the study—no surprise there. In addition, most of the studies have been rather small in terms of the number of participants and the research techniques used. To make matters worse, the studies are spread over a wide range of books and journals, making a fully informed judgment extremely difficult.

To fill this gap in the research literature on psychotherapy techniques, in 1977 Mary Lee Smith and Gene Glass at the University of Colorado undertook the task of compiling virtually all the studies on psychotherapy effectiveness that had been done up to that time and reanalyzing them. By searching through 1,000 various magazines, journals, and books, they selected 375 studies that had tested the effects of counseling and psychotherapy. The researchers then applied *meta-analysis*—a technique developed by Glass—to the data from all the studies in an attempt to determine overall the relative effectiveness of different methods. (A meta-analysis takes the results of many individual studies and integrates them into a larger statistical analysis so that the diverse evidence is combined into a, presumably, more meaningful whole.)

Theoretical Propositions

The goals of Smith and Glass's study were the following (p. 752):

1. To identify and collect all studies that tested the effects of counseling and psychotherapy.
2. To determine the magnitude of the effect of therapy in each study.
3. To compare the outcomes of different types of therapy.

The theoretical proposition implicit in these goals was that when this meta-analysis was complete, psychotherapy would be shown to be (a) effective and (b) differences in effectiveness of the various methods, if any, could be demonstrated.

Method

Although the 375 studies analyzed by Smith and Glass varied greatly in terms of the research method used and the type of therapy assessed, each study examined at least one group that received psychotherapy compared with another group that received a different form of therapy or no therapy at all (a control group). The magnitude of the *effect of therapy* was the most important finding for Smith and Glass to include in their meta-analysis. This effect size was obtained for any outcome measure of the therapy that the original researcher chose to use. Often, studies provided more than one measurement of effectiveness, or the same measurement may have been taken more than once. Examples of outcomes used to assess effectiveness were increases in self-esteem, reductions in anxiety, improvements in school work, and improvements in general life adjustment. Wherever possible, all the measures used in a particular study were included in the meta-analysis.

A total of 833 effect sizes were combined from the 375 studies. These studies included approximately 25,000 subjects. The authors reported that the average age of the participants in the studies was 22 years and that they had received an average of 17 hours of therapy from therapists who had an average of 3.5 years of experience.

Results

First, Smith and Glass compared all the treated participants with all the untreated participants for all types of therapy and all measures of outcome. They found that "the average client receiving therapy was better off than 75% of the untreated controls. . . . The therapies represented by the available outcome calculations moved the average client from the 50th percentile to the 75th percentile" (pp. 754–755). (*Percentiles* indicate the percentage of individuals whose scores on any measurement fall beneath the specific score of interest. For example, if you score in the 90th percentile on a test, it means that 90% of those who took the same test scored lower than you.) Furthermore, only 99 (or 12%) of the 833 effect sizes were negative (meaning the client was worse off than before therapy). The authors pointed out that if psychotherapy were ineffective, the number of negative effect sizes should be equal to or greater than 50%, or 417.

Second, various measures of psychotherapy effectiveness were compared across all the studies. These findings are represented in Figure 9.1.1, which clearly demonstrates that therapy, in general, was found to be significantly more effective than no treatment.

Third, Smith and Glass compared the various psychotherapy methods found in all the studies they analyzed using similar statistical procedures. Figure 9.1.2 is a summary of their findings for the more familiar psychotherapeutic methods.

Smith and Glass combined all the various methods into two "superclasses" of therapy: a *behavioral superclass*, consisting of systematic desensitization, behavior modification, and implosion therapy, and a *nonbehavioral superclass* made up of the remaining types of therapy. When they analyzed all the studies in which behavioral and nonbehavioral therapies were compared with no-treatment controls, all differences between the two superclasses disappeared (73rd and 75th percentile, respectively, relative to controls).

Figure 9.1.1 Combined effectiveness of all studies analyzed for four outcome measures. If no improvement had occurred, the clients would have had scores of 50. If their condition had become worse, their scores would have been below 50.

(Based on data from p. 756.)

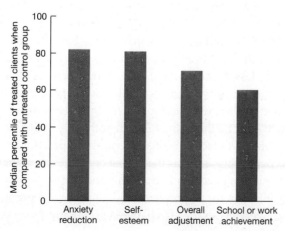

Figure 9.1.2 Comparison of the effectiveness of seven methods of psychotherapy. As in Figure 9.1.1, any score above 50 indicates improvement.

(Modified from data from p. 756.)

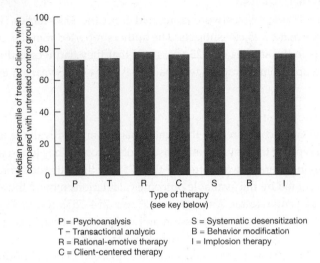

P = Psychoanalysis
T – Transactional analysis
R = Rational-emotive therapy
C = Client-centered therapy

S = Systematic desensitization
B = Behavior modification
I = Implosion therapy

Discussion

Overall, psychotherapy appeared to be successful in treating various kinds of problems (Figure 9.1.1). In addition, no matter how the different types of therapy were divided or combined, the differences among them were found to be insignificant (Figure 9.1.2).

Smith and Glass drew three conclusions from their findings. One is that psychotherapy works (hooray for that!). The results of the meta-analysis clearly support the assertion that people who seek therapy are better off with the treatment than they were without it. Second, "despite volumes devoted to the theoretical differences among different schools of psychotherapy, the results of research demonstrate *negligible differences* in the effects produced by different therapy types. Unconditional judgments of the superiority of one type or another of psychotherapy . . . are unjustified" (p. 760). Third, the assumptions researchers and therapists have made about psychotherapy's effectiveness are weak because the relevant information has been spread too thinly across multitudes of publications. Therefore, they suggested that their study was a step in the right direction toward solving the problem and that research using similar techniques deserves further attention.

Implications and Subsequent Research

The findings from Smith and Glass's study made the issue of psychotherapy effectiveness less confusing for consumers—but more confusing for therapists. Those who choose psychotherapy as a career often feel a personal investment in believing that one particular method (theirs) is more effective than others. However, the conclusions from Smith and Glass's study have been supported by subsequent research (Landman & Dawes, 1982; Smith, Glass, & Miller, 1980). One of the outcomes of this line of research was an increase in therapists' willingness to take an *eclectic* approach to helping their clients, meaning that in their treatment practices they combine methodologies from several psychotherapeutic methods and tailor their therapy to fit each individual client and each unique problem. In fact, 40% of all therapists in practice consider themselves to be eclectic. This percentage is by far the largest of all the other single approaches.

It would be a mistake to conclude from this and similar studies that all psychotherapy is equally effective for all problems and all people. These studies take a very broad and general overview of the effectiveness of therapy. However, depending on your personality and the circumstances of your specific problem, some therapies might be more effective for you than others.

The most important consideration when choosing a therapist may not be the type of therapy at all but, rather, your *expectations* for psychotherapy, the characteristics of your therapist, and the quality of the relationship between you and your therapist. If you *believe* that psychotherapy can help, and you enter the therapeutic relationship with optimistic expectations, the chances of successful therapy are greatly increased. The connection you feel with the therapist can also make an important difference. If you trust your therapist and believe he or she can truly help, you are much more likely to experience effective therapy.

Recent Applications

Smith and Glass's findings and methodology both continue to exert a strong influence on research relating to the efficacy of the many forms of therapeutic intervention for various psychological problems. This influence stems from their conclusions that most approaches to psychotherapy are equally effective, which they found using their meta-analytic research technique.

Examples of research that followed the methodological trail of Smith and Glass include a study to assess the effectiveness of group therapy in treating depression (McDermut, Miller, & Brown, 2001). The authors conducted a meta-analysis of 48 studies on group therapy and depression and found that, on average, those receiving treatment improved significantly more than 85% of those in an untreated comparison group. The researchers concluded that "Group therapy is an efficacious treatment for depressed patients. However, little empirical work has investigated what advantages group therapy might have over individual therapy" (p. 98). Based on Smith and Glass's research, you might predict that the effectiveness is likely to be similar for group and individual approaches to therapy, but further research would be needed for us to know for sure.

Another study demonstrating the diverse applications of the meta-analysis strategies described in Smith and Glass's article concerned various behavioral (e.g., non-medication) treatments for people who suffer from recurrent migraine and tension headaches (Penzien, Rains, & Andrasik, 2002). Through meta-analytic analyses, the researchers compared 30 years of studies of relaxation training, biofeedback, and stress-management interventions. Overall, they found a 35%–50% reduction in these types of headaches with behavioral strategies alone. This is an important finding because, as the authors point out, "the available evidence suggests that the level of headache improvement with behavioral interventions may rival those obtained with widely used pharmacologic (drug) therapies" (p. 163). Based on this finding, the authors suggest that if behavioral therapies for chronic headaches can be made more available and less expensive, more doctors, as well as their patients, might opt for nondrug treatment.

A study exemplifying the broad influence of the Smith and Glass's method and findings examined the effectiveness of psychotherapy for individuals who are diagnosed with mental retardation or intellectual disability (Prout & Nowak-Drabik, 2003). Their meta-analysis examined studies with widely varying research methodologies, styles of psychotherapy, and characteristics of the clients. Results across all the studies revealed a moderate, yet significant degree of benefit to clients with intellectual disability. The researchers concluded that "psychotherapeutic interventions should be considered as part of an overall treatment plan for persons with [intellectual disability]" (p. 82).

Conclusion

Smith and Glass's study was a milestone in the history of psychology because it helped to remove much of the temptation for researchers to try to prove the superiority of a specific method of therapy and encouraged them instead to focus on how best to help those in psychological pain. Today, research may concentrate more directly on exactly *which factors* promote the fastest, the most successful, and especially the most healing therapeutic experience.

Just as the most widely practiced forms of psychotherapy have varied throughout the history of people receiving therapy, one of the methods used most commonly today is known as *Cognitive Behavioral Therapy* or *CBT*. This approach to therapy is suggested for clients of all ages who continually and repetitively think in maladaptive ways that maintain ineffective and painful behaviors. By helping them to alter their negative thought processes, they are more likely to be successful in changing their unproductive and distressing behaviors. These clients also typically suffer from anxiety and depression for which they may take medications, but require psychotherapy in addition to the drug therapy (see Bhandari, 2018). However, as mentioned above, the odds are high that new forms of therapy and variations on existing techniques will come into use as we learn more about effectively treating people's psychological difficulties.

Bhandari, S. (2018). Mental health and psychotherapy: Types of psychotherapy. *WebMD*. Retrieved from https://www.webmd.com/mental-health/mental-health-psychotherapy

Landman, J., & Dawes, R. (1982). Psychotherapy outcome: Smith and Glass's conclusions stand up under scrutiny. *American Psychologist, 37*, 504–516.

McDermut, W., Miller, I., & Brown, R. (2001). The efficacy of group psychotherapy for depression: A meta-analysis and review of the empirical research. *Clinical Psychology: Science and Practice, 8*, 98–116.

Penzien, D., Rains, J., & Andrasik, F. (2002). Behavioral management of recurrent headaches: Three decades of experience and empiricism. *Applied Psychology and Biofeedback, 27*, 163–181.

Prout, H., & Nowak-Drabik, K. (2003). Psychotherapy with persons who have mental retardation: An evaluation of the effectiveness. *American Journal of Mental Retardation, 108*, 82–93.

Smith, M., Glass, G., & Miller, T. (1980). *The benefits of psychotherapy*. Baltimore, MD: Johns Hopkins University Press.

Wood, J. (2007). *Getting help: The complete & authoritative guide to selfassessment and treatment of mental health problems*. Oakland, CA: New Harbinger Publications.

Reading 9.2: Relaxing Your Fears Away

Wolpe, J. (1961). The systematic desensitization treatment of neuroses. *Journal of Nervous and Mental Diseases, 132*, 180–203.

9.2 Describe the process and applications of systematic desensitization

Before discussing this very important technique in psychotherapy called *systematic desensitization* (which means decreasing your level of anxiety or fear gently and gradually), the concept of *neuroses* should be clarified. The term *neuroses* is a somewhat outdated way of referring to a group of psychological problems for which extreme anxiety is the central characteristic. Today, such problems are usually called *anxiety disorders*. We are all familiar with anxiety and sometimes experience a high degree of it in situations that make us nervous, such as public speaking, job interviews, exams, and so on. However, when someone suffers from an anxiety *disorder,* the reactions are much more extreme, pervasive, frequent, and debilitating. Often such disorders interfere with a person's life so that normal and desired functioning is impossible. In other words, the anxiety begins to take over.

The most common anxiety-related difficulties are phobias, panic disorder, and generalized anxiety disorder. If you have ever suffered from one of these, you know that these kinds of anxiety can take control of your life. This reading's discussion of the work of Joseph Wolpe (1915–1997) in treating those disorders focuses primarily on phobias. The word *phobia* comes from *Phobos,* the name of the Greek god of fear. The ancient Greeks painted images of Phobos on their masks and shields to frighten their enemies.

A phobia is an *irrational* fear. In other words, it is a physical and mental fear reaction that is out of proportion to the reality of the danger: the fear reaction is bigger than any real danger. For example, if you are strolling down a path in the forest and suddenly happen upon a rattlesnake, coiled and ready to strike, you will feel fear (unless you're Harry Potter or something!). This is *not* a phobia but a normal, *rational* fear response to a real danger. On the other hand, if you are unable to go near the zoo because you might see a snake behind thick glass that would probably be considered a phobia. This may sound humorous to you, but it's not funny at all to those who suffer from phobias. Phobic reactions are extremely uncomfortable events that involve symptoms such as dizziness, heart palpitations, feeling faint, hyperventilating, sweating, trembling, and nausea. A person with a phobia will warily avoid situations in which the feared stimulus might be encountered. Often, this avoidance can interfere drastically with a person's desired functioning in life.

Phobias are divided into three main types. *Simple* (or *specific*) *phobias* involve irrational fears of animals (such as rats, dogs, spiders, or snakes) or specific situations, such as small spaces (*claustrophobia*) or heights (*acrophobia*). *Social phobias* are characterized by irrational fears about interactions with others, such as public speaking or fear of embarrassment. *Agoraphobia* is the irrational fear of being in unfamiliar, open, or crowded spaces, typically developing as a result of panic attacks that have occurred in those areas. Although the various types of phobias are quite different, they share at least two common features: They are all irrational, and they all are treated in similar ways.

Early treatment of phobias centered on the Freudian concepts of psychoanalysis. This view maintains that a phobia is the result of unconscious psychological conflicts stemming from childhood traumas. It further contends that the phobia may be substituting for some other, deeper fear or anger that the person is unwilling to face. For example, a man with an irrational fear of heights (*acrophobia*) may have been cruelly teased as a small boy by his father, who pretended to try to push him off a high cliff. Acknowledging this experience as an adult might force the man to deal with his father's general abusiveness (something he doesn't want to face), so he represses it, and it is expressed, instead, in the form of a phobia. In accordance with this Freudian view of the source of the problem, psychoanalysts historically attempted to treat phobias by helping the person to gain insight into unconscious feelings and release the hidden emotion, thereby freeing themselves of the phobia in the process. However, such techniques, although sometimes useful for other types of psychological problems, have proven relatively ineffective in treating phobias. It appears that even when someone uncovers the underlying unconscious conflicts that may have led to the phobia, the *phobia itself persists*.

Joseph Wolpe was not the first to suggest the use of the systematic desensitization behavioral technique, but he is generally credited with perfecting it and applying it to the treatment of anxiety disorders, especially phobias. The behavioral approach differs dramatically from psychoanalytic thinking in that it is not concerned with the unconscious sources of the problem or with repressed conflicts. Behavioral therapists typically do not especially care where the phobia originated. The fundamental idea of behavioral therapy is that you have *learned* an ineffective behavior (the phobia), and now you must *unlearn* it. This formed the basis for Wolpe's method for the treatment of phobias.

Theoretical Propositions

Earlier research by Wolpe and others had discovered that fear reactions in animals could be reduced by a simple conditioning procedure. For example, suppose a rat behaves fearfully when it sees a realistic photograph of a cat. If the rat is given food every time the cat is presented, the rat will become less and less fearful, until finally the fear response disappears entirely. The rat had originally been conditioned to associate the cat photo with fear. However, the rat's response to being fed was incompatible with the fear response. The fear response and the feeding response cannot both exist at the same time, so the fear was inhibited by the feeding response. This incompatibility of two responses is called *reciprocal inhibition* (when two responses inhibit each other, only one may exist at a given moment). Wolpe proposed the more general proposition that "if a response inhibitory to anxiety can be made to occur in the presence of anxiety-provoking stimuli . . . the bond between these stimuli and the anxiety will be weakened" (p. 180). He also argued that human anxiety reactions are quite similar to those found in the animal lab and that the concept of reciprocal inhibition could be used to treat various human psychological disorders.

In his work with people, the anxiety-inhibiting response was deep relaxation training rather than feeding. The idea was based on the theory that you cannot experience deep physical relaxation and fear at the same time. As a behaviorist, Wolpe believed that the reason you have a phobia is that you learned it sometime in your life through the process of classical conditioning, by which some object became associated in your brain with intense fear (see Reading 3.1 on Pavlov's research relating to classical conditioning). We know from the work of Watson (see also Reading 3.2 on Little Albert) and others that such learning is possible even at very young ages. To treat your phobia, you must experience a response (relaxation) that is inhibitory to fear or anxiety while in the presence of the feared object or situation. Will this treatment technique work? Wolpe's article reports on 39 cases randomly selected out of 150. Each participant's phobia was treated by the author using his systematic desensitization technique.

Method

Imagine that you suffer from acrophobia. This problem has become so extreme that you have trouble climbing onto a ladder to trim the trees in your yard or going above the second floor in an office building. Your phobia is interfering so much with your life that you decide to seek psychotherapy from a behavior therapist like Joseph Wolpe. Your therapy will consist of relaxation training, construction of an anxiety hierarchy, and desensitization.

RELAXATION TRAINING   The first several sessions will deal very little with your actual phobia. Instead, the therapist will focus on teaching you how to relax your body. Wolpe recommended a form of progressive muscle relaxation introduced by Edmund Jacobson in 1938 that is still common in therapy today. The process involves tensing and relaxing various groups of muscles (such as the arms, hands, face, back, stomach, legs, etc.) throughout the body until a deep state of relaxation is achieved. This relaxation training may take several sessions with the therapist until you can create such a state on your own. After the training, you should be able to place yourself in this state of relaxation whenever you want. Wolpe also incorporated hypnosis into the treatment for most of his cases to ensure full relaxation, but hypnosis has since been shown to be unnecessary for effective therapy because usually full relaxation can be obtained without it.

CONSTRUCTION OF AN ANXIETY HIERARCHY   The next stage of the process is for you and your therapist to develop a list of anxiety-producing situations or scenes involving your phobia. The list would begin with a situation that is only slightly uncomfortable and proceed through increasingly frightening scenes until reaching the most anxiety-producing event you can imagine. The number of steps in a patient's hierarchy may vary from 5 or 6 to 20 or more. Table 9.2.1 illustrates what might appear on your hierarchy for your phobia of heights, plus a hierarchy Wolpe developed with a patient suffering from claustrophobia, the latter adapted directly from his article.

DESENSITIZATION   Now you come to the actual "unlearning." According to Wolpe, no direct contact with your feared situation is necessary to reduce your sensitivity to them (something clients are very glad to hear!). The same effect can be accomplished through descriptions and visualizations. Remember, you developed your phobia through the process of association, so you will eliminate the phobia the same way. First, you are instructed to place yourself in a state of deep relaxation as you have been taught. Then the therapist begins with the first step in your hierarchy and describes the scene to you: "You are walking down the sidewalk and you come to a large grating. As you continue walking, you can see through the grating to the bottom 4 feet below." Your job is to imagine the scene while remaining completely relaxed. If this is successful, the therapist will proceed to the next step: "You are sitting in an office on the third floor . . .," and so on. If at any moment during this process you feel the slightest anxiety, you are instructed to raise your index finger (or some such signal). When this happens, the presentation of your hierarchy will stop until you have returned to full relaxation. Then the descriptions will begin again from a point further down the list while you maintain your relaxed state. This process continues until you are able to remain relaxed through the entire hierarchy. Once you accomplish this, you might repeat the process several times in subsequent therapy sessions. In Wolpe's work with his clients, the number of sessions for successful treatment varied greatly. Some people claimed to be recovered in as few as six sessions, although one took nearly a 100 (this was a patient with a severe phobia of death, plus two additional phobias). The average

Table 9.2.1 Anxiety Hierarchies

Acrophobia

1.   Walking over a sturdy bridge
2.   Sitting in a third-floor office near the window (not a floor-to-ceiling window)
3.   Riding an elevator to the 15th floor
4.   Watching rock climbers not using safety ropes
5.   Standing on a short step ladder to change a light bulb
6.   Sitting on a balcony with a railing of a fourth-floor apartment
7.   Sitting in the front row of the second balcony at the baseball park
8.   Standing on the fifth step of a ladder to trim trees in the yard
9.   Standing at the edge of the roof of a two-story building with no railing
10.   Riding a bike on a narrow mountain road
11.   Riding as a passenger in a car around curves on a narrow mountain road
12.   Standing at the edge of the observation platform of the Empire State Building

Claustrophobia

1.   Reading of miners trapped
2.   Having polish on fingernails without access to remover
3.   Being told of someone in jail
4.   Visiting and being unable to leave
5.   Having a tight ring on finger
6.   On a journey by train (the longer the journey, the more the anxiety)
7.   Traveling in an elevator with an operator (the longer the ride, the more the anxiety)
8.   Traveling alone in an elevator
9.   Passing through a tunnel on a train (the longer the tunnel, the greater the anxiety)
10.   Being locked in a room (the smaller the room and the longer the duration, the greater the anxiety)
11.   Being stuck in an elevator (the greater the time, the greater the anxiety)

(Modified from Wolpe, 1961, p. 197.)

number of sessions was around 12, which was considerably fewer than the number of sessions generally required for formal psychoanalysis, which usually lasted years.

The most important question relating to this treatment method is this: Does it work?

Results

The 39 cases reported in Wolpe's article involved many different phobias, including, among others, claustrophobia, storms, being watched, crowds, bright light, wounds, agoraphobia, falling, rejection, and snakes or snake-like shapes. The success of therapy was judged by the patients' own reports and by occasional direct observation. Generally, patients who reported improvement and gradual recovery described the process in ways that led Wolpe to accept their reports as credible. The desensitization process was rated as either completely successful (freedom from phobic reactions), partially successful (phobic reactions of 20% or less of original strength), or unsuccessful.

For the 39 cases, a total of 68 phobias were treated. Of these treatments (in a total of 35 patients), 62 were judged to be completely or partially successful. This was a success rate of 91%. The remaining 6 (9%) were unsuccessful. The average number of sessions needed for successful treatment was 12.3. Wolpe explained that most of the unsuccessful cases displayed special problems that did not allow for proper desensitization to take place, such as an inability to imagine the situations presented in the hierarchy.

Critics of Wolpe, mainly from the Freudian, psychoanalytic camp, claimed that his methods were only treating the *symptoms* and not the underlying *causes* of the anxiety. They maintained that new symptoms were bound to crop up to replace the ones treated in this way. They likened it to a leaking dike: When one hole is plugged, another eventually appears. Wolpe responded to criticisms and questions by obtaining follow-up reports at various times, over a 4-year period after treatment from 25 of the 35 patients who had received successful desensitization. Upon examining the reports he wrote, "There was no reported instance of relapse or new phobias or other neurotic symptoms. I have never observed resurgence of neurotic anxiety when desensitization has been complete or virtually so" (p. 200).

Discussion

The discussion in Wolpe's article focuses on responding to the skepticism of the psychoanalysts at the time his research was done. During the 1950s, psychoanalysis was still a very common and popular form of psychotherapy. Behavior therapies created a great deal of controversy as they began to make their way into the mainstream of clinical psychology. Wolpe pointed out that the desensitization method offered several advantages over traditional psychoanalysis (see p. 202 of the original study):

1. The goals of psychotherapy can be clearly stated in every case.
2. Sources of anxiety can be clearly and quickly defined.
3. Changes in the patient's reactions during descriptions of scenes from the hierarchy can be measured during the sessions.
4. Therapy can be performed with others present (Wolpe found that having others present, such as therapists in training, during the sessions did not interfere with the effectiveness).
5. Therapists can be interchanged if desired or necessary.

Subsequent Research and Recent Applications

Since Wolpe published this article and a book on the use of reciprocal inhibition in psychotherapy (Wolpe, 1958), the use of systematic desensitization has grown to the point that now it is usually considered the treatment of choice for anxiety disorders, especially phobias. This growth has been due in large part to more recent and more scientific research on its effectiveness.

A study by Paul (1969) treated college students who suffered from extreme phobic anxiety in public-speaking situations. First, all the participants were asked to give a short, ad-libbed speech to an unfamiliar audience. Their degree of anxiety was measured by observer's ratings, physiological measures, and a self-report questionnaire. The students were then randomly assigned to three treatment groups: (a) systematic desensitization, (b) insight therapy (similar to psychoanalysis), or (c) no treatment (control). Experienced therapists carried out the treatment in five sessions. All the participants were then placed in the same public-speaking situation, and all the same measures of anxiety were taken. Figure 9.2.1 summarizes the results. Clearly, systematic desensitization was significantly more effective in reducing anxiety on all measures. Even more convincing was that in a *2-year* follow-up, 85% of the desensitization group *still* showed significant improvement, compared with only 50% of the insight group.

Numerous studies on behavior therapy continue to cite Wolpe's early work as part of their theoretical underpinnings. His application of classical conditioning concepts to the treatment of psychological disorders has become part of intervention strategies in a wide range of settings. For example, one study (Fredrickson, 2000) relied in part on Wolpe's concept of reciprocal inhibition in developing a new treatment strategy for difficulties stemming primarily from negative emotions such as anxiety, depression, aggression, and stress-related health problems. Fredrickson proposes assisting and teaching patients with such psychological problems to generate more and stronger positive emotions, such as love, optimism, joy, interest, and contentment, which directly inhibit negative thinking. The author contends that

> Positive emotions loosen the hold that negative emotions gain on an individual's mind and body by undoing the narrowed psychological and physiological preparation for specific action. . . . Therapies optimize health and well being to the extent that they cultivate positive emotions. Cultivated positive emotions not only counteract negative emotions, but also broaden individuals' habitual modes of thinking, and build their personal resources for coping. (p. 1)

Another article resting on Wolpe's research studied the effectiveness of systematic desensitization for a condition many students know all too well: *math phobia* (Zettle, 2003). In this study Wolpe's treatment techniques were used to help students overcome

Figure 9.2.1 Results of treatment for anxiety. (Based on Paul, 1969.)

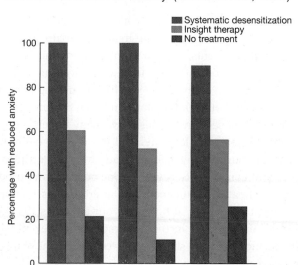

extreme levels of math anxiety. Participants were given instructions on progressive muscle relaxation and a tape to use to practice relaxing each day at home. Each student worked with the researcher to develop an 11-item math fear hierarchy containing items such as "being called upon by my math instructor to solve a problem at the blackboard" or "encountering a word problem I don't know how to solve on the final" (p. 205). The hierarchy was then presented to each student as described previously in this reading. To summarize briefly, it worked! At the end of the treatment, 11 out of 12 students "displayed recovery or improvement in their levels of math anxiety. . . . Furthermore, clinically significant reductions in math anxiety were maintained during the 2 months of followup" (p. 209).

Conclusion

Wolpe was quick to point out in his article that the idea of overcoming fear and anxiety was not new: "It has long been known that increasing measures of exposure to a feared object may lead to the gradual disappearance of the fear" (p. 200). In fact, you probably already knew this yourself, even if you had never heard of systematic desensitization prior to reading this chapter. For example, imagine a child who is about 13 years old and has a terrible phobia of dogs. This fear is probably the result of a frightening experience with a dog when the child was much younger, such as being jumped on by a big dog, being bitten by any dog, or even having a parent who was very afraid of dogs (phobias can be passed from parent to child through modeling). Because of these experiences, the child developed an association between dogs and fear. If you wanted to cure this child of the fear of dogs, how might you break that association? Many people's first response to this question is "Buy the child a puppy!" If that's what you thought, you have just recommended a form of systematic desensitization.

How about a more recent and very useful application of Wolpe's method? Dentist phobia. Now, granted, dentistry has improved greatly over the decades and is far less painful and traumatic overall. However, many people still suffer terrible dentist phobia which prevents them from obtaining the care they need. A 2016 study suggested that Wolpe's systematic desensitization is a helpful method to move these individuals past their phobia and into the dentist's chair (Appukuttan, 2016). Let's imagine for a moment (so to speak) how this might work. (1) First is the relaxation training (2) then comes the development of the fear hierarchy: (3) then getting into the car to drive to the dentist (4) next, walking from the car to the dentist's office (5) then entering the dentist's office (6) next, sitting in the waiting room (7) then, hearing other patients being worked on (8) then, hearing your name called by the hygienist (9) next, sitting down in the dentist's chair (10) opening your mouth for the work to begin (11) then hearing the sound of the drill or cleaning tool (some of you are freaking out already I bet). But you are not *experiencing* any of these events, you are simply making the list. Then, under deep relaxation, the therapist describes each step to you from least anxiety to most *while you maintain your deep relaxation.* If, at any stage you lose your deep relaxation, you signal the therapist to stop, regain your relaxed state, and then continue the process of visualization. After a number of sessions of this (how many depends on how strong the phobia), you are able to stay completely relaxed through the entire hierarchy. When you reach this point in your therapy, you are ready to make a trip to see the dentist. You will likely find that your anxiety is either gone or greatly reduced to the point of allowing you to get the treatment you need. And after a successful appointment, your anxiety will be reduced even more. If not, and your anxiety stays sky high, you can return to the behavior therapist for further treatment until it eventually is successful. Systematic desensitization has been shown repeatedly to be one of the most successful therapies "on the market".

Appukuttan, D. (2016). Strategies to manage patients with dental anxiety and dental phobia: Literature review. *Clinical, Cosmetic and Investigational Dentistry, 8,* 35–50.

Fredrickson, B. (2000). Cultivating positive emotions to optimize health and wellbeing. *Prevention and Treatment, 3* (article 00001a): 1–25. Retrieved February 3, 2008, at http://www.unc.edu/peplab/publications/cultivating.pdf

Paul, G. L. (1969). Outcome of systematic desensitization: Controlled investigation of individual technique variations and current status. In C. Franks (Ed.), *Behavior Therapy: Appraisal and Status.* New York: McGraw-Hill.

Wolpe, J. (1958). *Psychotherapy through reciprocal inhibition.* Palo Alto, CA: Stanford University Press.

Zettle, R. (2003). Acceptance and commitment therapy (ACT) vs. systematic desensitization in treatment of mathematics anxiety. *Psychological Record, 53,* 197–215.

Reading 9.3: Projections of Who You Are

Rorschach, H. (1942). *Psychodiagnostics: A diagnostic test based on perception.* New York: Grune & Stratton.

9.3 Explain the use and criticisms of the Rorschach assessment scale

Picture yourself and a friend relaxing in a grassy meadow on a warm summer's day. The blue sky above is broken only by a few white puffy clouds. Pointing to one of the clouds, you say to your friend, "Look! That cloud looks like a woman in a wedding dress with a long veil." To this your friend replies, "Where? I don't see that. To me, that cloud is shaped like a volcano with a plume of smoke rising from the top." As you try to convince each other of your differing perceptions of the same shape, the air currents change and transform the cloud into something entirely different. But why such a difference in what the two of you saw? You were looking at the same shape and, yet, interpreting it as two entirely unrelated objects.

Everyone's perceptions are influenced by their internal psychological factors, so perhaps the different objects found in the cloud formations revealed something about the personalities of the observers more than the object observed. In other words, you and your friend were *projecting* something about yourselves onto the cloud shapes in the sky. This is the concept underlying Hermann Rorschach's (1884–1922) development of his "Form Interpretation Test," better known as "the Inkblot Test." This was one of the earliest versions of a type of psychological assessment tool known as a *projective test.*

The two most widely used projective tests are the Rorschach Inkblot (discussed in this reading) and the *Thematic Apperception Test,* or *TAT* (see Reading 9.4, next). Both of these instruments are pivotal in the history of clinical psychology. Rorschach's test, first described in 1921, involves direct comparisons among various groups of mental illnesses and is often associated with the *diagnosis* of psychological disorders.

A *projective test* typically presents a person with a picture of an ambiguous shape or drawing and assumes that the person, in describing the image, will interpret it by *projecting* his or her inner or unconscious psychological processes onto it. In the case of Rorschach's test, the stimulus is nothing more than a symmetrical inkblot that is so ambiguous it can be perceived to be virtually anything. Rorschach suggested that what a person sees in the inkblot reveals a great deal about his or her internal psychological processes. He called this the *interpretation of accidental forms.* An often-told story about Rorschach's inkblots tells of a psychotherapist who is administering the test to a client. With the first inkblot card the therapist asks, "What does this suggest to you?" The client replies, "Sex." The same question is asked of the second card, to which the client again replies, "Sex." When the same one-word answer is given to the first five cards, the therapist remarks, "Well, you certainly seem to be preoccupied with sex!" To this the surprised client responds, "Me? Doctor, you're the one showing all the sexy pictures!" Of course, this story oversimplifies Rorschach's test, and sexual interpretations would, on average, be no more likely than any other.

Rorschach believed that his projective technique could serve two main purposes. One was that it could be used as a research tool to reveal unconscious aspects of personality. The other purpose, claimed somewhat later by Rorschach, was that the test could be used to diagnose various types of psychopathology.

Theoretical Propositions

The theory underlying Rorschach's technique proposed that in the course of interpreting a random inkblot, attention would be drawn away from the person so that his or her usual psychological defenses would be weakened. This, in turn, would allow normally hidden aspects of the person's psyche to be revealed. When the stimulus perceived is ambiguous (i.e., having few—or no—clues as to what it is), the interpretation of the stimulus must originate from the mind of the person doing the perceiving (for an expanded discussion of this concept, see Reading 9.4, next, on Murray's Thematic Apperception Test). In Rorschach's conceptualization, inkblots were about as ambiguous as you can get and, therefore, would allow for the greatest amount of projection from a person's unconscious.

Method

An examination of Rorschach's formulation of his inkblot test can be divided into two broad sections: the process he used to develop the original forms and the methods suggested for interpreting and scoring the responses made by participants or clients.

DEVELOPMENT OF THE TEST   Rorschach's explanation of how the forms were made sounded very much like instructions for a fun children's art project: "The production of such accidental forms is very simple: A few large inkblots are thrown on a piece of paper, the paper folded [in half], and the ink spread between the two halves of the sheet" (p. 15). However, the simplicity stopped there. Rorschach went on to explain that only those designs that met certain conditions could be used effectively. For example, the inkblot should be relatively simple and moderately suggestive of vague objects. He also suggested that the forms should be symmetrical, because asymmetrical inkblots are often rejected by participants as impossible to interpret. After a great deal of testing, Rorschach finally arrived at a set of 10 forms that made up his original test. Of these, five were black on white, two used black and red, and three were multicolored. Figure 9.3.1 contains four figures representative of the type Rorschach used.

ADMINISTRATION AND SCORING   Rorschach's form interpretation test is administered simply by handing a person each figure, one at a time, and asking "What might this be?" Participants are free to turn the card in any direction and to hold it as close to or as far from their eyes as they wish. The researcher or therapist administering the test, notes all the responses for each figure without prodding or making any suggestions. No time limit is imposed.

Rorschach pointed out that participants almost always think the test is designed to study imagination. However, he is very careful to explain that it is not a test of imagination, and a person's imaginative creativity does not significantly alter the result. It is, Rorschach claimed, a test of perception involving the processes of sensation, memory, and unconscious and conscious associations between the stimulus forms and other psychological forces within the individual.

Figure 9.3.1 Examples of accidental forms similar to the type used in Rorschach's Form Interpretation test.

(Science Museum/SSPL/The Image Works)

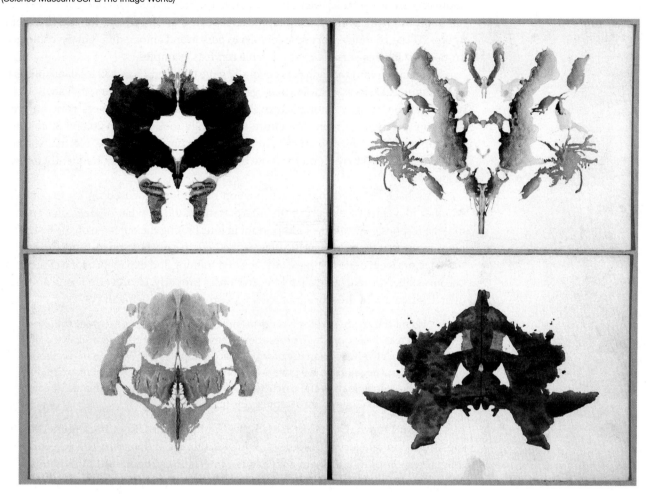

Rorschach listed the following guidelines for scoring his test subjects' responses to the 10 inkblots (p. 19):

1. How many responses were made? What was the reaction time; that is, how long did the person look at the figure before responding? How often did the participant refuse to interpret a figure?

2. Was the person's interpretation only determined by the shape of the figure, or were color or movement included in the perception?

3. Was the figure seen as a whole or in separate parts? Which parts were separated, and how were they interpreted?

4. What did the subject see?

Interestingly, Rorschach considered the content of the subject's interpretation the *least* important factor in the responses given to the inkblots. The following section summarizes Rorschach's observations, related to these four guidelines, of numerous subjects with a variety of psychological symptoms.

Results

To discover how various groups of people might perform differently on the inkblot test, Rorschach and his associates administered it to individuals from several psychological groups. These included, but were not limited to, normal individuals with varying amounts of education, schizophrenic patients, and individuals diagnosed as manic-depressive (now called *bipolar*).

Table 9.3.1 presents typical responses reported by Rorschach for the 10 inkblot figures. These, of course, vary from person to person and among different psychological groups, but the answers given in the table serve as examples.

Rorschach found that subjects generally gave between 15 and 30 total responses to the 10 figures. Depressed individuals generally gave fewer answers, those who were happy gave more, and among schizophrenics the number of answers varied a great deal from person to person. The entire test usually took between 20 and 30 minutes to complete, with schizophrenics taking much less time on average. Normal subjects almost never failed to respond to all the figures, but schizophrenics frequently refused to answer.

Rorschach believed that which portion of the form focused on by the subject, whether movement was part of the interpretation, and to what degree color entered into the responses were all very important in interpreting the outcome on the test, often more important than the specific objects the person saw. His suggestions for scoring those factors were quite complex and required training and experience for a clinician to become skilled in analyzing a person's responses properly. However, a useful and brief overall summary of the scoring process was provided by Gleitman (1991):

> Using the entire inkblot is said to indicate integrative, conceptual thinking, whereas the use of a high proportion of small details suggests compulsive rigidity. A relatively frequent use of white space is supposed to be a sign of rebelliousness and negativism. Responses that describe humans in movement are said to indicate imagination and a rich inner life; responses that are dominated by color suggest emotionality and impulsivity. (p. 684)

In regard to what a person actually sees in the inkblot, Rorschach found that the most common category of responses involved animals and insects. The percentage of animal responses ranged from 25% to 50%. Interestingly, depressed individuals were among those giving the greatest percentage of animal answers; artists were reported as giving the fewest.

Another category proposed by Rorschach was that of "original responses." These were answers that occurred fewer than once in 100 tests. Original responses were found most often among participants who were diagnosed as schizophrenic and least often among normal participants of average intelligence.

Table 9.3.1 Typical Responses to Rorschach's Inkblot Figures for an Average Normal Subject

Figure Number	Responses
I.	Two Santa Clauses with brooms under their arms
II.	A butterfly
III.	Two marionette figures
IV.	An ornament on a piece of furniture
V.	A bat
VI.	A moth or a tree
VII.	Two human heads or two animal heads
VIII.	Two bears
IX.	Two clowns or darting flames
X.	A rabbit's head, two caterpillars, or two spiders

(Modified from data from pp. 126–127.)

Discussion

In his discussion of the form interpretation test, Rorschach pointed out that originally it had been designed to study theoretical questions about the unconscious workings of the human mind and psyche. His notion that the test may also have had the potential to serve as a diagnostic tool came about accidentally. Rorschach claimed that his test was often able to indicate schizophrenic tendencies, hidden neuroses, a potential for depression, characteristics of introversion versus extroversion, and intelligence. He did not, however, propose that the inkblot test should substitute for the usual practices of clinical diagnosis but, rather, that it could aid in this process. Rorschach also warned that although the test can indicate certain unconscious tendencies, it cannot be used to probe the contents of the unconscious in detail. He suggested that other common psychological practices at the time, such as Freudian dream interpretation and free association, were superior methods for exploring the deep unconscious.

Criticisms and Subsequent Research

Numerous studies over the decades since Rorschach developed his test have drawn many of his conclusions into question. One of the most important criticisms relates to the *validity* of the test—whether it actually measures what Rorschach claimed it measured: underlying, unconscious psychological issues. Research has demonstrated that many of the response differences attributed by Rorschach to psychological factors can be more easily explained by such things as verbal ability, age of the person, intellectual level, amount of education, and even the characteristics of the person administering the test (see Anastasi & Urbina, 2007, for a more detailed discussion of these issues).

Taken as a whole, the many decades of scientific research on Rorschach's test do not provide a particularly optimistic view of its accuracy as a personality test or diagnostic tool. Nevertheless, the test remains in common use among clinical psychologists and psychotherapists. This apparent contradiction may be explained by the fact that Rorschach's inkblot technique is often employed in clinical use, not as a formal test but, rather, as a means of increasing a therapist's understanding of individual clients and opening up lines of communication during the therapeutic process. It is, in essence, an extension of the verbal interaction that normally occurs between a therapist and a client. In this less rigid application of the responses on the test, some clinicians feel that it offers helpful insights for effective psychotherapy.

Recent Applications

A review of recent psychological and related literature shows that the validity of the Rorschach assessment scale continues to be studied and debated (see Wood et al., 2003; Exner & Erdberg, 2005, for a comprehensive overview of this debate). Several studies from the psychoanalytic front have indicated that newer methods of administration and scoring may increase the scale's interscorer reliability and its ability to diagnose and discriminate among various psychological disturbances. For example, Arenella and Ornduff (2000) employed the Rorschach inkblot method to study differences in body image of sexually abused girls compared to nonabused girls from otherwise stressful environments. The researchers found that sexually abused girls responded to the Rorschach test in ways that indicated a greater concern about their bodies than did their nonabused counterparts. In a similar vein, researchers obtained Rorschach scores for a group of 66 psychopathic male youth criminal offenders between the ages of 14 and 17 (Loving & Russell, 2000). This study found that at least some of the standard Rorschach variables were significantly associated with various levels of psychopathology. The authors suggested that the Rorschach test may provide a valuable means of predicting which teens are at highest risk of violently criminal behaviors and, thereby, improve prevention and intervention strategies.

An intriguing development in the validity debate stems from a study comparing the Rorschach to a commonly used *objective* psychological test called the MMPI (*Minnesota Multiphasic Personality Inventory*) in evaluating sex offenders (Grossman et al., 2002). A common problem in testing sex offenders for psychological disorders is that they often deny having, or minimize the severity of, any such problems. This study found that sex offenders who were able to "fake good answers" on the MMPI and score normally on psychological profiles were exposed as psychopaths by the Rorschach: "These findings indicate that the Rorschach is resilient to attempts at faking good answers and may therefore provide valuable information in forensic settings where intentional distortion is common" (p. 484). Of course, the validity of this use of the Rorschach is equally open to questions about validity as is the original use of the test.

A 2015 study took a fresh look at the Rorschach test's connection with diagnosing depression and found some hopeful results (Mondal & Kumar, 2015). Using a specific scoring index (The DEPI) of how patients interpreted the forms, the study found that a score of 5 or more identified individuals suffering from depression. Moreover, a high score on the DEPI has been shown to correlate very highly with diagnoses of various emotional problems.

Conclusion

These studies, along with many others, demonstrate the enduring influence and use of Rorschach's work. Future studies, perhaps with modifications and wider applications of the Rorschach test, may lead researchers to the development and refinement of projective tests that offer both greater scientific validity and even more valuable therapeutic insights.

Anastasi, A., & Urbina, S. (2007). *Psychological testing,* 7th ed. Upper Saddle River, NJ: Prentice Hall.

Arenella, J., & Ornduff, S. (2000). Manifestations of bodily concern in sexually abused girls. *Bulletin of the Menninger Clinic, 64*(4), 530–542.

Exner, J., & Erdberg, P. (2005). *The Rorschach, advanced interpretation.* Hoboken, NJ: Wiley.

Gleitman, H. (1991). *Psychology,* 3rd ed. New York: Norton.

Grossman, L., Wasyliw, O., Benn, A., & Gyoerkoe, K. (2002). Can sex offenders who minimize on the MMPI conceal psychopathology on the Rorschach? *Journal of Personality Assessment, 78,* 484–501.

Loving, J., & Russell, W. (2000). Selected Rorschach variables of psychopathic juvenile offenders. *Journal of Personality Assessment, 75*(1), 126–142.

Mondal, A., & Kumar, M. (2015). A study on Rorschach depression index in patients suffering from depression. *Eastern Journal of Psychiatry, 18*(2), 12–18.

Wood, J., Nezworski, M., Lilienfeld, S., & Garb, H. (2003). *What's wrong with the Rorschach? Science confronts the controversial inkblot test.* New York: Wiley.

Reading 9.4: Picture This!

Murray, H. A. (1938). *Explorations in personality.* pp. 531–545. New York: Oxford University Press.

9.4 Evaluate the TAT interview as a diagnostic tool

In Reading 9.3, a method that some clinical psychologists have used to expose underlying aspects of personality, called the *projective test,* was discussed in relation to

Rorschach's inkblot technique. The idea behind Rorschach's test was to allow individuals to place or project their own interpretations onto objectively meaningless and unstructured forms. Also, in an attempt to draw conclusions about the participant's personality characteristics, Rorschach examined a person's focus on particular sections in the inkblot, the various specific features of that section, and perceptions of movement in the figure. The content of the subject's interpretation was also taken into account, but it was of *secondary* importance.

Several years after Rorschach developed his test, Henry A. Murray (1893–1988), at the Harvard Psychological Clinic, in consultation with his associate, Christiana D. Morgan (1897–1967), developed a different form of a projective test called the *Thematic Apperception Test*, or *TAT*, which focused *entirely* on the content of the subjects' interpretations (*apperception* means "conscious perception"). Rather than formless shapes like Rorschach's inkblots, the TAT consists of black-and-white drawings depicting people in various ambiguous situations. The client in therapy is asked to make up a story about the drawing. The stories are then analyzed by the therapist or researcher, hoping to reveal hidden unconscious conflicts or issues the client may have but be unaware of.

The theory behind the TAT is that when you observe human behavior, either in a picture or in real life, you will interpret that behavior according to the clues that are available in the situation. When the causes for the observed behavior are clear, your interpretation will not only be mostly correct, it will be in substantial agreement with other observers. However, if the situation is vague and it is difficult to find reasons for the behavior, your interpretation will more likely reflect something about yourself— about your own fears, desires, conflicts, and so on. For example, imagine you see the faces of a man and a woman looking up into the sky with different expressions on their faces: He looks terrified, but she is laughing. You find it difficult to interpret their emotional expressions. Upon looking more carefully, however, you see that they are waiting in line for a ride on "Kingda Ka," the tallest and fastest roller coaster in the world, located at Six Flags Great Adventure in New Jersey. Now you find it easier to speculate about the couple's behavior in this situation, and your analysis would probably be similar to that of other observers. Now imagine seeing the same expressions in isolation, without any situational clues to explain the behavior. If you were asked "What are these people experiencing?" your answer would depend on *your* internal interpretation of them and might reveal more about *you* than about the people you are observing. Furthermore, because of the ambiguity of the isolated behavior, different observers' answers would vary greatly (e.g., they're looking at a UFO, a ski run, small children playing on a high climbing toy, or an approaching rainstorm). These personal perception variations form the idea behind Murray and Morgan's Thematic Apperception Test.

Theoretical Propositions

The basic underlying assumption of the TAT, like that of the Rorschach test, is that people's behavior is driven by unconscious forces. Implicit in this notion is an acceptance of the principles of psychodynamic psychology developed originally by Freud (see the discussion of Freud's theories in Reading 8.2). This view contends that unconscious conflicts or issues (usually formed in childhood) must be exposed for accurate diagnosis and successful treatment of psychological problems. This was the purpose of Rorschach's inkblot test (discussed in Reading 9.3), and it was also the goal of Murray's TAT.

Murray wrote, "The purpose of this procedure is to stimulate literary creativity and thereby evoke fantasies that reveal covert and unconscious complexes" (p. 530). The way he conceived of this process was that a person would be shown ambiguous drawings of human behavior. In trying to explain the situation, the client would become less self-conscious and less concerned about being observed by the therapist. This would, in turn, cause the person to become less defensive and reveal (possibly without even being aware of it) inner wishes, fears, and past experiences that might have been repressed.

Murray also pointed out that part of the theoretical foundation for this test was that "a great deal of written fiction is the conscious or unconscious expression of the author's experiences or fantasies" (p. 531).

Method

In the TAT's original conceptualization, participants were asked to guess the events *leading up to* the scene depicted in the drawing and what they thought the outcome of the scene would be. After testing the method, it was determined that a great deal more about the psychology of clients could be obtained if they were simply asked to make up a story about the picture, rather than asked to guess the facts surrounding it.

Murray and Morgan developed the pictures to stimulate fantasies in people about conflicts and important events in their lives. Therefore, they decided that each picture should involve at least one person with whom everyone could easily identify. Through trial and error with several hundred pictures, a final set of 20 was chosen. Because the TAT is in common use today, many believe that widespread publication of the pictures might compromise its validity. However, understanding the test is difficult without being able to see the type of drawings chosen. Therefore, Figure 9.4.1 is one of the original drawings that was under consideration, but it was not ultimately chosen as one of the final 20 and has been made available to the public domain.

Murray conducted an early study of the TAT and reported the findings in his 1938 book. Participants were men between the ages of 20 and 30. Each participant was seated in a comfortable chair facing away from the experimenter (as has been commonly practiced by psychotherapists when administering the TAT). These are the exact instructions given to each participant:

> This is a test of your creative imagination. I shall show you a picture and I want you to make up a plot or a story for which it might be used as an illustration. What is the relation of the individuals in the picture? What has happened to

Figure 9.4.1 Example of a TAT card. How would *you* interpret this picture?

(Photo Researchers/Science History Images/Alamy Stock Photo)

them? What are their present thoughts and feelings? What will be the outcome? Do your very best. Because I am asking you to indulge your literary imagination, you may make your story as long and as detailed as you wish. (p. 532)

The experimenter handed the participant each picture in succession and took notes on what the participant said for each one. Each participant was given 1 hour. Due to the time limitations, most participants only completed stories for about 15 of the 20 drawings.

A few days later, the participants returned and were interviewed about their stories. To disguise the true purpose of the study, participants were told that the purpose of the research was to compare their creative experiences with those of famous writers. Participants were reminded of their responses to the pictures and were asked to explain what their sources for the stories were. They were also given a free association test, in which they were to say the first thing that came to mind in response to words spoken by the experimenter. These exercises were designed to determine to what extent the stories the participants made up about the drawings reflected their own personal experiences, conflicts, desires, and so on.

Results and Discussion

Murray and Morgan reported two main findings from their early study of the TAT. The first was the discovery that the stories the participants made up for the pictures came from four sources: (a) books and movies, (b) real-life events involving a friend or a relative, (c) experiences in the participant's own life, and (d) the participant's conscious or unconscious fantasies (see p. 533 of the original study).

The second and more important finding was that the participants clearly projected their own personal, emotional, and psychological existence into their stories. One such example reported by the authors was that most of the participants, who were students, identified the person in one of the drawings as a student, but none of the nonstudent participants did so. In another example, the participant's father was a ship's carpenter, and the participant had strong desires to travel and see the world. This fantasy appeared in his interpretations of several of the drawings.

For instance, when shown a drawing of two workers in conversation, the participant's story was "These two fellows are a pair of adventurers. They always manage to meet in out-of-the-way places. They are now in India. They have heard of a new revolution in South America and they are planning how they can get there. . . . In the end they work their way there on a freighter" (p. 534). Murray reports that, without exception, every person who participated in the study injected aspects of their personalities into their stories.

To illustrate further how the TAT reflects personal characteristics, one participant's responses were reported in detail. The participant "Virt" had emigrated to the United States from Russia after terrible childhood experiences during World War I, including persecution, hunger, and separation from his mother. Murray described picture number 13 of the TAT (not pictured here) as follows: "On the floor against the couch is the huddled form of a boy with his head bowed on his right arm. Beside him on the floor is an object which resembles a revolver" (p. 536). When Virt saw this drawing, his story about it was the following:

> Some great trouble has occurred. Someone he loved has shot herself. Probably it is his mother. She may have done it out of poverty. He being fairly grown up sees the misery of it all and would like to shoot himself. But he is young and braces up after a while. For some time he lives in misery, the first few months thinking of death. (p. 536)

It is interesting to compare this story with other, more recent stories made up by other clients about the same drawing:

1. *A 35-year-old junior high school teacher:* "I think that this is someone who has been put in prison for something he did not do. He has denied that he committed any crime and has been fighting and fighting his case in the courts. But he has given up.

Now he is completely exhausted, depressed, and hopeless. He made a fake gun to try to escape, but he knows this won't work either" (author's files).

2. *A 16-year-old high school student:* "This girl is playing hide-and-seek, probably with her brothers. She is counting from one to a hundred. She is sad and tired because she is never able to win and always has to be 'it.' It looks like the boys were playing some other game before because there's a toy gun here" (author's files).

You don't have to be a psychotherapist to make some predictions about the inner conflicts, motives, or desires that these three people might be projecting onto that one drawing. These examples also demonstrate the remarkably diverse responses that are possible on the TAT.

Criticisms and Related Research

Although the TAT uses stimuli that are very different from Rorschach's inkblot test, it has been criticized on the same grounds of poor reliability and validity (see Reading 9.3 on Rorschach's test for additional discussion of these issues). The most serious reliability problem for the TAT is that different clinicians offer differing interpretations of the same set of TAT responses. Some have suggested that therapists may unknowingly inject their own unconscious characteristics onto the participant's descriptions of the drawings. In other words, the interpretation of the TAT might, in some cases, be a projective test for the clinician who is administering it!

In terms of validity (i.e., the extent to which the TAT truly measures what it is designed to measure), several types of criticisms have been cited. If the test measures underlying psychological processes, then it should be able to distinguish between, say, normal people and people who are mentally ill, or between different types of psychological disorders. However, research has shown that it fails to make such distinctions. In a study by Eron (1950), the TAT was administered to two groups of male veterans. Some were students in college and others were patients in a psychiatric hospital. When the results of the TAT were analyzed, no significant differences were found between the two groups or among psychiatric patients with different illnesses.

Other research has questioned the ability of the TAT to predict a person's actual behavior. For example, if a person includes a great deal of violence in the stories and plots used to describe the drawings, this does not differentiate between aggression that merely exists in someone's fantasies and the potential for *real,* violent behavior. Some people can easily fantasize about aggression without ever expressing violent behavior, although for others, aggressive fantasies will predict actual violence. Because TAT responses do not indicate into which category a particular person falls, the test is of little value in predicting aggressive tendencies (see Anastasi & Urbina, 1996).

Another basic and very important criticism of the TAT (one that also has been directed at Rorschach's inkblot technique) relates to whether the projective hypothesis itself is valid. The assumption underlying the TAT is that people's stories about the drawings reveal something about their basic personalities and their ongoing unconscious, psychological processes. Scientific evidence suggests, however, that responses to projective tests such as the Rorschach and TAT may depend more on temporary and situational factors and lack reliability. What this means is that if you are given the TAT on Monday, just after work, when you've had a big fight with your boss, and then again on Saturday, just after you've returned from a relaxing day at the beach, the stories you make up for the drawings might be completely different on the two occasions. Critics argue that, to the extent that the stories are different, the TAT has only tapped into your temporary state and not your *real* underlying self.

As a demonstration of this criticism, studies have found variations in TAT performance relating to the following list of influences: hunger, lack of sleep, drug use, anxiety level, frustration, verbal ability, characteristics of the person administering the test, the attitude of the participant about the testing situation, and the participant's cognitive abilities. In light of these findings, Anne Anastasi, one of the leading authorities on psychological testing, wrote, "Many types of research have tended to cast doubt on the projective hypothesis. There is ample evidence that alternative explanations may account as well or better for the individual's responses to unstructured test stimuli" (Anastasi & Urbina, 1996).

Recent Applications

Every year, Murray's research and the TAT continue to be cited and incorporated into numerous studies of personality characteristics and their measurement. One study compared TAT responses of patients diagnosed with *dissociative disorders,* such as *traumatic amnesia* and *dissociative identity disorder* (previously known as *multiple personality disorder*), with those of other inpatients in a psychiatric facility (Pica et al., 2001). The researchers found that, among dissociative patients, responses to the TAT cards contained virtually no positive emotions and that the "testing behaviors of dissociative participants were characterized by switching, trance states, intrainterview amnesia (blocking out parts of the TAT interview *during* testing), and affectively loaded [highly emotional] card rejections" (p. 847).

Murray's 1938 work has also been incorporated into research on personality disorders, including *antisocial personality* (a disregard for other people's rights; lack of guilt or remorse), *avoidant personality* (chronic and consistent feelings of inadequacy), *borderline personality* (intense anger, very unstable relationships), and *narcissistic personality* (exaggerated sense of self-importance, great need for admiration). Some studies have found that the TAT is successful in differentiating among personality disorders and that TAT scores are consistent with scores on the MMPI (Minnesota Multiphasic Personality Inventory), a widely used and fairly well-validated objective personality assessment tool (Ackerman et al., 1999).

It is important to acknowledge that people's interpretation of ambiguous pictures is almost certain to vary across cultures. A study demonstrating this analyzed TAT responses of adolescents in Zambia and compared them to responses from a similar group of participants in Germany (Hofer & Chasiotis, 2004). These two groups, as you may imagine, are very diverse in terms of overall culture, beliefs, education, and life experiences. The authors found that the complexity of imagery and the interpretations given for the five TAT picture cards used in this study varied significantly between the two groups—so much so, in fact, that the authors suggested that using the TAT method for comparing diverse cultures on important psychological variables may be invalid.

What about a TAT using different sensory modalities? Nagle and Rani (2015) developed a *Sound Apperception Test* (the SAT—no not *that* SAT!) which used auditory projective testing (using ambiguous *sound* stimuli)! The SAT used 24 ambiguous, mixed sounds; six of the sounds were targeted at males (e.g., "airplane passing overhead and horse carriage passing") and six at females (e.g., "young children playing in playground and ambiguous conversation"). These sex-specific sounds were included because Murray had different sets of picture cards for men and women, which shared some of the same pictures, and the development of the SAT was patterned closely after the TAT. The remaining 12 sounds were played for both sexes (e.g., "baby crying and telephone ringing"; "plane takes off and bombing from plane").

Each sound was played for 30 seconds. Following the sound, participants were asked to write a brief story describing when the sound happened and some details about the situation in which the sound occurred.

The researchers determined the reliability of the SAT by administering the test to the same group of subjects 15 days apart and found it to be highly reliable. Interestingly, the validity of the SAT was determined by comparing it to interpretations of the TAT for the same subjects. The researchers concluded that the SAT is a valid and reliable test and is potentially useful in determining emotional disturbances in psychiatric patients.

Conclusion

One of the most remarkable aspects of projective tests such as the TAT and the Rorschach inkblot test (previous reading) is that, in spite of a massive body of evidence condemning them as invalid, unreliable, and possibly based on faulty assumptions, they are among the most frequently used psychological tests by therapists. The fact that clinicians continue to be enthusiastic about these tools while experimental psychologists grow increasingly wary is a key point of contention between those two groups (see Lilienfeld, Wood, & Garb, 2000, for a review of this issue). How can we reconcile this contradiction? The most common answer to this question is that the TAT and the Rorschach tests are often employed in psychotherapy *not* as formal diagnostic tools but rather as extensions of the early give-and-take between clinicians and their patients. It follows, then, that therapists apply these projective devices in very individual ways to open up channels of communication with clients and enter psychological domains that might have been avoided or hidden without the prompting by the stories on the TAT (see Cramer, 2006). As one practicing psychotherapist explains, "I don't score my clients' responses on the TAT or use them for diagnosis, but the drawings are a wonderful and valuable vehicle for bringing to light troubled areas in a client's life. The identification and awareness of these issues that flow from the TAT allow for more focused and effective therapy" (author's files).

Ackerman, S., Clemence, A., Weatherill, R., & Hilsenroth, M. (1999). Use of the TAT in the assessment of *DSM-IV* Cluster B personality disorders. *Journal of Personality Assessment, 73*(3), 422–442.

Anastasi, A., & Urbina, S. (1996). *Psychological testing,* 7th ed. New York: Macmillan.

Cramer, P. (2006). *Storytelling, narrative, and the Thematic Apperception Test.* New York: Guilford Press.

Eron, L. (1950). A normative study of the Thematic Apperception Test. *Psychological Monographs, 64* (9, Whole No. 315).

Hofer, J., & Chasiotis, A. (2004). Methodological considerations of applying a TAT type picturestory test in cross-cultural research: A comparison of German and Zambian adolescents. *Journal of CrossCultural Psychology, 35*(2), 224–241.

Lilienfeld, S., Wood, J., & Garb, H. (2000). The scientific status of projective techniques. *Psychological Science in the Public Interest, 1,* 27–66.

Nagle, Y. K., & Rani, E. K. (2015). Sound apperception test: Development and validation. *Global Journal of Human-Social Science Research, 15*(8), 48–54.

Pica, M., Beere, D., Lovinger, S., & Dush, D. (2001). The responses of dissociative patients on the TAT. *Journal of Clinical Psychology, 57,* 847–864.

Chapter 10
Social Psychology

 ## Learning Objectives

10.1 Relate Zimbardo's prison study to social behaviors in human incarceration

10.2 Explain how Asch's experiments determined factors that influence social conformity

10.3 Identify contexts associated with bystander intervention or inaction

10.4 Analyze the influence of the Milgram experiments on social psychology

Social psychology is the branch of psychology that looks at how your behavior is influenced by that of others and how their behavior is influenced by yours. It is the study of human interaction. This branch of psychology is vast and covers a wide array of topics, from romantic relationships to group behavior to prejudice, discrimination, and aggression. This is probably the area in psychology many nonpsychologists will find the most relevant to their personal lives. As humans, we spend most of our waking hours interacting with other humans in one way or another (either verbally or nonverbally), so we naturally seek to learn more about the psychological processes involved in our social relationships. Social psychology may also be the research domain that contains the greatest number of landmark studies.

The four studies chosen for this section clearly changed the field of psychology by (a) providing new insights into some extreme human social behavior; (b) sparking new waves of research to either confirm, refine, or contest theories and discoveries; and (c) creating heated controversy about research ethics that ultimately led to the ethical principles discussed in the preface of this book.

The first discussion reviews one of the most well-known studies in the history of psychology: Philip Zimbardo's "Stanford Prison Study," which-produced some startling revelations about the psychology of imprisonment. Second is a recounting of a crucial study that demonstrated the power of *conformity* in determining behavior. The third study revealed a surprising phenomenon called the *bystander effect*, which states that the more people who witness an emergency, the less likely anyone is to help. Fourth, we arrive at another famous and surprising milestone in our understanding of the extremes people may resort to in powerful situations: Stanley Milgram's famous study of blind obedience to authority.

Reading 10.1: A Prison by Any Other Name . . .

Zimbardo, P. G. (1972). The pathology of imprisonment. *Society, 9*(6), 4–8.
Haney, C., Banks, W. C., & Zimbardo, P. G. (1973). Interpersonal dynamics in a simulated prison. *International Journal of Criminology & Penology, 1*, 69–97.

10.1 Relate Zimbardo's prison study to social behaviors in human incarceration

Have you ever been imprisoned? Let's assume your answer (and mine) is "no." Do you know anyone who has spent time incarcerated? Maybe. Regardless, most of us know very little about the psychological effects of spending time in prison. You may have read articles, stories, or novels about prisons, and almost certainly you've seen prison life portrayed in movies and on TV. From this exposure, most people's only certainty is that prison is not a place we ever want to wind up! We know it is a horrific experience and it surely must produce strong reactions and even pathological behaviors among inmates. Most of us also believe that those who choose to be prison employees, such as guards and wardens, probably possess certain unique, personal characteristics. But how can behavioral scientists study systematically the psychological and emotional effects of the prison experience, for either the inmates or the employees?

As for most complex real-life situations, studying the psychology of prison life is at best a difficult challenge for researchers because the methods used must be correlational—that is, we can observe the prison environment, interview inmates and guards, gather information about prisoners after they are released, and then try to make assumptions based on these accounts. But we cannot scientifically control the prison environment to draw clear, valid conclusions about the real causes of the behaviors that we observe. Does prison change people, or were the people in the prison system already "different" going in? One way around this research dilemma might be to create a simulated "research prison" and place people into it either as "prisoners" or "guards." Sounds impossible? Perhaps this would be a difficult study to do today, but one famous psychologist, Philip Zimbardo, and his associates Craig Haney, Curtis Banks, and Dave Jaffe did just that over 40 years ago at Stanford University (the two articles listed at the beginning of this reading are the earliest discussions of their study). They wanted to create a simulated prison with randomly assigned, typical college students in the roles of "guards" and "prisoners." Their "prison" (which will be described in greater detail) was constructed in the basement of the psychology building on the Stanford campus.

Theoretical Propositions

Zimbardo was testing his belief that the environment around you, the situation, often determines how you behave more strongly than who you are—that is, your internal, dispositional nature. He contends that, although we may have certain inherent or internal behavioral *tendencies*, powerful situations can overcome those tendencies and lead us to engage in behaviors that are very different from our usual selves. Zimbardo and his associates set out to discover what happens to normal people who are placed into a *situation* that exerts great power over individuals: *prison*.

Except for their initial belief that the situation exerts strong effects over our behavior, the researchers did not formulate any specific hypotheses. To test the impact of situational forces, they randomly assigned each participant to be either a "guard" or a "prisoner" in this contrived prison. They believed that random assignment to either the role of guard or prisoner would result in significantly different reactions in the mock prison environment on behavioral measures of interpersonal interaction, emotional measures of mood and pathology, attitudes toward self, as well as other indices of coping and adaptation to this novel situation (Haney, Banks, & Zimbardo, 1973).

Method

SETTING Zimbardo's goal was to create a situation that would resemble a prison or jail as closely as possible; he brought in a consultant: an ex-convict who had been incarcerated for 17 years. Although for this study the prison would not be real and participants in the study would know this, Zimbardo wanted to be sure to *simulate* a real prison experience, realistically.

Using space in the basement of the psychology building at Stanford University, Zimbardo supervised a work crew as it transformed various rooms and hallways into a "prison." The prison had to be well-built because the study was planned to last for two weeks. Each end of a corridor was boarded up and the laboratory rooms became prison cells. To enhance realism, special cell doors were constructed with vertical bars for door windows and individual jail-cell numbers (see Figure 10.1.1). The enclosed hallway that ran along the cell rooms was the "prison yard" where prisoner–participants would be allowed out of their cells to eat and move around. At the end of the hall was a small closet that would eventually be designated as solitary confinement for prisoners who were troublemakers, rebellious, disrespectful to the guards, or otherwise uncooperative. The bathroom was down the hall, but the guards would lead prisoners there blindfolded so they would not become aware of their location (Zimbardo, 2007b). The "prison" was equipped with a hidden observation camera and an intercom system that allowed the experimenters to maintain supervision of the guards' and prisoners' behavior.

PARTICIPANTS   If you are not already familiar with this famous study, what you are about to read may surprise or even shock you. As you read on, try to put yourself into the mind-set of the participants. First, the researchers placed ads in local papers near Stanford University in Palo Alto, California, offering $15 per day (that would be about $75 today) for individuals to volunteer to participate in a research study about prison life. To ensure participants gave informed consent, volunteers were told about the general nature of the study and that during the study they might experience some violations of their personal privacy and civil rights and that the food they would receive might be minimal, although it would meet their basic nutritional needs. They all agreed to these provisions.

After extensive testing to screen out anyone with psychological problems or criminal backgrounds, 24 normal college-age men were selected from a group of nearly a hundred volunteers. Then, at random (by the flip of a coin), the men were divided into two groups: "prisoners" and "guards." Remember, Zimbardo's goal here was to separate internal, personality factors from the influence of the situation in determining behavior. Therefore, it was imperative for each group of participants, at the outset,

Figure 10.1.1 A typical "cell" at the "Stanford Prison."

(Philip G. Zimbardo, Inc.)

to be as identical, on average, as possible (Zimbardo, 2005). Then all the participants went home, having received no instructions, no training, and no preparation at all for what lay ahead.

PROCEDURE The goal of the study was to observe, record, and analyze the behavior of the prisoners and the guards. As mentioned, Zimbardo and his associates were looking for signs that the situations and roles into which these young men were placed would be strong enough to overcome their personal characteristics and behavioral tendencies as individuals.

The "Prisoners" Several days after the initial screening and selection, the participants assigned to the prisoner group were surprised at their homes on a Sunday morning by a knock on their door from an officer from the (real) Palo Alto Police Department. Each participant was "arrested" for armed robbery, searched, handcuffed, and whisked off to the station—sirens, lights, and all. Each prisoner was booked, fingerprinted, and placed blindfolded into a holding cell. Later, they were told that they were to be transported, still blindfolded, to the "Stanford County Jail" (this was the mock prison built in the psychology building basement).

When the prisoners arrived at the jail, the participants who were assigned to be guards proceeded to search (see Figure 10.1.2), strip, delouse (using an aerosol spray), and give each "inmate" a prison uniform consisting of a dress-like smock, each with a different four-digit number (these numbers would become the prisoners' names for the duration of the study), rubber sandals, a nylon stocking to wear over his hair at all times (to simulate head shaving, which occurs in most real prisons), and a chain wrapped around his ankle and padlocked (this was not attached to anything but was intended to serve as a reminder of prisoner status). Zimbardo pointed out that although these procedures varied from actual, real-life prison procedures, the idea behind them was to *simulate* the humiliation, repression, and entrapment inmates experience routinely in real prisons. The prisoners were assigned three to each small cell; each inmate had a cot with a thin mattress and one blanket. The three cots filled the space and there was virtually no extra room in the small cells.

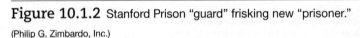

Figure 10.1.2 Stanford Prison "guard" frisking new "prisoner."
(Philip G. Zimbardo, Inc.)

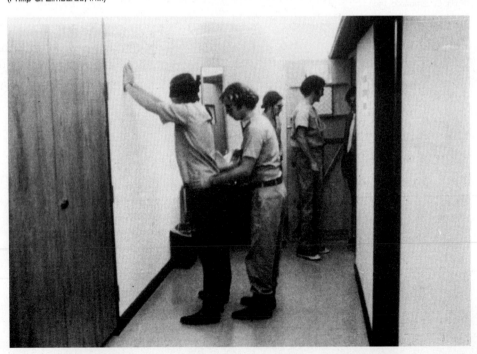

Table 10.1.1 "Prisoner" and "Guard" Behaviors and Reactions During the "Stanford Prison" Study

The "Guards"	The "Prisoners"
Used demeaning, degrading language with prisoners; harassed and intimidated them	Quickly became docile, subservient, and conformed to the rules set by the guards
Made humiliating comments to prisoners (e.g., "Prisoner 2354, go over and tell prisoner 2578 that you love him.")	Showed clear and early signs of trauma and depression, including crying and profound depression
Raucously awakened all prisoners in the middle of the night (every night) for "inmate counts"	Begged to be paroled
Frequently used push-ups as punishment for minor offenses (One guard stepped on a prisoner's back as he was attempting to carry out the push-up punishment.) Appeared to enjoy their sadistic control over the prisoners	Agreed to forfeit all payment in exchange for release
Shot a fire extinguisher (ice-cold CO_2) at prisoners to quell a rebellion	Experienced uncontrollable crying and rage and disorganized thinking
Placed prisoners in solitary confinement for entire nights Made visiting the bathroom a privilege, at times denying visits and placing a waste bucket in their cell	Planned and staged a "rebellion" that involved removing stocking caps, tearing off uniform numbers, barricading the cells with beds, and cursing and taunting the guards
Positioned an informant (a confederate of the experimenters) in the cells to spy on prisoners for signs of escape or rebellion plans	Designed an elaborate escape plan that never materialized
Stripped prisoners naked to achieve order following exposed escape plan; removed prisoners' beds and forced prisoners to give up blankets	Eventually gave up all attempts at rebellion and solidarity
Allowed "privileges" (better food, teeth brushing, washing, etc.) to prisoners at random in an effort to divide and conquer and to break prisoner camaraderie, trust, and solidarity	Assumed an every-man-for-himself attitude, abandoning solidarity with other prisoners
Forced prisoners to clean toilets with their bare hands, extended "night counts" to several hours long, increased number of push-ups: all as punishment for the attempted escape	Docilely accepted with increasing hopelessness the guards' degrading and sadistic treatment of them as the study progressed
Were creative and inventive in finding ways of breaking the prisoners' spirit	After 6 days, all became completely passive and dehumanized, robotlike

(Haney et al., 1973; Zimbardo, 1972; Zimbardo, 2005; Zimbardo, 2007b.)

The "Guards"   Unlike the prisoners, who were required to be in the prison 24/7 (they were incarcerated, after all), the guards worked 8-hour shifts—three men to a shift—and lived their normal lives when not on duty. They were given identical prison guard-style uniforms, nightsticks (although they were not allowed to strike prisoners), and reflective sunglasses designed to give them a menacing and anonymous appearance. Zimbardo explained that his idea for the mirrored sunglasses came from the 1967 film *Cool Hand Luke*, starring Paul Newman (Zimbardo, 2007). The guards received no specific training for their roles, and were merely charged with the responsibility of keeping the prisoners in line and maintaining order in the prison.

Results

This is one of the most researched, discussed, and analyzed studies in the history of psychology. (In 2015 it was made into a feature film starring Ezra Miller, Tye Sheridan, and Billy Crudup. If you are curious, it is typically available on Netflix.) The personality and behavioral changes that occurred in the guards and the prisoners were profound and alarming. To summarize the complex findings in the limited space available here, specific, representative behaviors of the participants are condensed in Table 10.1.1. More generally, however, here is what happened over the next several days in the "Stanford Prison."

Faster than anyone would have predicted, the true identities and personalities of the prisoners and guards seemed to vanish, and the roles they were being asked to play took over (remember they were assigned at random to be prisoners or guards). Within a day the line between "play" and real life became disturbingly blurred. As Zimbardo wrote of the participants in his original study (1972):

> The majority had indeed become "prisoners" and "guards," no longer able to clearly differentiate between role playing and self. . . . In less than a week, the experience of imprisonment undid (temporarily) a lifetime of learning; human values were suspended, self-concepts were challenged and the ugliest, most

base, pathological side of human nature surfaced. We were horrified because we saw some boys (guards) treat others as if they were despicable animals, taking pleasure in cruelty, while other boys (prisoners) became servile, dehumanized robots who thought only of escape, of their own individual survival and of their mounting hatred for the guards. (Zimbardo, p. 4)

Remember, this was a scientific study conducted by highly qualified, professional researchers, and it was rapidly taking on a life of its own. The participants, especially those given the role of prisoners, seemed to forget that they were college students with free will; they could have simply quit the study at any time, but they did not. After several days, many were pleading to be paroled, to be released, but when release was denied, they simply returned to their cells, dejected but obedient. The emotional breakdown and stress reactions of five of the prisoner–participants were so extreme that they became depressed, were unable to think clearly, and stopped eating. They had to be released from the study (or perhaps, more appropriately, from *the prison*) within the study's first several days.

Some of the guards took to tormenting the prisoners, apparently enjoying the power of their positions. Some of the guards were less strict and tried to be fair, but they never interfered with the more tyrannical guards and, more importantly, never went to the experimenters to suggest that the other guards might have gone "over the top" in their roles. Even Zimbardo himself forgot, at times, that he was in charge of a scientific study and found himself slipping into the role of "prison superintendent."

Recent Applications

As is true of Milgram's study of obedience (see Reading 10.4), Zimbardo's prison study has generated sweeping social and political effects over the 30-plus intervening years. It is difficult if not impossible to discuss Zimbardo's findings without acknowledging the political nature of the research. One of the most controversial and heated issues facing the United States, and most countries worldwide, is prison reform. Throughout history, the systematic abuse of prisoners has been well documented and continues to this day. The headline-history in the United States of prison riots, uprisings, rebellions, kidnappings, and murders from the time of Zimbardo's study to the present is filled with parallels, on a larger scale, to the events in that basement at Stanford. To aggravate further the potential for prisoner abuse, the number of inmates in U.S. prisons and jails grew from approximately 500,000 in 1980 to over 1.5 million in 2016 (Carson, 2018). This is the highest prisoner population of any country in the world. Moreover, since the mid-1970s the goal of rehabilitation in prisons has been generally abandoned (although the phrase *correctional facilities* is still in wide use) and replaced with the goals of punishment and removing offenders from the public (referred to as *incapacitation*). In 1998, Zimbardo and Haney analyzed how the prison system had changed since their study at Stanford. Here, in Zimbardo's words, was their conclusion at that time:

> Prisons continue to be failed social experiments using a dispositional [internal] model of punishment, and isolation of offenders rather than any basic rehabilitation practices that might reduce persistently high rates of recidivism. What our analysis revealed was that prison conditions had significantly worsened in the decades since our study as a consequence of the politicization of prisons, with politicians, prosecutors, DAs, and other officials taking a hard line on crime as a means of currying favor of an electorate made fearful of crime by media exaggerations. (Zimbardo, 2005)

As you have been reading this, you may have been thinking about the possible links between Zimbardo's prison study and some of the events that have occurred, over the last 20 years during the U.S. involvement in the Middle East. Several highly publicized reports, especially the prisoner abuse scandals at Abu Ghraib Prison in Iraq, the reports of detainee abuse at the Guantanamo detention camp in Cuba, and the use of torture (see Hooks & Mosher, 2005; Keller, 2006), have brought the "Stanford Prison Study" back into the spotlight. Zimbardo, in his book *The Lucifer Effect: Understanding How Good People Turn Evil* (2007a), has revisited the prison study and expanded his research and commentary on prisoner abuse beyond prisons to the larger concept of human evil. We are disbelieving that events such as Abu Ghraib and elsewhere could ever truly happen—that anyone, especially citizens of a free, democratic society, could have engaged in such sadistic treatment of other humans. How could this be? Psychologists, such as Zimbardo, and other social scientists have tried to help us understand; as the authors of one study about these abuses stated,

> Journalists have looked to social scientific research to understand the abuse in Iraq, Afghanistan and around the world. These accounts move away from an emphasis on a few "bad apples" and call into question an emphasis on punishing the lowest ranking soldiers. Zimbardo's (1972) research figures prominently in these accounts. He rejects out of hand the "bad apple" thesis, suggesting instead that the barrel is bad. Zimbardo faulted the Bush administration with a "failure of leadership" and emphasized that the abusive interrogation techniques and harsh treatment of prisoners were "authorized from the top down" by military commanders and by the highest-ranking officials in the Bush administration. (Hooks & Mosher, 2005, pp. 1632–1633)

In report after report from Iraq, Syria, Afghanistan, and Guantanamo, we have heard about and seen in graphic detail the horrendous abuses and torture of prisoners carried out by guards and interrogators, who, like Zimbardo's prison participants, are not, by all accounts, sadistic, brutal people. They are essentially normal people, perhaps not so different from you and me, who are drastically transformed by what may ultimately be the most powerful situational force of all for evil: war.

Conclusion

As mentioned, Zimbardo had planned for a 2-week study, yet he decided to call it off after only 6 days because the mock prison situation was so powerful that it had morphed, in alarming ways, into reality. These were no longer randomly assigned university students and experimenters; they had become their roles, had transformed into prisoners, guards, and wardens. These roles were so powerful that individual identities dissolved to the point that the participants, and even the experimenters, had difficulty realizing just how dangerous the behaviors in the "Stanford Prison" had become. Zimbardo wrote about his decision to halt the study as follows:

> I terminated the experiment not only because of the escalating level of violence and degradation by the "guards" against the "prisoners" . . . but also because I was made aware of the personal transformation that I was undergoing personally. . . . I had become a Prison Superintendent, the second role I played in addition to that of Principal Investigator. I began to talk, walk and act like a rigid institutional authority figure more concerned about the security of "my prison" than the needs of the young men entrusted to my care as a psychological researcher. In a sense, I consider that the most profound measure of the power of this situation was the extent to which it transformed me. (Zimbardo, 2005, p. 40; see also, Zimbardo, Maslach, & Haney, 1999)

Carson, A. (2018). Bureau of Justice Statistics. (2018). *Prisoners in 2016*. Retrieved from www.bjs.gov/index.cfm?ty=pbdetail&iid=6187.

Haney, C., Banks, W. C., & Zimbardo, P. G. (1973). Interpersonal dynamics in a simulated prison. *International Journal of Criminology & Penology, 1*, 69–97.

Hooks, G., & Mosher, C. (2005). Outrages against personal dignity: Rationalizing abuse and torture in the war on terror. *Social Forces, 83*(4), 1627–1645.

Keller, A. S. (2006). Torture in Abu Ghraib (Iraq prisoner abuse scandal, 2004). *Perspectives in-Biology and Medicine, 49*(4), 553–569.

Zimbardo, P. (2005). A situationist perspective on the psychology of evil: Understanding how good people are transformed into perpetrators. In A. Miller (Ed.), *The social psychology of good and evil: Understanding our capacity for kindness and cruelty* (pp. 21–50). New York: Guilford.

Zimbardo, P. (2007a). *The Lucifer Effect: Understanding how good people turn evil.* New York: Random House.

Zimbardo, P. (2007b). The Stanford Prison Experiment: A simulation study of the psychology of imprisonment conducted at Stanford University. Retrieved June 2, 2007, from http://www.prisonexp.org.

Zimbardo, P. G., Maslach, C., & Haney, C. (1999). Reflections on the Stanford Prison Experiment: Genesis, transformation, consequences. In T. Blass (Ed.), *Obedience to authority: Current-perspectives on the Milgram paradigm* (pp. 193–237). Mahwah, NJ: Erlbaum.

Reading 10.2: The Power of Conformity

Asch, S. E. (1955). Opinions and social pressure. *Scientific American, 193*(5), 31–35.

10.2 Explain how Asch's experiments determined factors that influence social conformity

Do you consider yourself to be a conformist, or are you more of a rebel? Most of us probably like to think that we are conformist enough not to be considered terribly strange or frightening, yet nonconformist enough to demonstrate that we are individuals and capable of independent thinking. Psychologists have been interested in the concept of conformity for decades. You can see why when you remember that psychological research focuses not only on explaining human behavior but also, and perhaps more importantly, on revealing the *causes* of it. The effect of people's willingness to conform to others can help us a great deal in understanding the sources of people's behavior.

When psychologists talk about conformity, they refer to individual behavior that adheres to the normative behavior patterns of a particular group of which that individual is a member. The usually unspoken rules or guidelines for behavior in a group are called *social norms*. If you think about it, you can probably remember a time in your life when you behaved in ways that were out of sync or in disagreement with your attitudes, beliefs, or morals. Chances are, whenever this occurred, you were part of a group in which everyone was behaving that way, so you went along with them. Conformity is a powerful force on our behavior and can, at times, *cause* us to behave in ways that, left to our own devices, we would never do. Therefore, conformity is clearly worthy of interest and study by behavioral scientists. However, no one undertook to study conformity scientifically until the early 1950s. Enter Solomon Asch. His experiments on conformity offered us a great deal of new information about conforming behavior and opened many doors for future research.

Theoretical Propositions

Suppose you are with a group of people you see often, such as friends or co-workers. The group is discussing some controversial social issue or political candidate. It quickly becomes clear to you that everyone in the group shares one view, which is the opposite of your own. At one point the others turn to you and ask for your opinion. What are you going to do? The choices you are faced with are to state your true views and risk the consequences of being treated as an outcast, to agree with the group consensus even though it differs from your opinion, or—if possible—to sidestep the issue entirely.

Asch wanted to find out just how powerful the need to conform is in influencing our behavior. Although conformity often involves general and vague concepts, such as agreeing with others' attitudes, ethics, morals, and belief-systems, Asch chose to focus on a much more obvious type: *perceptual conformity*—that is, the extent to which humans tend to conform with one another's perceptions and sensations of the world (what we see, hear, taste, smell, and touch). Asch chose to study conforming behavior on a simple visual comparison task so that he could examine this phenomenon in a controlled laboratory environment.

If conformity is as powerful a force as Asch and many others believed, researchers should be able to manipulate a person's behavior by applying group pressure to conform. This is what Asch set about testing in a very elegantly designed series of experiments, all incorporating a similar method.

Method

The visual materials consisted simply of pairs of cards with three different lengths of vertical lines (called comparison lines) on one card and a single standard line the same length as one of three comparison lines on the other card (see Figure 10.2.1). Here is how the experimental process worked. Imagine you are a participant who has volunteered to participate in a "visual perception study." You arrive at the experiment room and find seven other participants already seated in a row. You sit in the one empty chair at the end of the row. The experimenter then reveals a pair of cards and asks you to determine which of the three comparison lines is the same length as the standard line. You look at the lines and immediately decide on the correct response. Starting at the far end of the row away from you, each participant is asked individually for his or her answer. Everyone gives the correct answer, and when your turn comes you give the same obviously correct answer. The cards are changed, the same process happens, and—once again, no problem—you give the correct answer along with the rest of the group. On the next trial, however, something odd happens. The card is revealed and you immediately choose in your mind the correct response (this all seems very easy!), but when the other participants give their answers this time, they all choose the *wrong* line! And they all choose the *same* wrong line. Now, when it is your turn to respond again, you pause. You can't believe what is happening. Are all these other people blind? The correct answer is obvious. Isn't it? Have *you* gone blind? Or crazy? You now must make a decision. Do you maintain your opinion (after all, the lines are right in front of your nose), or do you conform and agree with the rest of the group?

As you have probably figured out by now, the other seven "participants" in the room were not participants at all but, rather, confederates of the experimenter. They were in on the experiment from the beginning, and the answers they gave were, of course, the key to this study of conformity. So, how did the real participants in the study answer?

Figure 10.2.1 An example similar to Asch's line judging task card.

SOURCE: Adapted from p. 32.

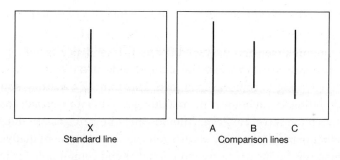

X
Standard line

A   B   C
Comparison lines

Results

Each participant took part in the experimental situation several times. Approximately 75% went along with the group's *incorrect* consensus at least once. For all trials combined, participants agreed with the group on the incorrect responses about one-third of the time. Just to be sure that the line lengths could be judged accurately, individuals in a control group of participants were asked simply to write down their answers to the line comparison questions. Participants in this group were correct 98% of the time.

Discussion and Related Research

The powerful effects of group pressures to conform were clearly demonstrated in Asch's study. If individuals are willing to conform to a group of people they hardly know about a clearly incorrect judgment, how strong must this influence be in real life, where groups exert even stronger forces and issues are more ambiguous? Conformity as a major factor in human behavior, the subject of widespread speculation for years, had now been scientifically established.

Asch's results were important to the field of psychology in two crucial ways. First, as discussed, the real power of social pressure to conform was demonstrated clearly and scientifically for the first time. Second, and perhaps even more important, this early research sparked a huge wave of additional studies that continue right up to the present. The body of research that has accumulated since Asch's early studies has greatly elaborated our knowledge of the specific factors that determine the effects conformity has on our behavior. Some of these findings follow:

1. *Social support.* Asch conducted his same experiment with a slight variation. He altered the answers of the confederates so that in the test condition one confederate of the seven gave the correct answer. When this occurred, only 5% of the participants agreed with the group consensus. Apparently, a single ally is all you need to "stick to your guns" and resist the pressure to conform. This finding has been supported by several later studies (e.g., Morris & Miller, 1975).

2. *Attraction and commitment to the group.* Later research demonstrated that the more attracted and committed you are to a particular group, the more likely you are to conform to the behavior and attitudes of that group (see Forsyth, 1983). If you like the group and feel that you belong with its members (they are called your *reference group*), your tendency to conform to that group will be extra strong.

3. *Size of the group.* At first, research by Asch and others demonstrated that the tendency to conform increases as the size of the group increases. However, upon further examination, it was found that this connection is not so simple. While it is true that conformity increases as the size of the group increases, this only holds for groups up to six or seven members. As the group size increases beyond this number, conformity levels off, and even decreases somewhat. This is shown graphically in Figure 10.2.2. Asch has suggested this happens because as the group becomes large, people may begin to suspect the other members of working together purposefully to affect their behavior and, in response, they become resistant to this obvious pressure.

4. *Sex.* Do you think men and women differ in their tendency or willingness to conform? Early studies that followed Asch's work indicated that women seemed to be much more willing to conform than men. This was such a strong and frequently repeated finding that it entered the psychological literature as an accepted difference between the sexes. However, later research drew this notion into question. It appears that many of the early studies (all conducted by men) inadvertently created testing conditions that were more familiar and comfortable for men in those

Figure 10.2.2 The relationship-between group size and conformity.

(Based on data from p. 35.)

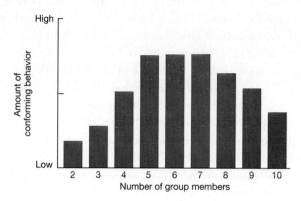

days than for women. Psychologists know that people will tend to conform more when placed in a situation where standards for appropriate behavior are unclear. Therefore, the finding of greater conformity among women may have simply been a systematic error caused by subtle (and unintentional) biases in the methods used (this is referred to as a research artefact). Research under better controlled conditions has failed to find this sex difference in conformity behavior (see Sistrunk & McDavid, 1971, for a discussion of these gender-related issues).

Numerous additional areas related to the issue of conformity also have been studied. These include cultural influences, the amount of information available when making decisions about conforming, personal privacy, and many others, including moral decisions—discussed further below.

Criticisms

Asch's work on conformity has received widespread support and acceptance. It has been replicated in many studies, under a wide variety of conditions. One criticism concerns whether Asch's findings can be generalized outside of the lab and to the real world. In other words, does a participant's answer in a laboratory about the length of some lines really have very much to do with conforming behavior in life? This is a valid criticism for all research about human behavior that is carried out in a controlled laboratory setting. What this criticism says is "Maybe the subjects were willing to go along with the group on something so trivial and unimportant as the length of a line, but in real life, and on important matters, they would not conform so readily." However, although real-life matters of conformity can certainly be more meaningful, it is equally likely that the pressures for conformity from groups in the real world are also proportionately stronger.

Recent Applications

An article examining why young adults continue to engage in unsafe sexual practices demonstrates how Asch's work continues to influence research on important social issues (Cerwonka, Isbell, & Hansen, 2000). The researchers assessed nearly 400 students between the ages of 18 and 29 on various measures of their knowledge of HIV/AIDS risk behaviors (such as failure to use condoms, multiple sex partners, alcohol and other drug use, and sexual history). Numerous factors were shown to predict high-risk sexual behaviors, including *conformity to peer group pressures*. You can see how an understanding of conformity pressures on people's choices about their sexual behaviors might be a valuable tool in fighting the continuing spread of STDs and HIV.

Another fascinating study incorporated Asch's 1955 article to examine why men are less likely than women to seek help, even when they are in dire need of it (Mansfield et al., 2003). This article begins with the following (old) joke: "Why did Moses spend 40 years wandering in the desert? Because he wouldn't ask for directions" (p. 93). This joke is (sort of) funny because it taps into a stereotype about men and help-seeking behavior. Of course, failure to ask for directions *usually* does not cause serious problems, but men also tend to resist seeking medical and mental health care, and that can be dangerous or even fatal. The authors suggest that one of the primary forces preventing men from seeking help is conformity: "In the context of help seeking, men may be disinclined to seek help if they believe they will be stigmatized for doing so. . . . If a man greatly admires the people in his life who discourage or speak badly of seeking help, he will be less likely to seek help himself" (p. 101).

Culture appears to play an especially important role in conformity (Bond & Smith, 1996). Research in collectivist countries, such as Japan or India, has consistently found higher levels of conformity than in individualistic countries, such as the United States (see Triandis's research on collectivist and individualistic cultures in Reading 7.4). Such findings add to the ever-growing body of evidence that psychological research must never overlook the impact of culture on virtually all human behaviors.

To what extent will people conform even on issues of morality? A study by Parsons (2016) addressed this question. The experimenter tested 60 participants (individually) each waiting in a room with two accomplices to the experimenter. They each heard descriptions read aloud by the experimenter and asked what was the right action to take. For example (you may have heard this one):

You are at the wheel of a trolley that has lost its brakes and is running down a hill out of control. Just ahead you see a fork in the tracks; to the right there are 5 workers repairing the tracks; to the left there is one worker working on the tracks. The trolley is set to take the right fork and, if you do nothing, will run over and injure and likely kill all 5 workers. You cannot stop the trolley, but you can hit a switch which will steer the trolley to the left fork which will likely kill the single worker. Should you hit the switch to avoid killing the 5 workers at the expense of the single worker's life? [Remember: if you do nothing, 5 people will be run over, but you won't have to bear as much responsibility as if you hit the button and kill one.]

The results were clear: when decisions were expressed privately, in writing, the responses to these dilemmas did not differ, but when expressed publically—that is, when the accomplices shared their identical moral "decisions" (these were planned as part of the experiment) with the participant, the participants' responses strongly conformed to the accomplices' decisions.

Bond, R., & Smith, P. (1996). Culture and conformity: A meta-analysis of studies using Asch's line-judgment task. *Psychological Bulletin, 119*(1), 111–137.

Cerwonka, E., Isbell, T., & Hansen, C. (2000). Psychosocial factors as predictors of unsafe sexual practices among young adults. *AIDS Education and Prevention, 12*(2), 141–153.

Forsyth, D. (1983). *An introduction to group dynamics*. Pacific Grove, CA: Brooks/Cole.

Mansfield, A., Addis, M., & Mahalik, J., (2003). Why won't he go to the doctor? The psychology of men's help-seeking. *International Journal of Men's Health, 2*, 93–109.

Morris, W., & Miller, R. (1975). The effects of consensus-breaking and consensus-preempting partners on reduction in conformity. *Journal of Experimental Social Psychology, 11*, 215–223.

Parsons, D., (2016). Social conformity to moral dilemmas. *2016 IPFW Student Research and Creative Endeavor Symposium*. 58. Retrieved from http://opus.ipfw.edu/cgi/viewcontent.cgi?article=1057&context=stu_symp2016

Sistrunk, F., & McDavid, J. (1971). Sex variable in conforming behavior. *Journal of Personality and Social Psychology, 17*, 200–207.

Reading 10.3: To Help or Not to Help

Darley, J. M., & Latané, B. (1968). Bystander intervention in emergencies: Diffusion of responsibility. *Journal of Personality and Social Psychology*, *8*, 377–383.

10.3 Identify contexts associated with bystander intervention or inaction

One of the most influential events in the history of psychological research was not a study at all but a violent and tragic event in New York City that was picked up by media news services across the United States. In 1964, a young woman, Kitty Genovese, was returning to her apartment in a quiet, middle-class neighborhood in Queens after closing the Manhattan bar that she managed. As she left her car and walked toward her building, she was viciously attacked by a man with a knife. As the man stabbed her several times, she screamed for help. One neighbor yelled out of his window for the man to "leave that girl alone," at which time the attacker began to run away. But then he turned, knocked Genovese to the ground, and began stabbing her again. The attack continued, and her screaming continued until *finally* someone telephoned the police. The police arrived 2 minutes after they were called, but Genovese was already dead and her attacker had disappeared. The attack had lasted 35 minutes. During their investigations, police found that 38 people in the surrounding apartments had witnessed the attack, but only 1 had eventually called the police. One couple (who said they assumed someone else had called the police) had moved two chairs next to their window to watch the violence.

Genovese's killer, Winston Moseley, died in prison in 2016 at the age of 81. He was denied parole 14 times during his 50+ years in prison.

If someone had acted sooner to help Genovese, she probably would have survived. New York City and the nation were appalled by the seeming indifference on the part of so many neighbors who had failed to try to stop this violent act. People attempted to find a reason for this inaction. They blamed the alienation caused by living in a large city; they blamed the neighborhood of Queens; they blamed basic human nature.

The Genovese tragedy sparked the interest of psychologists, who, as scientists, rather than looking to place blame for Moseley's actions, set out to try to understand what psychological forces might have been at work that prevented all those people from helping the victim. The concept of helping others falls into a research area of psychology that behavioral scientists call *prosocial behavior*, or behavior that produces positive social consequences. Topics falling into this research area include altruism, cooperation, resisting temptation, and helping behavior. If you witness an emergency situation in which someone may be in need of help, many factors affect your decision to step in and offer assistance. John Darley at New York University and Bibb Latané at Columbia University, both social psychologists, were among those who began to examine these factors. They termed the behavior of helping others in emergencies *bystander intervention* (or in the Genovese case, *nonintervention*).

Have you ever been faced with a true emergency? Contrary to what you may think from watching television and reading newspapers, emergencies are not very common. Darley and Latané estimated that the average person will encounter fewer than six emergencies in a lifetime. This is good and bad: good for obvious reasons, but bad because if and when you find yourself facing an emergency, you will have to decide what to do, without the benefit of very much experience. Society dictates that we should take action to help in emergencies, but often, as in the Genovese case, we do not. Could that be because we have so little experience that we simply do not know what to do? Is it because of the alienation caused by urban living? Or are humans, by nature, basically uncaring?

Following the Genovese murder, Darley and Latané analyzed the bystanders' reactions. They theorized that the large number of people who witnessed the violent event decreased the willingness of any one individual to step in and help. They decided to test their theory experimentally.

Theoretical Propositions

Your common sense might tell you that the higher the number of bystanders present during an emergency, the more likely it is someone will intervene. Darley and Latané hypothesized just the opposite: They believed that the reason no one took steps to help Kitty Genovese was a phenomenon they called *diffusion of responsibility*—that is, as the number of bystanders in an emergency increases, the greater is the belief that "Someone else will help, so I don't need to"—the responsibility for action is diffused among all those present. Have you ever witnessed an accident on a busy street or arrived at the scene of one soon after it has happened? Chances are that as you drove by you made the assumption that someone surely has called the police or an ambulance by now, and therefore you did not feel a personal responsibility to do so. But imagine discovering the same accident on a deserted country road with no one else around. Would your response be different? The answer for most of us is "yes."

The concept of diffusion of responsibility formed the theoretical basis for this chapter's study. The challenge was to recreate a Genovese-like situation in a controlled, laboratory-type situation so that it could be manipulated and examined scientifically. Darley and Latané were ingenious in designing experiments to do this.

Method

For obvious reasons, the actual events of the Kitty Genovese murder could never be recreated for experimental purposes. Therefore, the researchers needed to devise a situation that would approximate or simulate a true emergency so that the intervention behavior of bystanders could be observed. In this experiment, Darley and Latané told students in an introductory psychology class at New York University that they were interested in studying how students adjust to university life in a highly competitive, urban environment, as well as what kinds of personal problems they were experiencing. The students were asked to discuss their problems honestly with other students, but to avoid any discomfort or embarrassment, they would be in separate rooms and would speak with each other over an intercom system. This intercom, they were told, would only allow one student to speak at a time. Each student would be given 2 minutes, after which the microphone for the next student would be activated for 2 minutes, and so on.

All this was a cover story designed to obtain natural behavior from the participants and to hide the true purpose of the experiment. The most important part of this cover story was the way the students were divided into three different experimental conditions. The participants in group 1 believed that they would be talking with only one other person; those in group 2 believed there would be two other people on the intercom; and the group 3 participants were told that five other people were on the line. In reality, each participant was alone, and all the other voices they heard through the "intercom" were recorded.

Now that the size of the groups was varied, some sort of emergency had to be created. The researchers decided that a very realistically acted epileptic-seizure would be interpreted by most people as an emergency. As the discussions over the intercom system between the participants and the other "students" began, participants heard the first student, a male, tell about his difficulties concentrating on his studies and problems adjusting to life in New York City. He then added, with some embarrassment, that he sometimes had severe seizures, especially when under a lot of stress. Then the conversation switched to the next student. In group 1, the actual subject's turn came next, whereas in the other two conditions, the participant heard one or more other students speak before his or her turn. After the subject spoke, it was the first student's turn again. This is when the emergency occurred. The first student spoke normally as before but then began to have a seizure (remember, this was all on tape). Latané and Darley quote the seizure in detail in a later report as follows:

> I-er-um-I think I-I need-er-if-if could-er-er somebody er-er-er-er-er-er give me a little-er-give me a little help here because-er-I-er-I'm-er-h-h-having a-a-a real problem-er right now and I-er-if somebody could help me out it would-it would-er-er s-s-sure be good . . . because-er-there-er-ag cause I er-I-uh-I've got one of the-er-sei—zer-er-things coming on and-and-and I could really use some help so if somebody would-er give me a little h-help-uh-er-er-er-er c-ould somebody-er er-help-er-uh-uh-uh [choking sounds] . . . I'm gonna die-er-er . . . help-er-er-seizure [chokes, then quiet]. (pp. 95–96)

To the participants, this was clearly an emergency. They felt sure that the "student" was in trouble and needed help immediately. To analyze the responses of the participants, Darley and Latané measured the percentage of participants in each condition who helped the student in trouble (helping was defined as leaving the cubicle and notifying the experimenter of the problem). They also measured the amount of time participants waited to respond to the emergency and to try to help. Participants were given 4 minutes to respond, after which the experiment was halted and participants debriefed (explained the true purpose of the study, and that no one actually had a seizure).

Results

The findings from this study offered strong support for the researchers' hypothesis. As the number of others that participants believed were part of the study increased, the percentage who reported the seizure *quickly*—that is, as the attack was occurring—decreased dramatically (see Figure 10.3.1). Among those who *eventually* helped, the amount of delay in helping was greater when more bystanders were present. For group 1, the average delay in responding was less than 1 minute, whereas for group 3 it was over 3 minutes. The total number of participants who reported the seizure at all, either during or after it occurred, varied among the groups in a similar way. *All* the participants in group 1 reported the emergency, but only 85% of group 2 and 60% of group 3 did so *at any time* during the 4-minute period.

Figure 10.3.1 Number of participants in each condition who helped quickly during seizure.

(Based on data from p. 380.)

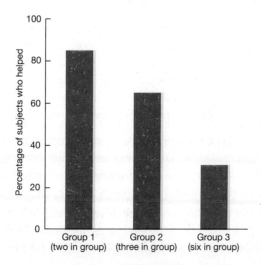

Discussion

As many did in the real-life case of Kitty Genovese, you might think that the participants in this study were simply uncaring toward the victim having the seizure. However, Darley and Latané are quick to point out that this was not true for the participants in groups 2 and 3 (or of Genovese's neighbors). All the participants reported experiencing a great deal of anxiety and discomfort during the attack and showed physical signs of nervousness (trembling hands, sweaty palms). The researchers concluded that the reason for their results must lie in the difference in the number of other people the participants believed were present. Whenever your behavior changes because of the presence of others, a psychological principle known as *social influence* is at work. Obviously, social influence played a significant role in this study, but we are still left wondering why. What was it about the presence of others that was so influential?

Darley and Latané claimed to have demonstrated and supported their theory of diffusion of responsibility. As the number of people in the group increased, the participants felt less personal or individual responsibility to take action. It was "easier" in groups 2 and 3 for the participants to assume that someone else would handle the problem. Moreover, people not only feel a shared responsibility for helping when others are present, but they also sense less potential guilt or blame if they do not help. Because we consider helping others to be a positive action in our culture, refusing or failing to help carries shameful connotations. If you are the only person present in an emergency, the negative consequences of not helping will be much greater than if others are there to bear some of the burden for nonintervention.

Another possible explanation for this type of social influence is something that psychologists have termed *evaluation apprehension*. Darley and Latané contended that part of the reason we fail to help when others are present is that we are afraid of being embarrassed or ridiculed. Imagine how foolish you would feel if you were to spring into action to help someone who did not need or want your help. I remember a time when, as a teenager, I was swimming with a large group of friends at a neighbor's pool. As I was about to dive from the board I saw the neighbor's 13-year-old daughter lying facedown on the bottom of the pool. I looked around, and no one else seemed to be aware of, or concerned about, this apparent emergency. Was she drowning? Was she joking? I wasn't sure. Just as I was about to yell for help and dive in for the rescue, she swam lazily to the surface. I had hesitated a full 30-seconds out of the fear of being wrong and feeling embarrassed for overreacting. Many of us have had experiences such as this. The problem is that they teach us the wrong thing: Helping others carries with it the possibility of looking foolish.

Significance of the Findings

From this and other studies, Darley and Latané became the leading researchers in the field of helping behavior and bystander intervention. Much of their early work was included in their book *The Unresponsive Bystander: Why Doesn't He Help?* (Latané & Darley, 1970). In this work, they outlined a model for helping behavior that has become widely accepted in the psychological literature on helping. They proposed five steps you and most people typically pass through before intervening in an emergency:

1. You, the potential helper, must first notice that an emergency event is occurring. In the study this reading examines, there was no question that something was wrong, but in the real world you may be in a hurry or your attention may be focused elsewhere, and you might completely fail to notice the event.

2. You must interpret the situation as one in which help is needed. This is a point at which fear of embarrassment exerts its influence. Again, in the present study, the situation was not ambiguous and the need for help was quite clear. In reality, however, most potential emergencies contain some degree of doubt or

ambiguity, such as in my swimming pool example. Or, imagine you see a man stagger and pass out on a busy city sidewalk. Is he sick, having a heart attack, or just drunk? How you interpret the situation will influence your decision to intervene. Many of those who failed to help in the Genovese case claimed that they thought it was a lover's quarrel and did not want to get involved.

3. You have to assume *personal* responsibility. You will usually do this if you are the only bystander. If others are present, however, you may instead place the responsibility onto them. This step was the focus of this chapter's experiment. The more people present in an emergency, the more diffused the responsibility and the less likely it is that help will occur.

4. If you assume responsibility, you then must decide what action to take. If you do not know what to do or you do not feel competent to take the appropriate action, you will be less likely to help. In Darley and Latané's study, this issue of competence did not play a part because all the participant had to do was report the seizure to the experimenter. But if a crowd were to witness a pedestrian being run over by a car, a member of the group who was a doctor, a nurse, or a paramedic would be more likely than others to intervene because he or she would feel more competent to know how to help.

5. After you've decided what action to take, you have to take it. Just because you know what to do doesn't guarantee that you will do it. Now, you will weigh the costs and benefits of helping. Are you willing to personally intervene in a fight in which one or both of the participants has a knife? What about victims of accidents—can you help them, or will you make things worse by trying to help (the competence issue again)? If you get involved, can you be sued? What if you try to help and end up looking like a fool? Many such questions, depending on the situation, may run through your mind before you actually take action.

Figure 10.3.2 illustrates how helping behavior may be short-circuited or prevented at any one of these stages.

Figure 10.3.2 Latané and Darley's-Model of Helping.

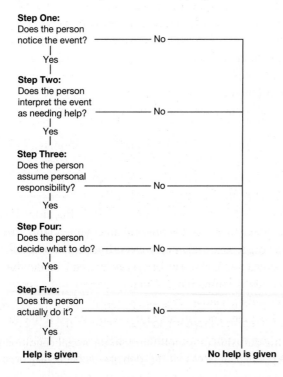

Subsequent Findings and Recent Applications

Both the Kitty Genovese murder and the experiment discussed in this reading involved groups of onlookers who were cut off from each other. What do you suppose would happen if the bystanders could see and talk to each other? Would they be more likely to intervene when they could be judged by others? Darley and Latané believed that, in some cases, even groups in close contact would be less likely than individuals to help. This would be especially true, they theorized, when the emergency is somewhat ambiguous.

For example, imagine you are sitting in a waiting room and smoke begins to stream in through a vent. You become concerned and look around at the others in the room. But everyone else appears quite calm and unconcerned. You think your reaction to the smoke must be exaggerated, and you decide against taking any action because if you take action and are wrong (maybe it wasn't smoke, just steam or something from the next room) you would feel sheepish and embarrassed. However, you don't realize that everyone in the room is feeling the same as you and hiding it, just as you are, to avoid embarrassment! Meanwhile, no one is doing anything about the smoke. Sound unbelievable? It's not.

Latané and Darley (1968) tested this idea by creating the situation just described. Psychology students volunteered to participate in interviews allegedly to "discuss some of the problems involved in life at an urban university." When they arrived for the interview, they were seated in a room and asked to fill out a preliminary questionnaire. After a few minutes, smoke began to seep into the room through a vent. For this study, the smoke was a special mixture of chemicals that would not be dangerous to the participants. After several minutes, the smoke became so thick that vision in the room was obscured. The researchers timed the participants to see how long they would wait to report the smoke. Some of the participants were in the room alone; others were with either two or three confederates, believed by the participant to be other subjects, who behaved very passively (as if it were no big deal) when the smoke appeared. Once again, Latané and Darley's results supported their theory. Of the participants in the alone condition, 55% reported the smoke within the first 2-minutes; only 12% of the participants in the other two groups did so. Moreover, after 4 minutes, 75% of the alone participants had acted, but no additional participants in the other groups ever reported the smoke.

Further evidence of the fear of embarrassment in people's hesitation to help others comes from a study that combined personality measures of shyness and *fear of negative evaluation* (FNE) with participants' willingness to help another (Karakashian et al., 2006). In this study, participants filled out scales to measure shyness and fear of negative evaluation. They were then given the opportunity to help a female confederate either alone or with two additional confederates in the room. In accordance with Darley and Latané's findings, participants' helping behavior decreased significantly with two other bystanders present, compared to the no-bystander condition, regardless of their scores on the personality tests. Beyond this, however, those who scored high on FNE and shyness were *less* likely to help in the no-bystander condition, but they were equally likely (or unlikely) to help when the two additional bystanders were present. This may seem counterintuitive to you—that is, someone who dreads being judged negatively or who is shy should be less likely to help in the presence of others—right? Not exactly. Think of it this way: If others are present, a shy person feels less pressure to help (due to diffusion of responsibility), so he or she, in essence, has an "excuse" to avoid helping just as the other bystanders do. On the other hand, if no other bystanders are present, that fear of (the potential for) negative evaluation kicks in and the shy person will be less likely to help than a non-shy person. The authors of the study stated it like this:

> Because of the diffusion of responsibility in the social condition [with others present], the participant faces little decision of whether to help or not. Here, FNE

does not become an issue, as there is little to no thought of helping, and in turn, no apprehension of being evaluated poorly. In the non-social condition [no other bystanders] the participant is left alone and has all the responsibility to help, and therefore must make a decision to act or not (Karakashian et al., 2006, p. 30).

Another study demonstrated the power of the bystander effect and diffusion of responsibility, not in real life, but in our *imaginations*. A study entitled *Crowded Minds: The Implicit Bystander Effect*, carried out by a team of researchers that included Darley, found that merely *imagining* being in a group changed helping behavior (Garcia et al., 2002). In this study, participants were asked to imagine that they were either part of a group of people or with only one other person. Then, all participants were asked to donate to a charity. The participants who imagined themselves in the presence of others donated significantly less money, and felt less personal accountability, than did those who imagined being with one other person. These findings imply that our brains immediately "leap" at the chance to assume less individual responsibility when we are part of a group.

To top off all these studies about the bystander effect, imagine this: You're in a bar; you and everyone else has "had a few." Suddenly there's a loud, major car accident outside the bar. Do you think, in your semi-inebriated state you would be more or less likely to rush out to see if you could help? Most people's inclination is to assume that the alcohol consumption would slow the bystanders' reaction to the emergency. However, an interesting study by Brommel et al. (2016) found that being tipsy actually reduces our attention to others and increases our fear of negative judgements by others and we are actually *faster* to help in an emergency when under the influence of alcohol.

Conclusion

The results of this body of research may seem rather pessimistic about our inclination to help others in need, but you should recognize that these studies deal with extremely specific situations in which people fail to help. Frequent examples may be found every day of people helping other people, of altruistic behaviors, and heroic acts. Darley and Latané's research is important, however, not only to explain a perplexing human behavior but also to help change it. Perhaps, as more people become aware of the bystander effect, they will make the extra effort to intervene in an emergency, even if others are present. In fact, research has demonstrated that those who have learned about the bystander effect (as you now have) are more likely to help in emergencies (Beaman et al., 1978). The bottom line is this: Never assume that others have intervened or will intervene in an emergency. *Always act as if you are the only bystander there.*

Beaman, A., Barnes, P., Klentz, B., & Mcquirk, B. (1978). Increasing helping rates through information dissemination: Teaching pays. *Personality and Social Psychology Bulletin, 4,* 406–411.

van Bommel, M., van Prooijen, J. W., Elffers, H., & Van Lange, P. A. (2016). Booze, bars, and bystander behavior: People who consumed alcohol help faster in the presence of others. *Frontiers in Psychology, 7,* 128. doi: 10.3389/2016.00128

Garcia, S., Weaver, K., Darley, J., & Moskowitz, G. (2002). Crowded minds: The implicit bystander effect. *Journal of Personality and Social Psychology, 83,* 843–853.

Karakashian, L., Walter, M., Christopher, A., & Lucas, T. (2006). Fear of negative evaluation affects helping behavior: The bystander effect revisited. *North American Journal of Psychology, 8*(1), 13–32.

Latané, B., & Darley, J. M. (1968). Group inhibition of bystander intervention in emergencies. *Journal of Personality and Social Psychology, 10,* 215–221.

Latané, B., & Darley, J. M. (1970). *The unresponsive bystander: Why doesn't he help?* New York: Appleton Century Crofts.

Reading 10.4: Obey at Any Cost?

Milgram, S. (1963). Behavioral study of obedience. *Journal of Abnormal and Social Psychology, 67,* 371–378.

10.4 Analyze the influence of the Milgram experiments on social psychology

If someone in a position of authority over you ordered you to deliver an electrical shock of 350 volts to another person, simply because the other person answered a multiple-choice question incorrectly, would you obey? Neither would I. If you met someone who was willing to do such a thing, you would probably think of him or her as cruel and sadistic. This study by Stanley Milgram of Yale University set out to examine the idea of obedience to authority and produced some disturbing findings.

Milgram's research on obedience joins Zimbardo's prison study (see Reading 10.1) as one of the most famous in all psychology's history. It is included in every general psychology text and every social psychology text. If you talk to students of psychology, most of them are familiar with these studies than others. Out of this study came a book by Milgram (1974) on the psychology of obedience, as well as a film about the research itself that is widely shown in college and university classes. In addition, a feature film, *Experimenter*, based on Milgram and his work, was released in 2015. Not only is this experiment referred to in discussions of obedience, but it has also influenced the entire debate about the ethics of involving human participants in psychological research.

Milgram's idea for this project grew out of his desire to investigate scientifically how people could be capable of carrying out great harm to others simply because they were *ordered* to do so. Milgram was referring specifically to the hideous atrocities committed during World War II and also, more generally, to the inhumanity that has been and is perpetrated by people following the orders of others. Milgram believed that in some situations, the human tendency to *obey* is so deeply ingrained and powerful that it cancels out a person's ability to behave morally, ethically, or even sympathetically.

When behavioral scientists decide to study some complex aspect of human behavior, their first step is to find a way to gain control over the behavioral situation so that they can approach it scientifically. This can often be the greatest challenge to a researcher, because many events in the real world are difficult to recreate in a laboratory setting. Milgram's problem was how to create a controlled situation in which one person would order another person to injure a third person physically, without anyone actually getting hurt. Now there's a researcher's challenge!

Theoretical Propositions

Milgram's primary theoretical basis for this study was that humans have a tendency to obey other people who are in a position of authority over them even if, in obeying, they violate their personal codes of moral and ethical behavior. He believed that, for example, many individuals who would never intentionally cause someone physical harm would inflict pain on a victim if ordered to do so by a person whom they perceived to be a powerful authority figure.

Method

The most ingenious portion of this study was the technique Milgram developed to test the power of obedience in the laboratory. Milgram designed a rather scary-looking shock generator: an electronic device with 30 toggle switches labeled with voltage levels starting at 30 volts and increasing by 15-volt intervals up to 450 volts (see Figure 10.4.1). These switches were labeled in groups such as *slight shock, moderate shock,* and *danger: severe shock.* The idea was that a participant could be ordered to administer electric

Figure 10.4.1 Milgram's experimental "shock" generator.

SOURCE: Alexandra Milgram.

shocks at increasing levels to another person. Before you conclude that Milgram was truly sadistic himself, this was a very realistic-*looking* simulated shock generator, but no one ever actually received any painful shocks (but the subjects *thought* they were administering them).

The participants for this study were 40 males between the ages of 20 and 50. They consisted of 15 skilled or unskilled workers, 16 white-collar sales-or businessmen, and 9 professional men. They were recruited through newspaper ads and direct-mail solicitation asking for volunteers to be paid participants in a study about memory and learning at Yale University. Each man participated in the study individually. To obtain an adequate number of participants, each man was paid $4.50 (remember, these were 1963 dollars, worth about $32 today). All participants were clearly told that this payment was simply for coming to the laboratory, and it was theirs to keep *no matter what happened after they arrived*. This was to ensure that participants knew they could withdraw at any time and did not feel coerced to behave in certain ways because they were worried about not being paid.

In addition to the participants, two other key participants were part of the study: a confederate (a 47-year-old accountant) posing as another participant and an actor (dressed in a gray lab coat, looking very official) playing the part of the experimenter.

As participants arrived at the social interaction laboratory at Yale, each was seated next to another "participant" (the confederate). Obviously, the true purpose of the experiment could not be revealed to participants because this would completely alter their behavior. Therefore, the experimenter told each participant a cover story explaining that this was a study on the effect of "punishment on learning." This is technically an ethical violation, but a necessary one if the experiment was to have any validity. The participants then drew pieces of paper out of a hat to determine who would be the teacher and who would be the learner. This drawing was rigged so that the true participant always became the teacher and the accomplice was always the learner. Keep in mind that the "learner" was a confederate in the experiment, as was the person playing the part of the experimenter.

The learner was then taken into the room next door and was, with the participant watching, strapped to a chair and wired up with electrodes (complete with electrode paste to "avoid any blisters or burns") connected to the shock generator in the adjoining room. The learner, although his arms were strapped down, was able to reach four buttons marked a, b, c, and d to answer questions posed by the teacher from the next room.

The learning task was thoroughly explained to the teacher and the learner. Briefly, it involved the learner memorizing connections between various pairs of words. It was a rather lengthy list and not an easy memory task. The teacher-subject would read the list of word pairs and then test the learner's memory of them. The teacher was instructed by the experimenter to administer an electric shock each time the learner responded incorrectly. Most important, for each incorrect response, the teacher was instructed to move up one level of shock voltage on the generator. All this was simulated so realistically that no participant suspected that the shocks were not really being delivered.

The learner-confederate's responses were preprogrammed to be correct or incorrect in the same sequence for all the participants. Furthermore, as the amount of voltage increased with incorrect responses, the learner began to shout his discomfort from the other room (in prearranged, prerecorded phrases, including the fact that his heart was bothering him), and at the 300-volt level, he pounded on the wall and demanded to be let out. After 300 volts, he became completely silent and refused to answer any more questions. (Remember, this was all theatre) The teacher was instructed to treat this lack of a response as an incorrect response and to continue the procedure.

Most of the participants would turn to the experimenter at some point for guidance on whether to continue the shocks. When this happened, the experimenter ordered the participant to continue, in a series of commands increasing in severity:

Command 1: Please continue.

Command 2: The experiment requires that you continue.

Command 3: It is absolutely essential that you continue.

Command 4: You have no other choice: You must go on.

A measure of obedience was obtained simply by recording the level of shock at which each participant refused to continue to deliver shocks. Because 30 switches were on the generator, each participant could receive a score of 0 to 30. Participants who went all the way to the top of the scale were referred to as *obedient subjects*, and those who broke off at any lower point were termed *defiant subjects*.

Results

Would the participants obey the commands of this experimenter? How high on the voltage scale did they go? What would you predict? Think of yourself, your friends, and people in general. What percentage do you think would deliver shocks all the way through the 30 levels? All the way up to the label: "450 volts—danger: severe shock"? Before discussing the actual results of the study, Milgram asked a group of Yale University senior psychology majors, as well as various colleagues, to make such a prediction. The estimates ranged from 0% to 3%, with an average estimate of 1.2%. That is, no more than three people out of 100 were predicted to deliver the maximum shock.

Table 10.4.1 summarizes the "shocking" results. Upon command of the experimenter, every participant continued at least to the 300-volt level, which was when the confederate banged on the wall to be let out and stopped answering. Most surprising is the number of participants who *obeyed* orders to continue all the way to the top of the scale.

Although 14 participants defied orders and broke off before reaching the maximum voltage, 26 of the 40 participants, or 65%, followed the experimenter's orders and proceeded to the top of the shock scale. This is not to say that the participants were calm or happy about what they were doing. Many exhibited signs of extreme stress and

Table 10.4.1 Level of Shock Delivered by Participants

Number of Volts to be Delivered	Number Who Refused to Continue at This Voltage Level
Slight shock	
15	0
30	0
45	0
60	0
Moderate shock	
75	0
90	0
105	0
120	0
Strong shock	
135	0
150	0
165	0
180	0
Very strong shock	
195	0
210	0
225	0
240	0
Intense shock	
255	0
270	0
285	0
300	5
Extreme intensity shock	
315	4
330	2
345	1
360	1
Danger: severe shock	
375	1
390	0
405	0
420	0
XXX– – –	
435	0
450	26

SOURCE: Adapted from Milgram, 1963, p. 376.

concern for the man receiving the shocks and even became angry at the experimenter. Yet they obeyed.

The researchers were concerned that some of the participants might suffer psychological distress from the ordeal of shocking another person, especially when the learner had ceased to respond for the last third of the experiment. To help alleviate this anxiety, after the participants finished the experiment, they received a full explanation (called a "debriefing") of the true purpose of the study and of all the procedures, including the deception that had been employed. In addition, the participants were interviewed as to their feelings and thoughts during the procedure and the confederate "learner" was brought in for a friendly reconciliation with each participant.

Discussion

Milgram's discussion of his findings focused on two main points. The first was the surprising strength of the participants' tendency to obey. These were average, normal people—not sadistic, cruel individuals in any way—who agreed to participate in an experiment about learning. Milgram points out that from childhood these participants had learned that it is immoral to hurt others against their will. So why did they behave this way? The experimenter was a person in a position of authority, but if you think about it, how much authority did he really have? He had no power to enforce his orders, and participants would lose nothing by refusing to follow orders. Clearly, it was the *situation* that carried a force of its own that somehow created an atmosphere of obedience.

The second key observation made during the course of this study was the extreme tension and anxiety manifested by the participants as they obeyed the experimenter's commands. Again, it might be expected that such discomfort could be relieved simply by refusing to go on, and yet this is not what happened. Milgram quotes one observer (who watched a participant through a two-way mirror):

> I observed a mature and initially poised businessman enter the laboratory smiling and confident. Within 20 minutes he was reduced to a twitching, stuttering wreck who was rapidly approaching a point of nervous collapse. . . . At one point he pushed his fist into his forehead and muttered, "Oh, God! Let's stop it." And yet he continued to respond to every word of the experimenter and obeyed to the end. (p. 377)

Milgram listed several points at the end of the article to attempt to explain why this particular situation produced such a high degree of obedience. In summary, from the point of view of the participant, his main points were that (a) if it is being sponsored by Yale, I must be in good hands, and who am I to question such a great institution; (b) the goals of the experiment appear to be important, and therefore, because I volunteered, I'll do my part to assist in the realization of those goals; (c) the learner, after all, also voluntarily came here and he has an obligation to the project, too; (d) hey, it was just by chance that I'm the teacher and he's the learner—we drew lots and it could have just as easily been the other way around; (e) they're paying me for this, I'd better do my job; (f) I don't know all that much about the rights of a psychologist and his participants, so I will yield to his discretion on this; and (g) they told us both that the shocks are painful but not dangerous.

Significance of the Findings

Milgram's findings have held up quite well in the 40-plus years since this article was published. Milgram himself repeated the procedure on similar participants outside of the Yale setting, on unpaid college student volunteers, and on women participants, and he found similar results each time.

In addition, he expanded further on his findings in this study by conducting a series of related experiments designed to reveal the conditions that promote or limit obedience (see Milgram, 1974). He found that the physical, and therefore emotional, distance of the victim from the teacher altered the amount of obedience. The highest level of obedience (93% going to the top of the voltage scale) occurred when the learner was in another room and could not be seen or heard. When the learner was in the same room with the participant and the participant was required to force the learner's hand onto a shock plate, the rate of obedience dropped to 30%. However, when the distance was less personal, obedience also dropped. In one condition, the experimenter was out of the room and telephoned his commands to the participant. In this case, obedience fell to only 21%.

On a more positive note, when participants were allowed to punish the learner by using any level of shock they wished, no one ever pressed any switch higher than 45 volts.

Criticisms

Although Milgram's research has been extremely influential in our understanding of obedience, it has also had far-reaching effects in the area of the *ethical treatment* of human participants. Even though no one ever received any shocks, how do you suppose you would feel if you knew that you had been willing to shock someone (possibly to death) simply because a person in a lab coat told you to do so? Critics of Milgram's methods (e.g., Baumrind, 1964; Miller, 1986) claimed that unacceptable levels of stress were created in the participants during the experiment. Furthermore, it has been argued that the potential for lasting negative effects existed. When the deception was revealed to participants at the end of their ordeal, they may have felt used, embarrassed, and possibly distrustful of psychologists or legitimate authority figures in the future.

Another line of criticism focused on the validity of Milgram's findings (e.g., Brief et al., 1995; Orne & Holland, 1968). One commonly cited basis for this criticism was that because the participants had a trusting and rather dependent relationship with the experimenter, and the laboratory was an unfamiliar setting, obedience found there did not represent obedience in real life. Therefore, critics claim, the results of Milgram's studies were not only invalid, but because of this poor validity the treatment his participants were exposed to could not be justified.

Milgram responded to these criticisms by surveying participants after they had participated. He found that 84% of his participants were glad to have participated, and only 1% regretted the experience. In addition, a psychiatrist interviewed 40 of the participants who were judged to have been the most uncomfortable in the laboratory and concluded that none had suffered any long-term effects. As to the criticism that his laboratory findings did not reflect real life, Milgram said, "A person who comes to the laboratory is an active, choosing adult, capable of accepting or rejecting the prescriptions for action addressed to him" (Milgram, 1964, p. 852).

The Milgram studies reported here have been a focal point in the ongoing debate over experimental ethics involving human participants. It is, in fact, arguable whether this research has been more influential in the area of the psychology of obedience or in policy formation on the ethical treatment of humans in psychological research (as summarized in this book's preface).

Recent Applications

The breadth of influence that Milgram's obedience project continues to exert on current research can best be appreciated through a brief annotated selection of recent studies that have been primarily motivated by Milgram's early methods and findings. As has been the case every year since the early 1960s when Milgram carried out his studies, these studies are divided between attempts to refine and elaborate on people's tendency to obey authority figures and the omnipresent debate about the ethics of using deception in research involving human participants.

Thomas Blass—a leading authority on the work and career of Stanley Milgram, and author of a biography of Milgram, *The Man Who Shocked the World* (Blass, 2009)—has reviewed all the research and social implications stemming from Milgram's obedience studies as of 2009 (Blass, 1999; 2009). In general, Blass has found universal support for Milgram's original findings, but, more importantly, he suggests that obedience rates have not changed significantly during the 40-plus years since Milgram first published his findings (as many might argue). This is contrary to many people's intuitive judgments that Americans, in general, have become less respectful of authority and more willing to rebel and fight back when ordered to perform behaviors with which they disagree.

Another question that often arises about Milgram's early studies concerns gender and the fact that all his original participants were male. Do you think, overall, that men or women would be more likely to obey an authority figure? Blass's review of later studies by Milgram and numerous others found *no difference* in obedience rates for males versus females.

A very pertinent application of Milgram's findings examined the psychological experience of "execution teams" charged with carrying out the death sentence in Louisiana State prisons (Osofsky & Osofsky, 2002). The researchers interviewed 50 correctional officers who were directly involved with executions. They found that, although exposed far more than most people to trauma and death, the participants were not found to be clinically depressed. They reported relying on religious beliefs, identification with their peer group, and their ability to diffuse responsibility to deal with painful emotions: "Nevertheless, the officers experience conflicted feelings and frequently report having a hard time carrying out society's 'ultimate punishment'" (p. 358).

On the ethics side, a study employed Milgram's research in examining potentially thorny ethical issues for social science research conducted on the Internet (Pittenger, 2003). Today, a great deal of research is conducted via the World Wide Web, and the number of such studies is likely to increase significantly in the future. Pittenger contends that researchers must be alert to potential ethical violations relating to invasion of privacy, obtaining informed consent, and using deceptive tactics online. "The Internet offers unique challenges to researchers," Pittenger writes. "Among these are the need to define the distinction between private and public behavior performed on the Internet, ensure mechanisms for obtaining valid informed consent from participants, performing debriefing exercises, and verifying the validity of data collected" (p. 45).

An important question is this: What should be done to protect participants from irresponsible, deceptive practices in psychological research, while at the same time allowing for *some* deception when absolutely necessary for scientific advancement? A study by Wendler (1996) suggested that participants in studies involving deception be given an increased level of "informed consent." (See the discussion of this concept in the preface to this book.) This enhanced informed consent would notify you of the study's *intention* to use deception before you agree to be a participant in the experiment, although you would not be aware of the exact nature of the deception. "This 'second order consent' approach to acceptable deception," claims Wendler, "represents our best chance for reconciling respect for participants with the occasional scientific need for deceptive research" (p. 87).

Recently researchers noticed that over the decades since Milgram's studies, Social Psychology texts have adopted an increasing friendly tone toward his findings and methods (Griggs & Whitehead, 2015). That is, less space is being allotted to stressing all the criticisms discussed in the previous paragraphs. This may be due to space issues in the expanding world of textbooks or possibly a more "friendly" writing style that lends itself less easily to criticisms, or perhaps simply the amount of time that has passed since these studies' questionable ethics occurred. Whatever the reason, this lack of attention to the ethics in a study that has been held up as an example of potentially major ethics violations (with which Milgram disagreed) is an egregious omission that should be addressed by textbook authors going forward. Until and unless that happens, this book will need to fill in the gaps.

Conclusion

Milgram historian Thomas Blass's (2002) remarks in a biographical review of Milgram's life and work provide a fitting conclusion to this reading:

> We didn't need Milgram to tell us we have a tendency to obey orders. What we didn't know before Milgram's experiments is just how powerful this tendency is. And having been enlightened about our extreme readiness to obey authorities, we can try to take steps to guard ourselves against unwelcome or reprehensible commands. (p. 73)

Baumrind, D. (1964). Some thoughts on the ethics of research: After reading Milgram's "Behavioral Study of Obedience." *American Psychologist, 19*, 421–423.

Blass, T. (1999). The Milgram paradigm after 35 years: Some things we now know about obedience to authority. *Journal of Applied Social Psychology, 29*(5), 955–978.

Blass, T. (2002). The man who shocked the world. *Psychology Today, 35*, 68–74.

Blass, T. (2009). *The man who shocked the world.* New York: Basic Books.

Brief, E., Collins, B., & Miller, A. (1995). Perspectives on obedience to authority: The legacy of the Milgram experiments. *The Society for the Psychological Study of Social Issues, 51*, 1–19.

Griggs, R. A., & Whitehead III, G. I. (2015). Coverage of Milgram's obedience experiments in social psychology textbooks: Where have all the criticisms gone? *Teaching of Psychology, 42*(4), 315–322.

Milgram, S. (1964). Issues in the study of obedience: A reply to Baumrind. *American Psychologist, 19*, 448–452.

Milgram, S. (1974). *Obedience to authority.* New York: Harper & Row.

Miller, A. G. (1986). *The obedience studies: A case study of controversy in social science.* New York: Praeger.

Orne, M. T., & Holland, C. H. (1968). On the ecological validity of laboratory deceptions. *International Journal of Psychiatry, 6*, 282–293.

Osofsky, M., & Osofsky, H. (2002). The psychological experience of security officers who work with executions. *Psychiatry: Interpersonal and Biological Processes, 65*, 358–370.

Pittenger, D. (2003). Internet research: An opportunity to revisit classic ethical problems in-behavioral research. *Ethics and Behavior, 13*, 45–60.

Wendler, D. (1996). Deception in medical and behavioral research: Is it ever acceptable? *Milbank Quarterly, 74*(1), 87.

Author Index

Subject Index